Hooked on Horror

Genreflecting Advisory Series

Diana Tixier Herald, Series Editor

Hooked on Horror

A Guide to Reading Interests in Horror Fiction

Anthony J. Fonseca
State Library of Louisiana
and
June Michele Pulliam
Louisiana State University

Foreword by Stine Fletcher
Mississippi State University

1999
Libraries Unlimited, Inc.
Englewood, Colorado

For Rosa, who sticks her tongue out at monsters.

Libraries Unlimited, Inc.
P.O. Box 6633
Englewood, CO 80155-6633
1-800-237-6124
www.lu.com

Library of Congress Cataloging-in-Publication Data

Fonseca, Anthony J.
   Hooked on horror : a guide to reading interests in horror fiction
/ Anthony J. Fonseca and June Michele Pulliam ; foreword by Stine
Fletcher, Mississippi State University.
     xxiii, 332 p. 19x26 cm. -- (Genreflecting advisory series)
     Includes bibliographical references and indexes.
     ISBN 1-56308-671-9
     1. Horror tales Bibliography. 2. Horror films Catalogs.
I. Pulliam, June Michele. II. Title. III. Series.
Z5917.H65F66 1999
[PN3435]
016.80883′ 8738--dc21   99-31441
                                                                   CIP

Contents

Part 4: Ready Reference, Criticism, and Other Helpful Information

Foreword

Horror Fiction in Library Collections

Stine Fletcher

As with other popular genres, the importance of horror fiction is often overlooked in libraries and institutions of higher education. The library profession has long considered horror as "popular" fiction, a lesser realm ruled over by public librarians trying to meet the demands of their patrons' leisure reading habits. Most library science literature on this genre centers around book reviews, "read-alike" lists, and subject interest lists, with little regard given to the genre's place in the collection or to its deeper social and psychological implications.

In addition, horror fiction, while so appealing to some readers, is repugnant to others, for its violence, for its warped psychology, or simply for its ability to question social mores and bring up uncomfortable and even disturbing issues. For whatever reasons, many readers view horror fiction as a kind of obscenity or sleaze—or even worse, as the literature of the occult. Under the twin specters of censorship and lack of funding, what librarian needs that kind of controversy in the library?

Despite these problems, horror fiction remains a staple to its large and devoted readership. Works by Anne Rice and Stephen King continue to top best-seller lists; publishers such as Tor and Kensington continue to publish; and readers continue to voraciously consume horror fiction. If the popularity of horror fiction alone is not reason enough to justify its inclusion in library collections, its role in popular culture is. Over the past decade, the academic study of horror fiction has grown substantially. The works themselves are areas for study either as artifacts of popular culture or as mirrors that reflect it; in turn, the incorporation of horror fiction into the university curriculum will likely spawn increased interest in public and academic library settings.

The bottom line is that we are public or academic librarians, and we realize that our job is to support our patrons' needs—in this case, the desire for works in a specific genre—even when this leads to concerns about the practicalities of supporting a popular fiction collection.

Preservation is the greatest concern and the greatest problem. Most items from the popular media were not produced with longevity in mind. Mass-market paperbacks are made of cheap paper and quickly fall victim to the slow burn of oxygen. Works of horror fiction that are never published as higher-quality hardback books are difficult to maintain in a usable state. The more popular works, which are published in hardcover, are easier to collect and conserve, but are also likely to be purchased by fans. So, although hardback books are the popular fiction medium that can be best maintained by a library, their feasibility and cost bring up another practical concern: budgetary constraints that can mandate paperback purchases in order to stretch collection development budgets for genre fiction.

Once a library decides to pursue collecting horror fiction, it must build and maintain that collection. In addition, it must provide patrons with access to that collection and must meet research needs that focus on the collection. This requires a well-developed reference collection focusing on the genre. Librarians, as a rule, do not collect in a subject area without relevant indexes and reference works. These works become especially important when one considers that the majority of librarians are largely unfamiliar with the genre. Some librarians are familiar with mystery, and others may be science fiction fans, but only a small percentage of library professionals read horror fiction.

Adding to the problem of disinterest and inexperience on the part of librarians, horror receives little treatment in library science literature. As expected, library resources that provide reviews of fiction and reference works for this genre do play a large role in collection development. They are useful tools for a librarian who is a fan of such fiction, and they are an absolute necessity for that majority of librarians who are not. Yet the two core works for fiction reviews for librarians are *Library Journal* and *Booklist*, and these widely used journals focus on providing (at best) short book reviews aimed at library personnel. Although both journals have separate sections for reviews of science fiction, which likely also includes works of fantasy, neither has a separate section for horror fiction reviews, leaving the inquisitive librarian to search through numerous unclassified reviews for a listing of horror fiction. The distinction of which titles are in the horror genre is also unclear in these two journals. To further complicate matters, in these two journals, the terms *horror* and *terror* are not necessarily used to describe horror fiction. One must assume from the author's name, and from the summary and/or title of the work, that it fits the genre. Occasionally there may be a comparison to another named horror author, and the librarian could use that comparison as an indicator; however, as stated earlier, the majority of librarians are not familiar with horror fiction beyond the popular name of Stephen King. To make matters worse, reviewers for these journals are not necessarily required to have a great deal of familiarity with the genre.

In addition, such review sources do not indicate what fans are reading, so for that a librarian must rely on fan magazines. Whereas science fiction reviews from fandom can easily be found in the popular magazines *Analog* and *Locus* (which also contain horror reviews and publication lists), horror reviews can be elusive to all but the most committed and persistent librarian. Review publications such as *Necrofile* from Necronomicon Press and *Cemetery Dance* are vital resources for reviews of horror fiction, but *Necrofile* is known only to hardcore fans, and *Cemetery Dance* is not likely to be taken seriously by many librarians (whose idea of horror may be affected by the public's negative perceptions of the genre). When such fan-oriented publications are located, they will be available to the librarian only if the library can justify and afford subscriptions to such magazines. The World Wide Web is another good source of horror fiction reviews, including the all-encompassing amazon.com mega-site. But again, specific horror sites are only known to fans of the genre, and Web sites are generally not acceptable review sources for librarians.

A librarian may have more luck in finding informative reviews for reference resources, but even in reference sources, horror fiction is not sufficiently covered. *American Reference Books Annual*, a core work for reference collection development, lists horror reference in its own category. However, review sources for reference works on horror do not necessarily require the reviewer to be familiar with this subject area. Without knowledge on the part of the reviewer, a review of a reference work can only describe the work and evaluate it on the basis of the basic features of a useful reference tool. The reviewer may be unaware of how comprehensive the content is, and of comparisons that could be made to similar reference works about the genre. In contrast, science fiction is well represented in the literature. Some of these reference works also cover the fantasy genre, and a few include horror as well, but horror is given the least emphasis. When all three genres are combined in a reference work, such as in Neil Barron's *What Fantastic Fiction Do I Read Next?* (Gale Research, 1998), horror invariably receives a less comprehensive treatment. Indeed, horror fiction, even horror film, has the fewest reference resources dedicated to it. An examination of index entries over time in *American Reference Books Annual* gives an overview of the availability and publishing trends of reference works for these three genres. Horror fiction works have the fewest entries, and in many years have no entries at all. Even entries for horror film are few. The lack of horror fiction reference resources greatly hampers efforts to build collections for and advise readers about this genre.

Deciding to collect and distribute horror fiction is just the beginning. The incredible rate of production of popular fiction makes it virtually impossible for one library to collect everything in the genre of horror fiction. This is a problem inherent in all collections of popular culture materials. Output is so prolific that it is hard to keep abreast of current and past materials and to keep up with collecting. The average library is certainly suited to a limited amount of collecting, and even then the collection may have to be specialized because of space and budgetary restrictions. Other dilemmas arise from the fact that, as mentioned previously, most titles are not published in hardcover, which makes them difficult to preserve, and these titles quickly go out of print. Librarians must also decide whether they will simply collect content (i.e., will they collect copies regardless of the edition?) or collect these works of fiction as artifacts in themselves. Changes in covers with various printings carry a great deal of information for a study in trends in the genre and for popular culture study in general.

Despite the impossibility of being comprehensive and the numerous concerns associated with such collections, the most basic reason for collecting remains: if no library collects these materials, then interested individuals will not have access to them, especially in the future. This is the need that *Hooked on Horror: A Guide to Reading Interests in Horror Fiction* attempts to address. The authors, an instructor of Horror Literature and Film and a fellow instructor turned cybrarian, have produced a comprehensive annotated guide to the current literature to help fill the horror reference void. Their resource enables librarians to more effectively collect, maintain, and circulate horror fiction. By organizing and describing some 1,000 titles published in recent years, *Hooked on Horror* gives its readers an overview of the genre and its subgenres, as well as insights into individual works. Fonseca and Pulliam strive to alleviate the pains of readers' advisory and horror fiction collection development by giving librarians a starting point. Not even the wisest of librarians can know everything, and no library can collect every title—but having this resource at hand is a step in the right direction.

Acknowledgments

We would like to thank our parents, Elta, Bob, and Mary; our families; and many of our friends and colleagues for their support and encouragement throughout this project, especially Patrick Abadie, John Lowe, Malcolm Richardson, Amy "Twilight" Montz, Lad Wells, Robin Roberts, Emily Toth, Waddell Laughlin, Kendra Kuss, and all of our Horror and Vampire Literature students, past and present. We are especially grateful to those who helped us procure information and suggested authors and titles to us from the get-go: David Faucheaux, Terre and Gary Ferguson, Stefan Dziemianowicz, and Elizabeth Miller. Finally, we are most appreciative of those people who actually made this project possible: Dana Watson, Connie Van Fleet, Ron Maas, and our editor, Barbara Ittner.

Preface

The Appeal of Horror

We wrote this near Halloween, when one of us (June, in her capacity as "Horror Queen" of Baton Rouge) was interviewed by a local television news program. She was asked the obvious questions: Why do people read horror and watch horror films? What makes people enjoy being scared? Her answer was that life is scary and uncertain, and horror at least allows us to experience the emotion of fear in a controlled setting. She went on to note that while the world of horror fiction is peopled with the ranks of the undead, with serial killers, with ghosts, and with mad scientists, the real world is populated by another type of horror: drunk drivers who carelessly take away the lives of our loved ones, child molesters who cruelly ruin young lives, and unscrupulous corporations that pollute the environment and downsize the workforce in the name of increased profits.

In horror fiction, such evildoers are made into monsters, and generally monsters can be killed or at least contained. In other words, Freddy Krueger may live to see another sequel, but we can leave the theater safe in the knowledge that we are beyond his pursuit. In a sense, horror allows us to face our fears and defeat them.

After the interview, we discussed her response and thought that perhaps we could approach this question from another angle. Our first-ever team-taught horror class was presented at Louisiana State University in 1995 (within two semesters, the class had become a staple on campus, as word of mouth got out that we weren't really vampires!). When we first met our class, though, we were pleasantly surprised by the diversity of the students. Given the nature of the genre and its fans, we expected a homogenous sea of "children of the night," eager to begin discussing the latest Dean Koontz maniac, Stephen King monster, or Anne Rice bloodsucker. In other words, we expected a group of mostly males who read horror and watched horror films because they enjoyed "the scare" or took perverse pleasure in witnessing the dismemberment of bodies. After all, this was the kind of reaction we always got after telling friends that we enjoyed the genre.

What we found was a class composed of honors students, athletes, older nontraditional students, goths, buzz-cut boys in baseball caps, body builders, girls with long wavy hair and blue fingernails, film buffs, pagans, Catholics, Southern Baptists, a few miscellaneous weird people who sat in the back—and one student who looked a lot like Stephen King. The most remarkable feature was that the class was mostly female. All were eager to read writers we had at that time heard little of—Poppy Z. Brite, Jeanne Kalogridis, Tanya Huff, and Michael Romkey—and many of them were pleasantly surprised that they enjoyed Bram Stoker's *Dracula*, Mary Shelley's *Frankenstein*, Kim Newman's *Anno Dracula*, and Elizabeth Hand's *Waking the Moon*. Amazingly, not one of these students had ever committed a murder, tortured an animal, had an insatiable desire to drink blood, or (as far as we know) harbored thoughts of torturing his or her professors and classmates. They were simply an eclectic collection of average people who had one thing in common: they all enjoyed reading and studying horror. Some liked the adrenaline rush associated with the production of fear; others emphasized the thematic concerns that could be read between the lines, taking a more intellectual approach; still others simply thought horror fiction was fun and exciting, suspenseful and entertaining. The point we are making here is that horror appeals to people in all walks of life, and for various reasons, not all associated with "the scare."

Of course, we are not the first to grapple with this question, as many cultural and literary critics have already attempted to describe the appeal of horror. William Patrick Day argues that people are simultaneously repulsed and attracted to horror, that it is sort of a fantastical manifestation of negative wish fulfillment (*In the Circles of Fear and Desire: A Study of Gothic Fantasy*, University of Chicago Press, 1985). In other words, a horror novel or film is like the accident that compels us to rubber-neck, even though we know in our hearts that we really don't want to see other humans broken and bloodied. Terry Heller takes a more physiological approach to the question of why we enjoy horror. He feels that horror gives people a safe adrenaline rush, like sky-diving with a parachute we know will always open, or riding a roller coaster (*The Delights of Terror: An Aesthetics of the Tale of Terror*, University of Illinois Press, 1987). People engage in these thrill-seeking activities because they allow the chance to transcend the drudgery of daily life and, in a sense, to come face-to-face with mortality and walk away. One could say that according to this theory, horror allows us to face our fears and master them. Critic Carol J. Clover, in contrast, looks at horror from a more psychological point of view. She notes that in slasher films, audience members are at various times encouraged to view the world from the perspective of both the monster and the victim (*Men, Women and Chain Saws: Gender in the Modern Horror Film*, Princeton University Press, 1992). This gives the horror fan a chance to experience fear vicariously from various points of view, and to emerge unscathed from the theater.

We feel that horror does all of these things—and also entertains and teaches. For example, Stephen King's novel *Carrie* gives a candid-camera view of a dysfunctional family that would be the quintessential guests on Jerry Springer (the episode entitled "My Mommy Is a Fundamentalist Freak Who Locks Me in the Closet," or "My Daughter Is the Spawn of Satan"). Carrie White's home life is painful to watch, yet the reader cannot turn away from Margaret White's savage abuse of her child in the name of religion. The reader, like Sue Snell, one of the only characters to survive Carrie's rampage on the night of the Black Prom, is able to walk among the exploding gas stations of Chamberlain, Maine, and watch people doing St. Vitus's dances of pain while stepping on downed power lines. Yet the reader finishes the book having vicariously faced down the monster, none the worse for wear. Simultaneously, the reader is invited to see the world through Carrie's eyes, and any of us who have been the picked-on child in school can sympathize with Carrie's corrosive anger, and know the literal meaning of the phrase "if looks could kill." Above all, the reader of *Carrie* experiences a good story told from multiple points of view by a talented young writer, and perhaps learns a bit of a lesson at the end about how, if it takes a village to raise a child, it also takes a village to create a monster. This is a lesson learned all too well from the past year's gun-toting children in Arkansas, Mississippi, Kentucky, Pennsylvania, Oregon, Colorado, and Georgia who have performed their own versions of Carrie's destruction of the town of Chamberlain.

The important thing for readers' advisors to remember when dealing with patrons who are horror fans is that they are not all of one type, and therefore they do not read horror for the same reasons. This means that they will not all enjoy the same writers. Those who are "goths" (those black-clad young adults who identify with gothicism and gothic industrial music) may prefer the decadence of Poppy Z. Brite and Caitlin R. Kiernan, whereas those who enjoy action adventure will certainly want books by Dean Koontz or P. N. Elrod. The more sophisticated horror fans (those who have read almost everything in the genre) will probably wish to find alternative literary works, by the likes of Kim Newman, Robert Poe, or Jeanne Kalogridis. Librarians should also keep in mind that these readers are not disturbed individuals who need counseling but are simply people who enjoy curling up with a scary or thought-provoking book. School librarians in particular should attempt to understand the reading tastes of their horror patrons, for it is in school libraries that horror works are often challenged and sometimes singled out for censorship. The bottom line they should keep in mind is that no child has ever murdered in the name of R. L. Stine or Christopher Pike. Children who go on rampages are usually products of dysfunctional homes and an aggressive society; such acts are rarely the result of reading scary stories. Rule number one of readers' advisory is one of Raganatham's Five Laws: Every reader his or her book. Understanding that horror appeals to more than simply the baser human emotions will help librarians to realize that horror patrons deserve their books of choice, and that no one individual or group has the right to tread on constitutional freedom of expression by preventing the match of that reader with a book of choice, even if that book is the latest by Stephen King or Anne Rice. In short, horror fans are not second-class readers simply because they are genre readers and enjoy scary books. They are potential library patrons with the same rights and privileges as the patron who seeks novels by Jane Austen, Zora Neale Hurston, William Faulkner, or Gabríel Garcia Márquez. *Hooked on Horror* is a tool that will allow librarians to grant horror patrons those rights and help patrons who read horror fiction find the books they enjoy.

Introduction

Purpose and Goal of This Book

General Information

Hooked on Horror is an in-depth treatment of the horror genre, a genre that has often been overlooked by literary critics, readers, and librarians. The consensus seems to be that "scary stories" are best left for children, to be told around campfires and published by presses that cater to young adults. Cutting our teeth in the academic world of English departments, we grew accustomed to the ivory-tower view that the works of Stephen King, Ramsey Campbell, and Anne Rice are simply not acceptable reading material, that the fiction of these writers is somehow inferior to that of authors who published Literature (with a capital L). Imagine our shared surprise when we discovered that some library directors and librarians also viewed horror fans as "genre" readers, and therefore as less serious than patrons who read the classics, the latest novels by Joyce Carol Oates or Toni Morrison, or the latest book on Oprah Winfrey's list. It is perhaps because of this attitude that very few readers' advisory tools exist for the horror genre. In fact, horror almost always gets grouped with science fiction and fantasy, which not only ghettoizes it by association but robs readers of even the possibility of comprehensive bibliographies and readers' advisory tools devoted solely to the genre. In other words, horror fiction usually gets less than one-third of the length of a book-length bibliography, when it gets any recognition whatsoever. It is this need for an in-depth, book-length source on horror fiction that this text addresses.

Hooked on Horror differs from Neil Barron's *What Fantastic Fiction Do I Read Next?* (Gale Research, 1998) and earlier bibliographies in the Genreflecting series because it deals *only* with horror fiction, without treating it as a subgenre of fantasy. Because it deals solely with horror, this book provides the reader with a more complete list of *annotated* novels, collections by single authors, and anthologies by diverse hands than currently exists anywhere else. Additionally, *Hooked on Horror* is written by two experts in the horror field who thoroughly enjoy their work, so the essays that begin each subgenre listing are enthusiastic and informative, and each annotation shows the care and seriousness used to emphasize the appeal of each work, based on its own merits.

Of course, the main function of a readers' advisory tool is to enable librarians to be conversant in an area of literature where they may have little or even no experience. This book attempts to fill that need by grouping books into subgenres and by suggesting similar titles for reader favorites. *Hooked on Horror* also leads readers' advisors to similar titles by identifying important subject headings for each work, subject headings not based on LOC or Sears headings but which pertain to the genre itself, and then matching these headings with other works that were assigned the same headings. In this way, items that may not be completely similar but that contain the same thematic concerns as the original book under consideration can be identified through an index that groups all occurrences of a given subject heading together. This book goes beyond the generalizations used in older readers' advisory texts for the genre, which group items under headings such as "Monsters," and then attempts to deconstruct readers' tastes as specifically as possible, grouping terms such as "Frankenstein's monster (character)," "subterranean monsters," and "werewolves." In other words, what we hope to accomplish with this text is to fill the need for a readers' advisory guide geared specifically toward horror fans, using their terminology and keeping in mind their preferences.

Hooked on Horror, however, is *not* a review source for horror fiction. We heartily acknowledge that one of the most daunting problems with selecting genre fiction of any type, horror fiction included, is that generally it is not reviewed in mainstream sources. *The New York Times Book Review* may condescend to review the latest best-sellers by Koontz or Rice, but only because readers would demand the blood of the reviewers if they failed to acknowledge these works. Library trade journals, such as *Kirkus Reviews*, *Booklist*, and *Library Journal*, consistently provide brief annotations with some evaluative content, but these summaries may prove inadequate for all purposes because these journals typically evaluate based on the circulation potential of works, not on quality. Nevertheless, we must also be emphatic in our belief that a readers' advisory guide, by its very nature, cannot also serve as a source for reviews. Librarians and readers in search of reviews are best served by examining genre-oriented periodicals such as *Necrofile: The Review of Horror Fiction*; *Horror: The Newsmagazine of the Horror and Dark Fantasy Field*; *Aberrations*; and *Cemetery Dance* (all briefly annotated in chapter 23 of this book). These are the best sources for horror reviews readily available to librarians. Another excellent source for horror reviews is the World Wide Web, with individual-run sites such as Dark Echo's Web page (darkecho.com) and HorrorNet (horrornet.com); also, the publishing mega-site amazon.com often provides substantive guest reviews, sometimes by published reviewers.

To reiterate, it is not the purpose of this book to evaluate the works included in it. This book is merely a descriptive list of available titles in print and titles that can be made available through interlibrary loan and other resource sharing. It should be supplemented with evaluative reviews from other sources.

Scope of This Guide

Focusing on horror fiction (as defined in chapter 1), this book offers users a guide to contemporary and classic works. Writing a bibliography of genre fiction is a daunting task. Many of the works are cursed with an ephemeral existence. Often first editions of horror texts are released in paperback, and sometimes second editions are not forthcoming. Only works by best-selling writers tend to enjoy what would be the publishing world's version of immortality. For this reason, we felt we must be selective in what recent works we chose to include and annotate in this guide.

Novels, Anthologies, Collections

We began with books currently in print and tried to be all-inclusive in this category. If it was in print, we examined a copy of the text and annotated it. This was done for novels, anthologies, and collections by single writers. We also realized that many books are available via interlibrary loan and publishers' backlists, and that these books might be requested by patrons. Thus, we set an arbitrary date of 1994 (approximately five years) as the parameter for publication date and attempted to identify all titles published from 1994 to 1998 that would probably be available in libraries. To this end, union catalogs of various state library systems and a few public library online catalogs provided us with a core list. Although we attempted to be inclusive in this category as well, we found that many works published since 1994 were unavailable, even through the publishers, forcing us to eliminate some titles. In essence, our philosophy for books published between 1994 and 1998 was this: if it is available somehow, it is included in this guide.

Second, we tried to identify all works that have achieved the status of "classic," such as Bram Stoker's *Dracula*, Mary Shelley's *Frankenstein*, and Richard Matheson's *I Am Legend*, even if some of these classics were currently out of print or temporarily between editions. As a note to the reader, we annotated the in-print version or a recent publication. We assumed that as more university curricula include horror classics—a trend that is sweeping the nation's universities—these works would be reissued by publishers. Finally, we attempted to include virtually every work by benchmark (best-selling or most popular) authors in the genre, such as Stephen King, Dean Koontz, Anne Rice, Ira Levin, and John Saul.

History, Criticism, and Reference

To make this book a complete representation of the genre, we also included the field's most prominent reference and critical works, as well as some of its better periodicals. In these cases, we were more flexible with inclusion, as many of these works were published by academic presses and therefore had a short publication run. For reference and critical works, we chose to include the "classics" by scholars such as Mike Ashley, Julia Briggs, William Patrick Day, and David Punter, among others. Works that are still in print, or are readily available, were also included. However, we did not attempt to be comprehensive in our selection of critical and reference texts, as they are not the primary focus of this guide.

Young Adult Titles

Young adult horror (YA titles) *are not* included, because the addition of such writers as R. L. Stine, Christopher Pike, and Annette Curtis Klaus would triple the number of titles in this guide. We are therefore leaving the compilation of a YA readers' advisory guide to horror to other bibliographers; it would take a book-length study, rather than the inadequate chapter listing that we would have been able to manage, to do the subgenre of YA horror justice. The only YA titles found in this guide are those commonly read by adults, such as Klaus's *The Silver Kiss* or John Saul's *Shadows*.

Horror and Film

Horror fiction has been greatly influenced by the film industry. What would have become of Mary Shelley's *Frankenstein* without Boris Karloff's movie performance? Because of this fact, and because an increasing number of libraries include videotapes in their collections, we decided to offer some patron information about horror film. However, because of the sheer number of horror films still available for purchase, we chose not to be all-inclusive in this category. This guide is, after all, primarily a *bibliography* of *written* horror. Only horror films on VHS that we consider important in having formed the genre—films that no library with a large horror readership should be without—were chosen for inclusion.

Of course, virtually all horror fans and most librarians are familiar with what are considered the "classics" of the genre, beginning with genre-defining (and refining) films such as Fritz Murnau's *Nosferatu* (1922), Tod Browning's *Dracula* (1931), James Whale's *Frankenstein* (1931), and Lambert Hillyer's *Dracula's Daughter* (1936). These are titles that all libraries with a large horror fan patronage should include in their collections, not only for the quality of filmmaking that each one represents, but also for the important role each of these films has played in changing the very landscape of the genre itself, by interpreting Bram Stoker's and Mary Shelley's works in ways they had not been before. If not for Bela Lugosi's portrayal of the suave, sophisticated Dracula, the Count could have never evolved into the sympathetic creature he became in 1992, when Francis Ford Coppola presented audiences with a Dracula who was more a victim of love than a creature of the night. Likewise, the image of the hideously pieced-together, flat-topped, bolt-necked, and inarticulate Boris Karloff has replaced Shelley's original creation: a tragic hero of sorts who was sensitive and intelligent, but nonetheless scorned by his maker and society in general because of his appearance.

Because well-made horror films often take the pulse of a society at a given moment in its cultural history, we also decided to include those films of the 1950s through the 1980s that so well captured the prevalent fears of the men and women of those eras. Masterpieces and pop culture icons such as Jack Arnold's *The Incredible Shrinking Man* (1957), Dan Siegel's *Invasion of the Body Snatchers* (1956), Alfred Hitchcock's *Psycho* (1960) and *The Birds* (1963), Brian dePalma's *Carrie* (1976), and Ridley Scott's *Alien* (1979) can also be found in this guide. In addition, we recognized the value of some of the B-movie counterparts of these classics, such as Nathan Juran's *Attack of the 50-Foot Woman* (1958), Herk Harvey's *Carnival of Souls* (1962), and George Romero's *Night of the Living Dead* (1968). These films bring to light our cultural preoccupation with changing gender roles (often viewed as emasculation), female sexuality, and women's rights, as well as our fears of McCarthyism, Communism, nature, the Cold War and its nuclear buildup, minority empowerment, and space exploration.

We were more selective in considering contemporary films for inclusion in this chapter, choosing mainly works that have received critical acclaim and those that tested the boundaries of the horror movie—sometimes making it art. Therefore, we included films such as Francis Ford Coppola's lush, stylized, and operatic *Bram Stoker's Dracula* (1992), Bernard Rose's ingenious metageneric *Candyman* (1992), Guillermo del Toro's Cannes Film Festival winner *Cronos* (1992), and Rusty Cundieff's extremely clever horror/comedy *Tales from the Hood* (1995).

Final Note

From the outset, we understood the impossibility of creating a comprehensive bibliography of any genre, so instead we set out to create what we considered a useful guide for librarians in readers' advisory and collection development officer capacities. Therefore, when considering content, we included all those novels that are generally classified as horror, as well as some that straddle genres but obviously fit the definitions we set forth for each subgenre. We did not include any young adult horror for the very practical reason explained earlier: such an inclusion would have rendered this bibliography unwieldy and impractical. We thus leave the monumental task of producing a bibliography of young adult horror to someone else.

Part 1

Introduction to Horror Fiction

Chapter 1

A Definition of Horror

Horror is not a genre, like the mystery or science fiction or the western. It is not a kind of fiction meant to be confined to the ghetto of a special shelf in the ghetto of libraries or bookstores. . . . [H]orror is an emotion.

—Douglas E. Winter, in the introduction to *Prime Evil*
(New York: *New American Library,* 1988)

Tragedy is when I cut my finger. Comedy is when you fall down the sewer and die. Horror is when you return from the dead and haunt me for laughing at your nasty trip down that sewer.

—June Pulliam's embellishment of an old saw

The Definition of Horror as Used in This Book

On the most basic level, a horror text is one that contains a monster, whether it be supernatural, human, or a metaphor for the psychological torment of a guilt-ridden human. These monsters can take on various forms. They can be the walking dead, the living-impaired who stumble around aimlessly chanting "Brains! Brains!" and snacking on anyone in heels who has the misfortune to trip on the terrain. They can be the vengeful ghost of a child molester, horribly disfigured through the vigilante justice of outraged parents—and fully equipped with twelve-inch razors for fingernails and the ability to invade his victims' dreams, cracking jokes as he slaughters the innocent. They can be angry strippers, once abused wives and mothers, who will now rid the world of men who would batter those they should protect. They can be the hideous and therefore unlovable creations of mad scientists who fancied themselves greater than God, but are nothing more than deadbeat dads creating illegitimate offspring that they refuse to love and parent. Or they can be preternaturally beautiful immortals who are physically, emotionally, and intellectually superior to the envious humans among whom they live—but who must nevertheless drink the blood of their admirers for survival.

Although a horror text must always contain a monster, for the purposes of our definition, and inclusion in this guide, a work of horror fiction does not necessarily have to have as its *raison d'être* the intention of producing fear in the reader. Of course, most works in the genre do, and readers' advisors will find that these types of horror works predominate in the listings in this guide. However, there are those that do not intend to induce fear. Anne Rice's Vampire Chronicles, for example, emphasize the philosophical dilemma of outliving friends and family while never growing old, and the uncertainty of an amoral universe. While these realizations about the nature of life, humanity, and divinity may be horrific to some, *The Vampire Lestat* has little in common with a novel like *Salem's Lot*, which has the loftiest of all goals: to scare readers into remembering to keep their feet covered with the blanket at night. Both novels are considered horror works by publishers, booksellers, bookstores, libraries, fans, professors who teach horror literature, and the authors themselves.

Our definition helped determine how we categorized the world of horror literature into its subgenres. Although various readers' advisory tools in the past have used either style-based categories (e.g., gothic horror, comic horror, splatterpunk, gentle reads, etc.) or a combination of style-based and monster-based (for want of a better term) categories, we have stuck strictly to subgenres according to the type of monster that predominates in the fictional text. Our reasoning is simple: we assumed that most readers who like a vampire novel like it because it has vampires, and that those who enjoy a psychological thriller starring a maniacal sociopath enjoy slashers with human monsters. Therefore, when these readers look for similar stories, in most cases they are literally looking for another work with a same or similar monster. In only two instances did we veer from this, and those are the subgenres of comic horror and splatterpunk. Because these two subgenres are defined mainly by their approach to the story, rather than by the story itself, we felt obliged to treat them differently. So, although comic horror and splatterpunk are not, according to our scheme of categorization, actual subgenres, they are treated as such for the purposes of practicality, to enhance the usefulness of this guide.

Defining Horror Fiction

Defining horror fiction is difficult because it is not all of one type. It would be easy if we could state that horror is fiction that contains threatening monsters, but that definition would preclude works of psychological horror, where the threat is perceived or implied—but is no less real. It would be easy if we could state that horror is fiction that intends to horrify, or that has the effect of scaring the reader, but this would not account for comic horror, nor works like Rice's Vampire Chronicles, which without a doubt belong to the genre. In addition, we could point out that horror fiction is the fiction of monsters, and that the word *monster* stems from the Latin words *monstrum* and *monere*, which mean, respectively, a portent or omen, often a divine warning, and "to warn." Therefore, horror fiction might be called fiction that attempts to warn its readers of a certain danger, of an action or belief that can have negative results. Nevertheless, after some careful thought, we decided that the best way to define horror as a genre is to describe its various subgenres. Of course, these subgenres are often insufficient in and of themselves to accurately describe a work of horror, but put together, like the pieces in a puzzle that create a whole picture, they help explain what horror is.

Ghosts and Haunted Houses: Dealing with Presences and Absences

Ghost and haunted-house stories are tales of guilt thought to be long buried in the unconscious mind. The ghost or the haunted house serves as a reminder to the person guilty of repressing knowledge of wrongdoing, as well as a portent to others who know nothing of that person's sin. The ghost often forcefully points out to the haunted individual the inadvisability of keeping this knowledge buried. Contrary to popular belief, ghosts do not necessarily reside in haunted houses. Ghosts exist to seek justice for a wrong they suffered in life, or to protect one of the living from harm. The haunted house, in contrast, can be likened to an abused child. It is a victim of events that either happened in the house itself or on the site of the house prior to its erection, and it now lashes out at its occupants, or sometimes cries for love.

Examples of ghost stories: Orson Scott Card, *Lost Boys*; Noel Hynd, *Cemetery of Angels*; Emily Brontë, *Wuthering Heights*.

Examples of haunted house stories: Shirley Jackson, *The Haunting of Hill House*; Orson Scott Card, *Homebody*.

Golems, Mummies, and Reanimated Stalkers: Wake the Dead and They'll Be Cranky

The dead can be purposefully reanimated, as with zombies, or reanimated by accident, as in George Romero's film *Night of the Living Dead*, in which the newly dead rise from their graves because of radiation released by a recent space probe. The dead can also be raised by the living who simply cannot accept the finality of death, as in Stephen King's *Pet Sematary*. The golem, another form of reanimated dead, can be seen in Mary Shelley's novel *Frankenstein*, and later in countless other works of fiction and film. But unlike the reanimated dead, golems are soulless, angry beings fashioned from human parts. They are not reanimated bodies, but rather crazy quilts of body parts, genes, souls, and the like.

> Examples: Anne Rice, *The Mummy, or Ramses the Damned*; Mary Shelley, *Frankenstein*; Dean Koontz, *Mr. Murder*.

Demonic Possession, Satanism, Black Magic, and Witches and Warlocks: The Devil Made Me Do It

Tales of black magic and demonic possession predate the Bible, and this subgenre of horror is arguably one of the oldest. Tales of demonic possession involve innocents possessed by demons, or by the Devil himself. Tales of Satanism and black magic can also be about witches, warlocks (note that not all witches practice black magic), and others who willingly become involved with dark forces. Most stories in this subgenre generally feature Catholics who have either lost their faith or see their brand of black magic as an extension of their faith. However, a few narratives feature Protestants.

> Examples: Ira Levin, *Rosemary's Baby*; William Peter Blatty, *The Exorcist*; Stephen King, *The Shining*.

Vampires and Werewolves: Children of the Night

Vampirism is the story of a creature of the night and his or her parasitic relationship with another. It has therefore been used as a metaphor for love, for the parent/child bond, for sexual relationships, and for power structures in general. Yet vampires are easily the most identifiable and often the most sympathetic—in short, the most appealing—of all horror's monsters, mainly because vampires must, in some way, resemble the humans on which they prey. In fact, vampirism is often represented as nothing more than superhuman immortality, with a little bloodlust thrown in for a good scare. Vampires often possess some sort of extraordinary power, such as the ability to hypnotize victims, to control the weather, to shapeshift, to control people's minds and bodies, or super strength and speed and/or the ability to fly (sort of an evil version of Superman). Finally, vampires are almost always erotic or sensual in some way, which is one of their greatest appeals.

Werewolves are related to vampires, and hence are included in this subgenre. The werewolf derives from vampire folklore that specified what particular beasts a vampire could turn into (usually bats and wolves). According to the same folklore, wolves are the pet dogs of vampires and do their bidding. In fact, in *Dracula* the Count refers to wolves as "the children of the night" when he praises their musical howling. This association with the vampire is what caused the werewolf to grow into a beast of its very own with its own literature.

> Examples: Bram Stoker, *Dracula*; Anne Rice's Vampire Chronicles; Poppy Z. Brite, *Lost Souls*; John Gideon, *Kindred*; Tom Holland, *Lord of the Dead*; Chelsea Quinn Yarbro's Saint-Germain series; Brian Stableford's Werewolves of London trilogy.

Mythological Monsters and "The Old Ones": Invoking the Gods

Every mythology has its monsters. From Kali the Destroyer in India, to the destructive one-eyed giant Cyclops in ancient Greece, to the Anglo-Saxon human-eater Grendel, to Lucifer in Christianity, every culture incorporates into its belief system some being that, although human-like, is nonetheless monstrous and destructive, often threatening entire populations. Narratives from this subgenre either represent the non-Christian gods as pure, monstrous Other, or tell of gods and goddesses supplanted by Christianity who now want their believers back.

Examples: H.P. Lovecraft's Cthulhu mythos stories; Elizabeth Hand, *Waking the Moon*; Dan Simmons, *Song of Kali*.

Maniacs and Sociopaths, or the Nuclear Family Explodes: Monstrous Malcontents Bury the Hatchet

This is a relatively new subgenre of horror simply because the nuclear family is a relatively new phenomenon, seeing its halcyon days in the post–World War II 1940s and 1950s. The nuclear, nonextended family was touted by psychologists as the norm and celebrated in situation comedies through the new medium of television. But Father doesn't always know best, and Mom isn't always content to stay home and clean the house while wearing pearls and her best Sunday dress. There's no one to turn to in this supposedly self-sufficient family when the stress of everyday life becomes too much; seriously disturbed children, and sometimes parents, are the result. Works in this subgenre play on the all-too-American fear that every family unit has a dark side that surfaces only behind closed doors, and that children from these types of families will grow up to turn order into chaos.

Examples: Robert Bloch, *Psycho*; Peter Straub's Blue Rose trilogy; Poppy Z. Brite, *Exquisite Corpse*; Gaston LeRoux, *Phantom of the Opera*; Susan Kay, *Phantom* (a rewriting of *Phantom of the Opera* that gives Eric a voice and makes him a much more sympathetic character).

Rampant Animals and Other Eco-Monsters: Mother Nature's Revenge

And man shall have dominion over all Earth's creatures … But what happens when those creatures, or even nature itself, strikes back? Horror fiction in this category shows the frightening result of humanity's tinkering with the forces of nature. Sometimes natural monstrosities aren't even the fault of humans; nature itself can be completely unpredictable and chaotic, and thus scary. The horror of Mother Nature's revenge serves as a reminder that we must face the consequences of our actions when we overuse the land and pollute the air and water, or violate what are at least perceived as being "natural" laws.

Examples: Stephen King, *Cujo*; Alfred Hitchcock, *The Birds*; Winifred Elze, *The Changeling Garden*.

Psychological Horror: It's All in Your Head

In these stories, there's no supernatural monster and there's no very real psychopath stalking an innocent—but what happens in someone's mind can be just as real and often just as terrifying. The source of terror can be guilt over one's actions, or living in proximity to a madman.

Examples: Daphne du Maurier, *Rebecca*; Theodore Rozak, *The Memories of Elizabeth Frankenstein*.

Small-Town Horror: Villages of the Damned

We all fear being the outsider, the stranger in a strange land, especially when that strange land is governed by laws different from our own, such as laws requiring human sacrifice to pagan gods or demons. This type of horror, often referred to as small-town horror, scares readers with the realization that once they are away from the sanity and security of home, anything is possible. Like antiquarian horror, it also reminds readers that sometimes it is best not to snoop around too much, lest something unspeakable be turned up. The fear of town secrets is as old as the idea of towns themselves. The proverbial skeleton in the closet is never as dangerous as the closet's owner, who does not want it to be found!

Examples: Robin Hardy and Anthony Shaffer, *The Wicker Man*; Thomas Tryon, *Harvest Home*; Phil Rickman, *Candlenight*.

Technohorror: Evil Hospitals, Military Screw-Ups, Scientific Goofs, and Alien Invasions

With the recent experiments in genetic cloning, technohorror once again will take its place among the most popular subgenres of horror fiction. People are naturally afraid of the unknown. Technohorror exploits that fear, especially when it results from scientific experimentation gone awry. More than any other horror subgenre, technohorror taps into Americans' (and others') fears—and the modern age's realization—that any seemingly benevolent discovery, such as Einstein's theory of relativity, can be transformed, Jekyll-and-Hyde fashion, into an element of destruction.

Examples: anything by Robin Cook or Michael Palmer; Stephen Bury, *The Cobweb*; James Whale's 1931 film of *Frankenstein*; Richard Matheson, *The Incredible Shrinking Man*.

Telekinesis and Hypnosis: Chaos from Control

In the nineteenth century, Dr. Anton Mesmer popularized the idea of mesmerism (later known as hypnotism), whereby an individual could get others to do his or her bidding through mind control. This pseudoscience, compounded with the reality that some charismatic individuals are able to exert an almost superhuman influence over others, gave rise to stories about evil individuals using their mental powers to control others. Telekinesis is another mind power. But whereas hypnotism requires the use of another person to accomplish the hypnotist's desires, telekinesis is more direct. The individual with telekinetic abilities can move objects with his or her mind. Furthermore, the person with telekinetic abilities is generally an angry outcast who, pushed beyond the limits of endurance, goes homicidally insane, wreaking havoc with those telekinetic abilities rather than with an AK-47.

Examples: Stephen King, *Carrie*; Barbara Erskine, *Lady of Hay*.

Splatterpunk: The Gross-Out

The newest subgenre of horror (emerging sometime in the late 1980s), splatterpunk is a style of writing more than a theme with any particular type of monster. It is also known by the name *extreme horror*. In the typical splatterpunk story, graphic sex and violence abound as a result of the decadent indulgences of bored mortals and immortals, rather than as shocking excesses of monsters that must be stopped. Punk, alternative, and heavy metal music are often part of the backdrop of a splatterpunk story. There are no reluctant vampires or antiheroes here—splatterpunk monsters revel in their monstrosity.

Examples: anything by Poppy Z. Brite or Michael Slade.

Comic Horror: Laughing at Our Fears

Many people do not realize that horror has almost always contained an element of the comic. Freddy Krueger may have been the first monster to crack jokes before disposing of his victims, although many might argue that lines such as "she has a nice neck" in *Nosferatu* can be seen as comic threats that predate Freddy's by more than fifty years. Nevertheless, humor in horror can be found in the understated reactions of Hrothgar's warriors to the monster Grendel in *Beowulf*, in the melodrama and irony of a good Poe tale, or in the stock stooge minor characters in early Universal Studios horror films such as *Dracula*, *Frankenstein*, and *Bride of Frankenstein*. Humor and horror also meet in the reactions of both the characters in horror texts and the readers/viewers of horror stories. The former, in their hurry to escape the monster, run into things, trip over themselves, and often make highly ironic comments foreshadowing their own deaths; the latter laugh nervously when their expectations are built up—and the mysterious noise turns out to be only a cat rummaging in a trash can. Despite this relationship between fear and laughter, true comic horror is a new and seldom-visited subgenre, by writers and readers alike.

Examples: Greg Kihn, *Horror Show*; Dan Simmons, *The Fires of Eden*.

Chapter 2

How to Use This Book

Most librarians would agree that the purpose of a good readers' advisory program is to encourage reading and improve circulation—by matching readers with books that they will enjoy. The job of the readers' advisor is often to interview readers and determine their reading tastes, based on limited information concerning the types of books these readers usually read, the topics and thematic concerns to which the readers are drawn, the writing styles that the readers enjoy and do not particularly like, the settings (geographic locations, periods in history, etc.) about which the readers most enjoy reading, and the writers these readers like and hate. Based on these interviews, a readers' advisor must be able to identify a list of books that the readers will more than likely enjoy. This is a daunting task in and of itself for general fiction, but the task becomes nearly impossible when a particular reader is one of those identified in our preface and chapter 3: a patron who reads almost exclusively in the horror genre. If the librarian who is serving as readers' advisor happens to be a horror fan personally, and happens to have read nearly everything written in the past five years in the genre, then that librarian will be able to identify five to ten books that this reader may enjoy.

Unfortunately, this is a monumental task, as it is for a readers' advisor working with a patron who reads almost solely in any genre. It requires that the readers' advisor have knowledge of virtually every book ever published in a genre, or at least of all books in print and available through interlibrary loan (ILL). Because it is unrealistic to expect any librarian to keep abreast of so many works, several publications exist for the sole purpose of helping readers' advisors to identify similar titles and authors to suit any given patron's reading tastes. These text-based and CD-ROM publications alert readers' advisors to the existence of available genre fiction that may be of interest to the reader. By using Libraries Unlimited's Genreflecting series, or perhaps Gale's What Do I Read Next? series of bibliographies, or the CD-ROM versions of these books (*NoveList* and *What Do I*

Read Next?), a readers' advisor can match a popular title, such as the latest best-seller by Stephen King, with other titles that have the same general appeal and will therefore more than likely appeal to the reader in question. These readers' advisory publications, until very recently, covered the full spectrum of genre fiction in a single volume, and were therefore unable to cover works in any particular genre extensively. This limits their usefulness for hardcore fans of a single genre, or those who often choose to read almost exclusively in a single genre (as most of us do).

As one of the pioneer works in the Genreflecting series, this book focuses solely on the horror genre. It attempts to list, annotate briefly, and match with similar titles virtually every readily available horror title, thereby giving readers' advisors and readers an in-depth look at the genre. Although it treats each of the subgenres of horror separately (such as Vampire Fiction, Technohorror, Small-Town Horror, Maniac Horror, etc.), it also links titles within a given subgenre with similar ones in other subgenres. Because approximately 75 percent of the titles listed in this bibliography were actually obtained from publishers and local (Louisiana) libraries, they were annotated based on firsthand experience with the text. This was particularly helpful because it resulted in annotations that go beyond the general blurblike description and briefly hint at the writing style and appeal possibilities of the majority of the works in this guide. Having the texts in hand also proved helpful in assigning subject headings for each entry. These headings serve two purposes: (1) to act as access points for titles, and (2) to allow readers to isolate themes, characters, settings, and so on—whatever most appealed to them about a work—and, based on that, locate similar texts.

As explained earlier, *Hooked on Horror* uses multiple layers of similarity to match texts. The most obvious is the subgenre designation itself. In other words, all works that deal mainly with vampires are grouped in the Vampire Fiction chapter, and all works dealing with technohorror (horror stemming from technology or scientific experimentation) are grouped together in the Technohorror chapter. This makes it easy for fans of "Vampire's Point of View" narratives and medical thrillers to find similar titles at a glance. Those readers, or their readers' advisor, need only skim the annotated list in the Vampire or Technohorror chapters.

The second layer of matching can be found at the end of many annotations, where a few similar titles are identified; these titles are the *most* similar to the one being matched by the librarian or reader. For the purposes of matching similar titles this way, we simply asked ourselves, "What title does this read most like?," either because of its thematic concerns, its plotline, or the writing style. The problem here, of course, is that these matches are highly subjective. Also, because some books are entirely unique and really cannot be matched, we were unable to assign similar titles to all texts.

Finally, subject headings were assigned to each entry. These heading identifiers are indexed so that any entries assigned to the same subject heading end up being grouped together in the index. In this respect, *Hooked on Horror* acts as a database (in print form) that links similar items based on key terms. For example, a fan of *Rosemary's Baby* may realize that the aspect of the novel that she most enjoyed was its setting, New York City, or the fact that one of the main characters was an actor, or that the main thrust of the story concerns demons and impregnation. Each of those possible access points is identified in a subject heading term, as indicated in the entry. All the readers or readers' advisor need do is find **Actor as Character**, **New York City**, **Demons**, or **Pregnancy** in the subject index, and they will find a list of all works that were assigned that subject term, followed by the page numbers on which those titles can be found in *Hooked on Horror*.

We've also added icons to indicate award-winning books: indicates a Bram Stoker award, indicates a Horror Guild award.

It is recommended that, as a first step in using this bibliography, the readers' advisor (and perhaps the reader) become familiar with the parameters of each of the subgenre chapters, by reading the overview of subgenres in chapter 1 and the essays that begin each chapter. It is also suggested that users of this bibliography familiarize themselves with the types of terms in the subject index, by simply scanning through some of its pages. This will help users get a feel for what types of match points for similar titles are possible, and will save those users time in the long run by preventing them from searching for terms that are not indexed. These subject headings, aside from being match points for finding similar titles, also serve as access points for readers who are not looking for a similar title, but need to find a work based on limited information. Therefore, a reader who has heard about the "Anita Blake" novels, but knows nothing other than the recurring character's name, will find that **Blake, Anita** is a character found in various Laurell K. Hamilton books, for which the page numbers are given. An additional feature of this book is the Short Story Index, which is organized by title. Each entry in this index consists of the story title, the author, and the anthology containing the story; page numbers will direct readers to the anthology. Readers can also look up the authors of short stories in the Author/Title Index.

We attempted to keep the overall searching/matching mechanisms of *Hooked on Horror* as simple as possible by generalizing and standardizing subject headings; by using extensive **See Also** cross-referencing in the keyword index; and by alphabetizing all entries, whether in the subgenre chapters or in the indexes, in the strictest and most literal form. Our hope is that we have put enough care and hard work into the making of this bibliographic reference tool that the readers' advisor and reader will be saved valuable time in searching.

We welcome any comments or suggestions from the users of this book. You can reach us via email at the following addresses:

junepulliam@earthlink.net

jpullia@lsu.edu

ajf2525@mailcity.com

Chapter 3

The Appeal of Horror Fiction

When we first began research for *Hooked on Horror*, we made "library runs" on a weekly basis; on each run, we would check out some thirty to fifty horror novels and short-story collections. We got some interesting stares from patrons and librarians alike. Of course, we recognized this reaction, because we have been receiving it from colleagues and friends for years: the raised eyebrows followed by statements such as, "I would never have guessed that you were into THAT stuff; it's just too weird." Unfortunately, this seems to be the prevalent belief about readers of the horror genre: that something, somehow, must be wrong with them because they enjoy novels with monsters and slashers. The truth is that horror fans are very ordinary people who happen to enjoy a particular type of fiction. They are no more likely to be psychologically disturbed than fans of any other genre. In fact, to assume that they are somehow "dark" or "violent" is to assume that readers of bodice-rippers enjoy narrowly avoiding rape, or that readers of detective fiction routinely solve crimes, or that readers of science fiction fly off in spaceships and visit other planets on a day-to-day basis. Of course we understand that horror fiction is not to everyone's taste; certainly we respect the preferences of those who choose not to read it. What we hope to achieve with this brief essay, and in *Hooked on Horror* as a whole, is a similar respect for fans of horror fiction. We hope to debunk many of the myths associated with horror fiction: that only young adults enjoy the genre, that the main readership is white teenage males, and that fans of horror fiction like only "pulp" writing.

We believe this is particularly important because horror-fiction fans, like fans of all other genre fiction, are often treated as second-class patrons. With the horror genre, though, the problem takes on a new dimension. Horror fiction is often equated with pornography, as if horror were some type of soft porn. In England, horror film was grouped with pornography for the purpose of the "Video Nasties" laws, which censor both genres. Although this type of censorship is unconstitutional in the United States, the misconceived horror/pornography conflation is just as prevalent on this side of the pond. Perhaps this is because most Americans define horror based on their knowledge of slasher B-flicks, which tend to be more marketable than well-made traditional horror films, and more prominent than horror literature in the collective American consciousness. These slasher flicks (such as *Friday the 13th* and *The Texas Chainsaw Massacre*) are usually marketed to young males, so of course they include much partial female nudity and sexual innuendo (these films also affirm the message that sex is scary and dangerous).

According to horror editor and scholar David Hartwell, although the main audience demographic group for horror/slasher films is teenage boys, women over age forty are the main consumers of horror literature. This popular misconception on the part of non-fans of the genre may derive from the mistaken belief that horror fans identify with the monster or killer in a horror text. Perhaps this is possible with a handful of slasher stories, where the viewer/reader sees the story from the killer's point of view. Logic, however, dictates the opposite: the vast majority of horror fans naturally identify with the victims rather than with the monsters. After all, horror is about what we fear, and about how those fears can be dealt with and defeated; this is the reason the "indestructible" monster is virtually always exterminated at the end of the typical horror story. It is also important for librarians to know that avid readers of the genre get more than a good scare out of these tales. Horror fiction aids its readers in dealing with both their private fears and the fears of society as a whole. After reading *The Exorcist*, for example, readers may have their fear of demons, and of losing their faith, allayed. Reading *It* may help readers to better understand and overcome their childhood fears, represented by the visage of a grotesque clown. Our point is that good horror fiction can do more than just scare readers: it can make them think about the human condition (Anne Rice's Vampire Chronicles); it can make them better understand societal fears (Stephen King's *Carrie* with its message about Americans' fear of the empowerment of women); it can cause them to reevaluate literary texts (Fred Saberhagen's *The Dracula Tape*).

Succinctly stated, our main aim in this chapter is to help librarians who do not read horror, for whatever reasons, to develop respect for the tastes of readers of the genre. These readers are as varied as the subgenres of horror itself, as diverse as the texts that constitute this bibliography. Some of them are college professors and honors students in our nation's universities, who love *Dracula*, *Frankenstein*, and Kim Newman's literate alternative fictions. Some are typical persons off the street, who have made Stephen King, Dean Koontz, and Anne Rice three of the best-selling authors in the world. Others are the black-clad goths who worship Caitlin R. Kiernan and Poppy Z. Brite. Still others are each librarian's friends and neighbors, who enjoy a good yarn like *Nazareth Hill*, *Bag of Bones*, the Millennium Quartet series, or the comic horror novels of Laurell K. Hamilton. Whoever they are otherwise, they are library patrons and deserve respect and equal treatment.

Chapter 4

A Brief History of the Horror Genre and Its Current Trends

Historically speaking, the first horror novel was published in 1764, when Horace Walpole penned the tale of a family curse, a damsel in distress, and a giant helmet that crushes humans. The popularity of *The Castle of Otranto* encouraged the publication of other gothic novels, one of which became the prototype for the erotic horror novel (M. G. Lewis's *The Monk*). These two works are discussed more at length in chapter 10. There were some early American gothic texts, such as those by Charles Brockden Brown and Washington Irving, but these bear little resemblance to what we now recognize as the horror text. It was not until the mid-1800s that two American writers, Edgar Allan Poe and Nathaniel Hawthorne, began publishing short fiction that for all practical purposes can be considered the literary ancestors of what we now call horror. Poe wrote often of maniacal killers, whereas Hawthorne examined the darkest recesses of the disturbed mind (psychological horror). Another American, Ambrose Bierce, known more for his fanciful weird fiction than for his horror fiction, later added the idea of cosmic horror and supernatural horror to the genre.

Monsters lay dormant until the 1930s, when Americans saw the resurgence of horror fiction in the form of pulp magazine publications. This was the decade of Lovecraftian horror and weird tales, with H.P. Lovecraft and Arthur Machen introducing the fears of the Old Ones, dark gods who reigned before humans inhabited the Earth and who want to regain their stronghold on the planet by bringing about the apocalypse. The preeminent texts of this decade were Lovecraft's Cthulhu tales and Machen's story of subterranean gods, *The White People*.

The most recent wave of popular horror began in 1968, when Ira Levin published *Rosemary's Baby*. Following the success of *Rosemary's Baby*, Levin, Stephen King, Anne Rice, Dean Koontz, and Peter Straub, produced one best-seller after another. Today's up-and-coming writers promise to keep the horror genre viable and exciting. Though the somewhat reduced number of horror titles published in the past few years may show some decline in popularity, the emergence of Poppy Z. Brite, Christa Faust, and Caitlin R. Kiernan has produced legions of new fans who have elevated these authors to cult status. In addition, Charles Grant and Robert R. McCammon, both of whom have been around awhile, seem to be hitting their strides when it comes to creating new stories based on familiar mythologies. Bentley Little and Orson Scott Card are reintroducing the weird tale (usually concerned with everyday life). Elizabeth Hand, Phil Rickman, and Tanarive Due are giving horror a multicultural voice, and Ramsey Campbell continues to awe the literary world by showing it that works of horror can be erudite as well as entertaining.

In the meantime, horror film continues to be a big draw at the box office, for example, *The Blair Witch Project*, *The Sixth Sense*, and the *Scream* and *I Know What You Did Last Summer* series. As is typical of the relationship between horror film and horror literature, the popularity of one seems to increase the popularity of the other (for a more detailed discussion of the relationship of horror film to horror literature, see the introduction to this book).

Current Trends

The following is a list of some of the current trends that we noticed in our readings for this bibliography.

Alternative Literature: The rewriting or retelling of classic works in the genre; may involve shifting the point of view, adding details omitted by the earlier work, or changing the story completely. Examples include Susan Kay's *Phantom* and Fred Saberhagen's *The Dracula Tape*.

Divine Warnings: Monsters go back to their etymological origins in serving as warnings to humans (the word "monster" derives from the Latin *monere*, which means to warn). Examples include Elizabeth Hand's *Waking the Moon,* Charles Grant's Millennium Quartet series, and Dan Simmons's *Fires of Eden.*

The Horror of Everyday Life: The monster and/or the supernatural is no longer necessary. Life itself, in its everyday ugliness and frightening lack of order and justice, is sufficiently horrifying. Examples include Bentley Little's *The Ignored* and Ramsey Campbell's *Nazareth Hill.*

Genre-Crossing: Horror texts cross over into other well-established genres such as action adventure, police procedural, detective fiction, and romance. (See the list of cross-genre horror novels in chapter 20.) Examples include Thomas Tryon's *Harvest Home,* the Headhunter series by Michael Slade, and the St. Germaine tales of Chelsea Quinn Yarbro.

Historical Horror: Historical figures are represented as monsters or monster-killers, adding a new dimension to their actions and often to the myths that surround them. Examples include Kim Newman's *Anno Dracula* and Dan Simmons's *Children of the Night.*

Intertextual Horror: Writers populate their fiction with characters created by other well-known writers, with characters from their own previous creations, and with characters from popular culture overall, creating a continuity of the horror universe. Examples include Brian Lumley's Necroscope and Blood Brothers series, and Theodore Rozak's *The Memoirs of Elizabeth Frankenstein.*

Splatterpunk: An over-the-top usage of violence, gore, sex, and cruelty—the typical splatterpunk anti-heroes relish their careers as monsters. Their exploits would shame Caligula. Examples include Poppy Z. Brite's *Exquisite Corpse* and Michael Slade's Headhunter series.

Part 2

An Annotated Bibliography of Horror Short-Story Collections

Chapter 5

Anthologies and Collections by Multiple Authors

To many horror fans, it is common knowledge that horror as a genre first took the literary form of the novel, with the publication of such books as *The Castle of Otranto, The Mysteries of Udolpho,* and *The Monk* in England in the late 1700s. However, it can be argued that those texts contained more dark fantasy and magical realism than they did horror. The first American examples of modern, psychological/supernatural horror—horror as we know it today—appeared in short-story form. In the mid-nineteenth century, Nathaniel Hawthorne made his mark in the horrific allegorical tale (perhaps the ancestor of the weird tale), and Edgar Allan Poe penned many a maniacal musing of a murderous madman.

Although few collections of short stories by a single author take their places on the shelves of local bookstores, as these are usually not big sellers, the short tale has proven marketable to publishers in the horror business. A countless number of short-story *anthologies*, collections that contain writings by various authors, can be found on the genre's best-seller lists at any given time. Perhaps this is because—and the format of *Hooked on Horror* is based on this supposition—fans of the genre tend to prefer tales that have quite a bit in common, whether they be in the same subgenre or are simply concerned with the same type of monster. For this reason, this chapter acknowledges the importance of anthologies intended for readers of particular subgenre fiction. Such anthologies are not only preferable to many horror fans, but are integral to the health and growth of the genre as well, for they allow readers to sample works by different authors and to gain an expanded understanding of the parameters of a given subgenre. In the long run, short-story anthologies encourage readers to pick up novels by writers who were unknown to them before they read that writer's short work.

Anthologies are also important to the marketability of the genre, because they allow writers who normally do not write horror fiction, and who may never have considered producing a novel in the genre, a chance to dabble in the supernatural and the psychotic. Glancing through the annotations in this chapter, readers will notice Isabel Allende, Eudora Welty, Fay Weldon, F. Scott Fitzgerald, Henry James, William Burroughs, Gabríel Garcia Márquez, Barbara Collins, John Cheever, and Woody Allen listed as authors of horror tales. In a best-case scenario, these "dabblings" could result in a renewed interest in horror by a writer who has much to offer the genre. Such was the case with Joyce Carol Oates, who wrote only short stories in the genre until recently. Her 1997 publication of *Zombie*, the disturbing diary of a psychopath, is one of the finest novel-length, first-person narrations by a maniac ever published, and will help give the genre more legitimacy in the eyes of its detractors. In other cases, the results of these dabblings could simply be the production of a fine horror text in the form of a short story. Works such as Robert Aickman's "Pages from a Young Girl's Journal," Oliver Onions's "The Beckoning Fair One," and Angela Carter's "The Company of Wolves" rival *any* vampire, ghost, or dark erotic novel published before or since their creation.

The bottom line is that, for whatever reason, there is a huge market for short-story anthologies, and fans of the genre cannot seem to get enough of them. Horror publishers, of course, have chosen to meet, and even exceed, reader demand for these collections. The result is a list of horror anthologies on almost any subject possible. In this chapter, we annotate as many of these anthologies as possible, concentrating mainly on those published in the last three years. We have also limited our annotations to the anthologies for which we were able to obtain the tables of contents.

Works in this category include such perpetually popular titles as *Love in Vein* and *Love in Vein II*, *Splatterpunks Over the Edge*, *Best Ghost and Horror Stories*, *Restless Spirits: Ghost Stories by American Women,* and various others, including *The Horror Writers Association Presents Robert Bloch's Psychos* and *Twists of the Tale* (horror stories about cats). In addition, we list here recent (published in the last two years) and notable anthologies that do not have a thematic bent, such as those edited by Ramsey Campbell, Charles L. Grant, David Hartwell, and Stefan Dziemianowicz (editor of *Necrofile*, the horror review journal). Our goal here is to raise awareness of the short story's place in the genre and to encourage collection development officers in libraries that have a strong horror readership to add these thematic anthologies to their collections.

Appeals: Brevity in the Reading Experience; Introduction to New Authors; Reading the "Classics"; Similar Monsters; Similar Thematic Concerns; Variety in the Reading Experience

Baldick, Chris (editor).

The Oxford Book of Gothic Tales. *New York: Oxford University Press, 1992. 526p.* A collection of gothic tales that spans more than 200 years, by well-known authors of the genre and well-known authors in general. Includes works by William Faulkner, Isabel Allende, Angela Carter, Jorge Luis Borges, Eudora Welty, Joyce Carol Oates, Isak Dinesen, Edgar Allan Poe, Nathaniel Hawthorne, Joseph Sheridan LeFanu, Robert Louis Stevenson, Thomas Hardy, Charlotte Perkins Gillman, and H.P. Lovecraft.

Feminism • Gothicism

Bloch, Robert (editor).

The Horror Writers Association Presents Robert Bloch's Psychos. *New York: Pocket Books, 1998. 373p.* Tales of maniacs in homage to Robert Bloch, the master of the subgenre. Contributors include Stephen King, Charles Grant, Ed Gorman, Richard Matheson, Yvonne Navarro, Billie Sue Mosiman, and Jane Yolen.

Brite, Poppy Z. (editor).

B H Love in Vein: Twenty Original Tales of Vampire Erotica. *New York: Harper Paperbacks, 1994. 396p.* Brite has brought together this genre's most powerful and seductive authors in an original collection of vampiric erotica. Includes contributions by well-known horror writers such as Melanie Tem and Kathe Koja. Winner of an International Horror Guild Award for Best Anthology, and includes Nancy Holder's "Café Endless: Spring Rain," a Bram Stoker short-story award-winner.

Love in Vein II: Eighteen More Original Tales of Vampire Erotica. *New York: Harper Prism, 1997. 375p.* Brite's second anthology of vampire erotica—if you loved *Love in Vein*, you'll love *Love in Vein II*. Contributors include Christopher Fowler, David J. Schow, Lucy Taylor, and Richard Laymon.

> *Eroticism • Gay/Lesbian/Bisexual Characters • Homoeroticism • Vampire as New Species • Vampire's Point of View*

Brownworth, Victoria A. (editor).

Night Bites: Vampire Stories by Women. *Seattle, Wash.: Seal Press, 1996. 259p.* The first collection of vampire stories by all female authors. Includes stories with unusual premises, including one set against a background of Afrocentric folklore, and a comic piece about the first Polish Jewish vampire.

> *Eroticism • Vampire's Point of View*

Collins, Nancy, Martin H. Greenberg, and Edward Kramer (editors).

Dark Love. *New York: ROC Books, 1996. 398p.* Twenty-two all-original tales of lust, obsession, and love in its darker forms, by Stephen King, Kathe Koja, Stuart Kaminsky, Ramsey Campbell, Michael Blumlein, and others.

> *Eroticism*

Cox, Michael (editor).

The Oxford Book of Twentieth-Century Ghost Stories. *New York: Oxford University Press, 1996. 425p.* This literate collection of 33 rarely anthologized tales by well-known authors of the genre epitomizes the rational twentieth century, a time when ghosts are allegedly extinct because we're all too technologically advanced to accept the existence of things unseen. Contributors include Robert Bloch, Joanna Russ, Fay Weldon, Robert Aickman, Elizabeth Bowen, F. Scott Fitzgerald, Oliver Onions, Edith Wharton, Angela Carter, and M. R. James.

Twelve Tales of the Supernatural. *New York: Oxford University Press, 1997. 188p.* A highly literate collection of ghost stories in which ordinary men and women are confronted with mysteries that defy nature and reason. Authors include M. R. James, Sheridan LeFanu, E. F. Bensen, and W. W. Jacobs.

Cox, Michael, and R. A. Gilbert (editors).

The Oxford Book of English Ghost Stories. *New York: Oxford University Press, 1986. 505p.* A collection of 42 highly literate ghost stories by well-known English authors. A good sampling of nineteenth- and twentieth-century examples of the genre. Contributions by Elizabeth Bowen, Robert Aickman, Sir Walter Scott, Joseph Sheridan LeFanu, Henry James, H.G. Wells, and Oliver Onions.

Victorian Ghost Stories. *New York: Oxford University Press, 1992. 497p.* A collection of 35 Victorian ghost stories by writers such as M. R. James, Henry James, Sheridan Le-Fanu, Mrs. Henry Woods, Charles Dickens, Rudyard Kipling, Elizabeth Gaskell, and Wilkie Collins.

Gothic Romance • Haunted Houses • Revenging Revenant

Dalby, Richard (editor).

The Mammoth Book of Victorian and Edwardian Ghost Stories. *New York: Carroll and Graf, 1995. 573p.* Forty ghost stories from the genre's golden age, 1839–1910, by writers such as Charles Dickens, Sheridan LeFanu, Henry James, Bram Stoker, M. R. James, F. Marion Crawford, and Ambrose Bierce.

Gothicism • Haunted Houses • Revenging Revenant

Daltow, Ellen (editor).

Twists of the Tale: An Anthology of Cat Horror. *New York: Dell, 1996. 366p.* Cats were worshipped in ancient Egypt, were hung for witchcraft in the Middle Ages, and are now the most popular pet in the United States. This collection of 23 stories by masters of the genre is a testament to the cat's popularity. Authors include William Burroughs, Stephen King, Kathe Koja, Joyce Carol Oates, and Tanith Lee. Similar title: *Dog-Gone Ghost Stories*, Karyn Kay Zweifel.

Cats

Daltow, Ellen, and Terri Windling (editors).

The Year's Best Fantasy and Horror: Ninth Annual Collection (1995). *New York: St. Martin's Press, 1996. 534p.* An impressive and thorough collection of 46 poems and short stories. The editors' comprehensive year-end summations of the genres and long list of honorable mentions make this a valuable reference source as well as a must-have collection of current horror and fantasy fiction. Contributors include Joyce Carol Oates, Nina Kiriki Hoffman, Charles de Lint, Peter Crowther, Stephen King, Ursula K. Le Guin, Tanith Lee, and S. P. Somtow.

The Year's Best Fantasy and Horror: Tenth Annual Collection (1996). *New York: St. Martin's Press, 1997. 534p.* Forty-three poems and short stories, including contributions by Tanith Lee, Angela Carter, Robert Silverberg, Thomas Ligotti, Gabríel Garcia Márquez, Charles de Lint, Dennis Etchison, Robert Olen Butler, and Jane Yolen. A must-have for any library with a serious horror collection.

The Year's Best Fantasy and Horror: Eleventh Annual Collection (1997). *New York: St. Martin's Press, 1998. 502p.* Forty-six poems and short stories, including contributions by Ray Bradbury, Charles de Lint, Jane Yolen, Joyce Carol Oates, Caitlin R. Kiernan, Douglas Clegg, Norman Partridge, and Vikram Chandra.

Fantasy • Magic • Science Fiction

Dziemianowicz, Stefan R., Martin H. Greenberg, and Robert Weinberg (editors).

The Mists from Beyond. *New York: ROC Books, 1995. 362p.* Twenty classic ghost stories by Peter Straub, Clive Barker, Edith Wharton, Ambrose Bierce, Bram Stoker, Shirley Jackson, Graham Greene, Ray Bradbury, John Updike, Joyce Carol Oates, Philip Jose Farmer, Harlan Ellison, and Charles Dickens.

Gelder, Ken (editor).

The Oxford Book of Australian Ghost Stories. *New York: Oxford University Press, 1996. 294p.* A wealth of nineteenth- and twentieth-century ghost stories by Australian authors, including Terry Dowling, W. W. Marcus Clarke, and Coo-Ee. The selections from this anthology do a fine job of representing Australian folklore.

> *Australia*

Gilliam, Richard, and Martin H. Greenberg (editors).

Phantoms of the Night. *New York: Daw Books, 1996. 390p.* Twenty-eight ghost stories by authors such as Billie Sue Mosiman, Owl Goingback, Edward E. Kramer, and Lisa Cantrell.

Gilliam, Richard, Martin H. Greenberg, and Edward E. Kramer (editors).

Confederacy of the Dead. *New York: ROC Books, 1995. 474p.* Twenty-five horror stories about the Civil War, by authors such as William S. Burroughs, Nancy A. Collins, and Anne McCaffrey.

> *War—American Civil War*

Grafton, John (editor).

Great Ghost Stories. *Mineola, N.Y.: Dover Books, 1992. 100p.* A brief anthology of 10 classic nineteenth- and early twentieth-century ghost stories, including "Dracula's Guest," Bram Stoker; "The Phantom Coach," Amelia B. Edwards; "Dickon the Devil," Sheridan LeFanu; "The Moonlit Road," Ambrose Bierce; and "The Monkey's Paw," W. W. Jacobs.

Grant, Charles L. (editor).

Gallery of Horror. *New York: New American Library, 1997. 416p.* A collection of 20 stories, including some classics not readily available elsewhere. Selections include "The Conqueror Worm," Stephen R. Donaldson; "Death to the Easter Bunny!," Alan Ryan; "The Rubber Room," Robert Bloch; "Petey," T. E. D. Klein; "The Sunshine Club," Ramsey Campbell; "Nunc Dimittis," Tanith Lee; "The Arrows," Chelsea Quinn Yarbro; and "Talent," Theodore Sturgeon.

> *Fantasy • Science Fiction*

Grant, Charles L., and Wendy Webb (editors).

Gothic Ghosts. *New York: St. Martin's Press, 1998. 256p.* Stories in the traditional vein, featuring characterization and atmosphere. Includes selections by Jessica Salmonson, Rick Hautala, Brian Stableford, Nancy Holder, and Lucy Taylor.

Greenberg, Martin H. (editor).

Dracula: Prince of Darkness. *New York: Daw Books, 1992. 316p.* A collection of all-original Dracula stories by such well-known horror, mystery, and fantasy writers as Richard Laymon, John Lutz, Brian Hodge, Rex Miller, F. Paul Wilson, Matthew J. Costello, Daniel Ransom, and P. N. Elrod.

Dracula (character)

Werewolves. *New York: Daw Books, 1995. 320p.* In this collection of 22 tales of werewolves, a psychiatrist has a patient who suffers from lycanthropy, a man willingly takes a gypsy potion to unleash "the beast within" for the sake of love, a woman picks up a stray werewolf from a dumpster, and the hordes of homeless children on the streets of Brazil are actually werewolves. Authors include Brian Hodge, Norman Partridge, Hugh Cave, Billie Sue Mosiman, Barbara Paul, and Peter Crowther.

Werewolves

White House Horrors. *New York: Daw Books, 1996. 316p.* An unusual collection of 16 stories about the presidency and the White House, from Thomas Jefferson's use of a writing machine with a mind of its own, to a voodoo-fueled attempt to seize control of Abraham Lincoln, to Harry Truman's confrontation with a 150-year-old ghost, to a president determined to mastermind his own exit from office. Includes stories by Billie Sue Mosiman, Brian Hodge, Barbara Collins, and Edward Lee.

Government Officials • History, Use of • Science Fiction • Washington, D.C.

Greenberg, Martin H., Frank McSherry, and Charles G. Waugh (editors).

Civil War Ghosts. *Little Rock, Ark.: August House, 1991. 205p.* A collection of ghost stories by nineteenth- and twentieth-century writers about the war where everyone took sides, even the dead. Selections include "An Occurrence at Owl Creek Bridge," Ambrose Bierce; "Iverson's Pits," Dan Simmons; and "The Drummer Ghost," John William DeForrest.

War—American Civil War

Greenberg, Martin H., and Lawrence Schimel (editors).

Tarot Fantastic. *New York: Daw Books, 1997. 315p.* Sixteen weird tales about tarot cards, with contributions by Lucy Taylor, Theresa Edgerton, Charles deLint, Billie Sue Mosiman, and Jane Yolen. Stories are reminiscent of the old *Twilight Zone* and *Night Gallery* television shows.

Fantasy • Tarot

Hartwell, David G. (editor).

The Dark Descent. *New York: Tor Books, 1987. 1,011p.* A collection of short stories that truly represent the diversity of the genre, with authors like Stephen King, M. R. James, H.P. Lovecraft, Shirley Jackson, Harlan Ellison, Nathaniel Hawthorne, Sheridan LeFanu, Ray Bradbury, Robert Aickman, Robert Bloch, Thomas Disch, Clive Barker, Edgar Allan Poe, Charlotte Perkins Gilman, William Faulkner, Joanna Russ, Dennis Etchison, D.H. Lawrence, Tanith Lee, Flannery O'Connor, Ramsey Campbell, Henry James, Charles Dickens, Joyce Carol Oates, Ambrose Bierce, Edith Wharton, and Philip K. Dick. Hartwell has assembled samplings from authors old and new, from high culture and low, and his anthology contains canonical works such as Poe's "The Fall of the House of Usher."

Fantasy • Science Fiction

Jones, Stephen (editor).

The Mammoth Book of Best New Horror, Volume 8. *New York: Carroll and Graf, 1997. 512p.* Annual collection of horror, terror, and dark fantasy showcasing both major and up-and-coming authors of the genre. Contributors include Poppy Z. Brite, Norman Partridge, Steve Rasnic Tem, Douglas Clegg, Thomas Ligotti, Thomas Tessier, Christopher Fowler, Karl Edward Wagner, and Terry Lamsley.

Fantasy

The Mammoth Book of Best New Horror, Volume 9. *New York: Carroll and Graf, 1998. 494p.* Annual collection of horror, terror, and dark fantasy showcasing both major and up-and-coming authors of the genre. Contributors include David J. Schow, Yvonne Navarro, Christopher Fowler, Thomas Ligotti, Brian Hodge, Ramsey Campbell, Caitlin R. Kiernan, and Kim Newman.

The Mammoth Book of Dracula: Vampire Tales for the New Millennium. *New York: Carroll and Graf, 1997. 512p.* This hundredth-anniversary tribute to Stoker's 1897 novel *Dracula* contains 33 stories, only 6 of which have been previously published. All stories include Dracula as a character. Contributors include Christopher Fowler, Thomas Ligotti, Ramsey Campbell, Manly Wade Wellman, Brian Lumley, Kim Newman, Hugh B. Cave, Roberta Lannes, Graham Masterton, Brian Stableford, and F. Paul Wilson.

Dracula (character) • Vampire Hunters • Vampire's Point of View

Kramer, Edward E. (editor).

Dark Destiny: Proprietors of Fate. *Clarkston, Ga.: White Wolf, 1995. 442p.* Twenty well-known names in the genre spin tales about historical figures as immortals who shape the fate of the world. A vampire assists Christ in resurrection; Alistair Crowley and Adolf Hitler battle one another with black magic during World War II; and the ghost of Archduke Francis Ferdinand possesses a man in post–World War I New Orleans in his quest to stop an immortal from thwarting Hitler's future rise to power. Contributors include Poppy Z. Brite, Charles L. Grant, Nancy Collins, Robert Weinberg, and Caitlin R. Kiernan.

Alternative History

Laudie, Catherine A. (editor).

Restless Spirits: Ghost Stories by American Women. *Boston: University of Massachusetts Press, 1997. 316p.* Twenty-two tales by some well-known, and some long-forgotten, American women writers. The stories are divided into five main themes: marriage, motherhood, sexual rivalry, madness, and widowhood or separation.

Leithauser, Brad (editor).

The Norton Book of Ghost Stories. *New York: W. W. Norton, 1994. 430p.* A collection of 28 stories arranged chronologically. Authors included are Henry James, M. R. James, Edith Wharton, Elizabeth Taylor, Oliver Onions, "Saki" (H.P. Munro), Elizabeth Bowen, W. F. Harvey, Shirley Jackson, V.S. Pritchett, Muriel Spark, Elizabeth Jane Howard, Marghanita Laski, Ann Bridge, Penelope Fitzgerald, John Cheever, A. S. Byatt, and Philip Graham.

Morrison, Robert, and Chris Baldick (editors).

Tales of Terror from Blackwood's Magazine. *New York: Oxford University Press, 1995. 298p.* A rare collection of gothic tales published in *Blackwood's Edinburgh Magazine* between 1817 and 1832. *Blackwood's,* one of the most important and influential literary-political journals of its time, was notorious for its shocking literary offerings. These tales "set a new standard of concentrated dread and precisely calculated alarm, and were to establish themselves as a landmark in the development of the short magazine story"—book jacket. Many of these tales are reminiscent of the works of Edgar Allan Poe. Contributors include Sir Walter Scott, John Galt, and William Godwin, half-brother of Mary Shelley.

The Vampyre and Other Tales of the Macabre. *New York: Oxford University Press, 1997. 278p.* A collection of 14 nineteenth-century English vampire tales previously published in pulp magazines of the time. Includes John Polidori's tale "The Vampyre," as well as stories by Sheridan LeFanu, Edward Bulwer-Lytton (writing as Edward Bulwer), Catherine Gore, Letitia Landon, and James Hogg.

Gothicism

Sammon, Paul M. (editor).

Splatterpunks over the Edge. *New York: Tor Books, 1995. 416p.* More "extreme horror" by acknowledged masters of the bizarre, such as Clive Barker, Martin Amis, Brian Hodge, Kathe Koja, Poppy Z. Brite, Nancy Holder, Melanie Tem, and Elizabeth Massie. A good mixture of best-selling, underground, and Stoker Award–winning authors of the genre.

Eroticism • Homoeroticism

Schimel, Lawrence, and Martin H. Greenberg (editors).

Blood Lines: Vampire Stories from New England. *Nashville, Tenn.: Cumberland House, 1997. 224p.* Ten vampire stories set in New England. Contributors include Manly Wade Wellman, H.P. Lovecraft, Chelsea Quinn Yarbro, and Hugh B. Cave.

New England

Southern Blood: Vampire Stories from the American South. *Nashville, Tenn.: Cumberland House, 1997. 203p.* Twelve vampire stories from the American South, with contributions by Dan Simmons, Billie Sue Mosiman, Manly Wade Wellman, and Brian Hodge.

The South

Slung, Michele (editor).

I Shudder at Your Touch. *New York: ROC Books, 1992. 408p.* Twenty-two weird tales about sex and horror, with representation of all subgenres of horror including vampire stories and ghost stories. Contributors include Stephen King, Michael Blumlein, Angela Carter, Thomas Disch, and Clive Barker.

Eroticism • Homoeroticism • Psychosexual Horror

Shudder Again. *New York: ROC Books, 1995. 363p.* The sequel to Slung's successful anthology, *I Shudder at Your Touch*, this collection contains another 22 stories about horror and desire. Contributors include Robert Bloch, Ray Bradbury, Ramsey Campbell, Harlan Ellison, Arthur Conan Doyle, J.G. Ballard, Nancy Collins, Lisa Tuttle, Thomas Ligotti, and Sarah Smith.

Eroticism • Homoeroticism • Psychosexual Horror

Stearns, Michael (editor).

A Nightmare's Dozen: Stories from the Dark. *San Diego, Calif.: Harcourt Brace, 1996. 239p.* An illustrated collection of dark fantasy featuring stories by horror/fantasy crossover authors such as Jane Yolen and Steve Rasnic Tem.

Fantasy

Stephens, John Richard (editor).

Vampires, Wine and Roses. *New York: Berkley, 1997. 384p.* A collection of 34 vampire tales by mostly literary writers, including a rare story by Anne Rice. Other authors included are William Shakespeare, Woody Allen, Edgar Allan Poe, Edith Wharton, Ivan Turgenev, Sir Walter Scott, Sir Arthur Conan Doyle, Alexander Dumas, John Keats, Voltaire, Jules Verne, Baudelaire, F. Scott Fitzgerald, H.P. Lovecraft, and Sting. Stephens's introduction discusses the history of vampires in print, from Sophocles to Marx to Virginia Woolf.

Wilson, F. Paul (editor).

Diagnosis: Terminal: An Anthology of Medical Terror. *New York: Forge, 1996. 349p.* A collection of medical terror by horror writers who don't generally dabble in this subgenre, including Chet Williamson, Billie Sue Mosiman, Karl Edward Wagner, Ed Gorman, and Thomas F. Monteleone.

> *Medical Horror*

Winter, Douglas E. (editor).

 Revelations. *New York: Harper Prism, 1997. 650p.* A collection of science-fiction/dark-fantasy/horror tales by contemporary writers well known for their contributions to the horror genre. Authors include Poppy Z. Brite, F. Paul Wilson, Charles Grant, Whitley Strieber, Elizabeth Massie, Richard Matheson, David J. Schow, Ramsey Campbell, Clive Barker, and Joe R. Lansdale. Winner of an International Horror Guild Award for Best Anthology.

> *Apocalypse • Fantasy • Science Fiction*

Our Picks

June's Picks: Any of *The Year's Best Fantasy and Horror Collections* (St. Martin's Press); *The Dark Descent,* David G. Hartwell (Tor Books); *Confederacy of the Dead,* Richard Gilliam, Martin H. Greenberg, and Edward E. Kramer (ROC Books); and *The Mammoth Book of Dracula: Vampire Tales for the New Millennium,* Stephen Jones, ed. (Carroll and Graf).

Tony's Picks: *Love in Vein: Twenty Original Tales of Vampire Erotica,* Poppy Z. Brite, ed. (Harper); *Gallery of Horror,* Charles L. Grant, ed. (New American Library); *Restless Spirits: Ghost Stories by American Women,* Catherine A. Laudie, ed. (University of Massachusetts Press); *Tales of Terror from Blackwood's Magazine,* Robert Morrison and Chris Baldick, eds. (Oxford University Press); *Revelations,* Douglas E. Winter, ed. (Harper Prism).

Chapter 6

Collections by Individual Authors

Short-story collections are particularly important for identifying writers who excel in the horror genre but who write exclusively, or almost exclusively, in the short-story format. As we noted in chapter 5, modern horror was born of the short-tale format, so in many ways these writers are the keepers of tradition in the genre. Yet more important is the fact that many of these authors—notably Edgar Allan Poe, Nathaniel Hawthorne, Edith Wharton, Sheridan LeFanu, H.P. Lovecraft, Angela Carter, Robert Aickman, and Thomas Ligotti—create nothing short of horror masterpieces using this brief literary form. Tales such as "The Tell-Tale Heart," "The Black Cat," "Young Goodman Brown," "Afterwards," *Carmilla*, "The Dunwich Horror," "The Rats in the Walls," "In the Company of Wolves," "No Stronger Than a Flower," "Pages from a Young Girl's Journal," and the Grimscribe tales have seldom been matched for their eloquence, atmosphere, and chilling effect.

This chapter annotates classics such as the tales of LeFanu and Poe, as well as collections by twentieth-century authors such as H.P. Lovecraft and Robert Aickman. It also identifies short-story collections by horror (and non-horror) novelists who dabble in the short-story genre on occasion, such as Clive Barker, Poppy Z. Brite, Isak Dinesen, Stephen King, Joyce Carol Oates, Peter Straub, Melanie Tem, and others. As in chapter 5, we have annotated collections only when it was possible to obtain the entire table of contents.

Appeals: Brevity of Reading Experience; Enjoyment of Writers Who Write Only Short Fiction in the Genre; Writer Loyalty

Aickman, Robert.

Cold Hand in Mine: Strange Stories. *New York: Scribner's, 1975. 215p.* This excellent collection of Hawthornesque strange tales contains a few of Aickman's classics: "The Swords," "The Hospice," and "Pages from a Young Girl's Journal," one of the best vampire short stories ever written. Also contains "The Real Road to the Church," "Niemandswasser," "The Same Dog," "Meeting Mr. Millar," and "The Clock Watcher." Aickman is a master of British subtlety.

Psychosexual Horror

Barker, Clive.

In the Flesh. *New York: Pocket Books, 1986. 187p.* One of Barker's best collections, featuring "The Madonna," "In the Flesh," and "Babel's Children." Each selection deals with the transformation of the human body into a monstrous creature. Also includes "The Forbidden," the story on which Bernard Rose based his script for the film *Candyman*.

Aliens • Demons

The Inhuman Condition. *New York: Pocket Books, 1987. 254p.* Five weird tales dealing with mortality, religion, and human desires for sex and violence. In "The Body Politic," human hands revolt against their masters and control the world. In "Revelations," a traveling evangelist and his long-suffering wife spend the night in a hotel room haunted by the ghosts of a faithless husband and the wife who was executed for his murder. In "Down, Satan!," a man who can't find God looks for the devil instead.

Religion—Christianity

Bloch, Robert.

Midnight Pleasures. *New York: Doubleday, 1987. 177p.* In these 14 short stories, a psychotic man, victimized by an overbearing mother, answers the "Jewish Question"; an artist cuckolds a wealthy South American painter and witnesses the spouse's bloody wrath; a middle-aged man must pay the price for a prank played when he was a child; and a bookseller discusses the existence of Count Dracula with an actual descendant of Abraham Van Helsing.

Revenge • Science Fiction

Bradbury, Ray.

Quicker Than the Eye. *New York: Avon, 1996. 261p.* Bradbury's first collection in 10 years, filled with the dark fantasy that made him a hallmark author.

Brite, Poppy Z.

Wormwood. *New York: Dell, 1995. 225p.* "In an old car rocking down a North Carolina highway with the radio on so loud you can't hear the music ... Behind a dusty Georgia carny show ... In a mausoleum in Baton Rouge, or an alley in Calcutta ... Here wanderers come to rest, the lost and lonely press their bodies up against each other, the heat rises, flesh yields, bones are bared, blood spills"—book jacket. An early example of Brite's poetic sense of the macabre and her eye for detail. Excellent.

Gay/Lesbian/Bisexual Characters • Homoeroticism • The South

Carter, Angela.

Burning Your Boats: The Collected Short Stories. *New York: Penguin, 1997. 462p.* An impressive volume of Carter's short fiction, including early work and previously unpublished stories. Carter is known for her ability to twist fairy tales and everyday events into uncanny, frightening landscapes that often contain biting social commentary.

Eroticism • Fairy Tales • Gothicism

Grimm, Jacob (editor).

Grimm's Grimmest. *San Francisco: Chronicle Books, 1997. 144p.* Twenty-two fairy tales based on the Grimm Brothers' 1822 edition (the contemporary horror literature of its day) before the stories became whitewashed Disney productions. Maria Tatar, a scholar of fairy tales who wrote the book's introduction, says that the stories in the genre are "the ancestors of our urban legends about vanishing hitchhikers and cats accidentally caught in the dryer or ... the preliterate equivalents of tabloid tales describing headless bodies found in topless bars."

Fairy Tales

Hynes, James.

Publish and Perish: Three Tales of Tenure and Terror. *New York: Picador, 1997. 338p.* Three tales of academic horror that pit arrogant American scholars against forces of evil beyond their control. Lots of dramatic irony and satire.

Academia

Jackson, Shirley.

The Lottery and Other Stories. *New York: Farrar, Straus & Giroux, 1982. 306p.* Twenty-five stories by the author of *The Haunting of Hill House*, in which the elitism and racism of the self-satisfied are exposed and the familiar is made uncanny. Includes "The Lottery," "The Daemon Lover," "Come Dance with Me in Ireland," and "A Fine Old Firm."

Human Sacrifice

King, Stephen.

Six Stories. *Bangor, Maine: Philtrum Press, 1997. 197p.* Dark fantasy by King, including two previously unpublished tales. Selections include "Lunch at the Gotham Cafe," "Autopsy Room Four," and "The Man in the Black Suit." A limited edition release.

Fantasy

Skeleton Crew. *New York: Putnam, 1985. 512p.* Psychological horror and campy weird tales reminiscent of B-movie horror flicks from the fifties and sixties. In the novella "The Mist," a supermarket becomes the last bastion of humanity as a sort of acid fog menaces humanity. In "Word Processor of the Gods," a man finds that he can change reality with the stroke of a key. In "The Monkey," a man's family and friends are unknowingly menaced by an unwholesome childhood toy.

Fantasy • Maine

Klein, T. E. D.

Dark Gods. *New York: Viking, 1986. 261p.* Lovecraftian horror tales, including the masterful urban horror story "Children of the Kingdom." Also: "Petey," "Black Man with a Horn," and "Nadleman's God."

Demons • New York City • Subterranean Monsters

Koontz, Dean.

Strange Highways. *New York: Warner Books, 1995. 561p.* Includes a novella about a young man who lives the same nightmare over and over again. Also includes "The Black Pumpkin," "Miss Attilla the Hun," "Down in the Darkness,"

"Ollie's Hands," "Snatcher," "Trapped," "Bruno," "We Three," "Hardshell," "Kittens," "The Night of the Storm," "Twilight of the Dawn," and "Chase."

Alcoholism • Time Travel

Lansdale, Joe R.

A Fist Full of Stories: and Articles. *Baltimore, Md.: CD Publications, 1996. 259p.* A quirky collection of some of Lansdale's short fiction, including "All American Hero," "Bar Talk," "Beyond the Light," "Billie Sue," "Change of Lifestyle," "Companion," "Drive In Date (the Play)," "Listen," "Master of Misery," "Mummy Buyer," "Old Charlie," "Pasture," "Personality Problem," "Story Notes," and "Two Bear Mombo (chapter six)."

LeFanu, Sheridan.

Through a Glass Darkly. *New York: Oxford University Press, 1872. 347p.* Five stories supposedly collected by LeFanu's character Dr. Hesselius, a "metaphysical doctor" who is a sort of precursor of Bram Stoker's Abraham Van Helsing. Stories include "Forever, Said the Duck," "The Hardened Criminals," "The Happy Man," "Light and the Sufferer," "Sleepy People," and "Vanilla Dunk."

Ligotti, Thomas.

Ⓑ **The Nightmare Factory.** *New York: Carroll and Graf, 1996. 551p.* A selection of works from four Ligotti collections—*Songs of a Dead Dreamer, Grimscribe, Noctuary,* and *Teatro Grottesco and Other Tales*—with a foreword by Poppy Z. Brite. Winner of a Bram Stoker Award. Similar title: *Cold Hand in Mine,* Robert Aickman.

Noctuary. *New York: Carroll and Graf, 1994. 194p.* In this book of eerie tales reminiscent of the stories of Edgar Allan Poe, Ligotti tells of a man compelled to kill children, the nature of horror, and an angel uncorrupted by dreams or thought.

Angels • Demons • Fantasy

Songs of a Dead Dreamer. *New York: Carroll and Graf, 1990. 275p.* Stories that run the full gamut of horror fiction, from the exotic and surreal to the domestic terrors populating every child's—and parent's—nightmares. Ligotti is a master of erudite dark fantasy that challenges the reader at many levels.

Dreams • Fantasy

Lovecraft, H.P.

Tales of H.P. Lovecraft: Major Works, edited by Joyce Carol Oates. *Hopewell, N.J.: Ecco Press, 1997. 328p.* Ten stories by Lovecraft, the master of weird tales who influenced modern-day masters of the genre such as Stephen King and Ramsey Campbell. The introduction, by editor Joyce Carol Oates, explains how "Lovecraft initiated the fusion of the gothic tale and what would come to be defined as science fiction." Stories in this collection include "The Call of Cthulhu," "At the Mountains of Madness," and "The Music of Erich Zann."

Science Fiction

Lumley, Brian.

The Horror at Oakdeene and Others. *Sauk City, Wis.: Arkham House, 1977. 229p.* Early work by the creator of the Necroscope series. Features "The Viking's Stone," "Aunt Hester," "No Way Home," "The Horror at Oakdeene," "The Cleaner Woman," "The Statement of Henry Worthy," "Darghud's Doll," and "Born of the Wind."

Haunted Houses • Magic

Matheson, Richard.

I Am Legend. *New York: Tor Books, 1995. 312p.* A reissue collection of weird tales by Richard Matheson, including his well-known vampire novella, *I Am Legend*, a tale of a postapocalyptic world overrun by vampires, which was later made into the film *The Omega Man*. Other stories included are "Dance of the Dead," "The Funeral," and "Dress of White Silk." Similar titles: *The Queen of Darkness*, Miguel Conner; *Bloodlust*, Ron Dee.

Apocalypse • Epidemic • Los Angeles, California • Science Fiction •
Vampire Hunters

The Incredible Shrinking Man. *New York: Tor Books, 1994. 373p.* A reissue of Matheson's classic novella, *The Incredible Shrinking Man*, a post–World War II tale of a man who begins shrinking after being sprayed by a mysterious radioactive mist. This novella was made into a film by Jack Arnold in 1957. Also in this collection are nine other stories, including "Duel" (made into a film in 1971 by Steven Spielberg) and "Nightmare at 20,000 Feet" (made into an episode of *The Twilight Zone*).

Science Fiction

Oates, Joyce Carol.

Haunted: Tales of the Grotesque. *London: Signet, 1994. 310p.* A collection of 16 tales by the modern mistress of the gothic and psychological horror.

Eroticism • Gothicism

Poe, Edgar Allan.

Selected Tales. *New York: Vintage, 1991. 436p.* Stories by the father of American psychological horror and the detective story. Included in this collection are "The Tell-Tale Heart," "The Masque of the Red Death," "The Pit and the Pendulum," "The Fall of the House of Usher," "The Black Cat," and "The Cask of Amontillado."

Simmons, Dan.

Lovedeath. *New York: Warner Books, 1993. 354p.* Five novellas: "Entropy's Bed at Midnight," "Dying in Bangkok," "Sleeping with Teeth Women," "Flashback," and "The Great Lover," all about the connection between love, sex, and death. Thoughtful and provocative first-person narratives.

Eroticism • War—World War I

Stoker, Bram.

Best Ghost and Horror Stories. *Mineola, N.Y.: Dover Books, 1997. 242p.* An original compilation of 14 of Stoker's stories from various earlier editions. Though not all the selections deal with the ghostly and supernatural, they are always bizarre, and some are equal to Poe at his best. Includes "The Dualists," "A Dream of Red Hands," "The Secret of the Growing Gold," and "Dracula's Guest," which was omitted from Stoker's 1897 novel *Dracula*. Introduction by Richard Dalby.

Fantasy • Gothicism

Midnight Tales. *Chester Springs, Pa.: Dufour Editions, 1995. 182p.* Some of Stoker's lesser works, collected and edited by Peter Haining and with a foreword by Christopher Lee. Stories include "Midnight Tales," "Bridal of Dead," "The Man from Shorrox," and "The Spectre of Doom."

Gothicism • Revenge

Straub, Peter.

Houses Without Doors. *New York: Signet Books, 1991. 454p.* A schoolboy hypnotizes his little brother and discovers a dark and deadly power. Straub's first collection of short fiction reflects his elegant, hard-edged approach to horror, both psychological and occult-oriented.

Wandrei, Donald.

Don't Dream: The Collected Horror and Fantasy of Donald Wandrei. *Minneapolis, Minn.: Fedogan & Bremer, 1997. 394p.* Includes "The Green Flame," "When the Fire Creatures Came," "The Fire Vampires," "The Lady in Grey," "A Scientist Divides," and "The Destroying Hoard," as well as some prose poems, essays, and marginalia.

> *Fantasy*

Wharton, Edith.

The Ghost Stories of Edith Wharton. *New York: Scribner's, 1997. 288p.* Eleven of Wharton's chilling tales, with Wharton's 1937 preface. Illustrated by Laszlo Kubinyi.

> *New England • United States—Nineteenth Century*

Zweifel, Karyn Kay.

Dog-Gone Ghost Stories. *Birmingham, Ala.: Crane Hill, 1996. 163p.* Storyteller Kay Zweifel has 13 ghost stories about dogs in this unusual anthology. Firehouse Annie, long gone from this world, still saves lives by giving advance warning of disasters. A two-headed dog patrols River Road at night, while a headless dog looks for mortal companionship. Similar title: *Twists of the Tale*, Ellen Daltow, ed.

> *Dogs*

Our Picks

June's Picks: *Burning Your Boats,* Angela Carter (Penguin); *Through a Glass Darkly,* Sheridan LeFanu (Oxford University Press); *I Am Legend* and *The Incredible Shrinking Man,* Richard Matheson (Tor Books); *Houses Without Doors,* Peter Straub (Signet Books).

Tony's Picks: *Cold Hand in Mine,* Robert Aickman (Scribner's); *Wormwood,* Poppy Z. Brite (Dell); *Dark Gods,* T. E. D. Klein (Viking); *Through a Glass Darkly,* Sheridan LeFanu (Oxford University Press); *Lovedeath,* Dan Simmons (Warner Books).

Part 3

An Annotated Bibliography of
Horror Novels and Films

Chapter 7

Ghosts and Haunted Houses: Dealing with Presences and Absences

Ambrose Bierce, in *The Devil's Dictionary* (Oxford, 1999), defined the word *ghost* as "the outward manifestation of an inward fear." Though humorous, Bierce's commentary on ghosts implies what writers of traditional ghost tales have known for a long time: most sightings are more a result of an individual's overactive imagination—fed by guilt, remorse, grief, or paranoia—than of actual visitations by otherworldly beings.

On one level, ghost and haunted-house stories can be viewed as tales of guilt, guilt often thought to be long buried in the unconscious mind. The ghost or haunted house serves as a portent, or warning, to the haunted person, who is often guilty either of actual wrongdoing or of having (repressed) knowledge of a wrongdoing. The poltergeist and possessed abode can also serve as a signal to others who know nothing of the past sin, thus reminding the haunted individual of the inadvisability of ignoring or burying this newly acquired knowledge in the unconscious mind. In this view, haunted houses may be interpreted as symbols of the psyche. Although ghosts and haunted houses often go hand in hand, in this chapter we include works concerned with either one type of supernatural visitation or the other, as we argue that, contrary to popular belief, ghosts do not necessarily reside in haunted houses, and ghosts have more of a purpose to their existence than do haunted houses.

A metaphorical comparison may better help explain the difference between the two: haunted houses are a sort of architectural version of abused children who lash out at the world. In contrast, the ghost's function is to educate the wrongdoer: the three ghosts in Dickens's "A Christmas Carol" teach Scrooge the meaning of Christmas; Hamlet's father's ghost tells him of a "murder most foul"; the ghost of Beloved in Toni Morrison's novel teaches Sethe to forgive her own past sins. Usually, as in the Dickens example, ghosts are created or summoned by the wrongdoer's transgression. The haunted house, however, is a victim of events that either happened in the house itself or on the site of the house prior to the house's erection. Hill House, in Shirley Jackson's novel, is haunted because its creator and original inhabitant, Hugh Crane, was a twisted New England Puritan who was incapable of love. Unlike ghosts, haunted houses don't try to educate later occupants about the wages of sin or repressed guilt; instead, they only lash out and scare anyone unfortunate enough to come under their roofs, sometimes with fatal consequences.

This chapter includes works that trace the ghost story from its literary beginnings, with Robert Louis Stevenson; to its development, by turn-of-the-century writers such as M. R. James, Henry James, Edith Wharton, and Oliver Onions; into the form we recognize today in the works of Shirley Jackson, Stephen King, and Peter Straub. Representative titles in this chapter include Kingsley Amis's *The Green Man*, Thomas M. Disch's *The Business Man*, Toni Morrison's *Beloved*, Peter Straub's *Ghost Story*, and others. This chapter also includes works that trace the beginnings of the literary haunted house in Britain, with the prototypes seen in *The Castle of Otranto* and *Northanger Abbey*. Also featured are novels showing how the Americanization of the haunted house led to the development of the haunted forest/landscape and the haunted mind, as seen in the fiction of Hawthorne, Poe, and Henry James. Notable titles in this chapter include Jay Anson's *The Amityville Horror*, Poppy Z. Brite's *Drawing Blood*, Shirley Jackson's *The Haunting of Hill House*, Stephen King's *The Shining*, and Peter Straub's *Ghost Story*.

Appeals: Affirms Human Beliefs of Life After Death; Simulates Childhood Stories and Campfire Stories; Universal Fear of "Bumps in the Night" When Nothing Is There; Universal Fear of Returning Dead

Amis, Kingsley.

The Green Man. *New York: Harcourt Brace, 1969. 252p.* (See chapter 19, "Comic Horror.")

Anson, Jay.

The Amityville Horror. *Englewood Cliffs, N.J.: Prentice-Hall, 1977. 207p.* The Lutz family moves into its dream house on 112 Ocean Avenue in Amityville, Long Island, despite knowing that the house was once the scene of a mass murder. When extremely strange, inexplicable events begin to occur, the Lutzes must face the fact that they own a haunted house. In this action-oriented, easily read novel, Anson adds his own touch to one of the best-known horror icons—the haunted suburban dwelling. Similar titles: *House of Echoes*, Barbara Erskine; *Poltergeist* and *Poltergeist II*, James Kahn; *The Voice in the Basement*, T. Chris Martindale; *The Basement*, Bari Wood.

Haunted Houses • New York State

Austen, Jane.

Northanger Abbey. *New York: Penguin, 1986. [First published in 1818.] 221p.* (See chapter 19, "Comic Horror.")

Aycliffe, Jonathan.
The Lost. *New York: Harper Prism, 1996. 264p.* (See chapter 9, "Vampires and Werewolves.")

Baldick, Chris (editor).
The Oxford Book of Gothic Tales. *New York: Oxford University Press, 1992. 526p.* (See chapter 5, "Anthologies and Collections by Multiple Authors.")

Barker, Clive.
In the Flesh. *New York: Pocket Books, 1986. 187p.* (See chapter 6, "Collections by Individual Authors.")

The Inhuman Condition. *New York: Pocket Books, 1987. 254p.* (See chapter 6, "Collections by Individual Authors.")

Bischoff, David.
The Crow: Quoth the Crow. *New York: Harper Prism, 1998. 256p.* (See chapter 18, "Splatterpunk.")

Blaylock, James P.
Winter Tides. *New York: Ace Books, 1997. 346p.* Ghost story about twins, one of whom drowns in an accident in which a friend is forced to choose between saving one or the other sibling. Now, a local psychic seems to be unwillingly channeling the dead twin. Erudite, with emphasis on characterization.

> *California • Revenging Revenant • Twins*

Bloch, Robert.
Lori. *New York: Tor Books, 1989. 282p.* When Lori Holmes returns home from college graduation, she finds her childhood home engulfed in flames, with her parents inside. Then Lori discovers that the family is bankrupt and that she is linked to a mysterious woman named Priscilla Fairmount. Priscilla's college yearbook photo has Lori's face—but the book was printed before Lori was born. Now she falls victim to horrifying nightmares in which she can feel the flesh rotting from her long-dead bones, can hear the dead calling to her; in her waking hours, she's drawn into a web of murder, deceit, and supernatural danger. Similar titles: *Drawing Blood*, Poppy Z. Brite; *Double Edge*, Dennis Etchison.

> *Revenge*

Midnight Pleasures. *New York: Doubleday, 1987. 177p.* (See chapter 6, "Collections by Individual Authors.")

Brite, Poppy Z.
The Crow: The Lazarus Heart. *New York: Harper Prism, 1998. 256p.* (See chapter 18, "Splatterpunk.")

Drawing Blood. *Dell: New York, 1994. 403p.* (See chapter 18, "Splatterpunk.")

Brontë, Emily.
Wuthering Heights. *New York: Cambridge University Press, 1997. 416p.* Catherine Earnshaw has loved Heathcliff ever since her father brought him home as a stray waif. But Catherine's father passes away, and when she comes of age, her brother refuses to countenance her relationship with the gypsy foundling, instead encouraging his sister to marry the more gently bred Edgar Linton. Heathcliff is driven mad by his thwarted love, and after Catherine's death seeks

to destroy the Linton and Earnshaw families. But revenge cannot calm Heathcliff, and he is forever haunted by Catherine's ghost at Wuthering Heights. First published in 1847 and considered a literary classic. Has inspired several films, including one directed by Luis Buñuel in 1954. Similar titles: *Beloved*, Toni Morrison; *The Phantom of the Opera*, Gaston LeRoux.

England • Gothic Romance • Revenge • Sibling Rivalry

Brust, Steven.

Agyar. *New York: Tor Books, 1993. 254p.* (See chapter 9, "Vampires and Werewolves.")

Campbell, Ramsey.

The Influence. *New York: Macmillan, 1988. 260p.* (See chapter 10, "Demonic Possession, Satanism, Black Magic, and Witches and Warlocks.")

Nazareth Hill. *New York: Doherty, 1997. 383p.* When eight-year-old Amy's father holds her up so she can see inside one of the windows of Nazarill—an old, decrepit building in Partington, England—she sees something move ... something spidery and ghostlike. Eight years later, her father is the caretaker of Nazarill, now a renovated hostelry. When one of Nazarill's tenants dies of heart failure, Amy suspects that the ghost she saw as a child is seeking revenge. But can she get anyone, even her own father, to believe her? A spellbinding novel. Recipient of an International Literary Guild Award for Best Novel. Similar titles: *Deadly Friend*, Keith Ferrario; *Passive Intruder*, Michael Upchurch; *Hell Fire*, John Saul; *Sacrifice*, John Farris; *Summer of Night*, Dan Simmons.

Haunted Houses • Parenting • Photographer as Character

Card, Orson Scott.

Homebody. *New York: HarperCollins, 1998. 291p.* Don Lark, a contractor specializing in fixer-uppers, can't get over the death of his two-year-old daughter, and fills his days and nights with work. But when he purchases a decaying mansion in Greensboro, North Carolina, he finds it difficult to avoid human contact. The mansion comes complete with a squatter and two elderly female neighbors who want Don to tear down the house, which they believe has a malign influence over them. And then there's the mysterious tunnel in the basement. Similar titles: *Lost Boys*, Orson Scott Card; *The Haunting of Hill House*, Shirley Jackson; *Cemetery of Angels*, Noel Hynd.

African-American Characters • Gothic Romance • Grieving • Haunted Houses • North Carolina

Lost Boys. *New York: HarperCollins, 1992. 528p.* Step Fletcher moves his devout Mormon family to the small town of Steuben, North Carolina, so that he can accept employment with Eight Bits, a software company. The Fletchers soon discover that their new North Carolina home is not Mayberry, but rather the site of a great evil that has their son Steven in its grip. Card's leisurely paced novel is laced with fascinating details of everyday Mormon life, and successfully interweaves the drama and horror of daily life with the supernatural. Similar titles: *Homebody*, Orson Scott Card; *Cemetery of Angels*, Noel Hynd; *The Haunting of Hill House*, Shirley Jackson; *Tainted Blood*, Andrew Billings.

Child Molesters • Computers • Marriage • North Carolina • Parenting • Religion— Christianity—Mormonism • Serial Killers

Treasure Box. *New York: HarperCollins, 1996. 372p.* (See chapter 10, "Demonic Possession, Satanism, Black Magic, and Witches and Warlocks.")

Chadbourn, Mark.

Scissorman. *London: Victor Gollancz, 1997. 352p.* (See chapter 11, "Mythological Monsters and 'The Old Ones.' ")

Clegg, Douglas.

The Children's Hour. *New York: Dell, 1995. 383p.* (See chapter 13, "Small-Town Horror.")

Codrescu, Andrei.

The Blood Countess. *New York: Simon & Schuster, 1995. 347p.* (See chapter 17, "Psychological Horror.")

Cody, Jack.

The Off Season. *New York: St. Martin's Press, 1995. 352p.* (See chapter 19, "Comic Horror.")

Collins, Nancy A.

Sunglasses After Dark. *New York: New American Library, 1989. 253p.* (See chapter 9, "Vampires and Werewolves.")

Tempter. *New York: Penguin, 1990. 299p.* (See chapter 9, "Vampires and Werewolves.")

Cox, Michael (editor).

The Oxford Book of Twentieth-Century Ghost Stories. *New York: Oxford University Press, 1996. 425p.* (See chapter 5, "Anthologies and Collections by Multiple Authors.")

Twelve Tales of the Supernatural. New York: Oxford University Press, 1997. 188p. (See chapter 5, "Anthologies and Collections by Multiple Authors.")

Cox, Michael, and R. A. Gilbert (editors).

The Oxford Book of English Ghost Stories. *New York: Oxford University Press, 1986. 505p.* (See chapter 5, "Anthologies and Collections by Multiple Authors.")

Victorian Ghost Stories. *New York: Oxford University Press, 1992. 497p.* (See chapter 5, "Anthologies and Collections by Multiple Authors.")

Dalby, Richard (editor).

The Mammoth Book of Victorian and Edwardian Ghost Stories. *New York: Carroll and Graf, 1995. 573p.* (See chapter 5, "Anthologies and Collections by Multiple Authors.")

Daltow, Ellen, and Terri Windling (editors).

The Year's Best Fantasy and Horror: Ninth Annual Collection (1995). *New York: St. Martin's Press, 1996. 534p.* (See chapter 5, "Anthologies and Collections by Multiple Authors.")

The Year's Best Fantasy and Horror: Tenth Annual Collection (1996). *New York: St. Martin's Press, 1997. 534p.* (See chapter 5, "Anthologies and Collections by Multiple Authors.")

David, James F.

Fragments. *New York: Tor Books, 1997. 381p.* (See chapter 15, "Technohorror.")

Disch, Thomas M.

The Business Man. *New York: Berkley, 1984. 325p.* (See chapter 19, "Comic Horror.")

Dziemianowicz, Stefan R., Martin H. Greenberg, and Robert Weinberg (editors).

The Mists from Beyond. *New York: ROC Books, 1995. 362p.* (See chapter 5, "Anthologies and Collections by Multiple Authors.")

Erskine, Barbara.

House of Echoes. *New York: Signet Books, 1996. 476p.* When Joss Grant inherits Belheddon Hall, all she knows of the house is that her two young brothers died there many years ago. But townspeople whisper of a curse on both the house and Joss's family, and laughter of young boys is heard in the house. After the birth of Joss's second son, mysterious bruises appear on both sons. Similar titles: *Houses of Stone*, Barbara Michaels; other titles by Barbara Erskine; *The Amityville Horror*, Jay Anson; *December*, Phil Rickman.

England • Haunted Houses • Revenging Revenant • Witchcraft

Midnight Is a Lonely Place. *New York: Signet Books, 1995. 447p.* All best-selling biographer Kate Kennedy wants is some peace and quiet, to recover from the breakup of her last relationship and to write her book. But when she escapes to a remote cottage on the English coast, she discovers an ancient grave containing a Celtic necklace, and soon eerie sounds of doors opening by themselves, shocking vandalism, and smells of musky perfume and damp earth are filling Kate's nights with fear. Similar titles: *Houses of Stone*, Barbara Michaels; other titles by Barbara Erskine; *December*, Phil Rickman; *Greely's Cove*, John Gideon.

England • Haunted Houses • Religion—Druidism • Revenging Revenant • Writer as Character

Etchison, Dennis.

Double Edge. *New York: Bantam, 1997. 272p.* A woman working on a documentary about Lizzie Borden soon finds herself at the center of a series of violent slayings. Has she awakened Borden's ghost, or is someone trying to get her? Similar title: *Lori*, Robert Bloch.

Borden, Lizzie (character)

Ferrario, Keith.

Deadly Friend. *New York: Leisure Books, 1994. 358p.* Georgie is a lonely little boy and has difficulty making friends—because he's dead. But he finds a friend in Bobby, another lonely little boy, whose Down's syndrome makes it difficult for him to have friends. Georgie is nothing if not loyal, and when the town bullies pick on Bobby and his socially inept, unpopular older brother, Georgie gives them the punishment they so richly deserve. Told from multiple points of view. Similar titles: *Comes the Blind Fury*, John Saul; *Nazareth Hill*, Ramsey Campbell; *My Soul to Keep*, Judith Hawkes.

Childhood • Mental Retardation • Revenging Revenant

Garfield, Henry.

Room 13. *New York: St. Martin's Press, 1997. 309p.* An English teacher moves to a small town in California to escape the scandals that plague her. She finds herself teaching in a haunted classroom, surrounded by strange colleagues and students. Erudite and humorous. Similar titles: *The Off Season*, Jack Cody; *Madeleine's Ghost*, Robert Girardi.

> *California • Haunted Houses • Mental Retardation • Teacher as Character • Werewolves*

Gelder, Ken (editor).

The Oxford Book of Australian Ghost Stories. *New York: Oxford University Press, 1996. 294p.* (See chapter 5, "Anthologies and Collections by Multiple Authors.")

Gideon, John.

Kindred. *New York: Jove Books, 1996. 419p.* (See chapter 9, "Vampires and Werewolves.")

Gilliam, Richard, and Martin H. Greenberg (editors).

Phantoms of the Night. *New York: Daw Books, 1996. 390p.* (See chapter 5, "Anthologies and Collections by Multiple Authors.")

Gilliam, Richard, Martin H. Greenberg, and Edward E. Kramer (editors).

Confederacy of the Dead. *New York: ROC Books, 1995. 474p.* (See chapter 5, "Anthologies and Collections by Multiple Authors.")

Girardi, Robert.

Madeleine's Ghost. *New York: Delacorte Press, 1995. 356p.* A young graduate student from south Louisiana moves to Brooklyn to accept a low-paying research job from a priest. In the meantime, he figures out that his apartment is haunted, and that the ghost wants him. Emphasis is on characterization, setting, and description. Similar title: *Room 13*, Henry Garfield.

> *Academia • Clergy as Character • Haunted Houses • New York City • Religion—Christianity—Catholicism*

Vaporetto 13. *New York: Delacorte Press, 1997. 197p.* Jack Squire, a currency trader on assignment from Washington, D.C., takes up residence in Venice, where he meets the mysterious Caterina, a woman who can reveal nothing of her past and who seems to possess Squire's very soul. Squire begins to suspect that Caterina lives between two worlds—the world of the living and that of the dead.

> *Cats • Gothic Romance • Venice, Italy*

Goshgarian, Gary.

The Stone Circle: A Novel. *London: Donald I. Fine, 1997. 296p.* (See chapter 10, "Demonic Possession, Satanism, Black Magic, and Witches and Warlocks.")

Grafton, John (editor).

Great Ghost Stories. *Mineola, N.Y.: Dover Books, 1992. 100p.* (See chapter 5, "Anthologies and Collections by Multiple Authors.")

Grant, Charles L., and Wendy Webb (editors).

Gothic Ghosts. *New York: St. Martin's Press, 1998. 256p.* (See chapter 5, "Anthologies and Collections by Multiple Authors.")

Graves, Elizabeth.

Black River. *New York: Berkley, 1992. 239p.* (See chapter 13, "Small-Town Horror.")

Greenberg, Martin H. (editor).

White House Horrors. *New York: Daw Books, 1996. 316p.* (See chapter 5, "Anthologies and Collections by Multiple Authors.")

Greenberg, Martin H., Frank McSherry, and Charles G. Waugh (editors).

Civil War Ghosts. *Little Rock, Ark.: August House, 1991. 205p.* (See chapter 5, "Anthologies and Collections by Multiple Authors.")

Gregory, Stephen.

The Cormorant. *Clarkston, Ga.: White Wolf, 1996. 147p.* (See chapter 17, "Psychological Horror.")

Hartwell, David G. (editor).

The Dark Descent. *New York: Tor Books, 1987. 1,011p.* (See chapter 5, "Anthologies and Collections by Multiple Authors.")

Hautala, Rick.

Dark Silence. *New York: Kensington, 1992. 477p.* A young boy is drawn to his family's old mill in Maine, unaware of the evil that has lurked there since the hanging of a witch in the 1600s.

Maine • Revenging Revenant • Secret Sin

Hawkes, Judith.

Julian's House. *New York: New American Library, 1991. 400p.* (See chapter 17, "Psychological Horror.")

My Soul to Keep. *New York: Signet Books, 1997. 416p.* After her marriage breaks up, Nan Lucas moves with her nine-year-old son to her grandmother's ranch in Tennessee. When her son's "imaginary friend" resurfaces after four years, Nan is at first worried. But when her son's friend starts leading him into danger, Nan begins to suspect that more than imagination is at work. Similar title: *Deadly Friend*, Keith Ferrario.

Parenting • Photographer as Character • Secret Sin • Tennessee

Hawthorne, Nathaniel.

The House of the Seven Gables. *New York: Oxford University Press, 1991. 328p.* (See chapter 17, "Psychological Horror.")

Herbert, James.

Haunted. *New York: Jove Books, 1990. 338p.* The surviving heirs of the Mariell family know that their country home is haunted by an unspoken horror from the past. Now they've challenged David Ash, a skeptical psychic investigator, to prove them wrong—to dismiss the chilling sounds of a child's distant laughter. But not even Ash can explain the shockingly real vision of a pale young girl whose irresistible embrace pulls him down beneath the weeds of the garden pond, and may trap him there forever. Similar title: *The Haunting of Hill House*, Shirley Jackson.

England • Haunted Houses • Parapsychology

Holder, Nancy.

> **Dead in the Water.** *New York: Bantam, 1994. 413p.* (See chapter 10, "Demonic Possession, Satanism, Black Magic, and Witches and Warlocks.")

Huff, Tanya.

> **Blood Debt.** *New York: Daw Books, 1997. 330p.* (See chapter 9, "Vampires and Werewolves.")

Hynd, Noel.

> **Cemetery of Angels.** *New York: Kensington, 1995. 412p.* Rebecca Moore and her family move from Connecticut to Los Angeles after someone tries to kill Rebecca. The reasonably priced fixer-upper they purchase abuts a cemetery, and is haunted by a ghost that, at first, only the children can see. Then the children disappear under mysterious circumstances, and the ghost begins communicating with Rebecca. In the cemetery next door, a 2,000-pound monument has been toppled—the body beneath seems to have blasted through the earth and disappeared. Eerie and atmospheric. Similar titles: *Lost Boys* and *Homebody,* Orson Scott Card; *The Haunting of Hill House*, Shirley Jackson.

> *Cemeteries • Los Angeles, California • Precognition • Reincarnation*

> **A Room for the Dead.** *New York: Pinnacle, 1994. 412p.* (See chapter 17, "Psychological Horror.")

Jackson, Shirley.

> **The Haunting of Hill House.** *New York: Farrar, Straus & Giroux, 1982. [First published in 1949.] 306p.* Four people spending a weekend at Hill House to study the paranormal find themselves haunted by a sinister spirit. To make matters worse, one of the guests, Eleanor, a shy young woman in her thirties, seems to have been singled out by the "house." Jackson shows her mastery of storytelling and characterization in this classic of the genre, which was later made into an effective film by Robert Wise (*The Haunting*, 1963). Written in her characteristic third-person objective style, but very effective. Similar titles: *Homebody* and *Lost Boys*, Orson Scott Card; *Cemetery of Angels*, Noel Hynd; *Haunted*, James Herbert; *Poltergeist* and *Poltergeist II*, James Kahn; *The Crying Child*, Barbara Michaels; *When the Wind Blows*, John Saul; *The Basement*, Bari Wood; *University*, Bentley Little; *Julian's House*, Judith Hawkes.

> *Haunted Houses • Parapsychology • Religion—Christianity—Protestantism • Suicide*

Kahn, James. The Poltergeist series.

> **Poltergeist.** *New York: Warner Books, 1982. 301p.* The Freelings' home in Cuesta Verde Estates is built atop a burial ground. Using the family television set, ghosts contact six-year-old Carole Anne. But what do the poltergeists want? Novelization of the 1982 film of the same name. Similar titles: *Poltergeist II*, James Kahn; *The Haunting of Hill House*, Shirley Jackson; *The Amityville Horror*, Jay Anson.

> *California • Haunted Houses • Revenging Revenant*

> **Poltergeist II.** *New York: Ballantine, 1986. 179p.* To escape the poltergeists, the Freelings move from Cuesta Verde, California, to Phoenix, Arizona. However, again they find themselves plagued by strange beasts and a vengeful ghost. An easy read, based on the 1986 film of the same name. Similar titles: *Poltergeist*, James Kahn; *The Haunting of Hill House*, Shirley Jackson; *The Amityville Horror*, Jay Anson.

> *Child Molesters*

Kearsley, Susanna.

The Shadowy Horses. *London: Vista, 1998. 316p.* Archaeologist Verity Grey joins an expedition launched by a wealthy eccentric who, for the past 40 years, has searched for the Ninth Legion of the Roman army, which mysteriously disappeared from Scotland about A.D. 115. The only evidence that the famed lost legion lies buried on the site comes from an eight-year-old boy, who regularly communes with a ghostly Roman sentinel who speaks to him in Latin. Strong on atmosphere. Similar titles: *Houses of Stone* and *House of Many Shadows*, Barbara Michaels; *Virgins and Martyrs*, Simon Maginn.

Archaeology • Precognition • Romans—Ancient • Scholars • Scotland

Kihn, Greg.

Shade of Pale. *New York: Forge, 1997. 256p.* A New York City psychiatrist, Jukes Wahler, who is searching for his sister, is visited by the Banshee, the Irish ghost of wronged womanhood. Soon others who have seen the Banshee die in a grisly fashion. Is Jukes next, and can he find his sister before she falls prey to a vicious serial killer? Similar title: *Horror Show*, Greg Kihn.

Banshee, The • New York City • Psychiatrist as Character • Serial Killers

King, Stephen.

Bag of Bones. *New York: Scribner's, 1998. 560p.* A writer of thriller novels returns to his lake home in Maine to investigate his wife's death. In the process, he leaves himself open to visitations from various ghosts. Vintage King.

Haunted Houses • Maine • Writer as Character

The Shining. *New York: Plume, 1977. 416p.* (See chapter 10, "Demonic Possession, Satanism, Black Magic, and Witches and Warlocks.")

The Tommyknockers. *New York: Signet Books, 1988. 747p.* (See chapter 10, "Demonic Possession, Satanism, Black Magic, and Witches and Warlocks.")

Kinion, Richard.

Sacrifice. *New York: Kensington, 1995. 380p.* After a terrible breakup with her boyfriend and a horrible accident that leaves her without one leg from the knee down, Alice Sterling, at the suggestion of her psychiatrist, Dr. Holly Ryan, takes up residence in the Taylor Watch House. Little does she know that the spirit of an evil seductress inhabits the house, and now it wants her body. Can Dr. Ryan's newly realized love for Alice save her? A clever twist on the romantic triangle, from a lesbian point of view. Similar title: *Witch*, Barbara Michaels.

Demons • Gay/Lesbian/Bisexual Characters • Haunted Houses • Psychiatrist as Character

Kiraly, Marie.

Leanna. *New York: Berkley, 1996. 341p.* (See chapter 10, "Demonic Possession, Satanism, Black Magic, and Witches and Warlocks.")

Klavan, Andrew.

The Uncanny. *New York: Crown, 1998. 343p.* (See chapter 19, "Comic Horror.")

Koontz, Dean.

The House of Thunder. *New York: Berkley, 1992. 253p.* (See chapter 17, "Psychological Horror.")

Strange Highways. *New York: Warner Books, 1995. 561p.* (See chapter 6, "Collections by Individual Authors.")

Laudie, Catherine A. (editor).

Restless Spirits: Ghost Stories by American Women. *Boston: University of Massachusetts Press, 1997. 316p.* (See chapter 5, "Anthologies and Collections by Multiple Authors.")

Laymon, Richard.

The Midnight Tour. *Baltimore, Md.: Cemetery Dance Publications, 1998. 596p.* (See chapter 17, "Psychological Horror.")

LeFanu, Sheridan.

Through a Glass Darkly. *New York: Oxford University Press, 1872. 347p.* (See chapter 6, "Collections by Individual Authors.")

Leithauser, Brad (editor).

The Norton Book of Ghost Stories. *New York: W. W. Norton, 1994. 430p.* (See chapter 5, "Anthologies and Collections by Multiple Authors.")

Lumley, Brian.

The Horror at Oakdeene and Others. *Sauk City, Wis.: Arkham House, 1977. 229p.* (See chapter 6, "Collections by Individual Authors.")

Maginn, Simon.

Virgins and Martyrs. *Clarkston, Ga.: White Wolf, 1996. 316p.* (See chapter 17, "Psychological Horror.")

Martindale, T. Chris.

Demon Dance. *New York: Pocket Books, 1991. 294p.* (See chapter 10, "Demonic Possession, Satanism, Black Magic, and Witches and Warlocks.")

Nightblood. *New York: Warner Books, 1990. 322p.* (See chapter 9, "Vampires and Werewolves.")

The Voice in the Basement. *New York: Pocket Books, 1993. 279p.* Mitch and Cathy Ballard are about to discover an evil presence lurking in their basement—one that produces graphically violent visions and humanoid monsters. Can the psychic bonds that exist between husband and wife defeat pure evil? Similar titles: *The Amityville Horror*, Jay Anson; *The Night Boat*, Robert R. McCammon; *The Basement*, Bari Wood.

Dreams • Haunted Houses • Indiana • Marriage

Masterson, Graham.

The House That Jack Built. *New York: Carroll and Graf, 1996. 384p.* (See chapter 10, "Demonic Possession, Satanism, Black Magic, and Witches and Warlocks.")

McCammon, Robert R.

The Night Boat. *New York: Pocket Books, 1980. 343p.* A young diver accidentally raises a sunken German U-boat in Coquina Harbor, the site of a pleasant Caribbean island community. After several trawlers and welders are mysteriously killed, the local voodoo priest suspects an evil presence in the submarine—the vengeful ghosts of the U-boat's crew. Similar titles: *The Voice in the Basement*, T. Chris Martindale; *Good Night, Sweet Angel*, Clare McNally; *Cry for the Strangers*, John Saul.

Cursed Objects • Maritime Horror • Nazism • Revenging Revenant • War—World War II

McDaniels, Abigail.

Althea. *New York: Kensington, 1995. 253p.* (See chapter 10, "Demonic Possession, Satanism, Black Magic, and Witches and Warlocks.")

Dead Voices. *New York: Kensington, 1994. 252p.* (See chapter 13, "Small-Town Horror.")

McFarland, Dennis.

A Face at the Window. *New York: Bantam, 1998. 309p.* Ex-alcoholic and addict Cookson Selway travels to England with his wife Ellen, a mystery writer. While staying at the Willerton Hotel, Selway meets three ghosts, leading to a relationship that strains his hold on reality. Emphasis on characterization and psychology. Similar titles: *Nazareth Hill*, Ramsey Campbell; *The Shining*, Stephen King; "The Beckoning Fair One," Oliver Onions; *Violin*, Anne Rice; *The Green Man*, Kingsley Amis.

Alcoholism • Haunted Houses • London, England • Marriage • Writer as Character

McNally, Clare.

Good Night, Sweet Angel. *New York: Tor Books, 1996. 344p.* Jean Galbraith's ex tries to kill her and her four-year-old in an attempted murder/suicide, but succeeds only in killing himself. But her problems are not over, for it seems that his ghost is now intent on finishing the job. Similar title: *The Night Boat*, Robert R. McCammon.

Domestic Violence • Suicide

Michaels, Barbara.

Ammie, Come Home. *New York: Berkley, 1993. [First published in 1969.] 252p.* (See chapter 10, "Demonic Possession, Satanism, Black Magic, and Witches and Warlocks.")

The Crying Child. *New York: Berkley, 1971, 289p.* When Jo McMullen's older sister suffers a nervous breakdown after a miscarriage, she joins her family on their small island estate. But the seclusion isn't therapeutic for Jo's sister. Instead, she is driven to near-madness by the sound of a child crying. And soon, other members of the family hear the child crying as well. Similar titles: *The Haunting of Hill House*, Shirley Jackson; *Houses of Stone*, Barbara Michaels.

Deformity • Grieving • Haunted Houses • Maine • Parapsychology • Revenging Revenant • Secret Sin

House of Many Shadows. *New York: Berkley, 1974. 293p.* After an accident that leaves her hearing strange voices, Meg just wants some peace in the country. But for Meg, country living is anything but quiet. She is plagued by strange visions while staying in her cousin's Victorian manor. Even more disturbing, she's not the only one to see these visions—Andy, the caretaker, sees them too. Like Michaels's other work, emphasis is on characterization and description. Similar titles: *Witch* and *Houses of Stone*, Barbara Michaels; *The Dead Zone*, Stephen King; *The Shadowy Horses*, Susanna Kearsley; *December*, Phil Rickman; *When the Wind Blows*, John Saul.

Gothic Romance • Haunted Houses • Pennsylvania • Secret Sin

Houses of Stone. *New York: Berkley, 1994. 384p.* Professor Karen Holloway finds a battered manuscript by Ismene, an unknown nineteenth-century female author—a potentially career-making discovery for Karen. In her own time, Ismene was scorned and silenced by family and friends for her proto-feminist ideas. Karen visits the alleged site of Ismene's home to perform further research, where she is harassed by jealous colleagues who would steal her discovery, through violence if necessary. Only Ismene can help Karen. A compelling ghost story about the trials of women in academia and of female authors throughout history. Similar titles: *Witch, House of Many Shadows*, and *The Crying Child*, Barbara Michaels; *Midnight Is a Lonely Place, House of Echoes*, and *Lady of Hay*, Barbara Erskine; *The Shadowy Horses*, Susanna Kearsley; *The House on the Borderland*, William Hope Hodgson; *Virgins and Martyrs*, Simon Maginn.

    Feminism • Haunted Houses • Scholars • The South

Witch. *New York: Berkley, 1973. 292p.* Ellen March bought a small country cottage, hoping to enjoy the bucolic charms of Chew's Corners, Virginia. Instead, she finds that the residents are fundamentalist zealots who believe her possessed by the original inhabitant of her house, a woman reputed to be a witch because she was skilled in the arts of healing and known to speak her mind. Ellen has been seeing a mysterious white cat and nebulous shapes on the periphery of her vision. A typical example of Michaels's flair for paralleling past and modern-day persecution of women. Similar titles: *Houses of Stone*, Barbara Michaels; *Midnight Is a Lonely Place, House of Echoes,* and *Lady of Hay*, Barbara Erskine; *The Other*, Thomas Tryon; *Sacrifice*, Richard Kinion.

    Cats • Dreams • Haunted Houses • Orphans • Religion—Christianity— Protestantism • Virginia

Mohr, Clifford.

Requiem. *New York: Berkley, 1992. 309p.* Little Bob Bauer suffered brain damage at birth and is severely retarded. But when one of his mother's neighbors gives him an old, broken guitar, a demonic spirit enters him. At first, it seems that Bob is improving, but his parents do not realize how evil the ghost Nico truly is. Similar titles: *Violin*, Anne Rice; *The Exorcist*, William Peter Blatty.

    Cursed Objects • Parenting • Savant Syndrome

Monahan, Brent.

The Bell Witch, An American Haunting: Being the Eye Witness Account of Richard Powell Concerning the Bell Witch Haunting of Robertson County, Tennessee. *New York: St. Martin's Press, 1997. 208p.* A fictional retelling of a real manuscript written by Tennessean Richard Powell in the nineteenth century, in which he recounted the story of a poltergeist visitation on the Bell family. Clever and unique. Similar title: *Beloved*, Toni Morrison.

    Family Curse • History, Use of • Poltergeists • Tennessee • United States—Nineteenth Century • Witchcraft

Morris, Mark.

The Immaculate. *Clarkston, Ga.: White Wolf, 1992. 411p.* (See chapter 17, "Psychological Horror.")

Morrison, Toni.

Beloved. *New York: Plume, 1987. 275p.* Sethe and her children cross the Ohio River to freedom in the 1840s, but are soon tracked by a bounty hunter. Sethe, determined that she and her children will never be slaves again, does the unthinkable—she attempts to help her entire family escape slavery through death. She succeeds in freeing her infant daughter Beloved in this manner, but ultimately she cannot be free from the curse of slavery or from Beloved's ghost, who returns to destroy the entire family. Winner of a Pulitzer Prize for Fiction in

1988, this book is a highly literate masterpiece that tells a story of slavery through the all-too-often dismissed genre of horror. Made into a film of the same name in 1998. Similar titles: *The Bell Witch*, Brent Monahan; *Wuthering Heights*, Emily Brontë.

> *African-American Characters • Grieving • Haunted Houses • Ohio • Parenting • Revenging Revenant • Slavery • United States—Nineteenth Century*

Newman, Kim.

Bad Dreams. *London: Carroll and Graf, 1991. 280p.* (See chapter 10, "Demonic Possession, Satanism, Black Magic, and Witches and Warlocks.")

Perucho, Joan.

Natural History (trans.). *New York: Knopf, 1988. 186p.* (See chapter 9, "Vampires and Werewolves.")

Powers, Tim.

Expiration Date. *New York: Tor Books, 1996. 381p.* An 11-year-old boy accidentally unleashes a frenzy of ghost hunting in Los Angeles. Powers uses multiple points of view to tell the stories of various characters, all of whom come together for a twisted ending.

> *Apocalypse • Fantasy • Los Angeles, California*

Rice, Anne.

Lasher. *New York: Knopf, 1993. 577p.* (See chapter 10, "Demonic Possession, Satanism, Black Magic, and Witches and Warlocks.")

Taltos: Lives of the Mayfair Witches. *New York: Ballantine, 1995. 480p.* (See chapter 10, "Demonic Possession, Satanism, Black Magic, and Witches and Warlocks.")

Violin. *New York: Knopf, 1997. 289p.* Following the death of her lover, Karl, Triana Becker seems to be losing her mind. A mysterious violinist on the streets of New Orleans forces her back into her painful past through his music, and his playing is relentless. As it turns out, violinist Stefan Stefanovsky is a ghost, damned by his hatred and guilt to wander aimlessly—and he wants Triana. One of the masters of the gothic and horror tale weaves a new version of the classic ghost story. Subtle in approach. Similar title: *Requiem*, Clifford Mohr.

> *Grieving • Music—Classical • New Orleans, Louisiana • Sibling Rivalry*

Rickman, Phil.

Candlenight. *New York: Berkley, 1995. 463p.* (See chapter 13, "Small-Town Horror.")

Curfew. *New York: Berkley, 1994. 625p.* (See chapter 10, "Demonic Possession, Satanism, Black Magic, and Witches and Warlocks.")

December. *New York: Berkley, 1994. 678p.* The ruins of a twelfth-century abbey in Wales mark the site of a bloody massacre. In December 1980, the Abbey has become a recording studio, and a hot young band called The Philosopher's Stone has gathered to tap into the site's dark history. The session ends in death and tragedy, and Philosopher's Stone agrees to destroy the session tapes and disband. But when the Abbey tapes resurface and friends start dying, it's time for a reunion. Similar titles: *House of Many Shadows*, Barbara Michaels; *House of Echoes* and *Midnight Is a Lonely Place*, Barbara Erskine; *University*, Bentley Little.

> *Goff, Max (character) • History, Use of • Lennon, John—Assassination of • Music—Rock Music • Religion—Christianity • Religion—Paganism • Wales*

Rusch, Kristin Kathryn.

The Devil's Churn. *New York: Dell, 1996. 320p.* (See chapter 13, "Small-Town Horror.")

Saul, John.

The Blackstone Chronicles. *New York: Ballantine, 1997. 527p.* The inhabitants of Blackstone, New Hampshire, are unaware that an evil presence lurks within the walls of the old Blackstone Asylum. But when the asylum is slated for demolition, various influential citizens of the community begin receiving cursed gifts, which lead to murder and madness. Who can stop the mysterious gloved hand from picking gifts from the asylum to send to Blackstone's citizenry? Books in the series: *An Eye for an Eye: The Doll*; *Twist of Fate: The Locket*; *Ashes to Ashes: The Dragon's Flame*; *In the Shadow of Evil: The Handkerchief*; *Day of Reckoning: The Stereoscope*; and *Asylum*. Similar titles: Stephen King's Green Mile series.

Cursed Objects • Haunted Houses • Journalist as Character • New England

Comes the Blind Fury. *New York: Dell, 1980. 383p.* Michelle has moved to Boston with her family, but she is optimistic about making new friends with the children there. Then she begins to hear voices and feel the touch of a ghostly presence, and her new, supernatural friend has terrible things to tell her about the other children. Similar title: *Deadly Friend*, Keith Ferrario.

Blindness • Boston, Massachusetts • Maritime Horror • Revenging Revenant

Cry for the Strangers. *New York: Dell, 1979. 415p.* (See chapter 13, "Small-Town Horror.")

Hell Fire. *New York: Bantam, 1986. 344p.* (See chapter 8, "Golems, Mummies, and Reanimated Stalkers.")

Nathaniel. *New York: Putnam, 1984. 343p.* After her husband, Mark, dies in a freak accident, Janet Hall learns of an old farmhouse he once owned. She and her son Michael take up residence there, but Michael soon discovers that the farmland is haunted—and that the ghost wants vengeance. Similar titles: *The Other*, Thomas Tryon; *The Influence*, Ramsey Campbell; *Black River*, Elizabeth Graves.

Revenging Revenant • Secret Sin

When the Wind Blows. *New York: Dell, 1990. 281p.* A nine-year-old moves with her family to an old house that harbors a dark past. Then she starts hearing voices in the third-floor nursery, indicating that maybe the house contains something even more insidious. Plot-driven. Similar titles: *House of Many Shadows*, Barbara Michaels; *The Haunting of Hill House*, Shirley Jackson.

Haunted Houses

Simmons, Dan.

The Fires of Eden. *New York: Putnam, 1994. 399p.* (See chapter 19, "Comic Horror.")

Somtow, S. P.

Darker Angels. *New York: Tor Books, 1998. 384p.* (See chapter 10, "Demonic Possession, Satanism, Black Magic, and Witches and Warlocks.")

Stoker, Bram.

Best Ghost and Horror Stories. *Mineola, N.Y.: Dover Books, 1997. 242p.* (See chapter 6, "Collections by Individual Authors.")

Midnight Tales. *Chester Springs, Pa.: Dufour Editions, 1995. 182p.* (See chapter 6, "Collections by Individual Authors.")

Straub, Peter.

Ghost Story. *New York: Simon & Schuster, 1979. 567p.* Five septuagenarians in New England share a terrible secret that is all but consuming them with guilt. When satanic slayings of animals begin to occur, and the old men begin to die of mysterious causes, the survivors suspect that an evil presence is haunting them. Can a young Hawthorne scholar save them? Can anything save the town against an evil older than humanity itself? Highly literate and complex. Similar titles: *Hell Fire*, John Saul; *Phantoms*, Dean Koontz; *Bad Dreams*, Kim Newman; *Summer of Night*, Dan Simmons; *Slippin' into Darkness*, Norman Partridge; *The Devil's Churn*, Kristin Kathryn Rusch.

New England • Reincarnation • Revenging Revenant • Secret Sin • Shapeshifters

Tessier, Thomas.

Fog Heart. *New York: St. Martin's Press, 1998. 320p.* (See chapter 17, "Psychological Horror.")

Tyson, Donald.

The Messenger. *St. Paul, Minn.: Llewellyn, 1993. 272p.* University students studying the paranormal awaken an evil spirit in the woods of Nova Scotia. Once the spirit has them trapped and snowbound in a cabin, can any of them survive?

Haunted Houses • Nova Scotia

Upchurch, Michael.

Passive Intruder. *New York: W. W. Norton, 1995. 369p.* A grim novel about the problems involved in modern relationships, in which a couple find themselves haunted by a mysterious woman who appears in all their vacation photos. Dark and disturbing, but psychologically intriguing. Similar title: *Nazareth Hill*, Ramsey Campbell.

Gay/Lesbian/Bisexual Characters • Photographer as Character

Walpole, Horace.

The Castle of Otranto. *Oxford: Oxford University Press, 1996. [First published in 1764.] 110p.* (See chapter 10, "Demonic Possession, Satanism, Black Magic, and Witches and Warlocks.")

Wharton, Edith.

The Ghost Stories of Edith Wharton. *New York: Scribner's, 1997. 288p.* (See chapter 6, "Collections by Individual Authors.")

Wilde, Oscar.

The Canterville Ghost. *Cambridge, Mass.: Candlewick Press, 1996. [First published in 1891.] 128p.* (See chapter 19, "Comic Horror.")

Wilhelm, Kate.

The Good Children. *New York: St. Martin's Press, 1998. 224p.* (See chapter 17, "Psychological Horror.")

Williamson, Chet.

The Crow: Clash by Night. *New York: Harper Prism, 1998. 256p.* William-son's contribution to the Crow mythology, with the ghost/hero facing off against terrorists. Similar titles: *The Crow: Quoth the Crow*, David Bischoff; *The Crow: The Lazarus Heart*, Poppy Z. Brite.

> *The Crow (character) • Gothicism • Terrorism*

Wood, Bari.

The Basement. *New York: Avon, 1995. 336p.* Myra Ludsen lives a privileged life in a wealthy Connecticut neighborhood, but she has one problem: she is positive that some evil force inhabits her basement. When her neighbor and her husband die cruel but mysterious deaths, others begin to believe. But can they stop the evil? Nice plot twists and a surprise ending. Similar titles: *The Haunting of Hill House*, Shirley Jackson; *The Amityville Horror*, Jay Anson.

> *Domestic Violence • Haunted Houses • New England • Revenge*

Wright, T. M.

A Manhattan Ghost Story. *New York: Doherty, 1984. 381p.* A photographer moves into a Manhattan apartment complex and instantly falls for a beautiful woman—who introduces him to a ghastly version of the city where the dead reign. Rises above its weak spots with subtlety and emotion.

> *Gothic Romance • New York City • Photographer as Character*

The School. *New York: Tor Books, 1990. 245p.* A young couple hopes to get over the death of their child by taking an old school and turning it into a bed-and-breakfast. However, the school has its own ghosts, and harbors an evil presence.

> *Grieving • Haunted Houses • Parenting*

Zweifel, Karyn Kay.

Dog-Gone Ghost Stories. *Birmingham, Ala.: Crane Hill, 1996. 163p.* (See chapter 6, "Collections by Individual Authors.")

Film

 7

Candyman. *Bernard Rose, dir. 1992. 98 minutes.* Candyman is the embodiment of the urban legend about "The Hook," an escaped lunatic with a hook for a hand who menaces young lovers in compromising positions. When two graduate students attempt to unearth the legend of Candyman, they find the real revenant, a black man who was lynched for miscegenation in the 1890s and now exacts revenge on those who would doubt his existence. Based on "The Forbidden" by Clive Barker, this movie stars Virginia Madsen and Tony Todd and has a score by Philip Glass.

> *African-American Characters • Chicago, Illinois • Racism • Reincarnation • Revenging Revenant*

J. D.'s Revenge. *Arthur Marks, dir. 1976. 95 minutes.* (See chapter 10, "Demonic Possession, Satanism, Black Magic, and Witches and Warlocks.")

A Nightmare on Elm Street. *Wes Craven, dir. 1984. 92 minutes.* When Freddy Krueger, a school janitor who molested children, is released from prison, a posse of enraged parents burn him to death. But the ghost of Freddy returns, entering children's dreams and causing them to die hideous deaths. Robert Englund stars.

Child Molesters • Dreams • Revenging Revenant

Rebecca. *Alfred Hitchcock, dir. 1940. (Black-and-white.) 130 minutes.* (See chapter 17, "Psychological Horror.")

The Shining. *Stanley Kubrick, dir. 1980. 142 minutes.* (See chapter 10, "Demonic Possession, Satanism, Black Magic, and Witches and Warlocks.")

Supernatural. *Victor Halperin, dir. 1933. (Black-and-white.) 60 minutes.* (See chapter 10, "Demonic Possession, Satanism, Black Magic, and Witches and Warlocks.")

Tales from the Hood. *Rusty Cundieff, dir. 1995. 98 minutes.* (See chapter 19, "Comic Horror.")

Our Picks

June's Picks: *Drawing Blood*, Poppy Z. Brite (Dell); *Wuthering Heights*, Emily Brontë (Cambridge University Press); *Lost Boys*, Orson Scott Card (HarperCollins); *Houses of Stone,* Barbara Michaels (Berkley); *Beloved,* Toni Morrison (Plume); *December,* Phil Rickman (Berkley).

Tony's Picks: *Nazareth Hill*, Ramsey Campbell (Doherty); *Cemetery of Angels*, Noel Hynd (Kensington); *The Night Boat*, Robert R. McCammon (Pocket Books); *Beloved*, Toni Morrison (Plume); *Violin*, Anne Rice (Knopf).

Chapter 8

Golems, Mummies, and Reanimated Stalkers: Wake the Dead and They'll Be Cranky

Burial customs are more than just accepted methods of dealing with the remains of our loved ones; they are also methods of keeping the dead from walking once more among the living, either in body or in spirit. Ancient Egyptians took great care that their dead rulers, who were thought to be divine, could successfully make the journey from this world to the next. Not only were the bodies carefully preserved through mummification, but the tomb was also stocked with everything the dead would need in the next world, such as food and slaves. Furthermore, precautions were taken against invaders who might derail this journey. When these precautions are not taken in the funeral process, the results can be disastrous—grave robbers can steal any jewelry or riches buried with the body or even appropriate the loved one's body. In the world of horror, which metaphorically reflects societal fears with its dark atmosphere and grotesque imagery, even more terrifying outcomes are possible. In these fictional worlds, the dead can rise, not as ghosts but in corporeal form, usually to take revenge upon those living who disappointed or angered them. In some instances, the dead rise from their graves to walk about and indiscriminately murder the living.

Modern stories about mummies involve the dead for whom the proper precautions were not taken, and who, when unearthed by naive archaeologists centuries later, roam the earth in search of what they need to rest. This is the case with Boris Karloff in the Universal Studios picture *The Mummy* and with Ramses the Damned in Anne Rice's mummy books. To make matters worse, it isn't just dead nobles who can be roused from their eternal slumbers—even the average Joe or Jane may become a reanimated corpse if circumstances are favorable for the creation of zombies.

Whether the dead are purposefully reanimated, as in Haitian voodoo, or are reanimated by accident, as in George Romero's film *Night of the Living Dead* (where the newly dead rise from their graves due to radiation released by a recent space probe), they are always dangerous to the living. Psychologically speaking, the dead often are raised by the living who simply cannot accept the finality of death, as in Stephen King's *Pet Sematary*.

The golem, originally a human form made out of clay (in imitation of Adam's creation), is another manifestation of the reanimated dead. But unlike a mummy or a zombie, the golem was never a human being with a soul. Instead, its creator bypassed the natural process of reproduction and instead made something monstrous that will ultimately attempt to destroy its maker. The original golem comes from a medieval Jewish folktale, in which a rabbi creates a large man of clay to protect his congregation from gentiles bent on making their lives miserable. But the golem, who has no soul, must be returned to the dust when he insists on being treated like a human. The most famous golem can be found in Mary Shelley's novel *Frankenstein*, in which Victor assembles a creature from parts stolen from the local charnel house. Instead of making a god among men, Victor makes a creature so hideous that all run from him. The tormented and lonely creature finally seeks to destroy his maker. Contemporary golem stories range from murderous fictional characters (created by the fictional writers in the tales) who take corporeal form, as in Stephen King's *The Dark Half,* to an assassin cloned from stolen DNA who is drawn to his genetic "twin," believing that this person has stolen his life, as in Dean R. Koontz's *Mr. Murder.*

The bottom line is that when the dead are raised, they're cranky; and soulless creatures will always be rebellious and angry children, bent on self-destruction and the destruction of their makers. Zombies almost always have a taste for human flesh, and (like the dead raised in King's novel) are ungrateful for their second chance at life, so they attempt to kill those who raised them. Golems are similarly ungrateful for their *first* chance at life, and usually attempt to erase their creators and the very act of their own creations. They may do so through murder, as in Shelley's novel, or may just kill indiscriminately, as in James Whale's 1931 film version of Shelley's novel.

Representative works in this subgenre include Mary Shelley's *Frankenstein*, Stephen King's *Pet Sematary*, and Dan Simmons's *Summer of Night*. Note that many of the more popular and influential of these fictions include films, such as *Frankenstein, Bride of Frankenstein, The Mummy* (and various versions thereof), *Night of the Living Dead, The Evil Dead*, and *Re-Animator*. These texts all teach us what Johnny learns the hard way early on in Romero's *Night of the Living Dead,* and Victor eventually learns (again the hard way) in Shelley's *Frankenstein*: that lack of respect for the ancestral dead and for our living creations can produce disastrous results.

Appeals: Emphasis on Creation and on Consequences of "Playing God"; Universal Fear of Graveyards and Zombies; Universal Fear of the Returning Dead

Harris, Allen Lee.

> **Let There Be Dark.** *New York: Berkley, 1994. 345p.* Matt Hardison always wanted to publish the story of the Shadowstealer, which he heard as a child from his aunt. What he doesn't realize is that the shadow monster with claws can get you only if you know about it and fear it—and his book has introduced the Shadowstealer to his home town. Similar title: *The Devil on May Street*, Steve Harris.
>
> *Gay/Lesbian/Bisexual Characters* • *Writer as Character*

King, Stephen.

The Dark Half. *New York: Signet Books, 1989. 484p.* Thad Beaumont, best-selling author of slasher novels, would like to say he has nothing to do with the series of monstrous murders that keep coming closer to his home. But how can Thad disown the ultimate embodiment of evil that goes by the name of one of his characters and signs its crimes with Thad's bloody fingerprints? Similar titles: *Mr. Murder*, Dean Koontz; *Cain*, James Byron Huggins; *Big Thunder*, Peter Atkins; *Escardy Gap*, Peter Crowther and James Lovegrove; *The Immaculate*, Mark Morris; *Created By*, Richard Christian Matheson.

Castle Rock, Maine • Pangborn, Alan (character) • Police Officer as Character • Slasher • Writer as Character

Koontz, Dean.

Mr. Murder. *New York: Berkley, 1993. 376p.* Marty Stillwater, well-known writer of murder mysteries, is being stalked by Alfie, his double, a genetically engineered hit man who, unknown to Marty, was cloned from Marty's DNA. Alfie is psychically drawn to Stillwater; he believes that Marty has stolen his life and memories and he aims to get them back. Similar titles: *The Dark Half*, Stephen King; *Cain*, James Byron Huggins; *Frankenstein*, Mary Shelley; *Savant*, Rex Miller; *Dr. Jekyll and Mr. Hyde*, Robert Louis Stevenson; *The God Project*, John Saul; *The Door to December* and *The Key to Midnight*, Dean Koontz.

Cloning • Organized Crime

Matheson, Richard Christian.

Created By. *New York: Bantam, 1993. 324p.* To satiate America's hunger for more sex and violence on television, a television writer creates "The Mercenary," a murderous fictional character who mutilates his victims. But then the Mercenary comes to life, and only his creator can stop him. Similar title: *The Dark Half*, Stephen King.

Hollywood, California • Serial Killers • Television • Writer as Character

Rice, Anne.

The Mummy, or Ramses the Damned. *New York: Ballantine, 1989. 436p.* As a mortal, King Ramses sought the elixir of life to bring eternal prosperity upon his people. But humans aren't meant to be immortal: his experiment failed, and Ramses himself was "doomed forever to wander the earth, desperate to quell hungers that can never be satisfied—for food, for wine, for women"—book jacket. Ramses is reawakened in Edwardian London, where he becomes Dr. Ramsey, an Egyptologist and close friend of heiress Julie Stratford, but the pleasures he enjoys with his new companion cannot soothe him. Similar titles: *The Vampire Lestat* and *Servant of the Bones*, Anne Rice; *The Jewel of Seven Stars*, Bram Stoker.

Egypt • London, England • Mummies • Religion—Ancient Egyptian

Roszak, Theodore.

The Memories of Elizabeth Frankenstein. *New York: Bantam, 1996. 425p.* (See chapter 17, "Psychological Horror.")

Saul, John.

Hell Fire. *New York: Bantam, 1986. 344p.* Philip Sturgess decides to reopen the old mill that his father once owned, though it has been locked up for years. Little does he know that he has released the town's ghosts—and one of them is angry enough to lure Philip's daughter and stepdaughter into the realm of violent murder. Subtle but effective horror. Similar titles: *Ghost Story*, Peter Straub; *The Influence* and *Nazareth Hill*, Ramsey Campbell; *The Other*, Thomas Tryon.

> *Revenging Revenant • Secret Sin*

Shelley, Mary.

Frankenstein. *New York: Knopf, 1992. 256p. [First published in 1817.]* Dr. Victor Frankenstein, who thirsts for knowledge that humans aren't meant to possess, forms a creature of spare parts from charnel houses. The result is a hideous being whose appearance terrifies humans, dooming the creature to loneliness. The creature's solitary condition causes him to destroy his maker and his maker's family. A literary classic that has inspired various films and alternative retellings. Similar titles: *Mr. Murder*, Dean Koontz; *Cain*, James Byron Huggins.

> *Diary Format • Frankenstein, Caroline (character) • Frankenstein, Dr. (character) • Frankenstein's Monster (character) • Lavenza, Elizabeth (character) • Mad Scientist • Revenge • Science Fiction • Switzerland*

Stoker, Bram.

The Jewel of Seven Stars. *New York: Carroll and Graf, 1989. 214p. [First published in 1903.]* An Egyptologist accidentally awakens the soul of the mummy, which then possesses his daughter. He can save her only by bringing the body of the mummy back to life. Similar titles: *The Mummy, or Ramses the Damned*, Anne Rice; *The Mummy* (film).

> *Archaeology • Mummies • Religion—Ancient Egyptian*

Yarbro, Chelsea Quinn.

Nomads. *New York: Bantam, 1984. 232p.* Dr. Eileen Flax is bitten in the emergency room by a badly mutilated victim. Afterwards, she begins having strange dreams. At the same time, Jean-Charles Pommier, a French-Canadian anthropologist, has stumbled onto a group of violent nomads who terrorize certain areas of the city. Neither realizes that they are dealing with supernatural beings who threaten their very lives. From a screenplay by John McTiernan. Similar titles: *Bethany's Sin*, Robert R. McCammon; *Carrion Comfort* and *Song of Kali*, Dan Simmons; *Lost Souls*, Poppy Z. Brite.

> *Gang Violence • Religion—Inuit • Violence—Theories of*

Film

Bride of Frankenstein. *James Whale, dir. 1935. (Black-and-white.) 75 minutes.* Boris Karloff reprises his role as Frankenstein's monster in this rendition of the second half of Mary Shelley's novel. The lonely and somewhat inarticulate creature, who evaded destruction in *Frankenstein*, now demands that his creator make him a mate. Starring Boris Karloff, Elsa Lanchester, and Colin Clive.

> *Frankenstein, Dr. (character) • Frankenstein's Monster (character) • Mad Scientist*

Frankenstein. *James Whale, dir. 1931. (Black-and-white.) 71 minutes.* James Whale's rendition of the first half of Mary Shelley's novel is set in the twentieth century. But in this film, Dr. Frankenstein's creation isn't a monster because of his creator's arrogance in usurping the powers of God, nor because of the intolerance of society at large. Instead, this creature is monstrous because he is made with inferior parts. If Dr. Frankenstein's bumbling assistant hadn't procured an abnormal brain, then presumably the creature would truly have been the new Adam. Starring Boris Karloff as the monster.

> *Frankenstein, Dr. (character) • Frankenstein's Monster (character) • Mad Scientist*

The Mummy. *Karl Freund, dir. 1932. (Black-and-white.) 72 minutes.* When the mummy's tomb is desecrated by archaeologists, he is reanimated and kills those responsible for disturbing his rest. He then discovers that the reincarnation of his mate is among the band of archaeologists. Boris Karloff stars as the mummy. Be sure to look for the zipper in the back of his mummy costume.

Mummies • Reincarnation • Revenging Revenant

Our Picks

June's Picks: *The Dark Half*, Stephen King (Signet Books); *Frankenstein*, Mary Shelley (public domain).

Tony's Picks: *The Dark Half*, Stephen King (Signet Books); *Mr. Murder*, Dean Koontz (Berkley).

Chapter 9

Vampires and Werewolves: Children of the Night

The most popular of all the horror subgenre monsters, vampires have evolved considerably over the years. Originally the vampire was a cousin to the werewolf, a monstrous, megalomaniacal foreigner that represented the Western European fear of The Other (vampires rose out of the mythology of Transylvania, what is today known as Romania). Over the years, the monster figure evolved into a suave, sophisticated, intelligent superhuman—and then de-evolved into a bloodthirsty superpunk who, like the werewolf, rips victims to shreds. There are very few famous werewolves in fiction, but notable vampires are plentiful, ranging from the monstrous *nosferatu* of *Varney the Vampire* and of Bram Stoker's *Dracula*; to the sophisticated aristocrat of Anne Rice's Vampire Chronicles; to the misunderstood teenage splatterpunk children of the night of Poppy Z. Brite's *Lost Souls*; to the mind-controlling, war-mongering succubi and incubi of Dan Simmons's *Carrion Comfort*; to the erudite and secretive professor of Suzy M. Charnas's *The Vampire Tapestry*; to the parasitic alien of Brain Lumley's *Necroscope*. Despite these differences, all vampires and werewolves are monsters because they must somehow feed on their victims' vital essences: flesh, blood, emotion, love, even violence.

In essence, vampirism is the story of a creature of the night and its parasitic relationship with another. Vampirism has been used as a metaphor for love, for the parent/child bond, for sexual relationships, and for power structures in general. Yet vampires are easily the most identifiable and often the most sympathetic—in short, the most appealing—of all horror's monsters, mainly because vampires must, in some way, resemble the humans on whom they prey. In fact, vampirism is often represented as a sort of dark godhood, nothing more than superhuman immortality with a little bloodlust thrown in for a good scare. The classical vampire is an ex-human, like the mummy, ghost, or werewolf, but only the vampire retains (and often eclipses) human beauty. Also, vampires often possess some kind of extraordinary powers: the ability to hypnotize victims, to control the weather, to shapeshift, to control people's minds and bodies. They may also have super strength, super speed, and/or the ability to fly. In general, they can range from superhuman predators to subhuman beasts. These states appeal to both sides of the human experience, both the times when we need to feel strong and invulnerable and the times when we feel weak and vulnerable and seek to deal with this vulnerability vicariously. Finally, vampires are almost always erotic or sensual in some way, which is one of their greatest appeals.

Of all vampire texts, Bram Stoker's narrative is the most widely known, and arguably the most influential in the genre. All later vampire narratives must pay some sort of homage to *Dracula*, with its skillful combination of traditional Eastern European vampire folklore and nineteenth-century British xenophobia. Later vampire narratives sometimes add to the Dracula mythology established by Stoker, sometimes refute it, and often do a little of both. Anne Rice's Vampire Chronicles feature both aristocratic and bourgeois vampires, but vampires who held titles while "warm" have less difficulty adapting to the undead lifestyle, as this lifestyle is really just an extension of aristocratic privilege. Stoker's vampires are frequently repulsive and incapable of loving; Rice's vampires are almost always preternaturally beautiful, and capable of passionate, platonic relationships. Kim Newman's *Anno Dracula* brings the legend back to its beginnings: it is an alternative history speculating about what Victorian England would have been like if Dracula had defeated Van Helsing and his party of vampire hunters. Newman incorporates facts about the "real" Dracula, Romanian Prince Vlad Tepes, into his representation of Dracula. Vampires have indeed come a long way, and writers in the subgenre are constantly rewriting the vampire myth anew, with the possibilities being endless.

And then there are werewolves, cousins to the vampires. The werewolf comes from traditional vampire folklore, in which the undead frequently assume the form of wolves to facilitate their nocturnal feedings. The werewolf is the alter ego of the suave, sophisticated vampire: if the vampire is a sort of monstrous superego, the werewolf is the raging id. The werewolf represents our most essential desires—for food, sex, comfort, even violence—in their most bestial form.

Appeals: Eroticism; Excellent Monster for Metaphor (Vampire Can Symbolize Almost Anything); Historical Romance; Homoeroticism; Memorable Recurring Characters; More Series Than Other Subgenres; Ongoing Dialogue of Immortality vs. Humanity; Presents the Bestial Side of Human Nature; Sex Appeal; Sympathetic, Sometimes Enviable "Monsters"

Aickman, Robert.

Cold Hand in Mine: Strange Stories. *New York: Scribner's, 1975. 215p.* (See chapter 6, "Collections by Individual Authors.")

Anscombe, Roderick.

The Secret Life of Laszlo, Count Dracula. *New York: Hyperion, 1994. 409p.* A young medical student, Laszlo Dracula, accidentally murders a prostitute. Twenty years later and in a new location, Laszlo again acts out his bloodlust, and becomes a serial murderer. Emphasis is on psychology and characterization. One of the few nonsupernatural versions of the Dracula tale. Similar titles: *The Blood Countess*, Andrei Codrescu; *The Lost*, Jonathan Aycliffe.

Diary Format • Mad Scientist • Medical Horror • Paris, France • Serial Killers • Sex Crimes

Aycliffe, Jonathan.

The Lost. *New York: Harper Prism, 1996. 264p.* Cambridge prep school teacher Michael Feraru takes a sabbatical to Romania, to claim the property his grandparents had abandoned after World War II. Once there, he discovers that he's a titled lord and owner of an ancient stronghold in the Transylvanian Alps, Castle Vlaicu, and heir to the secret of the *strogi,* or the undead. Similar titles: *The Blood Countess*, Andrei Codrescu; *The Secret Life of Laszlo, Count Dracula*, Roderick Anscombe; *Children of the Night*, Dan Simmons.

Diary Format • Romania

Bainbridge, Sharon.

Blood and Roses. *New York: Berkley, 1994. 280p.* Elegant bachelor Sir Geoffrey has captured the hearts of all the young ladies of London. However, one of his love interests begins to grow pale and weak, her blood drained away. Is there another vampire in England? A gentle read. Similar title: *Lord of the Dead*, Tom Holland.

Gothic Romance • Victorian England

Baker, Nancy.

The Night Insider: A Vampire Thriller. *New York: Fawcett, 1994. 312p.* A young Ph.D. student in history is given a lucrative assignment, but is soon kidnapped by murderers who have already killed her colleagues and who hold an ancient vampire captive. She can help the vampire escape by sacrificing her blood, but will it then offer her help? What will she do afterward, if she becomes one of the undead? Similar title: *Forever and the Night*, Linda Lael Miller.

Academia • Toronto, Ontario • Vampire's Point of View

Bergstrom, Elaine. The Austra Family Chronicles.

Blood Alone. *New York: Jove Books, 1990. 325p.* A prequel to *Shattered Glass,* *Blood Alone* chronicles Paul Stoddard's introduction to the Austra family, their involvement in World War II, and Laurence Austra's encounter with Nazism. Contains multiple plotlines and lots of characters, and holds together well. Similar title: *'48*, James Herbert.

Austra Family (characters) • Nazism • Vampire's Point of View • War—World War II

Shattered Glass. *New York: Jove Books, 1994. 372p.* Stephen Austra finds himself strangely attracted to his neighbor, which presents a real problem because he is a vampire. To further complicate matters, another vampire is murdering people in Stephen's current home town of Cleveland. Similar titles: Laurell K. Hamilton's comic vampire novels; *Suckers*, Anne Billson.

Artist as Character • Austra Family (characters) • Cleveland, Ohio • Gothic Romance • Wells, Helen (character)

Blood Rites. *New York: Jove Books, 1991. 332p.* Austra family inductee Helen Wells moves into the Canadian wilderness to escape the stress of living with humans, only to run afoul of a vengeful crime boss who engineers the kidnapping of her children. She must use all the Austra powers now to save her family—and herself.

Austra Family (characters) • Canada • Organized Crime • Vampire Clans • Wells, Helen (character)

Daughter of the Night. *New York: Jove Books, 1992. 323p.* In this, the fourth book about the Austra vampire clan, Bergstrom chronicles the life of Elizabeth Bathory, who is half Austra/vampire. Bathory takes up with the only Austra to be ostracized by her family, and perfects her methods of bloodshed. Also related is the story of the artist, Charles. Similar title: *The Blood Countess*, Andrei Codrescu.

Artist as Character • Austra Family (characters) • Bathory, Elizabeth de (character) • History, Use of • Vampire Clans • Vampire's Point of View

Billson, Anne.

Suckers. *New York: Atheneum, 1993. 288p.* This satire on the yuppie scene in East London pits a designer magazine consultant and her immortal boyfriend against a centuries-old jealous girlfriend. At stake: the cultural and economic future of England. Uneven, but has its moments. Emphasis is on plot and symbol. Similar titles: *Shattered Glass*, Elaine Bergstrom; *Burnt Offerings* and *Circus of the Damned*, Laurell K. Hamilton.

Economic Violence • Revenge

Bloch, Robert.

Midnight Pleasures. *New York: Doubleday, 1987. 177p.* (See chapter 6, "Collections by Individual Authors.")

Borchardt, Alice.

The Silver Wolf. *New York: Ballantine, 1998. 451p.* Historical romance/horror tale about a young girl named Regeane, who is part-human, part-werewolf, and her adventures in decadent 30 B.C. Rome. Heavy on description and characterization. Similar titles: *Pandora: New Tales of the Vampire*, Anne Rice.

Gothic Romance • History, Use of • Immortality • Rome, Italy • Werewolves

Boyd, Donna.

The Passion. *New York: Avon, 1998. 387p.* The murder of three "distinguished" humans/werewolves leads to this tale within a tale told by multimillionaire werewolf Alexander Devoncroix. Devoncroix relates how werewolves have always capitalized on the United States' market-driven economy and have run billion-dollar companies throughout history. Unusual and clever. Similar title: *Carrion Comfort*, Dan Simmons.

Eroticism • History, Use of • New York City • Werewolves

Brand, Rebecca [pseud. of Suzy McKee Charnas].

The Ruby Tear. *New York: Tor Books, 1998. 247p.* The Ruby Tear, a jewel on a par with the Hope Diamond, is the source of playwright/playboy Nic Griffin's family wealth, and has brought both financial success and untimely death to the Griffin men. Nic must have the final showdown with the vampire von Cragga, who holds the key to the mystery of the Griffin family curse. Written by Suzy McKee Charnas under a pen name. Strong on portrayal of the New York City theater world.

Actor as Character • Cursed Objects • Gothic Romance • New York City • Vampire's Point of View

Brite, Poppy Z.

Lost Souls. *New York: Bantam-Dell, 1992. 355p.* (See chapter 18, "Splatterpunk.")

(editor). Love in Vein: Twenty Original Tales of Vampire Erotica. *New York: Harper Paperbacks, 1994. 396p.* (See chapter 5, "Anthologies and Collections by Multiple Authors.")

(editor). Love in Vein II: Eighteen More Original Tales of Vampire Erotica. *New York: Harper Prism, 1997. 375p.* (See chapter 5, "Anthologies and Collections by Multiple Authors.")

Brownworth, Victoria A. (editor).

Night Bites: Vampire Stories by Women. *Seattle, Wash.: Seal Press, 1996. 259p.* (See chapter 5, "Anthologies and Collections by Multiple Authors.")

Brust, Steven.

Agyar. *New York: Tor Books, 1993. 254p.* John Agyar, a vibrant young man who has taken up residence in a haunted house in Philadelphia, is being framed for crimes he never committed—by the woman who turned him into a vampire. While hunkered down awaiting his fate, he philosophizes on life, death, and immortality. Subtle and highly clever, with lots of original "mechanics of vampirism" thrown in. Erudite. Similar title: *Bloodlist*, P. N. Elrod.

Haunted Houses • Philadelphia, Pennsylvania • Shapeshifters • Vampire's Point of View

Cacek, P. D.

Night Prayers. *Darien, Ill.: Design Image, 1998. 219p.* After a three-day binge, Allison Garrett finds herself turned into a vampire, and she has no idea how to survive as one. This satire, set in Los Angeles, exposes the underworld of Southern California life. Quirky and clever. Similar titles: *Blood Hunt* and *Bloodlinks*, Lee Killough; *The Making of a Monster*, Gail Peterson.

Clergy as Character • Los Angeles, California • Vampire Clans • Vampire Hunters • Vampire's Point of View

Cadnum, Michael.

The Judas Glass. *New York: Carroll and Graf, 1996. 320p.* A yuppified California lawyer receives an antique mirror in the mail—which leads to his death and resurrection as a vampire. Action-oriented.

California • Lawyer as Character • Vampire Hunters • Vampire's Point of View

Caine, Jeffrey.

Curse of the Vampire. *New York: Berkley, 1991. 247p.* Only Abraham Stroud—archae-ologist, psychic, detective, and vampire hunter—can save the small town of Andover, Maryland, from a centuries-old curse that possesses the very soul of the local hospital's administrative staff. In the meantime, though, the dead are rising—and children are disap-pearing. Similar title: *Greely's Cove*, John Gideon.

Medical Horror • Vampire Hunters

Charnas, Suzy McKee.

The Ruby Tear. *New York: Tor Books, 1998. 247p.* (See Rebecca Brand, *The Ruby Tear.*)

The Vampire Tapestry. *Albuquerque, N.M.: Living Batch, 1980. 285p.* Katje suspects anthropology professor Dr. Weyland of being a vampire. Little does she know how much of a predator this mild, unassuming, middle-aged man can become. Using multiple narra-tors and multiple points of view, Charnas weaves tales of five events in the life of the vam-pire. Unique for its creation of an entirely new vampire, the sole survivor of his species, this is a highly sensitive and beautifully poetic rendering of the vampire myth. Similar ti-tle: *My Soul to Keep*, Tanarive Due.

Vampire as New Species • Vampire Hunters • Vampire's Point of View • Weyland, Dr. Edward Lewis (character)

Clark, Simon.

Vampyrrhic. *London: Hoddard and Stoughton, 1998. 441p.* David Leppington returns to his ancestral home only to discover a dark family secret: the Leppingtons originated from a vampire clan created by the Norse god Thor. Will he give in to his genetics and become a bloodsucker? Similar title: *The Blood Countess*, Andrei Codrescu.

England • Family Curse • Religion—Christianity • Religion—Paganism • Vampire Clans

Codrescu, Andrei.

The Blood Countess. *New York: Simon & Schuster, 1995. 347p.* (See chapter 17, "Psy-chological Horror.")

Collins, Nancy A.

Ⓑ**Sunglasses After Dark.** *New York: New American Library, 1989. 253p.* Denise Thorne, heiress, is raped by a vampire, and after nine months in a coma she is reborn as Sonja Blue, a vampire who can inhabit dream worlds, who violently kills cruel humans, and who terminates ghosts and other revenants. Considered by critics and vampire fans to be one of the finest original vampire tales of the past decade. Unique and erudite. Recipient of a Bram Stoker Award. Similar title: *Tap, Tap: A Novel*, David Lozell Martin.

Blue, Sonja (character) • Dreams • Rape • Telepathy • Vampire's Point of View

Tempter. *New York: Penguin, 1990. 299p.* A failed, aging rock musician turns to a voo-doo priestess—and ultimately to a fettered vampire revenant bound on revenge—to make a musical comeback. But can he control Tempter (the evil vampire spirit) and the gods of voodoo once he calls on them? Suspenseful. Similar titles: *The Making of a Monster*, Gail Peterson; *Valentine, Vampire Junction,* and *Vanitas: Escape from Vampire Junction*, S. P. Somtow.

Music—Rock Music • New Orleans, Louisiana • Religion—Voodoo • Revenging Revenant

Wild Blood. *New York: New American Library, 1994. 298p.* A popular metal band's members are not quite human, and a young teenage fan finds himself dragged into its nightmare world of shapeshifting monsters. Suspenseful and graphic writing abound in this strange tale of a were-coyote. Similar titles: *Valentine, Vampire Junction,* and *Vanitas: Escape from Vampire Junction,* S. P. Somtow.

Music—Rock Music • Native American Characters • Shapeshifters • Werewolves

Conner, Miguel.

The Queen of Darkness. *New York: Warner Books, 1998. 276p.* Vampires arrange a nuclear holocaust on Earth to create artificial darkness and thin out their human opposition. Now that they rule, their greatest enemy is one of their own. Similar title: *I Am Legend,* Richard Matheson.

Byron, Lord George Gordon (character) • Nuclear Holocaust • Vampire's Point of View

Cooke, John Peyton.

Out for Blood. *New York: Avon, 1991. 313p.* Cooke subverts the typical vampire hunter tale by presenting us with Chris Calloway, a young vampire who is quickly going to discover that when it comes to bloodlust, no species can top the human race.

Vampire Hunters • Vampire's Point of View

Courtney, Vincent.

Vampire Beat. *New York: Pinnacle, 1991. 302p.* Homicide detective Christopher Blaze has just been transferred to the night shift, which is just fine with this Miami cop turned vampire. But his first assignment is to hunt down one of his own, who is leaving a trail of young, beautiful bodies. Similar title: *Bring on the Night,* Joy Davis and Don Davis.

Miami, Florida • Police Officer as Character • Serial Killers • Vampire's Point of View

Daltow, Ellen, and Terri Windling (editors).

The Year's Best Fantasy and Horror: Ninth Annual Collection (1995). *New York: St. Martin's Press, 1996. 534p.* (See chapter 5, "Anthologies and Collections by Multiple Authors.")

The Year's Best Fantasy and Horror: Tenth Annual Collection (1996). *New York: St. Martin's Press, 1997. 534p.* (See chapter 5, "Anthologies and Collections by Multiple Authors.")

Davis, Joy, and Don Davis.

Bring on the Night. *New York: Tor Books, 1993. 403p.* Cruel vampire Nathan Kane is being hunted by serial killer/vampire hunter Christian Danner, who is out for revenge. But Kane has a few surprises for his nemesis, and before he is done with Christian, he may even bring him over to the dark side. Action-oriented. Similar titles: *Vampire Beat,* Vincent Courtney; *Near Death,* Nancy Kilpatrick; *Forever and the Night,* Linda Lael Miller.

Music—Rock Music • Revenge • Vampire Hunters

Dee, Ron.

Bloodlust. *New York: Dell, 1990. 264p.* A vampire disguised as a traveling salesman is infecting housewives in St. Louis, including the wife of a minister. When the dead come back to reclaim the living, a plague of vampires occurs. Action-oriented; graphic sexuality. Similar title: *I Am Legend*, Richard Matheson.

> *Clergy as Character • Eroticism • Religion—Christianity • St. Louis, Missouri*

Dietz, Ulysses G.

Desmond: A Novel of Love and the Modern Vampire. *Los Angeles: Alyson Books, 1998. 331p.* Desmond, an openly gay vampire living the high life in the Bowery section of Brooklyn, has found a cure for his loneliness—a young student of antiques. But to have the student as a lover, Desmond will first have to reveal his dark secret, and then save the young man's life. Similar titles: *Interview with the Vampire* and *The Vampire Lestat*, Anne Rice.

> *Gay/Lesbian/Bisexual Characters • Gothic Romance • History, Use of • Homoeroticism • New York City • Vampire's Point of View*

Dvorkin, David.

Unquenchable. *New York: Kensington, 1995. 347p.* An ex-vampire turned mortal is being lured back into the realm of the undead by two seductive women, one who wants a soul mate and another who lives only for blood and flesh. Now he must make a tough decision.

> *Eroticism*

Elrod, P. N. The Jonathan Barrett series.

Red Death. *New York: Ace Books, 1993. 288p.* Seventeen-year-old Jonathan Barrett is sent from his colonial American home to Cambridge University in 1773, just three years before the Revolutionary War. There he meets Nora Jones, "an unearthly beauty whose lovemaking talents entrance him" and whose kiss "will leave him to eternally crave the blood of others"—book jacket. Similar titles: *Interview with the Vampire*, Anne Rice; *Death and the Maiden*, P. N. Elrod.

> *Barrett, Jonathan (character) • England • Gothic Romance • History, Use of • Vampire's Point of View • War—American Revolutionary War*

Death and the Maiden. *New York: Ace Books, 1994. 244p.* Vampire/hero Jonathan Barrett must turn to murderous means to protect his family from a scheming woman. Part of a series set during the Revolutionary War. Similar title: *Red Death*, P. N. Elrod.

> *Barrett, Jonathan (character) • History, Use of • Vampire's Point of View • War—American Revolutionary War*

Death Masque. *New York: Ace Books, 1995. 261p.* Jonathan Barrett flees the American colonial rebellion to visit England and search for the woman who made him into a vampire.

> *Barrett, Jonathan (character) • England • Vampire's Point of View • War—American Revolutionary War*

Elrod, P. N. The Vampire Files series.

Bloodlist. *New York: Ace Books, 1990.* The first novel in Elrod's The Vampire Files, in which Jack Flemming initially suspects he may become a vampire, and finds out for sure when he is killed in a gangland hit. Now, as a vampire, he is out for revenge. Similar titles: *Agyar*, Steven Brust; *Howl-o-ween*, Gary Holleman.

> *Flemming, Jack (character) • Organized Crime • Vampire's Point of View*

Lifeblood. *New York: Ace Books, 1990. 208p.* In this second in the series of The Vampire Files, Jack Flemming, journalist/vampire, must deal with a group of vampire hunters. Similar titles: *Chill in the Blood*, P. N. Elrod; *Guilty Pleasures*, Laurell K. Hamilton; *Of Saints and Shadows*, Christopher Golden; *Thorn*, Fred Saberhagen.

Flemming, Jack (character) • Journalist as Character • Vampire Hunters • Vampire's Point of View

Bloodcircle. *New York: Ace Books, 1998. [First published in 1990.] 202p.* Reissue of the third book in The Vampire Files series. Jack Flemming continues searching for the vampire who made him. Similar title: *The Vampire Lestat*, Anne Rice.

Flemming, Jack (character) • Vampire's Point of View

Art in the Blood. *New York: Ace Books, 1991. 208p.* Number four of The Vampire Files, this book follows the exploits of vampire/private investigator Jack Flemming, in a case where he must help find the killer of a young artist. Humorous and fun; an easy read. Similar titles: Laurell K. Hamilton's Anita Blake, Vampire Hunter series.

Flemming, Jack (character) • Vampire's Point of View

Fire in the Blood. *New York: Ace Books, 1991. 198p.* The fifth book of The Vampire Files, staring vampire private eye Jack Flemming.

Flemming, Jack (character) • Vampire's Point of View

Blood on the Water. *New York: Ace Books, 1992. 199p.* Vampire private eye Jack Flemming runs afoul of the Mafia in Chicago. Will his thirst for blood lead to a Mafia hit—on him? Part six of The Vampire Files.

Chicago, Illinois • Flemming, Jack (character) • Organized Crime • Vampire's Point of View

Chill in the Blood. *New York: Ace Books, 1998. 327p.* The seventh addition to The Vampire Files series, tales of the world's first undead private investigator. A mixture of comedy and hard-boiled detection, with the emphasis on Jack Flemming's character development. Similar titles: *Guilty Pleasures*, Laurell K. Hamilton; *Of Saints and Shadows*, Christopher Golden; *Thorn*, Fred Saberhagen.

Chicago, Illinois • Flemming, Jack (character) • History, Use of • Organized Crime • Private Investigator as Character

Farren, Mick.

The Time of Feasting. *New York: Tor Books, 1996. 384p.* In this action-oriented tale, vampire clan leader Victor Renquist has a few problems: His clan is getting restless during "The Time of Feasting," which occurs every seven years, and a young upstart vampire named Kurt wants to oust him as leader. When bodies start turning up all over New York City, Renquist realizes that Kurt and his followers are behind the slayings that threaten to expose the clan, and that something must be done before the humans catch on.

New York City • Vampire as New Species • Vampire Clans • Vampire's Point of View

Gideon, John.

Golden Eyes. *New York: Berkley, 1994. 457p.* History professor Sam Lansen returns to Oldenberg, Washington, to write the history of his boyhood town. Instead, he experiences a fight to the death with an ancient vampire who has chosen Oldenberg as the place to reproduce his kind when the time is right. Written from multiple points of view, including diaries of the dead and pieces of a Halloween "tale" about a nineteenth-century medicine woman, Queen Molly, and her encounter with the vampires. Similar titles: *Salem's Lot*, Stephen King; *Curse of the Vampire*, Jeffrey Caine; *Natural History*, Joan Perucho.

Native American Characters • Portland, Oregon • Shapeshifters • Vampire as New Species • Vampire Clans • Witches

Kindred. *New York: Jove Books, 1996. 419p.* Louis Kindred returned from Vietnam a quadriplegic and a changed man. In Vietnam Louis came face-to-face with absolute evil. He saw it in the eyes of trained killers, smelled it in the wake of spilled blood. Then he challenged it in a game of chance and won the darkest gift of all: immortality. Similar title: *Last Call*, Tim Powers.

Asian-American Characters • Cannibalism • Portland, Oregon • Shapeshifters • Vampire as New Species

Golden, Christopher.

Of Saints and Shadows. *New York: Jove Books, 1994. 391p.* A secret Catholic sect possesses an ancient book of the undead called *The Gospel of Shadows,* which reveals the secret world of vampires. The church used the book to cover up the truth—and to systematically destroy all such beings. Now the book has been stolen, and Peter Octavian, a private investigator and vampire, must solve the mystery. Similar titles: *Guilty Pleasures*, Laurell K. Hamilton; *Chill in the Blood* and *Lifeblood*, P. N. Elrod; *Thorn*, Fred Saberhagen.

Boston, Massachusetts • Private Investigator as Character • Religion—Christianity • Vampire's Point of View

Gottlieb, Sherry.

Love Bite. *New York: Warner Books, 1994. 277p.* A police detective with a terminal disease stumbles across a case that may offer a way to avoid death—victims are found completely drained of blood, the sign of a vampire/killer. Emphasis is on the romantic angle as much as on horror.

Gothic Romance • Immortality • Police Officer as Character • Serial Killers

Greenberg, Martin H. (editor).

Dracula: Prince of Darkness. *New York: Daw Books, 1992. 316p.* (See chapter 5, "Anthologies and Collections by Multiple Authors.")

Werewolves. *New York: Daw Books, 1995. 320p.* (See chapter 5, "Anthologies and Collections by Multiple Authors.")

Grimson, Todd.

Stainless. *New York: Harper Prism, 1996. 265p.* Relates the misadventures of slacker vampire Justine and her ex-rock star minion, Keith, as the two struggle with ennui in Los Angeles. Emphasis is on language, writing style, and characterization. Similar titles: *Lost Souls*, Poppy Z. Brite; *The World on Blood*, Jonathan Nasaw.

Actor as Character • California • Drugs • Music—Rock Music

Haley, Wendy.

This Dark Paradise. *New York: Diamond Books, 1994. 311p.* A wealthy, powerful southern family is haunted by the ghosts of past family members—and by family secrets. Unique in its creation of the southern vampire.

Family Curse • Georgia • Secret Sin • Vampire's Point of View

Hambly, Barbara.

Traveling with the Dead. *New York: Ballantine, 1995. 343p.* At the dawn of the twentieth century, the Austrian empire is secretly conspiring to make an alliance with the Undead for its own sinister ends. Dr. James Asher, mild-mannered professor of linguistics by day and agent in the service of Her Majesty's government by night, is the only one who can stop this alliance, and thereby prevent a different outcome to World War I. But behind every successful man there is a woman, and behind Dr. Asher is his wife, Lydia. Told alternately from the points of view of James and Lydia. Hambly demonstrates a thorough command of history in this tightly woven narrative. Similar titles: *Anno Dracula* and *Bloody Red Baron*, Kim Newman; *Slave of My Thirst*, Tom Holland.

Alternative History • Espionage • History, Use of • Victorian England • War—World War I

Hamilton, Laurell K., The Anita Blake, Vampire Hunter series.

Bloody Bones. *New York: Penguin, 1996. 370p.*

Blue Moon. *New York: Penguin, 1998. 342p.*

Circus of the Damned. *New York: Berkley-Ace, 1995. 329p.*

Guilty Pleasures. *New York: Penguin, 1993. 265p.*

The Killing Dance. *New York: Ace Books, 1997. 387p.*

The Laughing Corpse. *New York: Penguin, 1994. 293p.*

The Lunatic Cafe. *New York: Penguin, 1996. 369p.*

(For annotations of the Hamilton books, see chapter 19, "Comic Horror.")

Harbaugh, Karen.

The Vampire Viscount. *New York: Signet Books, 1995. 224p.* A young woman is given away in an arranged marriage, only to discover that her husband harbors a dark secret. Romance meets vampirism. A Signet Regency Romance. Similar titles: Chelsea Quinn Yarbro's Saint-Germain Chronicles; *The Ruby Tear*, Rebecca Brand.

Gothic Romance • Marriage

Hartwell, David G. (editor).

The Dark Descent. *New York: Tor Books, 1987. 1,011p.* (See chapter 5, "Anthologies and Collections by Multiple Authors.")

Herbert, James.

'48. *New York: Harper Prism, 1997. 368p.* In this alternative history, Hitler uses biological warfare to turn London into a ghost city, inhabited only by the few who survived the chemical attack—and those who want to feed on the survivors. Excellent description and fast-paced action. Similar titles: *Anno Dracula* and *Bloody Red Baron*, Kim Newman; *They Used Dark Forces*, Dennis Wheatley; *Blood Alone*, Elaine Bergstrom; *The Bargain*, John Ruddy; *Darkness on the Ice*, Lois Tilton.

Alternative History • Biological Warfare • Dogs • London, England • Nazism • War—World War II

Hill, William.

Dawn of the Vampire. *New York: Windsor, 1991. 480p.* An unused small-town cemetery that used to rest under a lake finally surfaces, and when it does the undead creatures in the graves come back to haunt the living. Now only a sportswriter, whose friends are being picked off one by one, can stop the carnage.

> *Cemeteries • Journalist as Character • Tennessee • Vampire as New Species • Vampire Clans*

Holland, Tom.

Lord of the Dead. *New York: Simon & Schuster, 1995. 342p.* Lord Byron, the real-life model for Dr. Polidori's *nosferatu* (Lord Ruthven) in the story *The Vampyre*, really *is* a vampire. He narrates the story of his undead existence to a "real-life" descendant of the fictional Ruthven. Being a vampire has only exacerbated his rakishness, and is the ultimate ruin of his friendship with Polidori and Shelley. Holland, a Byron scholar, cleverly blends fiction with facts about Byron and his friends, Dr. Polidori and Mary Shelley. Similar titles: *Slave of My Thirst*, Tom Holland; *Anno Dracula* and *Bloody Red Baron*, Kim Newman; any of Fred Saberhagen's vampire novels; *Among the Immortals*, Paul Lake; *The Stress of Her Regard*, Tim Powers; *Blood and Roses*, Sharon Bainbridge.

> *Alternative Literature • Byron, Lord George Gordon (character) • Eroticism • Greece • Incest • Polidori, John (character) • Shelley, Percy B. (character) • Vampire's Point of View*

Slave of My Thirst. *New York: Simon & Schuster, 1996. 421p.* The "real" story behind Bram Stoker's novel *Dracula* casts Stoker as Abraham Van Helsing, intent on saving England from the peril of vampires. But in this narrative, England isn't threatened by a predatory Transylvanian count with a penchant for London real estate. Instead, the threat is unknowingly imported by colonial soldiers in India who awaken the goddess Kali. Holland's novel is a literate piece of alternative literature told from multiple points of view. Similar titles: *Lord of the Dead*, Tom Holland; *Anno Dracula* and *Bloody Red Baron*, Kim Newman; any of Fred Saberhagen's vampire novels; *Song of Kali*, Dan Simmons; *Traveling with the Dead*, Barbara Hambly.

> *Alternative Literature • Epistolary Format • Eroticism • Jack the Ripper Murders • Kali (character) • Lilith (character) • Polidori, John (character) • Shapeshifters • Stoker, Bram (character) • Victorian England*

Holleman, Gary L.

Howl-o-ween. *New York: Leisure Books, 1996. 313p.* Bodyguard Cyrus Trigg finds himself involved with a client whose connections with "the Dark Man" threaten both their lives. Can he help his client transport millions of dollars in diamonds by her Halloween deadline, or will the dark forces that pursue them bring about their violent deaths? Similar title: *Bloodlist*, P. N. Elrod.

> *Cursed Objects • Memphis, Tennessee • Religion—Voodoo • Werewolves*

Huff, Tanya. The Blood series.

Blood Price. *New York: Daw Books, 1991. 272p.* The first volume of The Blood series begins the partnership of Vicki Nelson, a Toronto detective, and Henry Fitzroy, a romantic novelist. Here the two search for a 450-year-old vampire who is leaving too many corpses behind. Similar titles: Laurell K. Hamilton's Anita Blake, Vampire Hunter series.

> *Fitzroy, Henry (character) • Nelson, Vicki (character) • Toronto, Ontario • Vampire Hunters • Vampire's Point of View • Writer as Character*

Blood Trial. *New York: Daw Books, 1992. 304p.* A family of werewolves is being murdered, so they contact novelist Henry Fitzroy and detective Vicki Nelson to help them track down the killers. Part 2 of The Blood series. Similar titles: Laurell K. Hamilton's Anita Blake, Vampire Hunter series.

> *Fitzroy, Henry (character)* • *Nelson, Vicki (character)* • *Vampire's Point of View* • *Werewolves* • *Writer as Character*

Blood Lines. *New York: Daw Books, 1992. 271p.* A 3,000-year-old priest is attempting to usher in the reign of a destructive Egyptian god. Can Fitzroy and Nelson stop him before Toronto is destroyed? Part 3 of The Blood series. Similar titles: Laurell K. Hamilton's Anita Blake, Vampire Hunter series.

> *Fitzroy, Henry (character)* • *Nelson, Vicki (character)* • *Religion—Ancient Egyptian* • *Toronto, Ontario* • *Vampire's Point of View* • *Writer as Character*

Blood Pact. *New York: Daw Books, 1993. 332p.* The fourth novel in Huff's vampire detective series, *Blood Pact* pits Vicki Nelson, Mike Celluci, and Henry Fitzroy against a mad scientist who attempts to use her mother's corpse in a research experiment. Graphic and disturbing. Similar titles: Laurell K. Hamilton's Anita Blake, Vampire Hunter series.

> *Grieving* • *Fitzroy, Henry (character)* • *Mad Scientist* • *Nelson, Vicki (character)* • *Toronto, Ontario* • *Writer as Character*

Blood Debt. *New York: Daw Books, 1997. 330p.* In part 5 of The Blood series, Henry is seeing ghosts, so he calls Vicki Nelson in to help him figure out why. Similar titles: Laurell K. Hamilton's Anita Blake, Vampire Hunter series.

> *Fitzroy, Henry (character)* • *Nelson, Vicki (character)* • *Vampire's Point of View* • *Vancouver, British Columbia* • *Writer as Character*

Jacob, Charlee.

The Symbiotic Fascination. *Orlando, Fla.: Necro Publications, 1997. 243p.* The story of a shapeshifter who meets a reluctant vampire, and the relationship the two try to share. Subtle, with emphasis on characterization and psychology. Similar titles: *Interview with the Vampire* and *The Vampire Lestat*, Anne Rice.

> *Shapeshifters* • *Werewolves*

Jensen, Ruby Jean.

Vampire Child. *New York: Zebra, 1990. 285p.* Patrick Skein is a cold-blooded murderer of his own siblings, so he is sent to a boy's farm. There he undermines all authority and attempts to seduce the warden's daughter. Is Patrick incorrigible, or is his soul possessed by a creature of the night? Emphasis on atmosphere. Similar title: *Martin* (film).

> *Child Abuse* • *Psychosexual Horror*

Jones, Stephen (editor).

The Mammoth Book of Dracula: Vampire Tales for the New Millennium. *New York: Carroll and Graf, 1997. 512p.* (See chapter 5, "Anthologies and Collections by Multiple Authors.")

Kalogridis, Jeanne. Covenant with the Vampire series.

Covenant with the Vampire: The Diaries of the Family Dracul. *New York: Delacorte Press, 1994. 324p.* In multiple-point-of-view journal entries dated 50 years before Count Dracula comes to London (see Bram Stoker's *Dracula*), this novel relates how Vlad Tepes's great-nephew, Arcady, unwittingly joins forces with the *nosferatu*. The first in Kalogridis's trilogy that ultimately accounts for Van Helsing's obsession with the vampire. Similar titles: *Drakulya: The Lost Journal of Mircea Drakulya, Lord of the Undead*, Earl Lee; *The Blood of the Covenant* and *The Book of Common Dread*, Brent Monahan; *I, Vampire* and *The Vampire Papers*, Michael Romkey; *A Sharpness on the Neck*, Fred Saberhagen; *Thirst of the Vampire*, T. Lucien Wright.

> *Alternative Literature • Diary Format • Dracula (character) • History, Use of • Tepes, Vlad (character) • Transylvania • Tsepesh, Arkady (character)*

Children of the Vampire. *New York: Delacorte Press, 1995. 300p.* The second book of the Covenant with the Vampire series tells the story of Arkady Tsepesh's flight from Transylvania and his uncle Vlad, and of his transformation into the creature he most abhors. Enlisting the aid of a young Abraham Van Helsing, Arkady must fight off his bloodlust urges while keeping his whereabouts a secret—but the sudden appearance of his sister Zsusanna, also now a vampire, may jeopardize his life and the lives of his wife and child. Highly erotic. Told from multiple points of view. Similar titles: *Drakulya: The Lost Journal of Mircea Drakulya, Lord of the Undead*, Earl Lee; *I, Vampire* and *The Vampire Papers*, Michael Romkey; *A Sharpness on the Neck*, Fred Saberhagen; *Thirst of the Vampire*, T. Lucien Wright.

> *Alternative Literature • Dracula (character) • Eroticism • Homoeroticism • Tepes, Vlad (character) • Transylvania • Tsepesh, Arkady (character) • Tsepesh, Zsusanna (character) • Van Helsing, Abraham (character)*

Lord of the Vampires. *New York: Delacorte Press, 1996. 347p.* Abraham Van Helsing continues his war on all vampires, as his friend John Seward in London enlists his aid in saving a young woman's life. A clever retelling of Stoker's *Dracula*, this final book of the Covenant with the Vampire series traces Van Helsing's battle against Vlad Dracul, Elizabeth de Bathory, Zsusanna Tsepesh, and the master of all vampires. Similar titles: *Anno Dracula* and *Bloody Red Baron*, Kim Newman; *Drakulya: The Lost Journal of Mircea Drakulya, Lord of the Undead*, Earl Lee; *I, Vampire* and *The Vampire Papers*, Michael Romkey; *Thirst of the Vampire*, T. Lucien Wright.

> *Alternative Literature • Bathory, Elizabeth de (character) • Diary Format • Dracula (character) • Harker, Jonathan (character) • Harker, Mina Murray (character) • Holmwood, Arthur (character) • London, England • Seward, John (character) • Tepes, Vlad (character) • Transylvania • Tsepesh, Arkady (character) • Tsepesh, Zsusanna (character) • Van Helsing, Abraham (character)*

Kells, Sabine.

A Deeper Hunger. *New York: Leisure Books, 1994. 362p.* The paths of Cailie Wellington and Alec Creighton have crossed—again. This time, the immortal Creighton does not want to lose the woman whose body encapsulates the soul he has loved for centuries. Emphasis is on description and emotion, with more subtlety than horror.

> *Gothic Romance • Hawaii • Librarian as Character • Reincarnation*

Kemske, Floyd.

Human Resources. *North Haven, Conn.: Catbird Press, 1995. 223p.* (See chapter 19, "Comic Horror.")

Killough, Lee.

Blood Hunt. *New York: Tor Books, 1987. 319p.* One of the first vampire detective novels following the efforts of San Francisco investigator Garreth Mikaelin, who is unwillingly turned into a vampire while on a case.

> *Hypnotism • Immortality • Vampire's Point of View*

Bloodlinks. *New York: Tor, 1988. 345p.* Continuation of *Blood Hunt* where investigator Garreth Mikaelin searches for the person who turned him into a vampire.

Hypnotism • Immortality • Vampire's Point of View

Kilpatrick, Nancy.

Near Death. *New York: Pocket Books, 1994. 295p.* Vampire David Hardwick teams up with an ex-prostitute/junkie/vampire slayer to stop a fellow vampire's plans of world domination. As much a romance as it is a horror novel, with lots of erotic moments. Similar title: *Bring on the Night*, Joy Davis and Don Davis.

Drugs • Eroticism • Vampire's Point of View

Kimbriel, Katherine Elisha.

Night Calls. *New York: Harper Prism, 1996. 310p.* (See chapter 10, "Demonic Possession, Satanism, Black Magic, and Witches and Warlocks.")

King, Stephen.

Salem's Lot. *Garden City, N.J.: Doubleday, 1975. 439p.* Jerusalem's Lot is a town well acquainted with darkness and evil. After all, the sins of the town legend, Hubie Marsten, were kept alive in rumor and gossip. But there is a new evil in the Marsten house, in the form of Richard Throckett Straker, an antique furniture dealer who is also a vampire. Good on scares and suspense. Similar titles: *Golden Eyes*, John Gideon; *Needful Things*, Stephen King.

New England • Writer as Character

Kiraly, Marie.

Mina. *New York: Berkley, 1994. 325p.* Kiraly's novel begins after Stoker's *Dracula* ends: Mina Harker is finding out that married life with Jonathan isn't all she hoped it would be, and that her new husband doesn't share her passionate nature. Furthermore, Mina was never really cured of Dracula's bite—his "influence" continues to course through her veins. Mina craves human blood as well as satisfaction of her animal lusts, and must finally return to Dracula's castle to discover her true nature. Similar titles: *Phantom*, Susan Kay; *The Memoirs of Elizabeth Frankenstein*, Theodore Roszak; *Sisters of the Night: The Angry Angel*, Chelsea Quinn Yarbro.

Alternative Literature • Dracula (character) • Eroticism • Harker, Jonathan (character) • Harker, Mina Murray (character) • London, England

Klause, Annette Curtis.

Blood and Chocolate. *New York: Delacorte Press, 1997. 264p.* A teenage werewolf has fallen in love with a young human who is faced with a loved one's terminal illness. Now she must determine where her allegiance lies. A gentle read.

Grieving • Werewolves

Kramer, Edward E. (editor).

Dark Destiny: Proprietors of Fate. *Clarkston, Ga.: White Wolf, 1995. 442p.* (See chapter 5, "Anthologies and Collections by Multiple Authors.")

Lake, Paul.

Among the Immortals. *Brownsville, Ore.: Story Line, 1994. 301p.* The murder of a college professor leads a graduate student to suspect that Romantic poet Percy B. Shelley has returned as a murderous vampire. Satirical look at academia and publishing. Similar title: *Lord of the Dead*, Tom Holland.

> *Academia • San Francisco, California • Shelley, Percy B. (character) • Writer as Character*

Lee, Earl.

Drakulya: The Lost Journal of Mircea Drakulya, Lord of the Undead. *Tuscon, Ariz.: Sharp Press, 1994. 213p.* Dracula tells his own version of the famous Stoker tale here; Drakulya is actually the older brother of Vlad the Impaler, who assumes Vlad's identity after his death. Emphasis is on characterization and psychological accuracy.

> *Alternative Literature • Diary Format • Dracula (character) • England • Harker, Mina Murray (character) • Mistaken Identity • Tepes, Vlad (character) • Vampire's Point of View*

LeFanu, Sheridan.

Carmilla. *New York: Oxford University Press, 1872. 112p.* In this novella, a young girl, Laura, befriends the temptress Carmilla, a young aristocratic girl who is actually a vampire. This influential nineteenth-century tale is characterized by its highly descriptive prose and indirect style, as well as by its use of first-person narration in journal form, included in a frame-tale format. Extremely clever. Similar title: *Carmilla: The Return*, Kyle Marffin.

> *Diary Format • Homoeroticism • Karnstein, Carmilla (character) • Vampire Hunters*

Through a Glass Darkly. *New York: Oxford University Press, 1872. 347p.* (See chapter 6, "Collections by Individual Authors.")

Longstreet, Roxanne.

The Undead. *New York: Zebra, 1993. 318p.* A medical examiner is suspected by a colleague of being a vampire. This leads to a chase between vampire and hunter, a duel between friends.

> *Medical Horror • Police Officer as Character • Vampire Hunters*

Lumley, Brian. The Necroscope series.

Necroscope. *London: Grafton, 1986. 511p.* Young Harry Keogh discovers that he has a gift—he can converse with the dead and learn their knowledge and secrets. Unknown to Keogh, his destiny is tied to a sadistic Russian who "reads" the dead by playing in their entrails, as well as to an ancient, evil vampire.

> *Dragosani, Boris (character) • Espionage • Keogh, Harry (character) • Telepathy • Wamphyri, The (characters)*

Necroscope II: Wamphyri. *New York: Tor Books, 1988. 470p.* Harry Keogh thought he had destroyed Dragosani and therefore had killed off the vampires, but in a secluded English village, Yolian Bodescu is plotting the Wamphyri takeover of the world. Even with his newfound ability to transport himself anywhere instantly, is the Necroscope a match for the vampires?

> *Dragosani, Boris (character) • Espionage • Fantasy • Keogh, Harry (character) • Wamphyri, The (characters)*

Necroscope III: The Source. *New York: Tor Books, 1989. 505p.* Harry Keogh must find his missing wife and son, while fighting more vampires who want to rule humans. High on adventure and dark fantasy.

> *Keogh, Harry (character) • Vampire as New Species*

Necroscope: The Lost Years, Vol. I. New York: Doherty, 1995. 593p.

Necroscope: Resurgence: The Lost Years, Vol. II. *New York: Doherty, 1996. 414p.* Harry Keogh, a.k.a. The Necroscope, is back, and this time it's personal. Harry must save his family, and must do so while in another man's body. Once again, the vampires are at the center of Harry's problems, but this time he has the powers of space and time travel, as well as his ability to talk with the dead, to aid him in his battle. Lumley is extremely creative in this espionage/adventure/horror work, which brings his Necroscope mythology up-to-date. Destined to be a classic in the subgenre. Similar titles: others in Lumley's Necroscope series.

> *Espionage • Keogh, Harry (character) • Telepathy • Vampire as New Species • Wamphyri, The (characters)*

Lumley, Brian. The Vampire World trilogy.

Blood Brothers. *New York: Tor Books, 1992. 565p.* The first novel of Lumley's post-Necroscope series, *Blood Brothers* begins with the twin sons of Harry Keogh, Nathan and Nestor, and traces their encounters with the Wamphyri. Nathan discovers he is telepathic; Nestor believes himself to be Wamphyri. Continues in *The Last Aerie.*

> *Fantasy • Kiklu, Nathan (character) • Kiklu, Nestor (character) • Telepathy • Twins • Wamphyri, The (characters)*

The Last Aerie. *New York: Tor Books, 1994. 479p.* The sequel to *Blood Brothers,* which concerns itself with the ongoing battle between Harry Keogh's twin sons, Nathan and Nestor. Nathan finds himself trapped on Earth, while Nestor grows even more evil. Unique.

> *Espionage • Fantasy • Keogh, Harry (character) • Kiklu, Nathan (character) • Kiklu, Nestor (character) • Telepathy • Twins • Wamphyri, The (characters)*

Bloodwars. *New York: Doherty, 1995. 760p.* Part III of the Vampire World trilogy chronicles Nathan's attempts to use all his powers to combat his brother Nestor, now a vampire lord. High in creativity and action.

> *Fantasy • Kiklu, Nathan (character) • Kiklu, Nestor (character) • Vampire as New Species • Vampire's Point of View*

MacMillan, Scott.

Knights of the Blood. *New York: ROC Books, 1993. 350p.* A series of murders in 1970s Los Angeles leads a police detective to a priest who claims to be following the undead. The story unravels through several historical periods, with police procedural details in the forefront.

> *Clergy as Character • History, Use of • Los Angeles, California • Nazism • Police Officer as Character • Religion—Christianity—Catholicism • War—World War II*

Marffin, Kyle.

Carmilla: The Return. *Darien, Ill.: Design Image, 1998. 296p.* Retelling of the LeFanu classic about a female vampire who stalks a young girl, updated to occur in the twentieth century. Carmilla herself narrates this darkly erotic tale. Similar title: *Carmilla*, Sheridan LeFanu.

Alternative Literature • Homoeroticism • Karnstein, Carmilla (character)

Martin, David Lozell.

Tap, Tap: A Novel. *New York: Random House, 1995. 291p.* Roscoe Bird's childhood friend, Peter, shows up on his doorstep decades later; unfortunately, his arrival coincides with the actions of a serial killer who is murdering all of Roscoe's enemies. A suspenseful psychological thriller. Similar title: *Sunglasses After Dark*, Nancy Collins.

Revenge • Serial Killers • Washington, D.C.

Martindale, T. Chris.

Nightblood. *New York: Warner Books, 1990. 322p.* A Vietnam veteran is led by his brother's ghost to a small town in Indiana where evil resides. Can he protect the town's children from the horrible creatures who killed his brother?

Haunted Houses • Indiana

Martini, Steven Paul.

The List. *New York: Putnam, 1997. 438p.* Thriller author Abby Chandlis travels to New York and St. Croix with an ex-Marine who poses as her most recent book's author, to boost sales. But then Abby discovers disturbing facts about his past that might link him to the murders of her friends and confidants.

Mistaken Identity • Writer as Character

Matheson, Richard.

I Am Legend. *New York: Tor Books, 1995. 312p.* (See chapter 6, "Collections by Individual Authors.")

McCammon, Robert R.

They Thirst. *New York: Pocket Books, 1981. 562p.* Los Angeles is under siege: an albino ex–Hell's Angel is gunning down people in diners; a serial killer is clearing prostitutes off the streets; and zombielike people are robbing graves. And police officer Andy Palatzin finds himself faced with an evil that goes all the way back to his childhood. Complex, multiple plotlines intersect, with a large-scale faceoff between good and evil. Similar titles: *Children of the Night* and *Carrion Comfort*, Dan Simmons; *The Time of Feasting*, Mick Farren.

Journalist as Character • Los Angeles, California • Police Officer as Character • Serial Killers • Vampire Clans

McCuniff, Mara, and Traci Briery.

The Vampire Memoirs. *New York: Zebra, 1991. 432p.* Chronicles the life of a young woman who was once a fifth-century wife and mother—and is now a reluctant vampire running for her life in twentieth-century Los Angeles. The closest thing to a female version of *Interview with the Vampire*. Similar titles: *Interview with the Vampire* and *The Vampire Lestat*, Anne Rice.

Diary Format • Immortality • Los Angeles, California • Vampire Hunters • Vampire's Point of View

Michaels, Barbara.

Sons of the Wolf. *New York: Berkley, 1968. 282p.* After the death of their grandmother, Ada and Harriet are sent to live with Mr. Wolfson, a distant relative who is to be their guardian; after all, unmarried young ladies don't live alone in the nineteenth century. Mr. Wolfson, confined to a wheelchair, has two fierce dogs and two mysterious sons, one good and one evil. But evil runs rampant through Abbey Manor, especially at night. Similar title: *Guardian*, John Saul.

England • Gothic Romance • Werewolves

Miller, Linda Lael.

Forever and the Night. *New York: Berkley, 1993. 338p.* Romantic triangles and political intrigue color this "unwilling vampire" tale. Aidan Tremayne is made one of the undead by a controlling dominatrix/vampire, and now he has discovered the possibility of becoming human again. Similar titles: *The Night Insider*, Nancy Baker; *Bring on the Night*, Joy Davis and Don Davis.

Eroticism • Immortality • Vampire's Point of View

Monahan, Brent. The Book of Common Dread series.

The Book of Common Dread. *New York: St. Martin's Press, 1993. 328p.* Simon Penn, rare book curator, is entrusted with the care of a 3,000-year-old manuscript that accurately describes DNA, atoms, the heliocentric theory of the universe, and the existence of vampires. But the vampire's ability to exist among humans depends in part on human disbelief. Thus Vincent DeVilbiss has been sent by his makers to destroy this manuscript before his kind can be destroyed by humans, and before his makers' plans for the destruction of the human race can be thwarted. Clever and intricate tale, told from multiple points of view. Similar titles: *Memnoch the Devil*, Anne Rice; *Covenant with the Vampire*, Jeanne Kalogridis.

Librarian as Character • New Jersey • Penn, Simon (character) • Vampire's Point of View • Vanderveen, Frederika (character)

The Blood of the Covenant: A Novel of the Vampiric. *New York, St. Martin's Press, 1997. 320p.* This sequel to *The Book of Common Dread* begins with De Vilbiss's death and Simon and Frederika's escape with the scrolls of Ahriman. Can the two escape from their bounty hunter—an ancient vampire skilled in torture? Similar titles: *Memnoch the Devil*, Anne Rice; *Covenant with the Vampire*, Jeanne Kalogridis.

Penn, Simon (character) • Religion—Christianity—Catholicism • Vanderveen, Frederika (character)

Moore, Christopher.

Bloodsucking Fiends: A Love Story. *New York: Avon, 1996. 300p.* (See chapter 19, "Comic Horror.")

Morrison, Robert, and Chris Baldick (editors).

The Vampyre and Other Tales of the Macabre. *New York: Oxford University Press, 1997. 278p.* (See chapter 5, "Anthologies and Collections by Multiple Authors.")

Murphy, Pat.

Nadya. *New York: Tor Books, 1997. 382p.* Character study of a young descendant of European werewolves who is forced to come to the New World. In nineteenth-century America, she learns of humans' hatred for her species—and about the capacity to love. Sensitive treatment of difference.

> *History, Use of • Homoeroticism • Native American Characters • Religion— Native American • United States—Nineteenth Century • Werewolves*

Nasaw, Jonathan.

The World on Blood. *New York: Dutton, 1996. 341p.* Human vampires populate this novel, which deals with blood addictions, Vampires Anonymous meetings, and one vampire who wants to destroy V.A. Literate, original, erotic, and sexually graphic. Similar titles: *Stainless*, Todd Grimson; *The Hunger*, Whitley Strieber.

> *Eroticism • Obsession • San Francisco, California • Vampire's Point of View • Weiss, Selene (character) • Whistler, Jamie (character)*

Shadows. *New York: Dutton, 1997. 336p.* (See chapter 10, "Demonic Possession, Satanism, Black Magic, and Witches and Warlocks.")

Newman, Kim. The Anno Dracula series.

Anno Dracula. *New York: Avon, 1992. 409p.* What would have happened if Dracula had actually defeated Van Helsing? Kim Newman twists Stoker's narrative, using historical, literary, and popular-culture figures, to create an intricate rewriting of the *Dracula* story while including every known vampire myth. Recipient of an International Literary Guild Award for Best Novel. Similar titles: *'48*, James Herbert; *The Werewolves of London* and *The Angel of Pain*, Brian Stableford; *Traveling with the Dead*, Barbara Hambly; *Lord of the Vampires*, Jeanne Kalogridis; *The Bargain*, John Ruddy; *Seance for a Vampire* and *A Sharpness on the Neck*, Fred Saberhagen.

> *Alternative History • Alternative Literature • Beauregard, Charles (character) • Holmwood, Arthur (character) • Jack the Ripper Murders • London, England • Seward, John (character) • Tepes, Vlad (character) • Vampire's Point of View • Victorian England*

Bloody Red Baron. *New York: Avon, 1995. 370p.* This novel continues 20 years after *Anno Dracula* ends. Previously, the evil Prince Vlad had been chased from England, and all think he has been defeated. However, Vlad Tepes has been regrouping his forces in Germany, and has gotten one of his own vampires to assassinate Archduke Ferdinand and start World War I. Highly literate prose and a knowledge of history.

> *Alternative History • Alternative Literature • Beauregard, Charles (character) • Holmwood, Arthur (character) • London, England • Tepes, Vlad (character) • Vampire's Point of View • War—World War I*

Judgement of Tears: Anno Dracula 1959. *New York: Carroll and Graf, 1998. 240p.* In the third novel of this series, Vlad Tepes is set to marry yet again for political gain, this time in Rome, the Eternal City. But someone is murdering vampire elders, some born to darkness as long ago as the Middle Ages. Typical Newman, in that he demonstrates a thorough command of place and time and peppers his narrative with walk-on appearances by well-known historical figures and fictional characters. Featured in this novel are Gomez and Morticia Addams, James Bond, Father Merrin from *The Exorcist*, an enormous Orson Welles, and a gloomy Edgar Allan Poe who, after becoming a vampire, is now a hack screenwriter. Similar titles for both the second and third in the series: *'48*,

James Herbert; *The Werewolves of London* and *The Angel of Pain*, Brian Stableford; *They Used Dark Forces*, Dennis Wheatley; *Traveling with the Dead*, Barbara Hambly; *Lord of the Vampires*, Jeanne Kalogridis; *The Bargain*, John Ruddy.

> *Alternative History • Alternative Literature • Rome, Italy • Tepes, Vlad (character) • Vampire's Point of View*

Odom, Mel, and David S. Goyer.

Blade. *New York: Harper Paperbacks, 1998. 343p.* Novelization of the 1998 film of the same name. Blade, a half-human/half-vampire, struggles against his *nosferatu* half and protects humanity from those who see the human race as nothing more than cattle. His mixed heritage gives him an advantage over the "children of the night" in that he can walk in the sunlight.

> *Fantasy • Vampire Hunters • Vampire's Point of View*

Perucho, Joan.

Natural History (trans.). *New York: Knopf, 1988. 186p.* First published in Catalan in 1960, *Natural History* tells of the adventures of scientist Antoni de Montpalau, who travels to a small village to investigate the killings of villagers. There he runs into a powerful vampire. Similar title: *Golden Eyes*, John Gideon.

> *Dracula (character) • Espionage • Shapeshifters*

Peterson, Gail.

The Making of a Monster. *New York: Dell, 1993. 371p.* Kate is forced to move to Los Angeles when her husband takes a new job, and there she meets an actor who turns her into a vampire. To survive, she joins an underground band—and enjoys a series of killings. Similar titles: *Lost Souls*, Poppy Z. Brite; *Silk*, Caitlin R. Kiernan; *Tempter*, Nancy A. Collins; *Night Prayers*, P. D. Cacek.

> *Actor as Character • Los Angeles, California • Music—Rock Music*

Pike, Christopher.

The Season of Passage. *New York: Tor Books, 1993. 438p.* (See chapter 15, "Technohorror.")

Prescott, Steve, and James A. Moore.

Nuwisha. *Clarkston, Ga.: White Wolf, 1998. 72p.* (See chapter 11, "Mythological Monsters and 'The Old Ones.' ")

Reaves, Michael.

Night Hunter. *New York: Tor Books, 1995. 276p.* When a young hustler is found murdered in a hotel room, he becomes famous as the Night Hunter's first victim. Police detective Jake Hull doesn't believe in vampires ... yet. Reaves gives the reader a fascinating view of the characters that populate Hollywood's underbelly.

> *Gay/Lesbian/Bisexual Characters • Hollywood, California • Human Sacrifice • Religion—Druidism • Religion—Satanism*

Reines, Kathryn.

The Kiss. *New York: Avon, 1996. 293p.* Rebecca and Richard, two young lovers on the run in Europe, find themselves in the home of a charismatic count and countess. Little do they know that they are now the targets of vampires—who want to "turn" Rebecca and enslave Richard. Clever plot twists.

> *Eroticism • Germany*

Rice, Anne. The Vampire Chronicles.

Interview with the Vampire. *New York: Ballantine, 1977. 346p.* This first novel in Rice's Vampire Chronicles series contains the first-person confessions of reluctant vampire Louis, who, during a time of overwhelming grief, was seduced into the undead life by Lestat de Lioncourt. Transports readers into the world of the undead in the New Orleans of 200 years ago. An immensely popular book that led to Rice's own "immortality" on the best-seller list. Made into a film in 1995. Similar titles: *The Werewolves of London* and *The Angel of Pain*, Brian Stableford; *Desmond: A Novel of Love and the Modern Vampire*, Ulysses G. Dietz; *The Symbiotic Fascination*, Charlee Jacob; *The Vampire Memoirs*, Mara McCuniff and Traci Briery.

Armand (character) • Claudia (character) • Homoeroticism • Lestat de Lioncourt (character) • Louis (character) • New Orleans, Louisiana • Vampire's Point of View

The Vampire Lestat. *New York: Ballantine, 1985. 550p.* Second in Rice's Vampire Chronicles series. Details the vampire Lestat's undead and pre-undead existence, and his search for the meaning of life. Written in the first person from Lestat's point of view, this novel is a reaction to *Interview with the Vampire*, a tell-all book published by Lestat's former lover, Louis, which represents Lestat as a thoughtless bloodsucker. Similar titles: *The Werewolves of London* and *The Angel of Pain*, Brian Stableford; *The Mummy, or Ramses the Damned* and *Servant of the Bones*, Anne Rice; Anne Rice's Mayfair Witch novels; *Desmond: A Novel of Love and the Modern Vampire*, Ulysses G. Dietz; *The Symbiotic Fascination*, Charlee Jacob; *The Vampire Memoirs*, Mara McCuniff and Traci Briery.

Akasha and Enkil (characters) • Armand (character) • Claudia (character) • History, Use of • Homoeroticism • Lestat de Lioncourt (character) • Louis (character) • Marius (character) • Music—Rock Music • Vampire's Point of View

The Queen of the Damned. *New York: Ballantine, 1989. 491p.* The third book in the Vampire Chronicles picks up where *The Vampire Lestat* stopped with Akasha and Lestat. The mother of all vampirekind, Akasha, has freed herself from Enkil, her husband and jailer for the past 2,000 years, and has taken Lestat as an unwilling personal assistant to help carry out her plan to kill 9 out of every 10 men on earth. Similar titles: *The Werewolves of London* and *The Angel of Pain*, Brian Stableford; *Widow*, Billie Sue Mosiman; *The Calling*, Kathryn Meyer Griffith; *My Soul to Keep*, Tanarive Due; Anne Rice's Mayfair Witch novels.

Akasha and Enkil (characters) • Babylon • History, Use of • Homoeroticism • Lestat de Lioncourt (character) • Lightner, Aaron (character) • Louis (character) • Maharet and Mekare (characters) • Marius (character) • Religion—Ancient Egyptian • Talamasca • Vampire's Point of View

The Tale of the Body Thief. *New York: Ballantine, 1992. 435p.* Rice's fourth book in the Vampire Chronicles, and the third book "written" by Lestat. *The Tale of the Body Thief* concerns Lestat's adventures as a mortal. Bored with the undead life, Lestat longs to experience mortal pleasures once more, such as eating and making love, but he also rediscovers the mortification of being encased in human flesh. Similar titles: *The Werewolves of London* and *The Angel of Pain*, Brian Stableford.

Homoeroticism • Lestat de Lioncourt (character) • Louis (character) • New York City • Talamasca • Vampire's Point of View

Memnoch the Devil. *New York: Knopf, 1995. 354p.* This was apparently intended as the last of the novels in the Vampire Chronicle series. For centuries Lestat has doubted the existence of God and Satan, until Satan comes to him, shows him the world of the living and the dead, and asks him to be Satan's Second in Command. Similar titles: *The Werewolves of London* and *The Angel of Pain*, Brian Stableford; Anne Rice's Mayfair Witch novels.

> *Armand (character) • Claudia (character) • Homoeroticism • Lestat de Lioncourt (character) • Louis (character) • Maharet and Mekare (characters) • New Age • New York City • Religion—Christianity • Satan (character) • Vampire's Point of View*

Pandora: New Tales of the Vampire. *New York: Knopf, 1998. 288p.* This first-person narrative is a pseudohistorical romp through the Rome of Augustus Caesar and modern-day Paris, starring Pandora, an innocent Roman girl made into a vampire by Marius. Emphasis on historical accuracy rather than vampirism per se, with the main character being one of the few strong Rice-created females. Generally counted as a sixth novel in the Vampire Chronicles series. Similar titles: Chelsea Quinn Yarbro's Saint-Germain novels; *The Silver Wolf*, Alice Borchardt.

> *Akasha and Enkil (characters) • History, Use of • Homoeroticism • Marius (character) • Religion—Christianity • Rome, Italy • Vampire's Point of View*

The Vampire Armand: The Vampire Chronicles. *New York: Knopf, 1998. 384p.* This seventh novel in Rice's Vampire Chronicles begins at the end of *Memnoch the Devil*, the fifth novel in the series. Lestat lies unconscious on the floor of a cathedral after his encounter with Satan, and all the vampires of the world have gathered at his side. It is during this occasion that Marius bids Armand to take the opportunity to tell his life story. Similar titles: *Interview with the Vampire*, *The Vampire Lestat*, and *Pandora: New Tales of the Vampire*, Anne Rice.

> *Armand (character) • History, Use of • Homoeroticism • Lestat de Lioncourt (character) • Marius (character) • Religion—Christianity • Vampire's Point of View*

Romkey, Michael. The I, Vampire series.

I, Vampire. *New York: Fawcett, 1990. 360p.* Good and evil vampire clans led by famous historical figures, such as Julius Caesar and Lucretia Borgia, highlight this action-oriented exploration of immortality. Plot-driven and considered a "classic" text by many vampire enthusiasts. Similar titles: *Children of the Vampire*, *Covenant with the Vampire,* and *Lord of the Vampires*, Jeanne Kalogridis; *The Vampire Papers*, Michael Romkey.

> *History, Use of • Parker, David (character) • Vampire Clans • Vampire's Point of View*

The Vampire Papers. *New York: Fawcett, 1994. 433p.* In this much-awaited sequel to *I, Vampire,* vampire clans led by David Parker and John Wilkes Booth clash in the colonial South. Similar titles: *Children of the Vampire*, *Covenant with the Vampire,* and *Lord of the Vampires*, Jeanne Kalogridis; *I, Vampire*, Michael Romkey.

> *History, Use of • Parker, David (character) • The South • Vampire Clans • Vampire's Point of View*

The Vampire Princess. *New York: Fawcett, 1996. 339p.* The third book of the *I, Vampire* series deals with David Parker's vampire love, Princess Nicoletta Vittorini di Medusa. The two undead lovers attend a cruise aboard the "Atlantic Princess," and David once again finds himself pitted against evil.

Gothic Romance • Parker, David (character) • Vampire's Point of View

The Vampire Virus. *New York: Ballantine, 1997. 295p.* In the jungles of Costa Rica, an unknown virus is introduced to the world, with lethal results. When CDC doctor Bailey Herrison travels there to investigate, she also finds a centuries-old ruler who is slave to a centuries-old thirst. Similar title: *Slave of My Thirst*, Tom Holland.

Archaeology • Costa Rica • Epidemic • Vampire as New Species

Ruddy, John.

The Bargain. *New York: Knightsbridge, 1990. 293p.* Dracula, having signed a covenant with his fellow Romanians, finds it necessary to protect the country during World War II. He enlists a legion of vampire prostitutes—and ultimately the help of a fanged Eva Braun—to drive Nazism to its death. Original, with much homage paid to Stoker's novel. Similar titles: *'48*, James Herbert; *Anno Dracula* and *Bloody Red Baron*, Kim Newman; *They Used Dark Forces*, Dennis Wheatley.

Dracula (character) • Eroticism • Nazism • Romania • War—World War II

Rusch, Kristin Kathryn.

Sins of the Blood. *New York: Dell, 1994. 388p.* The tale of Cammie, a vampire hunter whose father was one of the undead, and Ben, a tall, beautiful predator. Unique version of vampirism as a medical affliction. Suspenseful and graphic. Similar title: *Daughter of Darkness*, Steven Spruill.

Music—Rock Music • Vampire Clans • Vampire Hunters

Ryan, Shawn.

Nocturnas. *New York: Simon & Schuster/Pocket Books, 1995. 438p.* Photojournalist Adam Chase, on assignment in Romania during the last days of Nicolae Ceaucescu, discovers that the doomed dictator is protected by a band of vampires. Jarek, the leader of Ceaucescu's vampires, is thousands of years old, and provided security for Napoleon Bonaparte and Julius Caesar. When Ceaucescu is overthrown, Jarek flees to the United States, where he is hunted by Adam, Adam's magic stick, and Adam's friends in the Romanian resistance. This action-oriented tale is told through multiple points of view. Similar titles: *Thorn*, Fred Saberhagen; *Children of the Night*, Dan Simmons.

Ceaucescu, Nicolae (character) • Florida • Romania • Vampire as New Species • Vampire Hunters

Saberhagen, Fred. The Dracula Tape series.

The Dracula Tape. *New York: Doherty, 1975. 280p.* Count Dracula sets the record straight in this novel that challenges Stoker's version of the tale. Clever and well written, in transcribed-tape-entry form. Similar titles: *Blood of the Impaler*, Jeffrey Sackett; *Seance for a Vampire*, Fred Saberhagen.

Alternative Literature • Diary Format • Dracula (character) • Harker, Mina Murray (character) • Seward, John (character) • Vampire's Point of View • Van Helsing, Abraham (character)

A Matter of Taste. *New York: Tor Books, 1990. 284p.* Angie Roban finally gets to meet her fiancée's "Uncle Matthew," an ancient vampire in hiding from vampire hunters. The only problem is she may have led the vampire killers to their prey. Chapters are related alternately from Angie's and Dracula's points of view. Similar titles: *A Sharpness on the Neck* and *A Question of Time*, Fred Saberhagen; *Anno Dracula* and *Bloody Red Baron*, Kim Newman; *Slave of My Thirst*, Tom Holland.

> *Chicago, Illinois • Dracula (character) • Keogh, Joe (character) • Vampire's Point of View*

Thorn. *New York: Tor Books, 1990. 299p.* Dracula shows his tender side in this novel, in which he pursues his lost love, Helen, for 500 years, from Renaissance Italy to the late twentieth-century United States. But Dracula also finds himself pursued by those who would steal the secrets of immortality from him. Dracula/Thorn's life in the fifteenth century is loosely based on the life of Vlad Tepes. Told from Thorn/Dracula's point of view, alternating between his present-day pursuit of Helen and the beginnings of that pursuit in fifteenth-century Italy. Similar titles: *Nocturnas*, Shawn Ryan; *Of Saints and Shadows*, Christopher Golden; *Chill in the Blood* and *Lifeblood*, P. N. Elrod; *Guilty Pleasures*, Laurell K. Hamilton.

> *Dracula (character) • History, Use of • Italy • Vampire's Point of View*

A Question of Time. *New York: Tor Books, 1992. 263p.* A voluptuous woman named Camilla leads Jake Rezner, a blue-collar-type CCC camp worker, into the lair of a malicious vampire, and ultimately into a time warp. Meanwhile, decades later, two private investigators who unknowingly work with a vampire search for a missing girl. Clever interweaving of story lines and popular characters in this genre. Similar titles: *A Matter of Taste* and *Seance for a Vampire*, Fred Saberhagen; Brian Lumley's Necroscope series.

> *Dracula (character) • Keogh, Joe (character) • Time Travel • United States—1930s*

Seance for a Vampire. *New York: Tor Books, 1994. 310p.* A Newgate prisoner survives a hanging—Russian vampires are loose in London in 1910. When a young woman is mysteriously killed, but her spirit is called up in a seance, Sherlock Holmes and Dr. Watson believe that she has become one of the undead. They enlist the help of Holmes's cousin, Count Dracula, to solve this mystery. Lenin and Rasputin have cameos. A well-written, clever addition to Saberhagen's Dracula Tape series. Narrated by Watson and Dracula. Similar titles: *The Dracula Tape*, Fred Saberhagen; *Anno Dracula*, Kim Newman; *Blood of the Impaler*, Jeffrey Sackett.

> *Dracula (character) • History, Use of • London, England • Parapsychology • Vampire's Point of View • Victorian England*

A Sharpness on the Neck. *New York: Tor Books, 1996. 349p.* On their honeymoon, Philip and June Radcliffe accidentally hit a hitchhiker, and soon find themselves kidnapped by Dracula himself. But their greatest danger is not the legendary vampire; rather, it is his brother Radu, another immortal who has hunted down a Radcliffe before. Clever, unique, and full of historical and literary allusions. Similar titles: *Anno Dracula*, Kim Newman; *Covenant with the Vampire*, *Children of the Vampire*, and *Lord of the Vampires*, Jeanne Kalogridis.

> *Dracula (character) • History, Use of • Tepes, Vlad (character) • Vampire's Point of View • War—French Revolution*

Sackett, Jeffrey.

Blood of the Impaler. *New York: Bantam, 1989. 340p.* Malcolm Harker, grandson of Mina Murray Harker, is discovering that he has inherited traces of vampirism from his grandmother's blood encounter with Dracula. He decides that the only way to fight this is to enlist the aid of the vampire Lucy Westenra, who can lead him to Dracula. Inventive appropriation of Stoker's character and text. Similar titles: *The Dracula Tape* and *Seance for a Vampire*, Fred Saberhagen.

> *Alternative Literature • Dracula (character) • Religion—Christianity—Catholicism • Tepes, Vlad (character) • Westenra, Lucy (character)*

Saul, John.

Guardian. *New York: Fawcett Columbine, 1993. 390p.* Mary Anne Carpenter, a newly divorced mother who lives in Cannan, New Jersey, learns that her best friends, the Wilkensons, have been murdered, apparently by some sort of animal. But when Mary Anne and her daughter Alison take in the orphaned Joey Wilkenson, a shocking truth is revealed. Suspenseful and raw; a no-holds-barred horror story. Similar titles: *The Wolfen*, Whitley Strieber; *Sons of the Wolf*, Barbara Michaels.

> *Animal's Point of View • New Jersey • Orphans • Werewolves*

Schimel, Lawrence, and Martin H. Greenberg (editors).

Blood Lines: Vampire Stories from New England. *Nashville, Tenn.: Cumberland House, 1997. 224p.* (See chapter 5, "Anthologies and Collections by Multiple Authors.")

Southern Blood: Vampire Stories from the American South. *Nashville, Tenn.: Cumberland House, 1997. 203p.* (See chapter 5, "Anthologies and Collections by Multiple Authors.")

Shayne, Maggie.

Born in Twilight. *New York: Silhouette Books, 1997. 378p.* Continuation of *Twilight Illusions, Twilight Phantasies,* and *Twilight Memories*. A young nun is transformed into a vampire, but she discovers that there are worse creatures than bloodsuckers—namely, the humans who hunt them.

> *Gothic Romance • Vampire Hunters • Vampire's Point of View*

Siciliano, Sam.

Blood Feud. *New York: Pinnacle, 1993. 315p.* Two vampires vow that they will not rest until one is destroyed.

> *Revenge • Vampire's Point of View*

Simmons, Dan.

Ⓑ **Carrion Comfort.** *New York: Warner Books, 1989. 883p.* In this extremely complex and lengthy narrative, mind-controlling vampires dictate human history by feeding off and magnifying the violence inherent in humans. Simmons's prose is multilayered, suspense-oriented, and erudite, and the story takes unexpected twists and turns at every juncture. This novel, which contains believable, multidimensional characters, is told through several points of view. Recipient of a Bram Stoker Award. Similar titles: *Nomads*, Chelsea Quinn Yarbro; *The Passion*, Donna Boyd.

> *Holocaust, The • Mind Control • Nazism • Televangelism • Vampire as New Species • Vampire's Point of View • Violence—Theories of*

Children of the Night. *New York: Putnam, 1992. 382p.* Kate Neuman, an American hematologist, is called to post-Ceaucescu Romania to treat an abandoned infant with a rare blood condition: the baby is able to digest blood to cure hemophilia. She takes the infant to the United States, but she is kidnapped and her loved ones are murdered. Kate must go back to Romania to discover the ultimate horror behind the infant's curse. Similar titles: *Nocturnas*, Shawn Ryan; *The Lost*, Jonathan Aycliffe.

> *AIDS • Ceaucescu, Nicolae (character) • Dracula (character) • History, Use of • O'Rourke, Michael (character) • Romania • Tepes, Vlad (character)*

Smith, Robert Arthur.

Vampire Notes. *New York: Ballantine, 1990. 241p.* A playwright who is commissioned to produce a historical drama suspects that the play's benefactor is a vampire, and his companion a serial killer.

> *History, Use of • Serial Killers • Werewolves • Writer as Character*

Somtow, S. P.

Moon Dance. *New York: Doherty, 1989. 564p.* Epic-length tale of a tribe of werewolves who travel to the United States from Europe during the 1800s, and then join the general American movement westward. Emphasis is on detail and description. Narrated by a werewolf/shapeshifter in an insane asylum. Similar titles: Brian Stableford's Werewolves of London trilogy.

> *Mental Institutions • Native American Characters • United States—Nineteenth Century • Werewolves • Writer as Character*

The Vampire Junction series.

Vampire Junction. *New York: Tor Books, 1995.* Not available for annotation.

> *Valentine, Timmy (character) • Vampire's Point of View*

Valentine. *New York: Tor Books, 1995.* [First published in 1992.] 438p. In this sequel to *Vampire Junction*, Timmy Valentine returns to Los Angeles to search for salvation. Graphic and action-oriented, with a rare child vampire as a main character.

> *Los Angeles, California • Valentine, Timmy (character) • Vampire's Point of View*

Vanitas: Escape from Vampire Junction. *New York: Tor Books, 1997. 384p.* Timmy Valentine has finally achieved his dream—mortality. But now his music lacks the heart that made him an undead star. Can he regain it by finally facing his past? Graphic sequel to *Vampire Junction* and *Valentine*. Similar titles to all three volumes: *Tempter* and *Wild Blood*, Nancy A. Collins.

> *Music—Rock Music • Valentine, Timmy (character) • Vampire's Point of View*

Spruill, Steven. The Rulers of Darkness series.

Rulers of Darkness. *New York: St. Martin's Press, 1995. 357p.* The exsanguinated body of a young woman is found near Washington's National Cathedral, and hematologist Dr. Katherine O'Keefe begins to suspect that the killer is a hemophage—a genetically mutated human with a need for blood. She also discovers that many people close to her share the disease, including her new love interest, Merrick Chapman, the detective assigned to the case, who also happens to be a vampire. First of a multi-volume set. Similar title: *Sins of the Blood*, Kristin Kathryn Rusch.

> *Medical Horror • Police Officer as Character • Serial Killers • Vampire as New Species • Vampire's Point of View • Washington, D.C.*

Daughter of Darkness. *New York: Bantam, 1997. 307p.* Dr. Jenn Hrluska is a hemophage whose life depends on feeding on the blood of humans. Until now, Jenn has survived by transfusing blood from sleeping victims. But when she finds "a freshly killed body of a stranger on her doorstep," she realizes that her father, Zane, has "left the body for her" as an invitation "to reclaim her destiny of taking blood by deadly force"—book jacket. Similar titles: *Sins of the Blood*, Kristin Kathryn Rusch; *Blood Work*, Fay Zachary.

Medical Horror • Vampire as New Species • Vampire's Point of View • Washington, D.C.

Stableford, Brian. The Werewolves of London trilogy.

The Angel of Pain. *New York: Carroll and Graf, 1991. 395p.* Volume two of the trilogy continues the chronicles of the fallen angels, who have infested Victorian London as werewolf-like creatures. Emphasis on sociology and psychology. Similar titles: Anne Rice's Vampire Chronicles; *The Exorcist* and *The Omen,* William Peter Blatty; *Anno Dracula* and *Bloody Red Baron*, Kim Newman; *Nuwisha*, Steve Prescott and James A. Moore; *Moon Dance*, S. P. Somtow.

Alternative History • Angels • Animals Run Rampant • Fantasy • Lydyard, David (character) • Victorian England • Werewolves

The Werewolves of London. *New York: Carroll and Graf, 1992. 467p.* The werewolves of London are the progeny of the fallen angels of biblical mythology. They live among humans and can take their shape, but see humans as a generally inferior species that the world would be better without. In this first book of the trilogy, the creators of the werewolves are awakened during an archaeological expedition to Egypt, and take human hosts to further their plot to rule the world. Similar titles: Anne Rice's Vampire Chronicles; *The Exorcist* and *The Omen,* William Peter Blatty; *Anno Dracula* and *Bloody Red Baron*, Kim Newman; *Nuwisha*, Steve Prescott and James A. Moore; *Moon Dance*, S. P. Somtow.

Alternative History • Angels • Animals Run Rampant • Antichrist, The (character) • Epistolary Format • Fantasy • London, England • Lydyard, David (character) • Victorian England • Werewolves

The Carnival of Destruction. *New York: Carroll and Graf, 1994. 433p.* The third book in this dark fantasy trilogy. It is now 1918, and David Lydyard finds himself coming closer to understanding the nature of the seven fallen angels. Similar titles: *Nuwisha*, Steve Prescott and James A. Moore; *Moon Dance*, S. P. Somtow.

Angels • Fantasy • Lydyard, David (character) • War—World War I • Werewolves

Steakley, John.

Vampire$. *New York: Penguin-ROC, 1990. 357p.* Jack Crow, a giant of a man who works for a special organization answerable directly to the Pope, is a vampire hunter extraordinaire. He leads Team Crow on various hunts across the United States, in this dark comedy starring lots of testosterone-based male characters and evil vampires. Made into the film *John Carpenter's Vampires.* Similar titles: Laurell K. Hamilton's comic vampire novels.

Religion—Christianity—Catholicism • Vampire Hunters

Stephens, John Richard (editor).

Vampires, Wine and Roses. *New York: Berkley, 1997. 384p.* (See chapter 5, "Anthologies and Collections by Multiple Authors.")

Stoker, Bram.

Best Ghost and Horror Stories. *Mineola, N.Y.: Dover Books, 1997. 242p.* (See chapter 6, "Collections by Individual Authors.")

Dracula. *New York: Oxford University Press, 1983.* [First published in 1897.] 380p. The mother of all vampire texts, Stoker's novel is one of the few horror novels that has stood the test of time. Count Dracula comes to England; feeds from, and subsequently infects with vampirism, the wives and girlfriends of his enemies; and plans to take over the country. The story unfolds through journal entries, phonograph recordings, and letters of the vampire hunters, as well as a few newspaper articles. The novel is unique in that the vampire never speaks for himself. Has inspired countless films and rewritings of Stoker's original tale.

> *Diary Format • Dracula (character) • Harker, Jonathan (character) • Harker, Mina Murray (character) • Holmwood, Arthur (character) • London, England • Renfield (character) • Seward, John (character) • Vampire Hunters • Van Helsing, Abraham (character) • Victorian England • Westenra, Lucy (character)*

Strieber, Whitley.

The Hunger. *New York: Avon, 1981.* 307p. For thousands of years, Miriam has enjoyed the love of numerous companions in darkness. But while Miriam is forever young, she cannot promise the same for her lovers—she can merely bestow eternal life trapped in a rotting husk of a body. Made into a film in 1983 by Tony Scott, brother of famous director Ridley Scott. Similar title: *The World on Blood,* Jonathan Nasaw.

> *Aging • Gay/Lesbian/Bisexual Characters • Homoeroticism • New York City • Religion—Ancient Egyptian • Vampire's Point of View*

The Wild. *New York: Doherty, 1991.* 378p. (See chapter 19, "Comic Horror.")

The Wolfen. *New York: William Morrow, 1978.* 252p. Two New York City police officers are killed and horribly mutilated. Then an old blind man is murdered. Soon detectives Becky Neff and George Wilson realize that a new race of super-hunters—the Wolfen—cohabit with humans in the city. Suspenseful. Written from both points of view, human and wolfen. Similar titles: *Cujo,* Stephen King; *Guardian,* John Saul.

> *Animals Run Rampant • Museums • New York City • Police Officer as Character • Werewolves*

Swiniarski, S. A.

Raven. *New York: New American Library, 1996.* 348p. A man wakes up in a storm drain with amnesia. Upon delving into his history, he begins to suspect that he has been turned into a vampire. A cross-genre work with elements of a murder mystery.

> *Amnesia • Vampire's Point of View*

Tem, Melanie.

Desmodus. *New York: Bantam-Dell, 1995.* 351p. In a highly imagistic narrative, Tem tells of the Desmodus family packing up their belongings and moving south to hibernate. But this is not an ordinary clan; it is a group of vampires (half-bat/half-human) led by a group of matriarchs. Can Joel, one of the few healthy male vampires in the clan, discover the terrible secret behind its existence? Similar title: *Bethany's Sin,* Robert R. McCammon.

> *Matriarchy • Vampire Clans • Vampire's Point of View*

Tilton, Lois.

Darkness on the Ice. *New York: Pinnacle, 1993. 286p.* A Nazi SS officer who happens to be a vampire is sent on a hellish mission to an arctic post. Now, with few enemy soldiers to use as food, he must face the necessity of feeding on his own men. Similar title: *'48,* James Herbert.

Nazism • Vampire's Point of View • War—World War II

Williams, Sidney.

Night Brothers. *New York: Pinnacle, 1989. 448p.* A vampire is loose in Bristol Springs, Louisiana, and she has the local animals doing her bidding—which includes attacking and mutilating humans.

Animals Run Rampant • Journalist as Character • Louisiana

Wright, T. Lucien.

Thirst of the Vampire. *New York: Pinnacle, 1992. 351p.* The vampire Philippe Brissot is carrying a grudge against the Marat family, and he has vowed to take his revenge on every heir. He is down to the last Marat, and the hunt is on. Similar titles: Jeanne Kalogridis's Covenant with the Vampire series.

Revenge • Vampire's Point of View

Yarbro, Chelsea Quinn. The Atta Olivia Clemens Series.

A Flame in Byzantium. *New York: Tor Books, 1987. 470p.* Atta Olivia Clemens flees sixth-century Rome because of war. In Constantinople, she is accused of sorcery. Her life depends on her being able to keep her identity as a vampire a secret while her private life is being probed in an investigation. Similar titles: The Vampire Chronicles, Anne Rice; The Saint-German Chronicles, Chelsea Quinn Yarbo.

Clemens, Atta Olivia (character) • Espionage • History, Use of • Rome, Italy • Vampire's Point of View

Crusader's Torch. *New York: Doherty, 1988. 459p.* The second of the Atta Olivia Clemens novels, in which Olivia returns to Rome from Tyre, traveling across deserts filled with Crusaders and seas besieged by pirates. Her only companion on the journey is a crazed knight who grows more mentally unstable with each day. Similar titles: The Vampire Chronicles, Anne Rice; The Saint-German Chronicles, Chelsea Quinn Yarbo.

Clemens, Atta Olivia (character) • Crusades, The • History, Use of • Rome, Italy • Vampire's Point of View

A Candle for D'Artagnan: An Historical Horror. *New York: Tor Books, 1989. 485p.* This, the third novel in the Atta Olivia Clemens series, takes readers to France during the reigns of Louis XIII and XIV. There, Olivia begins a romance with the musketeer D'Artagnan. As usual with Yarbro, the strength of this novel lies in its historical description.

Alternative Literature • Espionage • Gothic Romance • History, Use of • Paris, France • Three Musketeers (characters) • Vampire's Point of View

Yarbro, Chelsea Quinn. The Saint-Germain Chronicles.

Hotel Transylvania: A Novel of Forbidden Love. *New York: St. Martin's Press, 1978. 279p.* Saint-Germain must save Madeleine de Montalia, an independent young woman with whom he has fallen in love, from the clutches of an evil cult. Set in eighteenth-century France. Similar titles: The Vampire Chronicles, Anne Rice.

Cults • Gothic Romance • History, Use of • Paris • Religion—Satanism • Saint-Germain, Count Ragoczy de (character) • Vampire's Point of View

The Palace. *New York: St. Martin's Press, 1978. 376p.* In fifteenth-century Florence, Francesco Ragoczy da San Germano "builds himself a home that rivals the most sumptuous in the city. No one knows for sure what rituals take place in his palace, but people suspect many things. The stranger never eats in public, has no mirrors in his home—even his manner of lovemaking is strange"—book jacket. Similar title: *My Soul to Keep*, Tanarive Due.

> *Epistolary Format • Florence, Italy • History, Use of • The Inquisition • Saint-Germain, Count Ragoczy de (character) • Vampire's Point of View*

Blood Games: A Novel of Historical Horror. *New York: St. Martin's Press, 1979. 458p.* Saint-Germain shows up in ancient Rome, where he must come to terms with the cruelties and casual disregard for human life he encounters among his new countrymen. Similar titles: The Covenant with a Vampire series, Jeanne Kalogridis; The Vampire Chronicles, Anne Rice.

> *History, Use of • Rome, Italy • Saint-Germain, Count Ragoczy de (character) • Vampire's Point of View*

Path of the Eclipse. *New York: St. Martin's Press, 1981. 433p.* The fourth in Yarbro's series finds the alchemist vampire in medieval China with Buddhists, Muslims, and Hindus, all attempting to flee the wrath of the Mongols. Yarbro's gentle vampire protagonist is more human than human; he eschews violence, and can receive sexual gratification only through completely satisfying his partner. Yarbro's erudite style demonstrates a thorough knowledge of world history. Similar title: *My Soul to Keep*, Tanarive Due.

> *China • Epistolary Format • History, Use of • Religion—Buddhism • Religion—Christianity • Religion—Hinduism • Religion—Islam • Saint-Germain, Count Ragoczy de (character) • Vampire's Point of View*

Tempting Fate. *New York: St. Martin's Press, 1982. 690p.* In a series of letters intermixed with narration, Yarbro places Saint-Germain during the Russian Revolution, where he must help a Russian countess escape revolutionary forces, as well as help a young war orphan. Rich in description and history. Similar title: *My Soul to Keep*, Tanarive Due.

> *Epistolary Format • History, Use of • Saint-Germain, Comte Ragoczy de (character) • Vampire's Point of View • War—Russian Revolution*

Better in the Dark: An Historical Horror. *New York: Tor Books, 1993. 412p.* Saint-Germain is captured and taken to Saxony during the Dark Ages. There he begins a romance with a beautiful lady of King Otto's court, but once more is doomed to be hunted, this time as a witch. Similar title: *My Soul to Keep*, Tanarive Due.

> *Epistolary Format • Gothic Romance • History, Use of • Saint-Germain, Count Ragoczy de (character) • Vampire's Point of View*

Darker Jewels. *New York: Orb, 1995. 398p.* Saint-Germain is assigned to help Istaven Bathory, Transylvanian King of Poland, ward off the Ottoman Turks. En route, he runs into problems with suspicious clergymen, arranged marriages, and feuding nobles. Dense with period and place description. Similar title: *My Soul to Keep*, Tanarive Due.

> *Clergy as Character • Espionage • Gothic Romance • History, Use of • Poland, Sixteenth-Century • Religion—Christianity—Catholicism • Saint-Germain, Count Ragoczy de (character) • Vampire's Point of View*

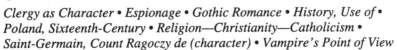

Mansions of Darkness: A Novel of Saint-Germain. *New York: Tor Books, 1997. 432p.* Saint-Germain travels to seventeenth-century Spanish America, where he runs into the forces of the Spanish Inquisition, as well as the usual vampire hunters. Yarbro weaves a tapestry of historical romance, vampire fiction, and anthropology. Similar title: *My Soul to Keep*, Tanarive Due.

> *Gothic Romance • History, Use of • The Inquisition • Native American Characters • Peru, Seventeenth-Century • Saint-Germain, Count Ragoczy de (character) • Vampire's Point of View*

Writ in Blood: A Novel of Saint-Germain. *New York: Tor Books, 1997. 543p.* Czar Nicholas sends Saint-Germain, who is residing in St. Petersburg, to deliver a top-secret peace proposal to Edward VI of England and Germany's Kaiser Wilhelm. Saint-Germain must contend with the political ambitions of the Czar's kinsmen, as well as the machinations of an ambitious arms manufacturer, Von Wolgast. Thoughtfully written historical novel in a series that rivals Rice's Vampire Chronicles. Similar title: *My Soul to Keep*, Tanarive Due.

> *Epistolary Format • Espionage • History, Use of • London, England • Saint-Germain, Count Ragoczy de (character) • Vampire's Point of View • War—World War I*

Blood Roses. *New York: Tor Books, 1998. 384p.* Saint-Germaine settles in a small French town in the fourteenth century, during the time of the black plague. Can he use his knowledge of healing without drawing suspicion to his true nature? Similar titles: The Vampire Chronicles, Anne Rice.

> *Epidemic • France, Fourteenth-Century • History, Use of • Saint-Germain, Count Ragoczy de (character) • Vampire's Point of View*

Yarbro, Chelsea Quinn. Sisters of the Night trilogy.

Sisters of the Night: The Angry Angel. *New York: Avon, 1998. 359p.* Yarbro begins her Sisters of the Night trilogy (about Dracula's three vampire concubines) with this novel about Kalene of Salonica. She is visited by Dracula, who wants her as one of his entourage. Emphasis on description, history, and characterization. Similar title: *Mina*, Marie Kiraly.

> *Alternative Literature • Angels • Dracula (character) • Gothic Romance • History, Use of*

The Soul of an Angel. *New York: Avon, 1999. 384p.* The follow-up to Yarbro's *The Angry Angel*, this traces the seduction of a wealthy sixteenth-century Venetian noblewoman by Count Dracula. Similar titles: The Covenant with a Vampire series, Jeanne Kalogridis; The Vampire Chronicles, Anne Rice; The Saint-Germain Chronicles, Chelsea Quinn Yarbro.

> *Alternative Literature • Dracula (character) • Gothic Romance • History, Use of • Italy*

Zachary, Fay.

Blood Work. *New York: Berkley, 1994. 277p.* (See chapter 14, "Maniacs and Sociopaths, or the Nuclear Family Explodes.")

Film

Blacula. *William Crain, dir. 1972. 92 minutes.* Manwalde, Ambassador of Ebonia, meets with Dracula to persuade him to stop supporting slave trading. Instead, Dracula makes Manwalde one of the undead, imprisoning him in a coffin to thirst eternally. Manwalde awakens 150 years later in 1970s Los Angeles, hungering for blood and the reincarnation of his long-deceased wife, who is now an Angeleno. William Marshall stars as the first African-American vampire in horror cinema history.

> *African-American Characters • Los Angeles, California • Reincarnation*

Bram Stoker's Dracula. *Francis Ford Coppola, dir. 1992. 130 minutes.* Coppola returns to the original source of the Dracula myth, drawing on Stoker's novel as well as the historical Vlad Tepes. Here Dracula is not so much an immortal monster, who must be destroyed at all costs, as a man who has defied death because his church and country have betrayed him. Gary Oldman, Winona Ryder, Anthony Hopkins, and Keanu Reeves star.

> *Dracula (character) • Harker, Jonathan (character) • Harker, Mina Murray (character) • London, England • Vampire's Point of View • Van Helsing, Abraham (character)*

Cronos. *Guillermo del Toro, dir. 1992. 92 minutes.* Mexican film in which an elderly antiques dealer, Jesus Gris, stumbles upon the Cronos device, the invention of a fourteenth-century alchemist, which makes the bearer immortal. In spite of several serious accidents and an attempt to embalm him, Jesus cannot die, and his discovery of the device has alerted the attention of an Anglo corporate mogul who will stop at nothing to steal it from Gris. Ron Perlman stars.

> *Immortality • Mexico • Weird Science*

Dracula. *Tod Browning, dir. 1931. (Black-and-white.) 75 minutes.* An adaptation of both Bram Stoker's novel and Hamilton Deane and John Balderston's stage play of Stoker's novel; this movie gave Bela Lugosi his first film role. As in Stoker's novel, Count Dracula comes to London via Transylvania, purchases a ruined abbey, and hopes to search for victims by night. Bela Lugosi's interpretation of Dracula is the suave cape-and-tuxedo-wearing creature of the night first seen in Deane and Balderston's stage play, rather than the hook-nosed and halitosis-plagued *nosferatu* of Stoker's tale.

> *Dracula (character) • Renfield (character) • Van Helsing, Abraham (character)*

Dracula's Daughter. *Lambert Hillyer, dir. 1936. (Black-and-white.) 71 minutes.* This film picks up where the 1931 version of *Dracula* left off, with Dr. Van Helsing having killed Count Dracula and believing that he has rid the world of vampires. But Dracula's daughter, Countess Marya Zaleska, claims her father's body, and soon several people are found mysteriously killed. Otto Kruger, Gloria Holden, and Marguerite Churchill star.

> *Family Curse • Homoeroticism • London, England*

The Hunger. *Tony Scott, dir. 1983. 100 minutes.* Miriam and John Blaylock are forever young and beautiful because they're vampires. But then John begins to age at an accelerated pace. Miriam must seek the help of an outsider, a scientist who studies aging, and who will be seduced by Miriam's promise of eternal youth. Catherine Deneuve, David Bowie, and Susan Sarandon star.

> *Aging • Gay/Lesbian/Bisexual Characters • Homoeroticism • New York City*

Interview with the Vampire. *Neil Jordan, dir. 1994. 123 minutes.* The film version of Anne Rice's novel of the same name, this movie sports an all-star cast, including Tom Cruise, Brad Pitt, Christian Slater, Antonio Banderas, and Kirsten Dunst.

> *Claudia (character) • Homoeroticism • Lestat de Lioncourt (character) • Louis (character) • New Orleans, Louisiana • Vampire's Point of View*

The Lost Boys. *Joel Schumacher, dir. 1987. 97 minutes.* A family moves to what they believe will be a peaceful town (Santa Carla, California), only to discover that they now reside in the murder capital of the world, and that the local gang is a pack of teenage vampires who, like Peter Pan, never want to grow up. Kiefer Sutherland and Dianne Wiest star.

California • Gang Violence • Vampire Clans

Nadja. *Michael Almereyda, dir. 1996. (Black-and-white.) 92 minutes.* Twin brother and sister vampires, children of Count Dracula, struggle against each other and against their own dual desires to be mortal and immortal. Set in modern-day New York City, this stylish parody of art films is also a remake of the 1936 *Dracula's Daughter.* Starring Peter Fonda and Elina Lowensohn.

Gay/Lesbian/Bisexual Characters • Homoeroticism • New York City • Renfield (character) • Twins • Vampire's Point of View

Nosferatu. *F. W. Murnau, dir. 1922. (Black-and-white.) 63 minutes.* This silent classic is an adaptation of Stoker's *Dracula.* Because of the complexities of German copyright law, Murnau's film had to change the names of the principals, but Count Orlock, his version of Count Dracula, is much closer to Stoker's idea of Dracula than the celluloid Dracula made famous by Bela Lugosi in 1931. Starring Max Schreck.

Germany

The Wolf Man. *George Waggner, dir. 1941. (Black-and-white.) 70 minutes.* A Universal Studios classic starring Lon Chaney, Jr., who is bitten by a vampire in wolf form (Bela Lugosi) and turned into a werewolf. Claude Rains also stars.

Werewolves

Our Picks

June's Picks: *Kindred,* John Gideon (Jove Books); *Lord of the Dead,* Tom Holland (Simon & Schuster); *Anno Dracula,* Kim Newman (Avon); *The Vampire Lestat,* Anne Rice (Ballantine).

Tony's Picks: *Lost Souls*, Poppy Z. Brite (Bantam-Dell); *The Vampire Tapestry*, Suzy McKee Charnas (Living Batch); *Children of the Vampire*, Jeanne Kalogridis (Delacorte Press); *Necroscope*, Brian Lumley (Grafton); *Anno Dracula*, Kim Newman (Avon); *The Queen of the Damned*, Anne Rice (Ballantine); *Carrion Comfort*, Dan Simmons (Warner Books).

Chapter 10

Demonic Possession, Satanism, Black Magic, and Witches and Warlocks: The Devil Made Me Do It

Tales of black magic and demonic possession go back as far as the Bible, so this subgenre of horror is arguably one of the oldest. Students of literature know that demons abound in the poetry of Milton and Blake, but it was not until the late 1700s that the earliest novel featuring demons was published: M. G. Lewis's *The Monk*, a study in necrophilia that set the stage early for the theme of the beautiful young woman as a demon in disguise. Nonetheless, the quintessential possession novel is a very recent one, William Peter Blatty's *The Exorcist*, the tale of a young girl possessed by the demon Pazuzu after ancient artifacts unearthed in Iraq unleash the creature's power. Whether they be about misled monks or demonic teenage girls, what makes tales of possession particularly frightening is that innocent humans are often possessed by demons, or even by the Devil himself.

Tales of Satanism and black magic can also take the form of stories about witches, warlocks, and other people who willingly become involved with dark forces. In Ira Levin's *Rosemary's Baby*, Guy Woodhouse sells his soul, and his wife's womb, to Satan, in exchange for worldly success as an actor. More contemporary possession/witchcraft tales include Anne Rice's *The Witching Hour*, *Taltos*, and *Lasher*, which concern themselves with 13 generations of Mayfair witches, and their profitable connection to the demon Lasher.

Interestingly, many stories in this subgenre feature Catholics who have either lost their faith or see their brand of black magic as an extension of their faith. Indeed, Satanism is more often than not represented as the polar opposite not of Christianity, but of Roman Catholicism, as in David Seltzer's *The Omen* (film), Ira Levin's *Rosemary's Baby*, and Whitley Strieber's *The Night Church*. Perhaps this is because Catholicism was at one point considered the universal version of Christianity and is therefore a good "default" religion for horror; perhaps it is because Catholicism is more ritual-oriented than other Christian sects, making it the perfect foil (polar opposite) of Satanism, which also values ritual; or perhaps it is because the original possession narratives were produced by a culture that demonized Catholicism, and the tradition or formula simply was continued by later writers.

Despite the prevalence of Catholicism in possession stories, other Christian sects have played an important role in the evolution of the subgenre. For example, a few narratives feature Protestantism as the religion that ushers in evil. Nathaniel Hawthorne's tales often feature upright, New England Puritans—and their connections with the Evil One. In Stephen King's *Needful Things*, town members unwittingly sell their souls to the devil, and Satan gains a toehold by first setting the Catholics and Protestants against one another. But no matter which sect is responsible for raising the devil, the bottom line of the possession tale is that the possessed characters are forgivable because they were not responsible for their actions while in this state.

Representative works in this subgenre include Clive Barker's *The Hellbound Heart* (the novel that spawned the Hellraiser series), John Buchan's *Witch Wood*, Ramsey Campbell's *Obsession*, Norah Lofts's *The Devil's Own*, Fritz Leiber's *Conjure Wife*, T. E. D. Klein's *The Ceremonies*, Gloria Naylor's *Linden Hills*, Peter Straub's *Shadowland* and *Floating Dragon*, and John Saul's *Shadows*, as well as various works by Anne Rice and Dennis Wheatley. Landmark works include William Peter Blatty's *The Exorcist*, Ira Levin's *Rosemary's Baby*, David Seltzer's *The Omen* (film), and Fred M. Stewart's *The Mephisto Waltz*.

Appeals: Believability (for Some); Curiosity Concerning the Occult; Familiarity with Satan/the Devil as Ultimate Monster; Identification with Innocent but Possessed Characters; Reaffirms the Universal Fear of Demons; Religious Connotations and Affirmation of Beliefs; Warning Texts—Beware of Digging Up Evil

Bachman, Richard [pseud. of Stephen King].

Thinner. *New York: New American Library, 1984. 282p.* Billy Halleck, an attorney who is 50 pounds overweight and pushing a heart attack, sideswipes an old gypsy woman as she crosses the street and then uses his professional wiles to avoid compensating the woman's family for her death. But one of the woman's clan curses Billy with the word "thinner," and Billy begins to lose weight uncontrollably. Similar title: *Evil Intent*, Bernard Taylor.

Curse • Maine • Revenge

Bacon-Smith, Camille. The Eye of the Daemon series.

Eye of the Daemon. *New York: Daw Books, 1996. 332p.* Bacon-Smith's first Kevin Bradley novel, in which the superhuman sleuth matches wits against equally unnatural kidnappers. Similar titles: Laurell K. Hamilton's comic vampire novels.

Bradley, Kevin (character) • Fantasy

The Face of Time. *New York: Daw Books, 1996. 318p.* Two Scotland Yard officers travel to a small town to track down a serial killer, only to find that their foe is more than human. A pleasant read.

England • Scotland Yard • Serial Killers

Eyes of the Empress. *New York: Daw Books, 1998. 304p.* The crystals of the Dowager Empress of China are disappearing, and a group of American detectives are called in to solve the case. However, they discover that the thief has ties beyond the natural world. Similar titles: Laurell K. Hamilton's comic vampire novels.

Bradley, Kevin (character) • Demons • Fantasy

Barker, Clive.

The Damnation Game. *New York: Putnam, 1987. 433p.* When Joseph Whitehead suspects that the demon Mamoulian is going to take him to the grave, he walls himself up in a fortress. But can Joe's bunker withstand the powers of Mamoulian, who wants revenge against the only human who has ever bested him—Joe? Barker's talent for drawing the reader into the horror is apparent in this page-turner.

Demons • Revenge

The Hellbound Heart. *New York: Harper, 1986. 164p.* When Frank, a playboy and thrill-seeker, decides that life holds no more pleasure for him, he experiments with Lamarchand's Box, which supposedly will summon the gods of pleasure. Instead, Frank summons demons of torture, and they want more than just Frank. Strong on action and eroticism, and characteristic of Barker's graphic style. Made into the film *Hellraiser*, which Clive Barker directed. Similar title: *Drawn to the Grave*, Mary Ann Mitchell.

Demons • Haunted Houses

Barker, Clive. The Book of the Art series.

The Great and Secret Show. *New York: Harper, 1989. 550p.* Randolph Jaffe, an employee of the U.S. Postal Service, discovers the Art through the dead letter office, kills his boss, and begins a cross-country trek. He discovers Fletcher, an old man who has the Art, and becomes Fletcher's pupil—until he has no further use for his teacher. After a battle, Fletcher and Jaffe and their armies of disembodied forces travel across the country, wreaking havoc in their paths. Creative and mesmerizing. Similar title: *All the Bells on Earth*, James P. Blaylock.

Fantasy • Rape

Everville. *New York: HarperCollins, 1994. 699p.* Various characters' desires for sex, love, truth, and sensuality come to life in this erotic, subtly humorous, yet mesmerizing and chilling sequel to *The Great and Secret Show*. Here, the monsters are those with human faces who threaten the desires of the main characters.

Demons • Domestic Violence • Eroticism • Oregon

Barry, Jonathan, with Whitley Strieber.

Cat Magic. *New York: Tor Books, 1986. 376p.* Maywell, New Jersey, is a small town populated by several communal covens of witches who practice white magic. The witches manage to coexist peacefully with the Christian residents until religious fanatic Brother Simon comes to town, bent on destroying the witches. And the witches are particularly vulnerable to destruction at this time, as their new coven leader is occupied navigating the borders between death and life. Barry and Strieber demonstrate a familiarity with pagan Celtic traditions, which are skillfully blended into the story. Similar titles: *The Black Cat*, Robert Poe; *Scarecrow*, Richard Tankersley Cuisak.

>   *Magic • New Jersey • Religion—Christianity—Protestantism • Religion—Paganism • Witches*

Beman, Donald.

The Taking. *New York: Leisure Books, 1997. 368p.* A retired professor of American literature is haunted by four women who may have something to do with the grisly deaths of his wife and son. He soon finds himself the centerpiece of a satanic ritual. Can he be saved before "the taking"? Suspenseful and descriptive, with emphasis on characterization.

>   *Academia • Cults • Human Sacrifice • New York State • Numerology • Religion— Satanism*

Blatty, William Peter.

The Exorcist. *New York: Bantam, 1971. 403p.* When 12-year-old Regan McNeil begins acting strangely, her mother suspects that she is possessed by demons. Could Regan's possession have something to do with Father Lankester Merrin's archaeological dig in northern Iraq? And will Merrin and Father Damien Karras, a young priest who is questioning his faith, be able to stop the demon? Made into a benchmark horror film in the 1970s by director William Friedkin. Similar titles: *The Blood of the Lamb*, Thomas F. Monteleone; *Dark Debts*, Karen Lynne Hall; *Sweet William*, Jessica Palmer; *Unholy Fire*, Whitley Strieber; *Phoenix Fire*, Elizabeth Forrest.

>   *Clergy as Character • Demons • Religion—Christianity—Catholicism*

Blaylock, James P.

All the Bells on Earth. *New York: Berkley, 1995. 376p.* A package accidentally delivered to businessman Walt Stebbins catapults him into the middle of a battle between good and evil, with three souls hanging in the balance. A light and enjoyable read. Similar titles: *The Great and Secret Show*, Clive Barker; *Hellboy: The Lost Army*, Christopher Golden.

>   *California • Clergy as Character • Cursed Objects • Demons*

Winter Tides. *New York: Ace Books, 1997. 346p.* (See chapter 7, "Ghosts and Haunted Houses.")

Bowker, David.

The Butcher of Glastonbury. *London: Victor Gollancz, 1997. 224p.* (See chapter 11, "Mythological Monsters and 'The Old Ones.' ")

Campbell, Ramsey.

Ancient Images. *New York: Tor Books, 1989. 311p.* Film editor Sandy Allan has a chance to work on a rare Lugosi/Karloff film that one of her colleagues has just located. But then her colleague mysteriously dies, and strange things begin to happen to those who are associated with the movie or the even rarer British short story on which it was based. Similar title: *Horror Show*, Greg Kihn.

>   *Cursed Objects • Horror Movie Industry*

The Influence. *New York: Macmillan, 1988. 260p.* After Heromine's Aunt Queenie dies, Heromine begins to suspect that her niece Rowan's new friend, Vichy, is somehow Queenie's ghost, and that Queenie's spirit is ultimately trying to possess Rowan's body. To stop this, Heromine must go out to her aunt's grave. But is Aunt Queenie fully dead? Similar titles: *Comes the Blind Fury, Hell Fire,* and *The Unloved,* John Saul; *The Homecoming,* Kimberly Rangel; *When Shadows Fall,* Brian Scott Smith.

Family Curse • Reincarnation • Wales

Nazareth Hill. *New York: Doherty, 1997. 383p.* (See chapter 7, "Ghosts and Haunted Houses.")

Card, Orson Scott.

Homebody. *New York: HarperCollins, 1998. 291p.* (See chapter 7, "Ghosts and Haunted Houses.")

Treasure Box. *New York: HarperCollins, 1996. 372p.* Reclusive millionaire Quentin Fears marries his dream woman after a whirlwind courtship. After a year of marriage, Quentin discovers that his wife doesn't exist—she is a sort of psychic holograph projected by someone who wants to manipulate him into opening a mysterious box containing something unspeakable and dangerous. Will he open the box and unleash its terror on the world? Compelling and original narrative written from Quentin's point of view. Similar titles: *Dawn Song,* Michael Marano; *The Demon and the Warlock,* Richard Perry; *Mask of the Sorcerer,* Darrell Schweitzer; *Dark Debts,* Karen Lynne Hall.

Demons • Grieving • Mind Control • Witches

Chadbourn, Mark.

The Eternal. *London: Victor Gollancz, 1996. 381p.* A young woman barely escapes a train crash, and notices a strange man walking away from it. She learns that he has traveled widely and is always seen leaving the scene of an accident. But when he comes after her and her hometown friends, can he be stopped? Similar title: *Bunker Man,* Duncan McLean.

Music—Rock Music • Religion—Paganism • Zombies

Codrescu, Andrei.

The Blood Countess. *New York: Simon & Schuster, 1995. 347p.* (See chapter 17, "Psychological Horror.")

de la Mare, Walter.

The Return. *New York: Dover Books, 1997. 193p.* [First published in 1922.] Arthur Lawford falls asleep on the grave of an eighteenth-century pirate, only to wake up and discover that his face is no longer his own. And though he believes himself to be essentially unchanged psychologically, he notices that another personality is insinuating itself into his consciousness. Similar titles: *Dr. Jekyll and Mr. Hyde,* Robert Louis Stevenson; *Rebecca,* Daphne du Maurier.

Alter Ego • England • Mind Control

Dedman, Stephen.

The Art of Arrow Cutting. *New York: Tor Books, 1997. 285p.* Photographer/drifter Michaelangelo Magistrale meets a beautiful woman named Amanda at a Greyhound bus station, and soon finds himself involved in a devious plot featuring goblins, a wizard, and the Japanese Yakuza. Clever. Similar title: *Kindred Rites,* Katherine Elisha Kimbriel.

Canada • Demons • Magic • Organized Crime • Photographer as Character

Disch, Thomas M.

The Priest: A Gothic Romance. *New York: Knopf, 1995. 303p.* (See chapter 19, "Comic Horror.")

Elze, Winifred.

The Changeling Garden. *New York: St. Martin's Press, 1995. 282p.* (See chapter 16, "Rampant Animals and Other Eco-Monsters.")

Erskine, Barbara.

House of Echoes. *New York: Signet Books, 1996. 476p.* (See chapter 7, "Ghosts and Haunted Houses.")

Midnight Is a Lonely Place. *New York: Signet Books, 1995. 447p.* (See chapter 7, "Ghosts and Haunted Houses.")

Etchison, Dennis.

Double Edge. *New York: Bantam, 1997. 272p.* (See chapter 7, "Ghosts and Haunted Houses.")

Ferrario, Keith.

Deadly Friend. *New York: Leisure Books, 1994. 358p.* (See chapter 7, "Ghosts and Haunted Houses.")

Forrest, Elizabeth.

Dark Tide. *New York: Daw Books, 1993. 368p.* (See chapter 16, "Rampant Animals and Other Eco-Monsters.")

Phoenix Fire. *New York: Daw Books, 1993. 364p.* An archaeological expedition in China unearths a 2,000-year-old demon that travels to Los Angeles to hunt down the mythological phoenix, for a battle to the death that will shake up the entire city. Similar title: *The Exorcist*, William Peter Blatty.

Archaeology • Demons • Los Angeles, California

Gideon, John.

Golden Eyes. *New York: Berkley, 1994. 457p.* (See chapter 9, "Vampires and Werewolves.")

Greely's Cove. *New York: Berkley, 1991. 422p.* (See chapter 11, "Mythological Monsters and 'The Old Ones.' ")

Golden, Christopher.

Hellboy: The Lost Army. *Milwaukie, Ore.: Dark Horse, 1997. 203p.* Based on the comic book series by Mike Mignola, this novel chronicles the battle of "Hellboy," a mutant human/demon summoned by the Nazis in World War II, and the evil magician Hazred. Contains some illustrations by Mignola. Similar titles: *All the Bells on Earth*, James P. Blaylock; *Dark Fall*, Dean Koontz; *Demon Dance*, T. Chris Martindale.

Archaeology • Demons • Egypt • Nazism • War—World War II

Goshgarian, Gary.

The Stone Circle: A Novel. *London: Donald I. Fine, 1997. 296p.* Archaeology professor Peter Van Zandt is hired to excavate a site where a new casino resort is scheduled to be erected. There he finds a miniature Stonehenge, and soon visions of his wife's ghost and of murder and human sacrifice are driving him to the edge. Unique, with emphasis on characterization. Similar titles: *Curfew*, Phil Rickman; *The 37th Mandala*, Marc Laidlaw.

> *Archaeology • Boston, Massachusetts • Dreams • Human Sacrifice • Religion—Paganism*

Gray, Muriel.

Furnace. *New York: Doubleday, 1997. 360p.* After a long haul on the road, truck driver Josh Spiller comes home to his live-in girlfriend Elizabeth, to discover that she is pregnant and planning on having an abortion. The two fight, and Josh goes back on the road. It is in this troubled state of mind that Josh drives through Furnace, Virginia, and runs over a baby in a stroller who was pushed into the street by a mysterious woman. Local law enforcement officials declare the tragedy an accident, but Josh insists on revealing the truth, which will entangle him in a deadly web of witchcraft. Gray's tale is enlivened by details about the lives of truckers. Similar titles: *Evil Intent*, Bernard Taylor; *The Death Prayer*, David Bowker; *The Count of Eleven*, Ramsey Campbell.

> *Demons • Human Sacrifice • Runes • Truck Driver as Character • Virginia • Witches*

Trickster. *New York: St. Martin's Press, 1994. 471p.* Former apprentice shaman Sam Hunt has denied his Kinchuinick heritage, believing that all Indians are pathetic losers who allowed the white man to take all and lock them up on reservations. But he must embrace this heritage if he is to defeat the Trickster, an evil spirit that has broken free of its container and begun murdering both Indians and whites. Gray's story is full of Kinchuinick and Cree lore, and is told through two main omniscient narratives, one set in present-day Alberta and one set in 1907. Similar titles: *Greely's Cove*, John Gideon; *Crota*, Owl Goingback; *The Purification Ceremony*, Mark T. Sullivan; *The Wendigo Border*, Catherine Montrose; *The Totem*, David Morrel.

> *Alberta, Canada • Demons • Native American Characters • Racism • Religion—Native American • Shapeshifters*

Greenberg, Martin H. (editor).

White House Horrors. *New York: Daw Books, 1996. 316p.* (See chapter 5, "Anthologies and Collections by Multiple Authors.")

Griffith, Kathryn Meyer.

The Calling. *New York: Kensington, 1994. 379p.* The vengeful spirit of a 2,000-year-old Egyptian queen takes over the body of a twentieth-century woman and seeks revenge against all men who treat women badly. Similar titles: *Widow*, Billie Sue Mosiman; *The Queen of the Damned*, Anne Rice; *Brand New Cherry Flavor*, Todd Grimson.

> *History, Use of • Religion—Ancient Egyptian • Revenge*

Grimson, Todd.

Brand New Cherry Flavor. *New York: Harper Prism, 1997. 352p.* A female filmmaker gets cheated out of an important directing job, so she goes to a witch doctor to find out how to get revenge using black magic. Soon, mysterious tattoos begin appearing on her body—and reality begins to change. Similar titles: *The Calling*, Kathryn Meyer Griffith; *Drawn to the Grave*, Mary Ann Mitchell.

> *Cursed Objects • Drugs • Feminism • Hollywood, California • Revenge*

Hall, Karen Lynne.

Dark Debts. *New York: Random House, 1996. 403p.* A family curse hangs over the Landrys because of the Satanism once practiced by its patriarch. Now the Landrys are dropping like flies, and it will take a New York priest, an exorcist, and a demonologist to save the remaining Landrys. Hall's strengths are in dialogue and psychology. Similar titles: *The Exorcist*, William Peter Blatty; *Treasure Box*, Orson Scott Card; *Unholy Fire*, Whitley Strieber.

Clergy as Character • Curse • Demons • Georgia • Religion—Christianity—Catholicism • Religion—Satanism

Hautala, Rick.

Dark Silence. *New York: Kensington, 1992. 477p.* (See chapter 7, "Ghosts and Haunted Houses.")

Hodgson, William Hope.

The House on the Borderland. *Westport, Conn.: Hyperion Press, 1976. [First published in 1908.] 186p.* A reissue of the 1908 classic about a diary found in an ancient stone house that leads to a tale of subterranean monsters. Emphasis is on atmosphere. Similar titles: *Houses of Stone*, Barbara Michaels; *Dark Gods*, T. E. D. Klein.

Diary Format • Ireland • Subterranean Monsters • Time Travel

Holder, Nancy.

Ⓑ **Dead in the Water.** *New York: Bantam, 1994. 413p.* The cruise begins aboard the *Pandora* with a message from the ship's captain: "This is how it will be when you drown." The situation only gets eerier and more frightening, as crew members and passengers alike fall into and out of nightmarish, violent alternative realities. If only they can stop Captain Reade, the demonic puppeteer of their nightmares. But no one, in any of Reade's previous lives, has stopped him before. Gory, but excellently written, literate horror. Recipient of a Bram Stoker Award. Similar titles: *Bad Dreams*, Kim Newman; *Cry for the Strangers*, John Saul.

Demons • Dreams • Hispanic-American Characters • Maritime Horror • Psychosexual Horror

Holder, Nancy, and Melanie Tem.

Witch-Light. *New York: Dell, 1996. 339p.* A highly erotic novel that follows the travels of a 22-year-old film student to the Southwest. Once Valerie gets to New Mexico to care for her dying father, she also finds a demon lover who will take her to the edges of reality and test the limits of love. Emphasis is on characterization and description.

Demons • Eroticism • Gothic Romance • New Mexico

Holland, Tom.

Slave of My Thirst. *New York: Simon & Schuster, 1996. 421p.* (See chapter 9, "Vampires and Werewolves.")

Huggins, James Byron.

Cain. *New York: Simon & Schuster, 1997. 400p.* (See chapter 11, "Mythological Monsters and 'The Old Ones.' ")

Jackson, Shirley.

The Haunting of Hill House. *New York: Farrar, Straus & Giroux, 1982. [First published in 1949.] 306p.* (See chapter 7, "Ghosts and Haunted Houses.")

Jensen, Ruby Jean.

Death Stone. *New York: Kensington, 1989. 315p.* A woman finds a mysterious ring at the bottom of a well. When she places it on her finger, she becomes possessed by a maniacal murderer. Similar title: *The Stress of Her Regard*, Tim Powers.

Cursed Objects • Serial Killers

Vampire Child. *New York: Zebra, 1990. 285p.* (See chapter 9, "Vampires and Werewolves.")

Kahn, James.

Poltergeist II. *New York: Ballantine, 1986. 179p.* (See chapter 7, "Ghosts and Haunted Houses.")

Kihn, Greg.

Horror Show. *New York: Tor Books, 1996. 274p.* (See chapter 19, "Comic Horror.")

Kimbriel, Katherine Elisha.

Kindred Rites. *New York: Harper Prism, 1997. 359p.* Alfreda Sorensson must overcome a kidnapping and poltergeists when she goes back home to the village of Sun Return. In addition, she will have to pit white magic against black magic in this historical dark fantasy. Similar title: *The Art of Arrow Cutting*, Stephen Dedman; *Beneath a Mountain Moon*, Silver Raven Wolf.

Fantasy • History, Use of • Magic • Poltergeists

Night Calls. *New York: Harper Prism, 1996. 310p.* A young girl who is a gifted practitioner of magic must save her community from vampires and werewolves that attack them on their way west. Narrated by the heroine. Similar title: *Greely's Cove*, John Gideon.

Fantasy • Magic • United States—Nineteenth-Century • Werewolves

King, Stephen.

Christine. *New York: Viking, 1983. 526p.* Dennis (the narrator of this first-person tale) has a best friend named Arnie Cunningham, a high-school loser whose only talent is his mechanical ability. Enter Christine, a vintage Plymouth possessed by an angry spirit. One of King's more character-driven, psychological works.

High School • Revenge

Cujo. *New York: Plume, 1981. 277p.* (See chapter 16, "Rampant Animals and Other Eco-Monsters.")

Desperation. *New York: Viking, 1996. 690p.* (See chapter 13, "Small-Town Horror.")

Needful Things. *New York: Penguin, 1991. 690p.* (See chapter 11, "Mythological Monsters and 'The Old Ones.' ")

The Shining. *New York: Plume, 1977. 416p.* Alcoholic ex-teacher Jack Torrance has a second chance at life and at saving his relationship with his family: he has been hired as the innkeeper/overseer for the Overlook Hotel during the off-season winter months. The hotel itself has different ideas: it wants to add the psychic power that Jack's son Danny possesses to its own powers, and it will stop at nothing, not even at supplying Jack with liquor. Who will win Jack's soul, the Overlook or his family? A classic haunted-house tale. Made into a film of the same name directed by Stanley Kubrick. Similar titles: *Nazareth Hill*, Ramsey Campbell; *The Green Man*, Kingsley Amis; *A Face at the Window*, Dennis McFarland; *Counterparts*, Nicholas Royle.

> *Alcoholism • Haunted Houses • Telepathy*

The Tommyknockers. *New York: Signet Books, 1988. 747p.* Unbeknownst to the residents of Haven, Maine, aliens have come to their small town and given the residents extraordinary powers. After Bobbi Anderson stumbles across a metal object that had been buried for millennia, the town becomes a very dangerous place for outsiders. Similar titles: *University*, Bentley Little; *Titus Crow: In the Moons of Borea* and *Elysia, The Coming of Cthulhu*, Brian Lumley; *The Demon and the Warlock*, Richard Perry; *The Forbidden Zone*, Whitley Strieber.

> *Aliens • New England*

King, Stephen, and Peter Straub.

The Talisman. *New York: Viking, 1984. 644p.* A young boy becomes involved with the occult and black magic. Will it cost him his soul?

> *Music—Jazz • Parapsychology*

Kinion, Richard.

Sacrifice. *New York: Kensington, 1995. 380p.* (See chapter 7, "Ghosts and Haunted Houses.")

Kiraly, Marie.

Leanna. *New York: Berkley, 1996. 341p.* Hailey Martin, a divorced writer looking for a new start, takes an apartment in the French Quarter in New Orleans. The apartment is haunted by Leanna, the woman murdered there eight years before. Leanna possesses Hailey through dreams, and allows her to relive Leanna's life. Hailey welcomes the possession, eager to learn more of Leanna's violent and passionate life and to solve the mystery of her murder, hoping to use the story as the basis for her next best-seller. But there are others who would silence Leanna's ghost and anyone enabling it to tell its tale. Written from multiple points of view. Similar titles: *Madeline After the Fall of Usher*, Marie Kiraly; *Ammie, Come Home*; Barbara Michaels; *Voodoo Child*, Michael Reaves.

> *Dreams • Eroticism • Haunted Houses • New Orleans, Louisiana • Religion— Voodoo • Revenge • Twins*

Madeline After the Fall of Usher. *New York: Berkley, 1996. 407p.* Kiraly continues the story of twins Madeline and Roderick from Poe's "The Fall of the House of Usher." Edgar Allan Poe is visited by Pamela, whose son has been stolen away by her late husband's grandmother, Madeline Usher. Madeline is a sorceress, who survived while her twin brother Roderick did not, because she hasn't denied her supernatural gifts and her unnatural passions. Similar titles: *Leanna*, Marie Kiraly; *Ammie, Come Home*, Barbara Michaels; *Sineater*, Elizabeth Massie; *The Lighthouse at the End of the World*, Stephen Marlowe; *Return to the House of Usher*, Robert Poe.

> *Incest • New Orleans, Louisiana • Poe, Edgar Allan (character) • Religion— Paganism • Twins • Usher, Madeline (character) • Usher, Roderick (character)*

Klavan, Andrew.

The Uncanny. *New York: Crown, 1998. 343p.* (See chapter 19, "Comic Horror.")

Klein, T. E. D.

The Ceremonies. *New York: Viking, 1984. 502p.* (See chapter 11, "Mythological Monsters and 'The Old Ones.' ")

Koontz, Dean.

Cold Fire. *New York: Berkley, 1991. 421p.* Jim Ironheart has been suffering from visions—visions that allow him to see when disaster will occur in time to prevent the tragedy. But can he and a young reporter who has taken a personal interest in him survive a showdown with evil? Similar title: *The Dead Zone*, Stephen King.

Dreams • Journalist as Character • Precognition

Dark Fall. *New York: Berkley, 1984. 371p.* Two detectives, Jack Dawson and Rebecca Chandler, are called in to investigate brutal gangland slayings. Dawson soon realizes that a practitioner of black magic named Lavelle is summoning creatures from the depths of hell to exact revenge. And now Lavelle has threatened Dawson by promising to have his children brutally murdered if he does not back off the case. The final 70 pages are a masterpiece of suspense. Similar titles: *Hellboy: The Lost Army*, Christopher Golden; *Demon Dance*, T. Chris Martindale.

Demons • New York City • Organized Crime • Police Officer as Character • Religion—Voodoo

Hideaway. *New York: Putnam, 1992. 384p.* Hatch Harrison dies in a car accident, but is revived by a brilliant doctor some 75 minutes later. Unfortunately, when he comes back from the afterlife, Hatch brings with him a demon that uses his body as a place to hide away. Suffice it to say that no one had better anger Hatch Harrison, or more specifically, his inner demon. The first 100 pages are incredible—Koontz at his absolute best—and the book never lets up. Similar title: *The Dead Zone*, Stephen King.

Artist as Character • Demons

The Mask. *New York: Berkley, 1992. [First published in 1981.] 305p.* Paul and Carol want nothing more than to have beautiful, perfect children, and then one day an accident grants their wish. They now have Jane, a homeless teenage girl who seems to be the perfect daughter. But Jane has a hidden agenda that may involve murder. Emphasis on plot makes this a fast and easy read. Similar titles: *The Dark One*, Guy N. Smith; *The Fifth Child*, Doris Lessing.

Demons • Matricide/Patricide • Parenting

Winter Moon. *New York: Random House, 1994. 472p.* When heroic police officer Jack McGarvey and his family inherit the Quartermass Ranch in Montana from someone they've never met, they consider themselves lucky. Little do they know what happened to its previous owner, Eduardo Fernandez, an old farmer who saw something in the moon. Builds up nicely to a gory, horrific climax. More subtle and traditional than Koontz's usual, but well written.

Aliens • Hispanic-American Characters • Police Officer as Character • Zombies

Laidlaw, Marc.

Ⓗ The 37th Mandala. *New York: St. Martin's Press, 1996. 352p.* Derek Crowe, a hack who wants to make money off New Age philosophy, unwittingly awakens an evil force when he converts followers using a mandala that is historically connected to Cambodia's killing fields. The monsters are Lovecraftian and the emphasis is on psychology and sociology. Recipient of an International Horror Guild Award for Best Novel. Similar titles: *Curfew*, Phil Rickman; *The Stone Circle*, Gary Goshgarian.

California • Cursed Objects • New Age

Laudie, Catherine A. (editor).

Restless Spirits: Ghost Stories by American Women. *Boston: University of Massachusetts Press, 1997. 316p.* (See chapter 5, "Anthologies and Collections by Multiple Authors.")

Levin, Ira. The Rosemary's Baby books.

Rosemary's Baby. *New York: Bantam, 1991. [First published in 1967.] 262p.* Young marrieds Guy and Rosemary Woodhouse move into their dream apartment in the Bramford, where they hope to start a family. But they don't believe Rosemary's friend and mentor, Hutch, when he tells them about the Bramford's sinister past, which includes proper Victorian spinsters who practiced cannibalism and a man who claimed to have conjured up Satan. Rosemary also isn't prepared to believe that the sweet old couple next door are practicing Satanists with designs on her womb. Made into a film of the same name directed by Roman Polanski. Similar titles: *The Night Church*, Whitley Strieber; *Harvest Home*, Thomas Tryon; *The Maddening*, Andrew Neiderman.

Actor as Character • Marriage • New York City • Pregnancy • Religion—Christianity—Catholicism • Religion—Satanism • Woodhouse, Rosemary (character)

Son of Rosemary. *New York: Dutton, 1997. 256p.* Rosemary Woodhouse awakens from a long coma to learn that her demonic son is now a charismatic religious leader preaching messages of peace and hope. Yet she also notes that demonic look he had in his eyes as an infant. The sequel to *Rosemary's Baby*.

Antichrist, The (character) • Incest • New York City • Religion—Satanism • Televangelism • Woodhouse, Rosemary (character)

Lewis, Matthew.

The Monk. *New York: Oxford University Press, 1998. [First published in 1796.] 445p.* A well-respected clergyman is tempted by Satan in this novel, one of the ancestors of erotic horror. A chilling character study of the degeneration of a human being and his soul. Similar titles: *Exquisite Corpse*, Poppy Z. Brite; *Rosemary's Baby* and *Son of Rosemary*, Ira Levin.

Clergy as Character • Eroticism • Necrophilia • Satan (character) • Shapeshifters

Little, Bentley.

Dominion. *New York: Signet Books, 1996. 416p.* (See chapter 11, "Mythological Monsters and 'The Old Ones.' ")

The Store. *New York: Signet Books, 1998. 431p.* (See chapter 11, "Mythological Monsters and 'The Old Ones.' ")

University. *New York: Signet Books, 1995. 416p.* (See chapter 18, "Splatterpunk.")

Maginn, Simon.

Virgins and Martyrs. *Clarkston, Ga.: White Wolf, 1996. 316p.* (See chapter 17, "Psychological Horror.")

Martindale, T. Chris.

Demon Dance. *New York: Pocket Books, 1991. 294p.* A medicine woman bent on revenge against her people's oppressors raises an army of the dead, leading to a faceoff against a legendary frontiersman, a revered medicine man, and a young daughter of the range. Similar titles: *Hellboy: The Lost Army*, Christopher Golden; *Dark Fall*, Dean Koontz.

> *Native American Characters • Religion—Native American • Revenge • United States—Nineteenth Century*

Where the Chill Waits. *New York: Warner Books, 1991. 332p.* Four hunters travel into the forest, unaware of the evil presence that awaits them there. Only the strong will survive, but what will they bring back with them?

> *Demons • Hunter as Character*

Masterson, Graham.

The House That Jack Built. *New York: Carroll and Graf, 1996. 384p.* Lawyer Craig Bellman takes up with textile merchant Jack Beliaas, an evil man who likes to destroy people, drive workers to suicide, and exploit women. And Craig is well on his way to becoming Jack's minion. Similar title: *The Store*, Bentley Little.

> *Demons • Economic Violence • Haunted Houses • Lawyer as Character • New York City • Sex Crimes • Suicide*

Matheson, Richard.

I Am Legend. *New York: Tor Books, 1995. 312p.* (See chapter 6, "Collections by Individual Authors.")

McCammon, Robert R.

Bethany's Sin. *New York: Pocket Books, 1980. 344p.* (See chapter 11, "Mythological Monsters and 'The Old Ones.' ")

Stinger. *New York: Pocket Books, 1995. [First published in 1988.] 538p.* (See chapter 15, "Technohorror.")

Usher's Passing. *New York: Simon & Schuster, 1992. 407p.* (See chapter 12, "Telekinesis and Hypnosis.")

McDaniels, Abigail.

Althea. *New York: Kensington, 1995. 253p.* A little girl finds an antique doll in an old Louisiana house that her family has just moved into. Little does she or her mother know of the reign of terror that the doll will unleash upon them. Clever and unique. Similar title: *The Cormorant*, Stephen Gregory.

> *Cursed Objects • Haunted Houses • Louisiana*

McGill, Gordon.

Omen IV: Armageddon 2000. *New York: Signet Books, 1982. 216p.* Although Damien Thorne is dead, his spirit lives on in the body of his young son. But there is one stumbling block in Damien's plan for Armageddon: the new CEO of Thorne Industries, Paul Buher. An easy but interesting read.

> *Antichrist, The (character) • Demons • Religion—Christianity*

Michaels, Barbara.

Ammie, Come Home. *New York: Berkley, 1993. [First published in 1969.] 252p.* A playful seance leads to the possession of a young girl and frightening consequences. Reissue of a 1969 classic known for its descriptive passages and effective mood. Similar titles: *Leanna* and *Madeline After the Fall of Usher*, Marie Kiraly.

Parapsychology • Parenting • Seances

The Dark on the Other Side. *New York: Berkley, 1988. 290p.* Linda Randolph has everything a woman could want—beauty; money; a house full of servants; a famous, handsome, and adoring husband—so why does she desperately want to escape? Gordon Randolph, famous author and politician who has never lost a race, has not used conventional methods to obtain his position in this world. An alliance with the forces of darkness gives him an unfair advantage over all. Written from multiple perspectives. Similar title: *Rebecca*, Daphne du Maurier.

Dogs • Psychiatrist as Character • Shapeshifters • Witchcraft

Mitchell, Mary Ann.

Drawn to the Grave. *New York: Leisure Books, 1997. 313p.* When Carl becomes terminally ill, he cannot face his own mortality, so he searches the world for help. In the Amazon rain forest, he finds a cure that requires him to become intimately acquainted with his victim before stealing her life. But Carl's arrogance has made him overlook the desire of his latest victim to survive and wreak vengeance. As Beverly decays, she plots to take back what was stolen from her. Graphic and original. Recipient of an International Horror Guild Award for Best First Novel. Similar titles: *The Hellbound Heart*, Clive Barker; *Brand New Cherry Flavor*, Todd Grimson; *The Picture of Dorian Gray*, Oscar Wilde.

Aging • Eroticism • Immortality • Magic • Revenge

Mohr, Clifford.

Requiem. *New York: Berkley, 1992. 309p.* (See chapter 7, "Ghosts and Haunted Houses.")

Monahan, Brent.

The Bell Witch, An American Haunting: Being the Eye Witness Account of Richard Powell Concerning the Bell Witch Haunting of Robertson County, Tennessee. *New York: St. Martin's Press, 1997. 208p.* (See chapter 7, "Ghosts and Haunted Houses.")

Monteleone, Thomas F.

Night of Broken Souls. *New York: Warner Books, 1997. 384p.* Ex–CIA assassin Harford Nichols becomes one of many people who find their dreams invaded by the memories of Nazi death camp victims. But when the spirit of Josef Mengele enters Nichols's body, he becomes a murderous lunatic bent on ethnic cleansing. Similar titles: *Carrion Comfort*, Dan Simmons; *Cujo*, Stephen King; *Supernatural* (film).

Central Intelligence Agency • Dreams • Mengele, Josef (character) • New York City • Psychiatrist as Character • Religion—Judaism

Murrey, Mary.

The Inquisitor. *New York: Lapwing Books, 1997. 238p.* (See chapter 17, "Psychological Horror.")

Nasaw, Jonathan. The World on Blood series.

The World on Blood. *New York: Dutton, 1996. 341p.* (See chapter 9, "Vampires and Werewolves.")

Shadows. *New York: Dutton, 1997. 336p.* Someone has attempted to kill Selene Weiss and her friends, some of whom happen to be vampires. Luckily, Selene is a witch, practiced in all forms of magic and prophecy, and can use her powers to discover who wants her dead and to save her friends. Nasaw's characters are complex and compelling, and the powers of his vampires and witches are not grounded in the supernatural. Similar title: *The World on Blood*, Jonathan Nasaw.

> *California • Eroticism • Weiss, Selene (character) • Whistler, Jamie (character) • Witchcraft*

Naylor, Gloria.

Linden Hills. *New York: Ticknor and Fields, 1985. 304p.* Linden Hills, an upper-middle-class black suburb, and its creator, Luther Nedeed, are known far and wide. Once a patch of rocky soil next to a cemetery, home to the people respectable society had disowned, Linden Hills has been transformed into a place that African Americans sell their souls to live in. During the last days of the year, though, a son of a Linden Hills resident and an inmate of the nearby slum of Putney Wayne discover the private horrors of the neighborhood, and find out what Luther has locked in his basement. Similar titles: *Galilee*, Clive Barker; *The Long Lost*, Ramsey Campbell.

> *African-American Characters • Detroit, Michigan • Gay/Lesbian/Bisexual Characters • Magic*

Newman, Kim.

Bad Dreams. *London: Carroll and Graf, 1991. 280p.* American journalist Anne Nielson goes to London to investigate the mysterious death of her drug- and violence-addicted sister, Judi. Judi's body has been drained of all its youth and vitality, thanks to Hugh Farnham, the monster who invades dreams and kills in them. Now Anne is in danger, because Hugh, and others like him, are part of the Wind, an immortal specter that feeds on humans. Truly scary and graphic. Similar titles: *Dead in the Water*, Nancy Holder; *Ghost Story*, Peter Straub.

> *Dreams • Drugs • London, England • Sadomasochism*

The Quorum. *New York: Carroll and Graf, 1994. 311p.* Four young British lads become involved with Derek Leech, a Mephistopheles-like multimedia mogul, who delivers fame and money in the form of phenomenal success. As Valentine's Day, 1993, rolls around, it is time for the young men, now extremely successful, to face their damnation. Written in Newman's usual erudite style, with multiple points of view. Similar titles: *The Devil on May Street*, Steve Harris; *Dominion* and *University*, Bentley Little.

> *London, England • Music—Rock Music • Private Investigator as Character • Satan (character)*

Palmer, Jessica.

Sweet William. *New York: Pocket Books, 1995. 342p.* A four-year-old's soul is slowly being taken over by evil forces that reside in his parents' home. Here, the battle between good and evil is waged on a small but effective scale. Similar title: *The Exorcist*, William Peter Blatty.

> *Demons • Haunted Houses • Parenting*

Perry, Richard.

The Demon and the Warlock. *Huntington, W.Va.: University Editions, 1994. 199p.* (See chapter 11, "Mythological Monsters and 'The Old Ones.' ")

Pike, Christopher.

The Cold One. *New York: Doherty, 1995. 349p.* Adult horror novel, by noted young adult novelist Pike, about a menacing evil being who destroys any human it comes into contact with. The first of what promises to be a multivolume work.

Demons • Immortality • Los Angeles, California • Shapeshifters

Powers, Tim.

Expiration Date. *New York: Tor Books, 1996. 381p.* (See chapter 7, "Ghosts and Haunted Houses.")

Last Call. *New York: William Morrow, 1992. 479p.* Ex–professional gambler Scott Crane now finds himself in the game of his life, with playing cards being replaced by a tarot deck and his soul as the ante. A truly unique and inventive work; Powers's erudite writing style and eye for American culture shine. Similar title: *Kindred*, John Gideon.

Las Vegas, Nevada • Replicants • Tarot

Rangel, Kimberly.

The Homecoming. *New York: Leisure Books, 1998. 360p.* As a teenager, Darby Jayson and her friends had a Halloween slumber party in the vacant Samuel Blue house, infamous as the site of a grisly serial killing. While Samuel Blue is being executed in a Texas prison, Darby's friends are murdered in the house in a fashion similar to Blue's own killing style. Darby, one of the survivors of the massacre, can't remember who the killer is, but she is tormented by horrifying dreams of that night. More disturbing still, a full 10 years later, similar murders continue to be committed in Darby's vicinity. Similar titles: *Supernatural* (film); *The Influence*, Ramsey Campbell.

Alcoholism • Amnesia • Serial Killers • Slasher • Texas

Reaves, Michael.

Voodoo Child. *New York: Tor Books, 1998. 352p.* A veritable soap opera of a horror novel; this offering by Hollywood screenwriter Reaves deals with voodoo, betrayal, murder, and love. Various story lines intersect in New Orleans, where a priest practicing black-magic voodoo resides. Action-oriented. Similar title: *Leanna*, Marie Kiraly.

Human Sacrifice • Music—Jazz • New Orleans, Louisiana • Religion—Voodoo

Rice, Anne. The Mayfair Witches series.

The Witching Hour. *New York: Ballantine, 1991. 1,038p.* After the death of her natural mother, Rowan Mayfair returns to New Orleans to discover her family and their legacy—the legacy of the Mayfair witches and their relationship with the spirit Lasher. For 12 generations Lasher has allowed the family to prosper, and now Rowan, the thirteenth generation of Mayfair witches, must pay the price for that prosperity. Written in Rice's usual romantic, detailed style. Similar titles: Anne Rice's Vampire Chronicles; *Reborn*, F. Paul Wilson.

Lasher (character) • Lightner, Aaron (character) • Mayfair, Rowan (character) • New Orleans, Louisiana • Religion—Christianity—Catholicism • Talamasca • Witches

Lasher. *New York: Knopf, 1993. 577p.* In this second novel in the series, Rice tells of the Mayfairs being haunted by Lasher, a spirit. In return for a favor granted to the Mayfair clan, Lasher is guaranteed possession of the body of the first strong witch born to the family. Can the women of the family survive Lasher's attempts to create a child strong enough for his spirit to inhabit? Similar titles: Anne Rice's Vampire Chronicles.

Lasher (character) • Mayfair, Rowan (character) • New Orleans, Louisiana • Revenging Revenant • Talamasca • Witches

Taltos: Lives of the Mayfair Witches. *New York: Ballantine, 1995. 480p.* Continues the tale begun in *The Witching Hour* and *Lasher*; Ashlar, a member of a race of mythic, immortal giants, teams up with the Mayfair witches to battle an evil force. A critical success as well as a success with Rice fans who love her ornate description and epic adventure. Similar titles: Anne Rice's Vampire Chronicles.

> *Alternative History • Immortality • Mayfair, Rowan (character) • New Orleans, Louisiana*

Rickman, Phil.

Curfew. *New York: Berkley, 1994. 625p.* New-Age billionaire Max Goff wants to replace the ancient standing stones that once surrounded Crybbe, and turn it into a sort of psychic Lourdes where people will flock to feel the Great Life Force. But Goff doesn't understand the dark forces he's unleashing. Similar titles: *University*, Bentley Little; *The Stone Circle*, Gary Goshgarian; *The 37th Mandala*, Marc Laidlaw.

> *Goff, Max (character) • Human Sacrifice • New Age • Religion—Paganism • Wales*

December. *New York: Berkley, 1994. 678p.* (See chapter 7, "Ghosts and Haunted Houses.")

Russell, Jay S.

Burning Bright. *New York: St. Martin's Press, 1998. 288p.* Private investigator Marty Burns must join forces with a ragtag group of misfits in London in order to battle neofascists who worship chaos and hope to bring it about. Lighter than Russell's *Celestial Dogs* and more quickly paced.

> *Burns, Marty (character) • London, England • Religion—Hinduism • Religion—Paganism*

Saul, John.

Black Lightning. *New York: Ballantine, 1993. 438p.* (See chapter 14, "Maniacs and Sociopaths, or the Nuclear Family Explodes.")

Comes the Blind Fury. *New York: Dell, 1980. 383p.* (See chapter 7, "Ghosts and Haunted Houses.")

Darkness. *New York: Bantam, 1991. 341p.* In a small Florida town called Villejeune, dark and unnatural forces are at work. There, the Dark Man and his children have long menaced the gloomy and mysterious depths of the swampland with their evil blood rites. The problem is that the Dark Man needs more children, and he doesn't mind "borrowing" them from the locals. Can Michael Sheffield and Kelly Anderson, two local teens, escape the fate that has befallen so many before them? Similar title: *Shadow Man*, Dennis Etchison.

> *Aging • Florida • Weird Science*

Nathaniel. *New York: Putnam, 1984. 343p.* (See chapter 7, "Ghosts and Haunted Houses.")

Suffer the Children. *New York: Dell, 1977. 378p.* In the small seaside community of Port Arbello, children are disappearing. Little Elizabeth and her disturbed, dark sister Sarah seem to be at the middle of the disappearances, as does a child rape/murder that occurred 100 years before. Graphic and disturbing at times, but a well-written horror version of *Alice in Wonderland*. Similar titles: *It*, Stephen King; *Neverwhere*, Neil Gaiman.

> *Alcoholism • New England • Reincarnation*

The Unloved. *New York: Bantam, 1988. 311p.* (See chapter 17, "Psychological Horror.")

The Unwanted. *New York: Bantam, 1987. 339p.* After Cassie Winslow's mother dies, she is adopted by her mother's ex-husband's family, and is sent to the small community of False Harbor, where she does not fit in. The townspeople think she is weird, and some suspect she is a witch, especially after her pet cat and hawk begin attacking people. Heavy on description, characterization, and plot twists. Similar title: *Carrie*, Stephen King.

> *Cats • High School • New England • Witchcraft*

Simmons, Dan.

The Fires of Eden. *New York: Putnam, 1994. 399p.* (See chapter 19, "Comic Horror.")

Summer of Night. *New York: Putnam, 1991. 555p.* A truly frightening novel about the escapades of six teens who discover that death reigns supreme at Old Central, the oldest elementary school in Elm Haven, Illinois, and that the dead still walk through the town. What chance do they have? Even their parents don't believe the horrors they've witnessed. One of Simmons's best. Introduces a variety of characters who appear as adults in his later novels. Similar titles: *Ghost Story*, Peter Straub; *Nazareth Hill*, Ramsey Campbell.

> *Childhood • Cooke, Cordie (character) • Cursed Objects • O'Rourke, Michael (character) • Religion—Christianity—Catholicism • Subterranean Monsters • Zombies*

Siodmak, Curt.

Donovan's Brain. *New York: Carroll and Graf, 1942. 160p.* (See chapter 15, "Techno-horror.")

Smith, Brian Scott.

When Shadows Fall. *New York: Leisure Books, 1997. 320p.* A young man questions the sudden death of a favorite aunt, only to discover that her friends are involved in satanic rituals. He witnesses what he believes to be a sacrifice and, unfortunately, is seen in the process. Now he must fight for his own life. Similar title: *The Influence*, Ramsey Campbell.

> *Human Sacrifice • Religion—Satanism*

Smith, Guy N.

The Dark One. *New York: Kensington, 1995. 252p.* The Garleys agree to take care of a troubled teenager while his parents go on vacation, and they find out too late that he is in league with dark forces. Now they are trapped, and the boy has raised hungry demons. Similar titles: *The Mask*, Dean Koontz; *The Fifth Child*, Doris Lessing.

> *Religion—Satanism • Satan (character)*

Somtow, S. P.

Darker Angels. *New York: Tor Books, 1998. 384p.* An extremely complex tale that weaves stories within stories starring historical figures, shapeshifting slaves, and voodoo shamans who want to raise the dead to form an invincible army. Clever and historically accurate; narrated from multiple points of view.

> *Alternative History • History, Use of • Racism • Religion—Voodoo • Shapeshifters • Slavery • United States—Nineteenth-Century • War—American Civil War*

Stoker, Bram.

The Jewel of Seven Stars. *New York: Carroll and Graf, 1989. 214p.* (See chapter 8, "Golems, Mummies, and Reanimated Stalkers.")

Straub, Peter.

Floating Dragon. *New York: Putnam, 1983. 515p.* (See chapter 14, "Maniacs and Sociopaths, or the Nuclear Family Explodes.")

If You Could See Me Now. *New York: Pocket Books, 1977. 328p.* Early Straub chiller about the pact made between two young lovers. When Miles returns to his home town 20 years afterward, he suspects that he will not be meeting the seductive Allison of his youth, but a savage demon ruled by revenge. High on suspense and thrills.

Demons • Parapsychology • Revenge

Shadowland. *New York: Berkley, 1981. 468p.* Two teenage friends, Tom Flanagan and Del Nightingale, spend a summer as apprentices to a magician, to polish up their amateur act. But then horrible events begin to occur at the boys' school, where they are picked on regularly. Is black magic at the core of these "accidents"?

High School • Magic

Strieber, Whitley.

The Night Church. *New York: Simon & Schuster, 1983. 279p.* In the streets of Queens, after dark, a flock of alternative Catholics meet in the local church to worship in rituals where good and evil come together in the gray areas between black and white morality. For Jonathan Banion and Patricia Murray, however, the Cult of the Night Church is a horrifying threat, for it intends to use them to give birth to a new god. Narrated using multiple techniques. Plot twists to the final page. Similar titles: *Rosemary's Baby*, Ira Levin; *Waking the Moon*, Elizabeth Hand.

Cults • Demons • Epistolary Format • New York City • Pregnancy • Rape • Religion—Christianity—Catholicism

Unholy Fire. *New York: Penguin, 1992. 327p.* Father John Rafferty is being tested by a demon who dances in the aisles of his church. This demon will stop at nothing—not seduction, not even murder by incineration—to destroy a young priest in Greenwich Village. Narrated both in third person and in the demon's voice. Similar titles: *The Exorcist*, William Peter Blatty; *Dark Debts*, Karen Lynne Hall.

Demons • Eroticism • New York City • Religion—Christianity—Catholicism

Taylor, Bernard.

Evil Intent. *New York: Leisure Books, 1996. 351p.* Jack and Connie think their dreams have come true when they inherit a quaint country house in Valley Green, a small English village. Now the entire family can move from cramped quarters in London and enjoy the pleasures of small-town life. But Valley Green is also home to John Callow, director of the local amateur opera company and a neighbor from Hell. People who run afoul of him die horribly and mysteriously. Told from multiple points of view. Similar titles: *Furnace*, Muriel Gray; *Mommy*, Max Allan Collins; *The Death Prayer*, David Bowker; *The Count of Eleven*, Ramsey Campbell.

Actor as Character • England • Music—Opera • Revenge • Runes

Tryon, Thomas.

Night Magic. *New York: Simon & Schuster, 1995. 286p.* A young actor/magician trying to make it in New York meets a strange old man during one of his performances, and his life is changed forever. In this macabre retelling of "The Sorcerer's Apprentice," ex-actor Thomas Tryon (in his final novel) shows that magical powers can corrupt, and often lead to horrifying events. Similar title: *Rosemary's Baby*, Ira Levin.

Actor as Character • Magic • New York City

Walpole, Horace.

The Castle of Otranto. *Oxford: Oxford University Press, 1996. [First published in 1764.] 110p.* Considered one of the first, if not *the* first-ever, horror work. *The Castle of Otranto* traces the fate of the cursed family of Manfred, Prince of Otranto, and their haunted castle. Similar title: *Northanger Abbey*, Jane Austen.

Castles • Haunted Houses • Italy

Wheatley, Dennis.

They Used Dark Forces. *London: Mandarin Paperbacks, 1995. 511p.* On a cloudless night in June 1943, Gregory Sallust parachutes into Nazi Germany. His mission is to penetrate the secrets of Hitler's "V" rockets. But before he can reach his objective, he becomes unwillingly involved with Ibrahim Malacou—hypnotist, astrologer, and disciple of Satan. Though their long and uneasy partnership is sustained by a common hatred of the enemy, their decision to use occult forces to destroy Hitler will imperil Gregory's immortal soul. Similar titles: *Bloody Red Baron*, Kim Newman; *'48*, James Herbert; *The Bargain*, John Ruddy.

Germany • History, Use of • Magic • Nazism • War—World War II

Wilde, Oscar.

The Picture of Dorian Gray. *New York: Penguin, 1985. [First published in 1891.] 269p.* When handsome young Dorian Gray sees a portrait that has been painted of him, he bitterly regrets that he must someday grow old. He wishes that the painting would age and that he would always keep his youth. Dorian's wish comes true, and he becomes a sort of dark Peter Pan who can never grow up, and never embrace adult heterosexuality. Similar titles: *Drawn to the Grave*, Mary Ann Mitchell; *The House of the Seven Gables*, Nathaniel Hawthorne.

Aging • Victorian England

Wilson, F. Paul.

The Keep. *New York: Berkley, 1981. 406p.* A World War II platoon stationed in the Transylvanian Alps unearths a malicious demon, and the massacre begins. Do humans stand a chance against supernatural evil? Similar titles: *Nightworld* and *Reborn*, F. Paul Wilson.

Demons • Magda (character) • Rasalom (character) • War—World War II

Nightworld. *New York: Jove Books, 1993. 328p.* Final novel in the series begun with *The Keep*. Like *The Keep*, concerned with the ultimate battle of good versus evil. Gory and suspenseful, with the emphasis on action. Similar titles: *The Keep* and *Reborn*, F. Paul Wilson.

Apocalypse • Magda (character) • Rasalom (character) • Subterranean Monsters

Reborn. *New York: Berkley, 1990. 342p.* When Jim Stevens, a struggling writer who grew up an orphan, inherits a Nobel Prize–winning geneticist's Victorian mansion, he is unaware of a pact made between the previous owner and the forces of evil. And now that Jim has a child, it is time to honor the pact. Similar titles: *The Witching Hour*, Anne Rice; *The Keep* and *Nightworld*, F. Paul Wilson.

Antichrist, The (character) • Cloning • Demons • Writer as Character

Wolf, Silver Raven.

Beneath a Mountain Moon. *St. Paul, Minn.: Llewellyn, 1995. 343p.* A young witch returns home, only to be greeted by the disappearance of her grandmother and a group of Dark Men who use magic to hurt others. Similar title: *Kindred Rites*, Katherine Elisha Kimbriel.

Clergy as Character • Witchcraft

Wood, Bari.

The Basement. *New York: Avon, 1995. 336p.* (See chapter 7, "Ghosts and Haunted Houses.")

Film

J. D.'s Revenge. *Arthur Marks, dir. 1976. 95 minutes.* A mild-mannered law student is possessed by the spirit of J. D., a small-time thug murdered nearly 40 years ago, who requires someone to tell his tale to bring his killers to justice. One of the few horror films with African Americans as main characters. Joan Pringle and Louis Gossett, Jr., star.

African-American Characters • New Orleans, Louisiana • Revenging Revenant

Rosemary's Baby. *Roman Polanski, dir. 1968. 134 minutes.* A very faithful adaptation of Ira Levin's novel of the same name. *Rosemary's Baby* is about a man who makes a pact with the devil: his wife will bear Satan's child in exchange for worldly success. Mia Farrow, John Cassavetes, and Ruth Gordon star.

New York City • Pregnancy • Religion—Christianity—Catholicism • Religion— Satanism • Woodhouse, Rosemary (character)

The Shining. *Stanley Kubrick, dir. 1980. 142 minutes.* Adapted from Stephen King's novel of the same name. Jack Nicholson stars as a recovering alcoholic and abusive father and parent, Jack Torrance. After losing his teaching position for assaulting one of his pupils, Torrance is given a second chance as winter caretaker of the Overlook Hotel, isolated in the Rocky Mountains. But the isolation and the hotel's ghosts push Jack over the edge and make him attempt to kill his wife and son. Shelley Duvall and Scatman Crothers also star.

Alcoholism • Colorado • Haunted Houses

Supernatural. *Victor Halperin, dir. 1933. (Black-and-white.) 60 minutes.* A woman who is executed for murdering her lovers vows that she will return from the dead. When she does, she possesses the body of Carole Lombard, a virginal heiress, and causes her to misbehave.

Parapsychology • Serial Killers

Our Picks

June's Picks: *Furnace*, Muriel Gray (Doubleday); *Trickster*, Muriel Gray (St. Martin's Press); *Rosemary's Baby*, Ira Levin (Bantam); *Drawn to the Grave,* Mary Ann Mitchell (Leisure Books); *Curfew,* Phil Rickman (Berkley); *Evil Intent*, Bernard Taylor (Leisure Books).

Tony's Picks: *Dead in the Water*, Nancy Holder (Bantam); *Hideaway*, Dean Koontz (Putnam); *Rosemary's Baby*, Ira Levin (Bantam); *Suffer the Children*, John Saul (Dell); *Summer of Night*, Dan Simmons (Putnam).

Chapter 11

Mythological Monsters and "The Old Ones": Invoking the Dark Gods

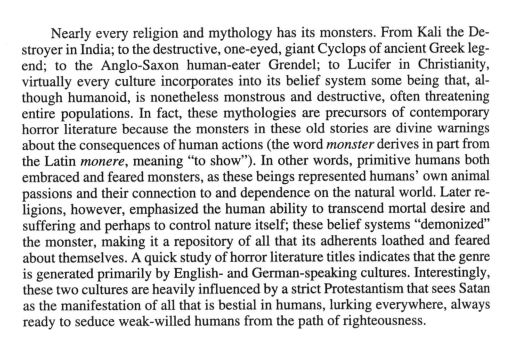

Nearly every religion and mythology has its monsters. From Kali the Destroyer in India; to the destructive, one-eyed, giant Cyclops of ancient Greek legend; to the Anglo-Saxon human-eater Grendel; to Lucifer in Christianity, virtually every culture incorporates into its belief system some being that, although humanoid, is nonetheless monstrous and destructive, often threatening entire populations. In fact, these mythologies are precursors of contemporary horror literature because the monsters in these old stories are divine warnings about the consequences of human actions (the word *monster* derives in part from the Latin *monere*, meaning "to show"). In other words, primitive humans both embraced and feared monsters, as these beings represented humans' own animal passions and their connection to and dependence on the natural world. Later religions, however, emphasized the human ability to transcend mortal desire and suffering and perhaps to control nature itself; these belief systems "demonized" the monster, making it a repository of all that its adherents loathed and feared about themselves. A quick study of horror literature titles indicates that the genre is generated primarily by English- and German-speaking cultures. Interestingly, these two cultures are heavily influenced by a strict Protestantism that sees Satan as the manifestation of all that is bestial in humans, lurking everywhere, always ready to seduce weak-willed humans from the path of righteousness.

Because of the raw power they possess, mythological monsters make great fodder for horror fiction writers. One could say that they are ready-made symbols of all we fear. Just by itself, the Christian Bible is an inexhaustible source of evil portents, impish monsters, ghoulish harbingers of death (e.g., the Four Horsemen of the Apocalypse), and hellish overlords. Even human biblical characters, such as the murderous Cain, have appeared in horror fiction. (Some vampire mythologies see Cain as the father of all vampires, as it was he who first slew his brother.) Still other writers prefer to populate their fictional worlds with monsters from other cultures and other mythologies. In *Song of Kali*, Dan Simmons sends the reader to a Calcutta that is overrun with poverty, violence, and a grotesque zombie version of an immortal poet. In John Farris's *Sacrifice*, family bonds are tested in Guatemala, where Native American gods demand a human sacrifice. In Elizabeth Hand's *Waking the Moon*, the wrath of the pagan goddess, silenced for centuries by patriarchal religions, is awakened and visited upon mere mortals. This divine retribution is the catalyst for a new religious movement for the millennium, a belief system that incorporates all that was good about both the matriarchal and the patriarchal religions. Douglas Preston and Lincoln Child, in *The Relic* and *Reliquary*, create a horrific world in which a tribal mythical monster/protector is accidentally loosed upon urban areas of the United States. The list of dark gods who are accidentally or purposefully invoked goes on and on.

But what of recent, fictional mythologies, populated with monsters that began as the creations of horror-fiction writers and became cultural icons afterwards? Some writers, such as H.P. Lovecraft, found set mythologies to be too constraining, so they created their own mythological monsters. One of the most famous of all these (bowing to perhaps only Godzilla, an "imported" mythological creation), Lovecraft's Cthulhu mythos has become so ingrained in the American horror subconscious that later writers—and Hollywood directors—have based entire texts on the reawakening of Cthulhu or the accidental reading of *The Necronomicon*, which some fans argue is only half fiction.

Whether a mythological monster is based on an existing mythology or is created by a horror writer, readers are reminded that "the old ones"—the old deities—are ever present and can be summoned at any time, even accidentally. Their eagerness to invade the human world when awakened by an innocent is what makes them so frightening; they remind us of the consequences of our actions, regardless of our intentions. Representative works in this subgenre include the weird tales of two of the masters of pulp horror fiction, H.P. Lovecraft and Arthur Machen. To give a good sense of the subgenre's evolution, we have also annotated in this section more recent works, novels such as Dean Koontz's *Phantoms*, Dan Simmons's *Song of Kali*, T. E. D. Klein's *The Ceremonies*, and others.

Appeals: Believability (for Some); Complexity; Familiarity with Monsters from Mythology and Religion; Learning About Other Cultures and Their Gods/Mythologies; Tendency to Be Thought-Provoking

Bowker, David.

The Butcher of Glastonbury. *London: Victor Gollancz, 1997. 224p.* A 13-year-old girl hears her family being savagely dismembered in the next room, and the local police, Scotland Yard, and even the FBI are clueless as to the killer's identity. When similar murders occur in this usually peaceful small town, Chief Superintendent Vernon Laverne must rely on his astral projection abilities to solve the crime. A literate thriller in the tradition of *The X-Files*. Similar title: *Scissorman*, Mark Chadbourn.

England • Federal Bureau of Investigation • Human Sacrifice • Kali (character) • Police Officer as Character • Reincarnation • Religion—Hinduism

Chadbourn, Mark.

Scissorman. *London: Victor Gollancz, 1997. 352p.* In the amoral 1980s, stock dealer Jon Summers recovers in his childhood home from a drug- and stress-induced nervous breakdown. This house has always been magical, but as of late the magic has become somewhat darker. The door to somewhere else has been opened and the Scissorman has been released—and he's now slicing up people who had worked with Jon. As Jon's wife and best friend plot his downfall, it's a toss-up as to whether somewhere else or the real world is filled with more evil. A literate, darker version of C.S. Lewis's classic *The Lion, the Witch, and the Wardrobe*. Similar titles: *The Butcher of Glastonbury*, David Bowker; *Demogorgon*, Brian Lumley; *The Immaculate*, Mark Morris.

> *Economic Violence • Fairy Tales • Fantasy • Haunted Houses • Human Sacrifice • London, England • Shapeshifters*

Chapman, Stepan.

The Troika. *Tallahassee, Fla.: Ministry of Whimsy Press, 1997. 251p.* An evil psychiatrist/angel tortures three souls by forcing them to exist in a surreal physical environment. Unique in approach and vision.

> *Afterlife • Angels • Dreams • Fantasy • Shapeshifters*

Clark, Simon.

Vampyrrhic. *London: Hoddard and Stoughton, 1998. 441p.* (See chapter 9, "Vampires and Werewolves.")

Clegg, Douglas.

The Halloween Man. *New York: Leisure Books, 1998. 360p.* (See chapter 13, "Small-Town Horror.")

Clements, Mark A.

Lorelei. *New York: Leisure Books, 1995. 298p.* Washington attorney Don Westerman disappears, and his mutilated corpse shows up in New Orleans. His wife launches an investigation that reveals a trail of mutilated men and a young seductress named Lorelei. Nice mix of the psychological and the supernatural. Similar titles: *The Undine*, Michael O'Rourke; *The Stress of Her Regard*, Tim Powers.

> *Alcoholism • Federal Bureau of Investigation • New Orleans, Louisiana • Serial Killers • Sex Crimes*

Collins, Nancy A.

Tempter. *New York: Penguin, 1990. 299p.* (See chapter 9, "Vampires and Werewolves.")

Disch, Thomas M.

The M. D. *New York: Knopf, 1991. 401p.* William Michaels is visited as a child by the god Mercury, who grants him the power to cure or afflict as he chooses. But the gods never give a gift without a price. In the future, William is able to cure AIDS, but a much more terrible disease takes its place and lays humanity to waste. Similar titles: *The God Project*, John Saul; *The Sisterhood*, Michael Palmer; *The Tooth Fairy*, Graham Joyce; *Sacrament*, Clive Barker; *Insomnia*, Stephen King; *The Halloween Man*, Douglas Clegg.

> *AIDS • Apocalypse • Childhood*

Due, Tanarive.

My Soul to Keep. *New York: HarperCollins, 1997. 352p.* An African immortal must deal with human feelings of love for and loyalty toward his human family when his fellow immortals wish him to sever all connections to protect the secret of their existence. Emphasis is on characterization and psychology, but well-thought-out plots, the use of historical fact, and a suspenseful climax make this not only unique, but also very enjoyable. Similar titles: *The Vampire Tapestry*, Suzy M. Charnas; *Interview with the Vampire* and *Servant of the Bones*, Anne Rice; Chelsea Quinn Yarbro's Saint-Germain Chronicles; *Shadows*, Kimberly Rangel.

African-American Characters • Immortality • Journalist as Character • Magic • Marriage • Miami, Florida • Religion—Christianity

Farris, John.

Sacrifice. *New York: Tor Books, 1994. 320p.* Greg Walker is an all-American, devout Baptist family man who will go to any extreme to protect his innocent 17-year-old daughter. However, a near-death experience soon reveals that Greg has a dark past. Extremely clever story conception. Emphasis on action. Similar title: *Nazareth Hill*, Ramsey Campbell.

Guatemala • Reincarnation • Religion—Native American

Forrest, Elizabeth.

Phoenix Fire. *New York: Daw Books, 1993. 364p.* (See chapter 10, "Demonic Possession, Satanism, Black Magic, and Witches and Warlocks.")

Gaiman, Neil.

Neverwhere. *New York: Avon, 1997. 337p.* Dark fantasy about a London businessman who finds an alternate reality in the subway system. All he wants to do is escape, but his destiny lies with the strange creatures there. Gaiman's rewriting of *Alice in Wonderland* for grown-ups is extremely literate and visual. Similar titles: *The Devil on May Street*, Steve Harris.

Angels • Fantasy • London, England • Subterranean Monsters

Gideon, John.

Greely's Cove. *New York: Berkley, 1991. 422p.* Nothing much happens in Greely's Cove, which makes it the ideal place for an ancient evil to hibernate until it can reproduce and wreak havoc on the world. Suddenly strange things happen—townspeople disappear without a trace, and an autistic boy is miraculously cured and demonstrates wisdom beyond his years. Well written and suspenseful. Told from multiple points of view. Similar titles: *Jago*, Kim Newman; *Candlenight* and *Curfew*, Phil Rickman; *Midnight Is a Lonely Place*, Barbara Erskine; *Trickster*, Muriel Gray; *Night Calls*, Katherine Elisha Kimbriel; *The Children's Hour*, Douglas Clegg; *Thunder Road*, Chris Curry.

Alchemy • Savant Syndrome • Washington (state) • Witches

Goingback, Owl.

Crota. *New York: Donald I. Fine, 1996. 292p.* A small Missouri town is terrorized by a demonic beast with a hunger for humans and other animals. Only the famed hunter Jay Little Hawk, with the aid of the town sheriff and an old shaman, can bring down the beast. A fast read. Well paced. Similar titles: *Trickster*, Muriel Gray; *The Purification Ceremony*, Mark T. Sullivan; *The Wendigo Border*, Catherine Montrose.

Demons • Missouri • Native American Characters • Religion—Native American • Subterranean Monsters

Grant, Charles. The Millennium Quartet.

Only two of the four books in the series have been released prior to publication of this book.

Symphony. *New York: Tor Books, 1997. 332p.* The first of the Millennium Quartet novels, about a group of maniacal murderers who hitchhike across the country with a strange, shadowy driver, committing mass murder on the way. Their goal is to usher in the apocalypse by murdering a small-town minister on the East Coast. Cleverly written to correspond with the movements of a symphony, with emphasis on character and mood. Similar titles: *Waking the Moon*, Elizabeth Hand; *Jago*, Kim Newman; *The Sea King's Daughter*, Barbara Michaels; *Song of Kali*, Dan Simmons; *Dominion*, Bentley Little; *Escardy Gap*, Peter Crowther and James Lovegrove; *A Dry Spell*, Susan Moloney.

> *Apocalypse • Clergy as Character • Music—Classical • New England • Religion—Christianity*

In the Mood. *New York: Forge, 1998. 304p.* Volume 2 of the Millennium Quartet, in which writer John Bannock becomes obsessed with mass murder and thereby finds himself a target for "the four horsemen." Can he stop them before a worldwide famine ushers in the apocalypse? Based on music, like Grant's earlier novel *Symphony*, but on big-band rather than classical. Similar title: *Song of Kali*, Dan Simmons.

> *Antichrist, The (character) • Apocalypse • Clergy as Character • Natural Disasters • New Orleans, Louisiana • Serial Killers • Writer as Character*

Hand, Elizabeth.

Waking the Moon. *New York: Harper Prism, 1996. 495p.* Since long before the fall of Rome, the Benandanti, a secret brotherhood, has controlled every government, country, church, and institution in the world to keep at bay the ancient blood cult of the Moon Goddess. But as the millennium approaches, the Moon Goddess prepares to make her return and, with the help of her New-Age feminist followers, overthrow the old patriarchal order. Narrative is compelling, demonstrating a thorough knowledge of the ancient goddess religions. Similar titles: *Jago*, Kim Newman; *Dominion*, Bentley Little; *The Sea King's Daughter*, Barbara Michaels; *Harvest Home*, Thomas Tryon; *Bethany's Sin*, Robert R. McCammon; *Requiem*, Graham Joyce; *Symphony*, Charles Grant; *Renaissance Moon*, Linda Nevins; *The Night Church*, Whitley Strieber; *The Wicker Man*, Robin Hardy and Anthony Shaffer.

> *Apocalypse • Feminism • Human Sacrifice • Matriarchy • New Age • Religion— Ancient Egyptian • Religion—Christianity • Religion— Paganism • Washington, D.C.*

Winterlong: A Novel. *New York: Bantam, 1990. 442p.* A twin brother and sister are seduced by a charismatic character named Death, in this dark fantasy that chronicles how their travels to a realm of speaking beasts threaten the end of the world. Similar titles: *From the Teeth of Angels*, Jonathan Carroll.

> *Apocalypse • Death (character) • Fantasy • Genetics • Twins • Weird Science*

Harris, Steve.

The Devil on May Street. *London: Vista, 1998. 381p.* Steve Warner and his best friend, Johnny Kane, see a boy on a swing vanish into thin air, only to reappear moments later. When they stand under the power lines on the vacant lot on May Street, they are transported back to 1972, where they find the mysterious house that once stood on the spot and encounter their young parents. Meanwhile, some grisly murders are occurring back in the present, and Steve's parents are caught performing mysterious rituals. An absorbing read. Similar titles: *The Quorum*, Kim Newman; *The Cipher*, Kathe Koja; *Let There Be Dark*, Allen Lee Harris; *Lightning*, Dean Koontz; *Neverwhere*, Neil Gaiman; *Silk*, Caitlin R. Kiernan.

> *Childhood • Drugs • England • Fantasy • Satan (character) • Secret Sin • Time Travel*

Holland, Tom.

Slave of My Thirst. *New York: Simon & Schuster, 1996. 421p.* (See chapter 9, "Vampires and Werewolves.")

Huggins, James Byron.

Cain. *New York: Simon & Schuster, 1997. 400p.* An Army scientist creates a cyborg killing machine from an ex–CIA agent—but her plans backfire when an evil spirit enters the body of her super-soldier and it goes on a killing rampage. Action-oriented. High on suspense. Similar titles: *Mr. Murder*, Dean Koontz; *The Dark Half*, Stephen King; *Frankenstein*, Mary Shelley.

> *Apocalypse • Central Intelligence Agency • Cyborgs • Epidemic • Experiments— Military • Religion—Christianity • Roswell, New Mexico • Satan (character)*

Johnstone, William W.

Rockabilly Hell. *New York: Kensington, 1995. 302p.* In the past 40 years, more than 500 people have disappeared along Route 61, where music greats like Elvis and Jerry Lee Lewis played in smoke-filled roadside clubs. A sheriff's deputy stumbles onto this mystery, which will take him into hell. Similar titles: *Rockabilly Limbo*, William W. Johnstone; *Swan Song*, Robert R. McCammon.

> *Apocalypse • Music—Rock Music • Police Officer as Character*

Rockabilly Limbo. *New York: Kensington, 1996. 302p.* In this continuation of *Rockabilly Hell*, old-time rock-and-roll becomes "the dance of death," causing a tide of violence to sweep America. Ex–deputy sheriff "Cole" Younger is on the run with some other survivalists attempting to stop this tide, which threatens to bring about the end of the world. Similar titles: *Rockabilly Hell*, William W. Johnstone; *Swan Song*, Robert R. McCammon.

> *Apocalypse • Music—Rock Music • Police Officer as Character • Religion— Christianity*

Joyce, Graham.

Requiem. *New York: Tor Books, 1995. 286p.* Newly widowed Tom Webster travels to Jerusalem, but finds no refuge from his grief or his guilt about his own dark desires. Instead, he is given a fragment of the Dead Sea Scrolls, which proclaims that Christ believed that humans should celebrate the flesh and that women should be the equal of men. Meanwhile, a mysterious wraith in the form of an old woman haunts Tom. Literate and original. Similar titles: *The Blood of the Lamb*, Thomas Monteleone; *Waking the Moon*, Elizabeth Hand; *Child of the Light, Child of the Journey*, Janet Berliner and George Guthridge.

> *Eroticism • Jerusalem • Religion—Christianity • Religion—Islam • Religion— Judaism*

The Tooth Fairy. *New York: Tor Books, 1998. 320p.* As a young boy, Sam awakened one night to find an eerie presence in his room, which he believed to be the tooth fairy. This sinister being follows him throughout his life, often taking the form of a seductress. Challenges the harmless "myths" we learn in childhood. Similar title: *The M. D.*, Thomas M. Disch.

> *Childhood • Fantasy*

Kiernan, Caitlin R.

Silk. *New York: Penguin, 1998. 353p.* (See chapter 17, "Psychological Horror.")

Kihn, Greg.

Shade of Pale. *New York: Forge, 1997. 256p.* (See chapter 7, "Ghosts and Haunted Houses.")

King, Stephen.

Needful Things. *New York: Penguin, 1991. 690p.* Castle Rock, Maine, is a peaceful little town. It's not exactly Mayberry, but everyone agrees to keep certain secrets and to disagree on the fine points of theology and morality in order to keep the peace. Then Leland Gaunt comes to town and opens a curiosity shop in a vacant building on Main Street. Leland's store carries everyone's heart's desire, but the prices are ones they can't afford. Similar titles: *The Store*, Bentley Little; *The Devil's Advocate*, Andrew Neiderman; *Salem's Lot*, Stephen King.

> *Castle Rock, Maine • Pangborn, Alan (character) • Police Officer as Character • Religion—Christianity—Catholicism • Religion—Christianity— Protestantism • Satan (character)*

Kleier, Glenn.

The Last Day. *New York: Warner Books, 1997. 484p.* A young woman walks out of the Negev Desert and proclaims herself to be the new Messiah. Is she a new Christ, or the Antichrist? Suspenseful, with lots of plot twists. Similar title: *The Calcutta Chromosome*, Amitav Ghosh.

> *Antichrist, The (character) • Apocalypse • Biological Warfare • Genetics • Journalist as Character • Science Fiction*

Klein, T. E. D.

The Ceremonies. *New York: Viking, 1984. 502p.* A dark force is awakening in a small New Hampshire town: the Old One, Satan himself, is hatching a new scheme to bring about the world's end. However, he needs a virgin and a scholar of the occult to complete his plans, so he assumes a pleasant disguise as a harmless old man. A very clever and haunting novel by one of the new Lovecraftian masters of the genre. Similar titles: *Titus Crow: In the Moons of Borea* and *Elysia, The Coming of Cthulhu*, Brian Lumley; *The House on the Borderland*, William Hope Hodgson.

> *Apocalypse • Librarian as Character • New England • Satan (character) • Tarot*

Koontz, Dean.

Phantoms. *New York: Putnam, 1983. 352p.* One of Koontz's best. More than half of the residents of Snowfield, California, have mysteriously either disappeared or died. Dr. Jennifer Paige, her 14-year-old sister Lisa, and Sheriff Bryce

Hammond must get to the bottom of these strange occurrences, while they avoid being gruesomely killed by It, the shapeshifting creature that seems to know each person's innermost fears. Similar title: *Ghost Story*, Peter Straub.

Computers • History, Use of • Satan (character) • Shapeshifters • Subterranean Monsters

Twilight Eyes. *New York: Berkley, 1985. 451p.* (See chapter 15, "Technohorror.")

Little, Bentley.

Dominion. *New York: Signet Books, 1996. 416p.* Unlike most teenage boys, Dion Semele has no interest in sex and alcohol, because of the daily example set by his alcoholic, nymphomaniac mother. But that changes when he moves to Napa, California, and meets Penelope Danaem, beautiful and virginal daughter of six co-mothers who run the local winery. Suddenly, people are found hideously murdered, the townspeople can't get enough of Danaem wine, and people engage in an old-fashioned carnival during which they indulge their desires to touch, and sometimes rend and consume, flesh. Similar titles: *Waking the Moon*, Elizabeth Hand; *Jago* and *The Quorum*, Kim Newman; *Symphony*, Charles Grant; *Serial Killer Days*, David Prill; *The Wild*, Whitley Strieber.

California • Cults • Eroticism • High School • Human Sacrifice • Religion—Paganism

The Store. *New York: Signet Books, 1998. 431p.* Juniper, Arizona, is a pleasant small town, but economic life on Main Street is ruined when a retail giant, The Store, comes to town. The Store has sufficient economic muscle to undersell small-business competition in Juniper; even worse, it can persuade the town council to exempt The Store from local sales taxes and build roads for it at city expense. Evil lurks within The Store. Employees behave mysteriously. Dead animals are found on the premises every day. Townspeople who oppose The Store disappear. Highly original. A compelling and fun read. Similar titles: *Needful Things*, Stephen King; *The Stepford Wives*, Ira Levin; *The Mailman* and *The Ignored*, Bentley Little; *The Devil's Advocate*, Andrew Neiderman; *The House That Jack Built*, Graham Masterson; *Obsession*, Ramsey Campbell.

Arizona • Cults • Demons • Fantasy • Mind Control • Zombies

University. *New York: Signet Books, 1995. 416p.* (See chapter 18, "Splatterpunk.")

Lumley, Brian.

Demogorgon. *New York: Tor Books, 1987. 345p.* A petty thief in London accidentally discovers the epitome of all evil—the Demogorgon—and to avoid being devoured by it, he must find some way to defeat it. But to stop the Demogorgon from taking over the Earth, he must first penetrate its disguises. Similar title: *Scissorman*, Mark Chadbourn.

Apocalypse • Demons • London, England • Shapeshifters

Titus Crow: In the Moons of Borea and Elysia, The Coming of Cthulhu. *New York: Tor Books, 1997. 380p.* In this, the third volume of the Titus Crow series, Cthulhu rises from slumber to attempt the destruction of humanity once again. Titus Crow and his sidekick, Laurent de Marigny, with the help of a few other Lumley creations from earlier works, must stop Cthulhu. As always, Lumley is inventive in his intertextual use of his own created worlds. Similar titles: *The Ceremonies*, T. E. D. Klein; *The Forbidden Zone*, Whitley Strieber; *The Tommyknockers*, Stephen King.

Cthulhu (character) • Fantasy • Religion—Native American • Time Travel

Marano, Michael.

Dawn Song. *New York: Tor Books, 1998. 384p.* A succubus visits Boston and takes up residence in an apartment complex so she can learn about human emotions (by killing her human lovers). However, she ends up as part of a strange army of humans and demons, readied for the battle between Belial and Leviathan. Graphic and disturbing; downright scary. Similar titles: *Treasure Box*, Orson Scott Card; *The Demon and the Warlock*, Richard Perry.

Alchemy • Boston, Massachusetts • Demons • Gay/Lesbian/Bisexual Characters • Psychosexual Horror

McCammon, Robert R.

Bethany's Sin. *New York: Pocket Books, 1980. 344p.* Evan Reid and his family move to a small town in Pennsylvania called Bethany's Sin. When Evan starts asking too many questions about the town's name and the docility of its male citizens, he becomes the victim of a ritualistic hunt. Truly unique plotline; suspenseful. Similar titles: *Desmodus*, Melanie Tem; *Harvest Home*, Thomas Tryon; *Waking the Moon*, Elizabeth Hand; *Widow*, Billie Sue Mosiman; *Nomads*, Chelsea Quinn Yarbro; *The Wicker Man*, Robin Hardy and Anthony Shaffer.

Amazon Warriors • Archaeology • Writer as Character

⑤ Swan Song. *New York: Pocket Books, 1996. 956p.* Epic struggles of good versus evil populate this post–nuclear holocaust novel, which follows the escapades of a ragtag bunch of survivors who must protect the savior known as Swan, a young girl, from the Man with the Scarlet Eye. Recipient of a Bram Stoker Award. Similar titles: *The Stand*, Stephen King; *Rockabilly Limbo* and *Rockabilly Hell*, William W. Johnstone.

Apocalypse • Demons • God—Christian God (character) • Nuclear Holocaust • Satan (character)

Michaels, Barbara.

The Sea King's Daughter. *Boston: G. K. Hall, 1976. 445p.* A young woman is lured to a Greek island by her archaeologist father, but forces slumbering beneath the surface threaten her existence. Similar titles: *Waking the Moon*, Elizabeth Hand; *Jago*, Kim Newman; *Symphony*, Charles Grant; *Dominion*, Bentley Little.

Greece • Natural Disasters • Subterranean Monsters

Monteleone, Thomas F.

⑤ The Blood of the Lamb. *New York: Tor Books, 1992. 421p.* The Catholic Church cloned Christ in 1968. Now, just in time for the upcoming millennium, this clone, Father Peter Carenza, is traveling across the United States in a Winnebago, performing miracles to ever-increasing crowds of adoring followers—and these miracles are both terrifying and awesome. Told through multiple points of view. Recipient of a Bram Stoker Award. Similar titles: *The Exorcist*, William Peter Blatty; *The Boys from Brazil*, Ira Levin; *Requiem*, Graham Joyce.

Clergy as Character • Cloning • Journalist as Character • Religion—Christianity—Catholicism

Montrose, Catherine.

The Wendigo Border. *New York: Tor Books, 1995. 278p.* Darcy Jacobi has a unique ability to converse with spirits, but when her friends at the Esoteric Society convince her she can channel her mother's spirit, they are setting her up to cross the border into the realm of demons. Only a Guardian of the Wendigo Border can protect her now. Similar title: *Trickster*, Muriel Gray.

Demons • Fantasy • Religion—Native American

Neiderman, Andrew.

The Devil's Advocate. *New York: Pocket Books, 1997. 320p.* Kevin Taylor, an up-and-coming legal advocate, joins the prestigious law firm of John Milton and Associates. Then he begins to notice that attorneys of the firm win every case they fight, even if the client is obviously guilty. What power does Taylor's employer hold over the justice system? Made into a movie by Taylor Hackford in 1997. Similar title: *Needful Things*, Stephen King; *The Store*, Bentley Little.

Lawyer as Character • New York City • Satan (character)

Nevins, Linda.

Renaissance Moon: A Novel. *New York: St. Martin's Press, 1997. 288p.* A university professor's daughter takes to heart her father's words that the pagan goddess of the moon, Artemis, is the true matriarch of humanity. She becomes a psychotic hunter, using her hatred for men as motivation for her rampages. Emphasis is on narrative development and historical/literary reference. Similar titles: *Waking the Moon*, Elizabeth Hand.

Academia • Human Sacrifice • Religion—Christianity—Catholicism • Religion—Paganism • Writer as Character

O'Rourke, Michael.

The Undine. *New York: Harper Paperbacks, 1996. 354p.* The Japan America Corporation has captured some fairies and kept them hidden in a sort of biosphere outside of Los Angeles, in an attempt to discover their secrets. The fairies, capable of shapeshifting from irresistibly beautiful, sexually insatiable human females to hideous gargoyle-like beasts, soon escape and torment humans for sport. These are not Tinkerbell fairies—they are ravenous succubi who prey on human males. Similar titles: *Dominion*, Bentley Little; *Lorelei*, Mark A. Clements.

Asian Characters • Eroticism • Fantasy • Government Officials • Los Angeles, California

Peretti, Frank.

The Oath: A Novel. *Dallas, Tex.: Word Books, 1995. 549p.* An evil dragon lives outside of Hyde River, feeding off the townspeople's lack of faith. Can wildlife biologist Steve find enough faith to defeat it? One of the few Christian fiction horror efforts.

Religion—Christianity—Protestantism • Secret Sin

Perry, Richard.

The Demon and the Warlock. *Huntington, W.Va.: University Editions, 1994. 199p.* A novel in the Lovecraftian tradition, about a brother and sister who are the unwitting pawns of an evil warlock. Can the two of them save each other before an old, evil being is awakened, or will they become the sacrifices it needs to free itself? Similar titles: *Dawn Song*, Michael Marano; *Treasure Box*, Orson Scott Card; *The Tommyknockers*, Stephen King.

Demons • Witches

Powers, Tim.

The Stress of Her Regard. *New York: Ace Books, 1989. 470p.* Powers fictionalizes the intersecting lives of Byron, Shelley, and Keats, telling the story of their obsession with female lamia, or shapeshifters. These beautiful "women" who haunt the dreams of the Romantic poets are actually eons-old, unmerciful mythological creatures whose tender embraces drain the life from their victims. Imaginative and thought-provoking, and strong on character development and image. Similar titles: *Lorelei*, Mark A. Clements; *Lord of the Dead*, Tom Holland; *Deathstone*, Ruby Jean Jensen.

> *Alternative Literature • Byron, Lord George Gordon (character) • History, Use of • Shapeshifters • Shelley, Percy B. (character)*

Prescott, Steve, and James A. Moore.

Nuwisha. *Clarkston, Ga.: White Wolf, 1998. 72p.* The forces of good and evil, of creation and destruction, fight to the finish in this violent tale. Unique in that the *garau*, or werewolf children of Gaia (Mother Earth), fight for the side of good. Similar titles: Brent Stableford's Werewolves of London trilogy.

> *Apocalypse • Gaia (character) • Garou, The (character) • Shapeshifters*

Preston, Douglas, and Lincoln Child.

The Relic. *New York: Tor Books, 1995. 474p.* A horrible monster that feeds on human brain tissue is loose in the New York Museum of Natural History. Can Margo Green, graduate student/museum researcher, discover the museum monster's secret and destroy it before the opening reception of a new exhibit? Action-oriented. Lots of cliffhanger scenes. Made into a movie in 1997 by Peter Hyams. Similar titles: *Reliquary*, Douglas Preston and Lincoln Child; *Jurassic Park*, Michael Crichton.

> *Federal Bureau of Investigation • Genetics • Green, Margo (character) • Museums • New York City*

Reliquary. *New York: Doherty, 1997. 382p.* In this sequel to *The Relic*, Natural History Museum curator Margo Green is called out to Manhattan to investigate two unearthed, abnormal skeletons. When brutal murders begin occurring, FBI agent Pendergast and scientist Dr. Frock are called in as well, and they all discover the ultimate horror behind the museum monster. Similar titles: *The Relic*, Douglas Preston and Lincoln Child; *Jurassic Park*, Michael Crichton.

> *Federal Bureau of Investigation • Green, Margo (character) • Museums*

Rangel, Kimberly.

Shadows. *New York: Leisure Books, 1996. 368p.* Selene deMarca has managed to quell the evil part of her genetics, her "shadow" self, for 25 years. But she is the last fertile female of her kind, and the last male Shadow needs her to perpetuate the species. To complicate matters, Reese Christian, a bounty hunter, is also after Selene. A love story played out in a gothic atmosphere. Similar title: *My Soul to Keep*, Tanarive Due.

> *Eroticism • Shapeshifters*

Rice, Anne.

Servant of the Bones. *New York: Random House, 1996. 387p.* In ancient Babylon, Azriel is sacrificed to become the Servant of the Bones, so that his people may return to Jerusalem. But the story doesn't end for Azriel, who is condemned to an immortal life and can relieve some of the loneliness of his condition only by telling his story to Jonathan, and helping his chosen scribe to foil a modern-day evan-gelical plot. Similar titles: *The Mummy, or Ramses the Damned* and *The Vampire Lestat*, Anne Rice; *My Soul to Keep*, Tanarive Due.

> *Babylon • History, Use of • Religion—Judaism*

Taltos: Lives of the Mayfair Witches. *New York: Ballantine, 1995. 480p.* (See chapter 10, "Demonic Possession, Satanism, Black Magic, and Witches and Warlocks.")

The Witching Hour. *New York: Ballantine, 1991. 1,038p.* (See chapter 10, "Demonic Possession, Satanism, Black Magic, and Witches and Warlocks.")

Russell, Jay S.

Celestial Dogs. *New York: St. Martin's Press, 1997. 272p.* Private investigator Marty Burns takes up with an Uzi-toting woman to battle demons. Russell combines Japanese mythology, popular culture, and the mean streets of Los Angeles in this satire/horror tale. Similar titles: Laurell K. Hamilton's Anita Blake, Vampire Hunter series.

> *Burns, Marty (character) • Demons • Los Angeles, California*

Schweitzer, Darrell.

Mask of the Sorcerer. *London: New English Library, 1995. 421p.* A 13-year-old boy goes on a mythic journey into the underworld, which transforms him into a sorcerer. As he loses his humanity and becomes a new creature, he uses his talents to torture and brutally murder those who oppose his will. Graphic. Very clever. Similar title: *Treasure Box*, Orson Scott Card.

> *Fantasy • Revenge*

Simmons, Dan.

The Fires of Eden. *New York: Putnam, 1994. 399p.* (See chapter 19, "Comic Horror.")

Lovedeath. *New York: Warner Books, 1993. 354p.* (See chapter 6, "Collections by Individual Authors.")

Song of Kali. *New York: Doherty, 1985. 311p.* According to journalist Robert Z. Luczak, "some places are too evil to be allowed to exist. . . . Calcutta is such a place." Amid the homeless beggars and the violent thugs, Luczak discovers an evil that is beyond human comprehension: a cult of killers so unmerciful that skinning people alive is within their realm. And it is just possible that these killers, worshippers of the goddess Kali, are scheming to infect the world with their cruelty. Similar title: *Nomads*, Chelsea Quinn Yarbro; *In the Mood* and *Symphony*, Charles Grant.

> *Cults • India • Journalist as Character • Parenting • Religion—Hinduism • Violence—Theories of*

Spencer, William Browning.

Resume with Monsters. *Sag Harbor, N.Y.: Permanent Press, 1995. 212p.* (See chapter 19, "Comic Horror.")

Strieber, Whitley.

The Forbidden Zone. *New York: Wilson and Neff, 1993. 415p.* Strieber updates Lovecraft's Cthulhu mythos in this tale about a physicist whose experiments loose tentacled monsters on a small New York town. Dr. Brian Kelley, a scientist, is awakened one night by the sound of someone screaming; he later finds that the screaming is coming from underground. Within a week, Kelley's pregnant wife almost miscarries, one of his neighbors is attacked by swarming flies, and many are killed. Has one of Kelley's experiments gone awry, or are demons finding their way out of Hell? Similar titles: *Titus Crow: In the Moons of Borea* and *Elysia, The Coming of Cthulhu*, Brian Lumley; *The Tommyknockers*, Stephen King.

> *Cthulhu (character) • New York State • Pregnancy • Subterranean Monsters • Weird Science*

Swanwick, Michael.

Jack Faust. *New York: Avon, 1997. 337p.* Medieval scholar Johannes Faust sells his soul for knowledge, and he swears to lead humanity out of the Dark Ages—but can humanity handle this new knowledge? Erudite alternative history/literature that explores timeless ideas. Similar title: *The Tortuous Serpent*, Donald Tyson.

> *Aliens • Alternative History • Alternative Literature • Faust Legend • Satan (character)*

Tyson, Donald.

The Tortuous Serpent: An Occult Adventure. *St. Paul, Minn.: Llewellyn, 1997. 480p.* Tyson mixes history and dark fantasy in this Elizabethan tale of magician John Dees and alchemist Edward Kelley. The two and their wives, Jane and Joanna, travel across Europe in pursuit of a grimoire (a book of spells) that, in the wrong hands, will release the mythological Lilith's hideous, monstrous children. Fast-paced and suspenseful. Similar title: *Jack Faust*, Michael Swanwick.

> *Alchemy • Apocalypse • England • Espionage • Lilith (character) • Religion—Judaism*

Williams, Sidney.

Azarius. *New York: Pinnacle, 1989. 446p.* An ex-angel masquerading as a human is intent upon murdering a priest. Can an out-of-work reporter and a radio host find him before it is too late?

> *Angels • Clergy as Character • Journalist as Character*

Wilson, F. Paul.

The Tomb. *New York: Tor Books, 1998. 448p.* A repairman of "situations" must deal with Bengali demons and a cursed necklace.

> *Demons • India*

Wright, T. M.

Little Boy Lost. *New York: Tor Books, 1992. 247p.* An estranged mother, who happens to be a mythological demon, kidnaps one of her sons and threatens the life of the other. Told in flashbacks and surreal dream visions.

> *Demons • Diary Format • Dreams*

Film

Hellraiser. *Clive Barker, dir. 1987. 94 minutes.* Barker directed this film version of his own novel, *The Hellbound Heart*. When Frank, a playboy and thrill-seeker, decides that life holds no more pleasure for him, he experiments with Lamarchand's Box, which supposedly will summon the gods of pleasure. Instead, Frank summons demons of torture, and they want more than just Frank.

   Demons • Eroticism

Tales from the Hood. *Rusty Cundieff, dir. 1995. 98 minutes.* (See chapter 19, "Comic Horror.")

Our Picks

June's Picks: *My Soul to Keep*, Tanarive Due (HarperCollins); *Waking the Moon*, Elizabeth Hand (Harper Prism); *The Devil on May Street*, Steve Harris (Vista); *The Store*, Bentley Little (Signet Books).

Tony's Picks: *My Soul to Keep*, Tanarive Due (HarperCollins); *Symphony*, Charles Grant (Tor Books); *Phantoms*, Dean Koontz (Putnam); *The Relic*, Douglas Preston and Lincoln Child (Tor Books); *Song of Kali*, Dan Simmons (Doherty).

Chapter 12

Telekinesis and Hypnosis: Chaos from Control

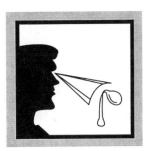

In the nineteenth century, Dr. Anton Mesmer popularized the idea of mesmerism (later known as hypnotism), whereby an individual could get others to do his or her bidding through mind control. This pseudoscience, compounded with the reality that some charismatic individuals are able to exert an almost superhuman influence over others, gave rise to stories about evil people using their mental powers to control others. One of the first fictional examples of this was a vampire, Count Dracula, who in Bram Stoker's novel used the power of mesmerism over his victims. In the twentieth century, it was widely believed that hypnotism could be used to access an individual's unconscious mind and, it was hoped, cure that person's psychological problems. But if hypnotism could allow someone to access another's unconscious mind, then it had the potential for great evil as well as great good. In the past 100 years, we have witnessed far too many "charismatic" individuals wreak havoc—and feed our fears of mind control. People such as Adolf Hitler, Jim Jones, and David Koresh, to name a few, proved that it is possible for one individual to *psychologically* and *emotionally* control the wills of many, with terrifying results. Robert Silverberg's short story, "Passengers," illustrates the principle of mind control and the questions it raises about the nature of free will. In his story, unseen aliens come to a seemingly orderly Earth and attach themselves to individuals, causing them to behave in socially unacceptable ways that are more than likely manifestations of their repressed unconscious desires.

Telekinesis is another type of mental control. Whereas hypnotism requires the use of another person to accomplish the hypnotist's desires, the individual with telekinetic abilities can move objects with his or her mind. What makes this power frightening is that typically the telekinetic person is an angry outcast who, pushed beyond the limits of endurance, goes berserk, wreaking havoc with telekinetic abilities rather than with an AK-47. Stephen King's novel, *Carrie,* is an excellent example of the subgenre. Carrie, the butt of all jokes in high school and the recipient of extreme abuse at the hands of her fundamentalist Christian mother, explodes when her classmates play one too many jokes on her, using her telekinetic abilities to destroy the town and half of its citizens.

Horror tales about mental control remind their readers that the loss of free will is always possible, sometimes with catastrophic results. It is a subgenre particularly geared toward American readers, for it threatens the loss of liberty, of the ability to control one's own actions and destiny. Representative works in this subgenre include King's *Carrie,* Peter Straub's Blue Rose series, Clive Barker's *Cabal,* Curt Siodmak's *Donovan's Brain,* Dean Koontz's *Strangers,* Owen Brookes's *Deadly Communion,* and George C. Chesbro's *Veil.*

Appeals: Fascination with ESP, Telepathy, Hypnosis, Mind Control; Fascination with the Human Brain's Potential, and Fear of It as Well; Often Contain Sympathetic Characters Empowered with Telekinetic Abilities (Vicarious Empowerment); Pseudo-Scientific Appeal

Amos, Beth.

Cold White Fury. *New York: HarperCollins, 1996. 355p.* After an automobile accident that kills his father, Tanner Bolton is left with a small piece of metal in his head—and the ability to read minds and converse with the dead. So why is a secret organization of right-wing professionals attempting to kill him and his mother? Emphasis is on character over action. Similar title: *Firestarter,* Stephen King.

Medical Horror • Telepathy • Weird Science

Barker, Clive.

Cabal. *New York: Poseidon, 1988. 377p.* Aaron Boone is hypnotized by Decker, his psychiatrist, into believing he is a serial killer. Thus, he runs away, hunted by the police, and finds himself in the monster-inhabited town of Meridian. When he himself becomes a monster and is hunted by Decker and the police, Boone realizes that humans are the true monsters in this supernatural realm. Full of twists and surprises. Similar title: *Sick,* Jay R. Bonansigna.

Alter Ego • Hypnotism • Meridian • Psychiatrist as Character

Galilee. *New York: HarperCollins, 1998. 432p.* (See chapter 17, "Psychological Horror.")

Clark, Leigh.

Evil Reincarnate. *New York: Tor Books, 1994. 351p.* (See chapter 14, "Maniacs and Sociopaths, or the Nuclear Family Explodes.")

Clegg, Douglas.

Dark of the Eye. *New York: Pocket Books, 1994. 325p.* An accident has left an 11-year-old girl with the power of life and death. Can she escape the forces that want to exploit her power: the government, an impish demon, and her mad scientist father? Similar title: *Jumpers,* R. Patrick Gates.

Demons • Mad Scientist

Collins, Nancy A.

Sunglasses After Dark. *New York: New American Library, 1989. 253p.* (See chapter 9, "Vampires and Werewolves.")

Craig, Kit.

Twice Burned. *New York: Berkley, 1995. 343p.* (See chapter 14, "Maniacs and Sociopaths, or the Nuclear Family Explodes.")

David, James F.

Fragments. *New York: Tor Books, 1997. 381p.* (See chapter 15, "Technohorror.")

Erskine, Barbara.

Lady of Hay. *New York: Delacorte Press, 1986. 540p.* Journalist Joanna Clifford is doing a story about people being hypnotized into remembering their past lives. As part of her research, she herself undergoes the process, only to discover that in the twelfth century, she was Lady Matilda deBarose, coveted and later persecuted by the evil King John. The true horror begins when Jo finds that her past insists on invading her present, and that Matilda can possess her body at will and force Jo to re-experience this past life. Jo discovers that the past isn't something gone and forgotten, but a force that shapes our present lives. Similar titles: *Houses of Stone*, Barbara Michaels; *Copper Moon*, Roxanne Conrad; *The Hollow Man*, Dan Simmons.

> *Gothic Romance • London, England • Reincarnation • Wales • Writer as Character*

Hamilton, Laurell K.

Burnt Offerings. *New York: Ace Books, 1998. 400p.* (See chapter 19, "Comic Horror.")

Hynd, Noel.

Rage of Spirits. *New York: Pinnacle, 1998. 416p.* In the year 2003, a Reaganesque president of the United States slips into a coma at the will of Carl Einhorn, a cross between the Unabomber and Hannibal Lecter. Meanwhile, the vice president, a firm believer in astrology, fears that an old curse placed on him may affect his move into the White House.

> *Astrology • Curse • Government Officials • Science Fiction • Washington, D.C.*

Kahn, James.

Poltergeist II. *New York: Ballantine, 1986. 179p.* (See chapter 7, "Ghosts and Haunted Houses.")

King, Stephen.

Carrie. *New York: Signet Books, 1975. 245p.* Carrie White is abused by her fanatically religious mother and by her peers at school. She is the perpetual foulup. But Carrie also has telekinetic powers that have lain dormant since she was five years old. Now, with the traumatic onset of her first menstrual period, Carrie's telekinetic powers resurface, and she uses them in self-defense against her tormentors. The novel is a combination of multiple first-person narratives, which are collected in several fictional critical works that recount Carrie's amazing powers. Made into a movie of the same name by Brian dePalma. Similar titles: *Second Child* and *The Unwanted*, John Saul; *The Night of the Moonbow*, Thomas Tryon; *Dragon Tears*, Dean Koontz.

> *Child Abuse • Documentary Techniques • High School • Maine • Religion— Christianity—Protestantism • Revenge*

Firestarter. *New York: New American Library, 1981. 404p.* An English instructor and his wife volunteer for a government experiment that involves a classified hallucinogen. Afterward, they find they have special telepathic powers and, later, that their daughter has telekinetic abilities. When the instructor begins to suspect that the government doctors are more dangerous than they look, all hell breaks loose. Similar titles: *Cold White Fury*, Beth Amos; *The Door to December*, Dean Koontz.

> *Experiments—Military • Mind Control • Parenting • Telepathy*

The Shining. *New York: Plume, 1977. 416p.* (See chapter 10, "Demonic Possession, Satanism, Black Magic, and Witches and Warlocks.")

Koontz, Dean.

The Door to December. *New York: Penguin, 1985. 510p.* When Laura answers her door one day, police officers tell her that her nine-year-old daughter, kidnapped by her father years before, has been located. As it turns out, nine-year-old Melanie has *not* been found, but the mutilated body of her father has been. When Melanie is finally located, Laura discovers that her daughter has been the guinea pig for sensory deprivation experiments—and that someone wants Melanie killed. Similar titles: *The Eyes of Darkness* and *Mr. Murder*, Dean Koontz; *Firestarter*, Stephen King.

> *Parenting • Weird Science*

Dragon Tears. *New York: Putnam, 1993. 377p.* A young man discovers that he can use his telekinetic/telepathic powers to become "a new God," and he takes it upon himself to "thin out the herd" of humanity by ridding it of its handicapped and destitute. Similar title: *Carrie*, Stephen King.

> *Drugs • Eugenics*

The Eyes of Darkness. *New York: Putnam-Berkley, 1981. 369p.* This early Koontz effort tells of a grieving mother who is haunted by her son's accidental death. A year after 12-year-old Danny was horribly mangled and killed in an accident, Tina Evans sees him in a car. And when strange things begin happening in Danny's old room, Tina is faced with the possibility that her son is still alive. Fast-paced and suspenseful. Similar titles: *The Door to December*, Dean Koontz; *A Small, Dark Place*, Martin Schenk.

> *Experiments—Military • Las Vegas, Nevada • Telepathy*

The Mask. *New York: Berkley, 1992. [First published in 1981.] 305p.* (See chapter 10, "Demonic Possession, Satanism, Black Magic, and Witches and Warlocks.")

Lumley, Brian.

Blood Brothers. *New York: Tor Books, 1992. 565p.* (See chapter 9, "Vampires and Werewolves.")

The Last Aerie. *New York: Tor Books, 1994. 479p.* (See chapter 9, "Vampires and Werewolves.")

Necroscope: The Lost Years, Vol. I, and **Necroscope: Resurgence: The Lost Years, Vol. II.** *New York: Doherty, 1995 and 1996. 593p. and 414p.* (See chapter 9, "Vampires and Werewolves.")

McCammon, Robert R.

Usher's Passing. *New York: Simon & Schuster, 1992. 407p.* The Usher family, made famous by Edgar Allan Poe, amassed its vast fortune by dealing in armaments, and this fortune has continued to multiply well into the twentieth century. But the Usher family has become wealthy not only because of its members' financial acumen, but also because of their natural telekinetic abilities. Now the Usher patriarch is dying, and his children are fighting over who will take over the family business and whether the Ushers should continue to profit from "blood money."

Alternative Literature • North Carolina • Revenge • Sibling Rivalry

Newman, Kim.

Jago. *New York: Carroll and Graf, 1991. 534p.* The tiny English village of Alder is dominated by a bizarre religious community known as the Agapemone. And now dreams—and nightmares—are beginning to come true, and at the heart of it all is the Reverend Anthony Jago, spiritual leader of the Agapemone, a man with unparalleled telepathic powers that can control collective reality. Newman's novel features a motley cast of characters described in highly literate prose. Similar titles: *Greely's Cove*, John Gideon; *Symphony*, Charles Grant; *Waking the Moon*, Elizabeth Hand.

Apocalypse • Cults • Dreams • England • Mind Control • Telepathy

Schenk, Martin.

A Small, Dark Place. *New York: Villard Books, 1997. 340p.* A young couple in Kansas runs into financial problems, so they decide to stage a false "child in the well" crisis with one of their children. The only problem is that another life-form lives in that well, and it alters their child drastically, giving the now angry girl supernatural powers. Original. Similar title: *The Eyes of Darkness*, Dean Koontz.

Kansas • Revenge

Simmons, Dan.

The Hollow Man. *New York: Bantam, 1992. 293p.* Jeremy Brenen is a telepathic sponge, whose wife acts as his filter for the thoughts of others. When she dies, he is overwhelmed by the flood of others' thoughts. So Jeremy tries to run away from his chaotic loneliness, but his travels across America only lead him to see life as more brutal and dark than ever. Can anything save him from his nightmare world? Told in both third- and first-person narratives. This is suspense at its best and horror on an individual scale. Similar titles: *Lady of Hay*, Barbara Erskine.

Scholars • Science Fiction • Telepathy

Siodmak, Curt.

Donovan's Brain. *New York: Carroll and Graf, 1985. [First published in 1942.] 160p.* (See chapter 15, "Technohorror.")

Wood, Bari.

The Basement. *New York: Avon, 1995. 336p.* (See chapter 7, "Ghosts and Haunted Houses.")

Film

Carrie. *Brian dePalma, dir. 1976. 97 minutes.* A faithful adaptation of Stephen King's first novel of the same name; stars Sissy Spacek, Piper Laurie, John Travolta, Amy Irving, Nancy Allen, and Betty Buckley. Carrie is made into a misfit by her fanatically fundamentalist mother and spends her young life as the butt of everyone's jokes in the small town of Chamberlain, Maine. Carrie's mother believes that sexual intercourse, even between married couples, is a sin, and that menstruation is God's sign that a woman has strayed from the path of righteousness, so she never speaks with her daughter about the facts of life. Thus, when 16-year-old Carrie begins her first period while showering with the other girls in the locker room, she believes that she is bleeding to death. When the other girls tease her about her ignorance, Carrie's telekinetic powers are reawakened, and her anger toward the peers who pick on her culminates in their destruction.

Child Abuse • Maine • Religion—Christianity—Protestantism • Revenge

Our Picks

June's Picks: *Lady of Hay,* Barbara Erskine (Delacorte Press); *Carrie,* Stephen King (Signet Books); *Jago,* Kim Newman (Carroll and Graf).

Tony's Picks: *Cabal,* Clive Barker (Poseidon); *Fragments,* James F. David (Tor Books); *Carrie,* Stephen King (Signet Books); *Dragon Tears,* Dean Koontz (Putnam); *Jago,* Kim Newman (Carroll and Graf).

Chapter 13

Small-Town Horror: Villages of the Damned

In our late twentieth-century world, chaos, ignorance, and superstition have allegedly been replaced by scientific knowledge and enlightenment. We place a higher value on human life than ever before, shunning cannibalism, torture, and (in some areas) even capital punishment. We know that disease is not an outward manifestation of sin, but something spread by viruses and bacteria, and we have found that many diseases can be cured or controlled by drugs. Or at least, this is the official story of the state of civilization. But civilization has not been an unqualified success. There exist, even in our country, isolated communities, and sometimes even more isolated individuals, that are untouched by twentieth-century values, technology, and rationalism. The Amish and the Mennonites scorn modernity, and often live without electricity or television or cars. Members of some religious sects refuse to seek medical care for sick children, believing that God alone can cure illness. There are several towns off southern interstates that people are advised to avoid because they are Klan strongholds and unwary travelers may fall victim to the peculiar brands of justice that prevail in these areas.

This chapter presents the type of horror, often referred to as small-town horror, that scares the reader with the realization that there are places where "normal" civilization does not rule; where anything, no matter how horrific, is possible. We have probably all experienced this fear at least once in our lives, as we traveled along deserted highways and the barren scenery is interrupted momentarily by a miniature town. In *Scarecrow*, Richie Tankersley Cusick relates one such tale, of a woman who takes a wrong turn down a deserted road and faces life-threatening consequences because of it.

The relative isolation of these places makes them a perfect setting for horrific events, which almost always occur (as slasher films teach us) in isolated areas or to isolated people. After all, the killing of wives and their replacement with robots, à la Ira Levin's *The Stepford Wives;* or the creation of zombies, as in Elizabeth Graves's *Black River*, could only happen in small, insulated communities, where truly "no one can hear you scream"—or, more specifically, where those who hear you scream have been in on the horror all along. This is the realization that ultimately dawns on the foolish police lieutenant in Robin Hardy's *The Wicker Man*: that no matter how civilized *his* society (the United Kingdom proper) may be, once he is on Summerisle, a pagan community in Scotland, he no longer makes the rules, but is at the mercy of the locals. In Elizabeth Massie's novel, *Sineater,* members of a rural Appalachian community punish those who would abolish their quaint custom of keeping one individual living on the fringes of their society for the purpose of taking into himself the sins of the dead. These tales also remind us of our own powerlessness within society, and of the dependence of the individual upon the others who make up a community or state. This stands in stark contrast to the American myth of "rugged individualism," which implies that any one person can stand alone against the forces of conformity, even when those forces are evil.

Like antiquarian horror, small-town horror reminds readers that sometimes it is best not to snoop around too much, lest something unspeakable be turned up. The fear of town secrets is as old as the idea of towns themselves; the proverbial skeleton in the closet is almost never as dangerous as the closet's owner who does not want the secret to be found. The quintessential example of this subgenre is Thomas Tryon's *Harvest Home*, in which a "citified" family stumbles into a New England town where sacrifices are still made to Dionysus. In fact, most horror tales of this type, such as Tryon's *Harvest Home* or T. E. D. Klein's *The Ceremonies*, take place in small New England towns that are isolated and therefore outside of the laws of order. Phil Rickman's *Candlenight*, set in Wales, is a recent example of small-town horror. In Rickman's tale, the conquering English still have not succeeded in trampling Welsh nationalism or the old Celtic deities.

Of course, sometimes even going home again can be horrific, if home happens to be an isolated community with dark secrets. We see this in Douglas Clegg's *The Children's Hour*, a novel in which a writer returns to his home in West Virginia (a state known for its isolation from the outside world) to discover an overwhelming evil that he could not understand as a child.

Novels in this chapter include Elizabeth Graves's *Black River*, a tale of grieving, voodoo, and evil; Bentley Little's *The Mailman*, a novel that explores the power the Postal Service holds over ordinary humans; Phil Rickman's *Candlenight*, which relates the story of a mysterious Welsh village where few strangers are welcome; and Thomas Tryon's *The Other*, perhaps the best evil-twin novel ever penned. Fine exemplars of the small-town horror subgenre include Tryon's haunting study of a New England village with a dark secret, *Harvest Home*; and Stephen King's recent best-seller concerned with traveling through the Nevada desert, *Desperation*.

Appeals: Identifiable Settings; Plays on Sense of Helplessness in New Environment; Tendency for Nonformulaic Endings (Hero Does Not Always Win); Universal Fear of Isolation; Universal, "Real" Fear That All Have Felt; "Us Against the World" Theme

Bachman, Richard [pseud. of Stephen King].

The Regulators. *New York: Dutton, 1996. 466p.* An Ohio suburb finds itself being dragged into a twisted and murderous version of reality, thanks to the visions of an eight-year-old autistic boy and a van full of maniacs.

Ohio • Savant Syndrome • Suburbia

Billings, Andrew.

Tainted Blood. *New York: Jove Books, 1997. 535p.* Widower Peter Cochran promised his wife on her deathbed that he would never have anything to do with her parents, but he has fallen on hard times and could use a hand. Little does he know that moving what remains of his family to the small Oregon home town of his late wife will put all their lives in jeopardy. Similar title: *Lost Boys*, Orson Scott Card.

Child Molesters • Oregon • Secret Sin • Serial Killers

Brite, Poppy Z.

Drawing Blood. *New York: Dell, 1994. 403p.* (See chapter 18, "Splatterpunk.")

Card, Orson Scott.

Lost Boys. *New York: HarperCollins, 1992. 528p.* (See chapter 7, "Ghosts and Haunted Houses.")

Chadbourn, Mark.

The Eternal. *London: Victor Gollancz, 1996. 381p.* (See chapter 10, "Demonic Possession, Satanism, Black Magic, and Witches and Warlocks.")

Clegg, Douglas.

The Children's Hour. *New York: Dell, 1995. 383p.* A writer takes his wife and children to his home town in West Virginia to visit his dying mother. While there, he begins hearing voices and unearths a horrifying evil that the town has kept secret for decades. Descriptive prose, but suspenseful as well. Similar titles: *Greely's Cove*, John Gideon; *Thunder Road*, Chris Curry; *The Devil's Churn*, Kristin Kathryn Rusch.

Demons • Grieving • Secret Sin • West Virginia • Writer as Character

The Halloween Man. *New York: Leisure Books, 1998. 360p.* Stony Crawford accidentally let an evil force loose in Stonehaven, a small town with many dark secrets. Now, as an adult, Crawford is beginning to realize his heritage and his relationship to the Halloween Man. Similar title: *The M. D.*, Thomas M. Disch.

Childhood

Cody, Jack.

The Off Season. *New York: St. Martin's Press, 1995. 352p.* (See chapter 19, "Comic Horror.")

Conrad, Roxanne.

Copper Moon. *New York: Onyx, 1997. 348p.* (See chapter 17, "Psychological Horror.")

Cooke, John Peyton.

Haven: A Novel of Anxiety. *New York: Mysterious Press, 1996. 456p.* A young doctor fresh out of medical school takes a job in a small Idaho town to pay off grad school debts, and finds herself faced with dead bodies and eerie neighbors. Heavy on atmosphere. Similar title: *The Neighborhood*, S. K. Epperson.

Idaho • Journalist as Character • Medical Horror • Secret Sin

Crowther, Peter, and James Lovegrove.

Escardy Gap. *New York: Tor Books, 1996. 500p.* (See chapter 17, "Psychological Horror.")

Curry, Chris.

Thunder Road. *New York: Pocket Books, 1995. 499p.* A small-town police chief and a local cowboy must join forces to fight an unseen evil entity before the town of Madelyn is engulfed by it. Emphasis is on plot. Similar titles: *The Children's Hour*, Douglas Clegg; *Greely's Cove*, John Gideon; *The Devil's Churn*, Kristin Kathryn Rusch.

Apocalypse • Police Officer as Character • Religion—Christianity

Cusick, Richie Tankersley.

Scarecrow. *New York: Pocket Books, 1990. 280p.* A young woman gets into an accident while traveling, and finds herself held prisoner on an isolated farm owned by a quaint, rural family. She discovers that their old-fashioned beliefs go back to some dark practices. Similar titles: *Harvest Home*, Thomas Tryon; *Cat Magic*, Jonathan Barry with Whitley Strieber; *The Maddening*, Andrew Neiderman.

Religion—Paganism

Epperson, S. K.

Green Lake. *New York: Fine Books, 1996. 263p.* A widow moves into her sister's rural cabin in Kansas and finds herself in a strange neighborhood of molesters, kidnappers, blackmailers, and other grotesques. Humorous, with emphasis on characterization and plot twists. Similar title: *The Neighborhood*, S. K. Epperson.

Child Molesters • Kansas • Native American Characters

Farris, John.

Sacrifice. *New York: Tor Books, 1994. 320p.* (See chapter 11, "Mythological Monsters and 'The Old Ones.' ")

Garfield, Henry.

Room 13. *New York: St. Martin's Press, 1997. 309p.* (See chapter 7, "Ghosts and Haunted Houses.")

Gideon, John.

Golden Eyes. *New York: Berkley, 1994. 457p.* (See chapter 9, "Vampires and Werewolves.")

Greely's Cove. *New York: Berkley, 1991. 422p.* (See chapter 11, "Mythological Monsters and 'The Old Ones.' ")

Goingback, Owl.

Crota. *New York: Donald I. Fine, 1996. 292p.* (See chapter 11, "Mythological Monsters and 'The Old Ones.' ")

Gorman, Edward.

Black River Falls. *New York: Leisure Books, 1997. 352p.* The boy everyone picks on finds himself in a strange predicament when he vows to protect a young, beautiful girl. But then one day he learns of a dark secret that will change his home town forever.

High School • Secret Sin

Grant, Charles.

Symphony. *New York: Tor Books, 1997. 332p.* (See chapter 11, "Mythological Monsters and 'The Old Ones.' ")

Graves, Elizabeth.

Black River. *New York: Berkley, 1992. 239p.* After her husband's death, Kay Abbott and her daughter Chloe move to Abaton, a small town in the Florida panhandle. There, in the swamplike Black River region, they find themselves confronted by the town's evil secrets, including the walking dead. Atmospheric, with attention paid to character, setting, and dialogue. Similar titles: *Nathaniel*, John Saul; *Harvest Home*, Thomas Tryon; *Dead Voices*, Abigail McDaniels; *The Devil's Churn*, Kristin Kathryn Rusch.

Florida • Grieving • Matriarchy • Parenting • Racism • Religion—Voodoo

Gray, Muriel.

Furnace. *New York: Doubleday, 1997. 360p.* (See chapter 10, "Demonic Possession, Satanism, Black Magic, and Witches and Warlocks.")

Hardy, Robin, and Anthony Shaffer.

The Wicker Man. *New York: Pocket Books, 1978. 239p.* Police officer Neil Howie receives an anonymous note reporting the disappearance of a young girl from the community of Summerisle, Scotland. What he discovers there are pagan fertility rituals and many deadly secrets. A masterpiece of a story that reads easily. Adapted from a film of the same name by Robin Hardy. Similar titles: *Harvest Home*, Thomas Tryon; *Waking the Moon*, Elizabeth Hand; *Bethany's Sin*, Robert R. McCammon.

Human Sacrifice • Police Officer as Character • Religion—Christianity— Protestantism • Religion—Paganism • Scotland

Harris, Allen Lee.

Let There Be Dark. *New York: Berkley, 1994. 345p.* (See chapter 8, "Golems, Mummies, and Reanimated Stalkers.")

Hawkes, Judith.

My Soul to Keep. *New York: Signet Books, 1997. 416p.* (See chapter 7, "Ghosts and Haunted Houses.")

Holder, Nancy, and Melanie Tem.

Witch-Light. *New York: Dell, 1996. 339p.* (See chapter 10, "Demonic Possession, Satanism, Black Magic, and Witches and Warlocks.")

Jackson, Shirley.

The Lottery and Other Stories. *New York: Farrar, Straus & Giroux, 1982. 306p.* (See chapter 6, "Collections by Individual Authors.")

Johnstone, William W.

Rockabilly Hell. *New York: Kensington, 1995. 302p.* (See chapter 11, "Mythological Monsters and 'The Old Ones.' ")

Rockabilly Limbo. *New York: Kensington, 1996. 302p.* (See chapter 11, "Mythological Monsters and 'The Old Ones.' ")

Kimball, Michael.

Undone. *New York: Avon, 1996. 416p.* (See chapter 17, "Psychological Horror.")

King, Stephen.

Carrie. *New York: Signet Books, 1972. 245p.* (See chapter 12, "Telekinesis and Hypnosis.")

The Dead Zone. *New York: Viking, 1979. 426p.* When a small-town schoolteacher emerges from a lengthy coma, he finds that he is able to see into the future. Now he must stop a charismatic political candidate, who will ultimately destroy the world, from winning public office. Made into a film of the same name starring Christopher Walken.

Castle Rock, Maine • Government Officials • Precognition • Teacher as Character

Desperation. *New York: Viking, 1996. 690p.* Companion novel to the Richard Bachman work, *The Regulators,* in which burnt-out novelist John Marinville has a run-in with the law while traveling with his family to Nevada. But this is no ordinary incident of police brutality—the sheriff who lies in wait on Route 50 is actually a shapeshifting alien. Similar titles: *The One Safe Place* and *The Last Voice They Hear*, Ramsey Campbell.

Alcoholism • God—Christian God (character) • Nevada • Police Brutality • Shapeshifters

It. *New York: Viking, 1986. 1,138p.* (See chapter 17, "Psychological Horror.")

Needful Things. *New York: Penguin, 1991. 690p.* (See chapter 11, "Mythological Monsters and 'The Old Ones.' ")

Salem's Lot. *Garden City, N.J.: Doubleday, 1975. 439p.* (See chapter 9, "Vampires and Werewolves.")

The Tommyknockers. *New York: Signet Books, 1988. 747p.* (See chapter 10, "Demonic Possession, Satanism, Black Magic, and Witches and Warlocks.")

Klein, T. E. D.

The Ceremonies. *New York: Viking, 1984. 502p.* (See chapter 11, "Mythological Monsters and 'The Old Ones.' ")

Koontz, Dean.

Midnight. *New York: Putnam, 1989. 383p.* (See chapter 15, "Technohorror.")

Night Chills. *New York: Berkley, 1983, © 1976. 367p.* (See chapter 15, "Technohorror.")

Phantoms. *New York: Putnam, 1983. 352p.* (See chapter 11, "Mythological Monsters and 'The Old Ones.' ")

Lansdale, Joe R.

The Nightrunners. *New York: Carroll and Graf, 1995. [First published in 1987.] 241p.* (See chapter 14, "Maniacs and Sociopaths, or the Nuclear Family Explodes.")

Levin, Ira.

The Stepford Wives. *New York: Random House, 1972. 145p.* Joanna Eberhart and her husband travel to the idyllic town of Stepford, where she notices that the women are a bit too enthusiastic about homemaking and being perfect. Little does she realize that there is a dark reason for their behavior. Made into a classic TV movie by the same name. Similar titles: *The Store*, Bentley Little; *Harvest Home*, Thomas Tryon.

Feminism • Marriage • Replicants • Suburbia

Ligotti, Thomas.

Grimscribe: His Lives and Works. *New York: Carroll and Graf, 1991. 214p.* (See chapter 17, "Psychological Horror.")

Little, Bentley.

The Mailman. *New York: Penguin, 1991. 320p.* The mailman of a small, lazy town commits suicide, and his replacement is pure evil. At first, people receive only good news in the mail, but later everyone in town gets threatening letters, bad news, and gory photos of mutilated bodies. Can the mailman be stopped before he drives everyone to the brink of insanity? Original and clever, a hard book to put down. Similar titles: *The Ignored*, *The Store*, and *University*, Bentley Little.

Child Molesters • Demons

The Store. *New York: Signet Books, 1998. 431p.* (See chapter 11, "Mythological Monsters and 'The Old Ones.' ")

Martindale, T. Chris.

Nightblood. *New York: Warner Books, 1990. 322p.* (See chapter 9, "Vampires and Werewolves.")

Massie, Elizabeth.

Sineater. *New York: Leisure Books, 1998. 396p.* (See chapter 14, "Maniacs and Sociopaths, or the Nuclear Family Explodes.")

McCammon, Robert R.

Bethany's Sin. *New York: Pocket Books, 1980. 344p.* (See chapter 11, "Mythological Monsters and 'The Old Ones.' ")

Stinger. *New York: Pocket Books, 1988. 538p.* (See chapter 15, "Technohorror.")

McDaniels, Abigail.

Dead Voices. *New York: Kensington, 1994. 252p.* An idyllic Louisiana town seems like the right place to raise children, so Gail and Roger move to New Falls Church near Lake Boudreaux. Little do they know that an evil creature lurks in the lake—and it can summon ghostly voices of the dead. Similar titles: *Black River*, Elizabeth Graves; *Water Rites*, Guy N. Smith.

Demons • Louisiana • Maritime Horror

Michaels, Barbara.

Witch. *New York: Berkley, 1973. 292p.* (See chapter 7, "Ghosts and Haunted Houses.")

Moloney, Susan.

A Dry Spell. *New York: Delacorte Press, 1997. 385p.* (See chapter 17, "Psychological Horror.")

Morrel, David.

The Totem. *New York: Warner Books, 1995. 365p.* In the small rural area of Potters Field, Wyoming, strange and deadly occurrences suggest the awakening of an evil presence that threatens to bring about the end of the town. First, cattle are mutilated; then people are found without faces. Can the local police chief stop the slaughter? Similar title: *Trickster*, Muriel Gray.

> *Animals Run Rampant • Wyoming*

Morris, Mark.

The Immaculate. *Clarkston, Ga.: White Wolf, 1992. 411p.* (See chapter 17, "Psychological Horror.")

Neiderman, Andrew.

The Maddening. *New York: Berkley, 1987. 312p.* When Stacey Oberman turned off the main highway, she never realized the danger she and her young daughter were in. Before she can react, she is kidnapped and locked away in a room by a backwoods couple who need a young child—her child. Similar title: *Rosemary's Baby*, Ira Levin.

> *Grieving*

Palmer, Michael.

Critical Judgment. *New York: Bantam, 1996. 450p.* (See chapter 15, "Technohorror.")

Peretti, Frank.

The Oath: A Novel. *Dallas, Tex.: Word Books, 1995. 549p.* (See chapter 11, "Mythological Monsters and 'The Old Ones.' ")

Prill, David.

Serial Killer Days. *New York: St. Martin's Press, 1996. 208p.* (See chapter 19, "Comic Horror.")

The Unnatural. *New York: St. Martin's Press, 1996. 237p.* (See chapter 19, "Comic Horror.")

Rickman, Phil.

Candlenight. *New York: Berkley, 1995. 463p.* Unlike other parts of Wales, the ancient village of Y Groes has resisted outsiders and outside influences and stuck to its traditions. Outsiders stupid enough to try to make a home in Y Groes are killed; the descendants of its people are lured back to the village, and kept there by force if necessary. Similar titles: *Greely's Cove*, John Gideon; *Harvest Home*, Thomas Tryon.

> *Religion—Paganism • Wales*

Curfew. *New York: Berkley, 1994. 625p.* (See chapter 10, "Demonic Possession, Satanism, Black Magic, and Witches and Warlocks.")

Rusch, Kristin Kathryn.

The Devil's Churn. *New York: Dell, 1996. 320p.* A young man shows up in the yard of an aging woman, and she recognizes him as her childhood sweetheart—who was killed 50 years earlier during a coastal storm. Young Spence Chadwich's body was never found, so the stranger could be him, yet he has not aged in 50 years. What the town of Dory Cove does not realize is that dark forces are at work, and Spence's appearance is only the beginning. Similar titles: *Ghost Story*, Peter Straub; *The Children's Hour*, Douglas Clegg; *Thunder Road*, Chris Curry; *Black River*, Elizabeth Graves.

> *Maritime Horror • Oregon • Secret Sin*

Russo, John A.

Return of the Living Dead. *Edmonton, Alberta: Commonwealth Publications, 1997. 184p.* (See chapter 15, "Technohorror.")

Saul, John.

The Blackstone Chronicles. *New York: Ballantine, 1997. 420p.* (See chapter 7, "Ghosts and Haunted Houses.")

Cry for the Strangers. *New York: Dell, 1979. 415p.* Eerie tale of a beach community haunted by a murderous evil presence that will not allow town visitors to live. Character- and atmosphere-oriented, and quite scary. Graphic at times. Similar titles: *Dead in the Water*, Nancy Holder; *The Night Boat*, Robert R. McCammon; *Dark Tide*, Elizabeth Forrest.

Maritime Horror • New England • Revenging Revenant • Secret Sin

The Unwanted. *New York: Bantam, 1987. 339p.* (See chapter 10, "Demonic Possession, Satanism, Black Magic, and Witches and Warlocks.")

Schmidt, Dan.

Silent Scream. *New York: Leisure Books, 1998. 368p.* (See chapter 14, "Maniacs and Sociopaths, or the Nuclear Family Explodes.")

Simmons, Dan.

Summer of Night. *New York: Putnam, 1991. 555p.* (See chapter 10, "Demonic Possession, Satanism, Black Magic, and Witches and Warlocks.")

Smith, Guy N.

Water Rites. *New York: Kensington, 1997. 256p.* The small town of Hapwas has a hidden deadly secret: something is alive in its reservoir. But when people begin dying mysteriously and children start to disappear, it becomes obvious that the barbed-wire fence around the reservoir cannot contain it. Similar title: *Dead Voices*, Abigail McDaniels.

Maritime Horror • Subterranean Monsters

Taylor, Bernard.

Evil Intent. *New York: Leisure Books, 1996. 351p.* (See chapter 10, "Demonic Possession, Satanism, Black Magic, and Witches and Warlocks.")

Tryon, Thomas.

Harvest Home. *New York: Knopf, 1973. 403p.* When Theodore, Beth, and Kate Constantine move to a small New England town called Cornwall Coombe, they think they have found paradise. However, Theodore soon begins to suspect that the townsfolk harbor dark secrets, which they would prefer he not find out. When he starts to lose his wife and child to the town doctor/matriarch, the Widow, Theodore realizes that he must dig up town skeletons (literally and figuratively) to save himself and his loved ones. A truly unique plotline, with lots of detection thrown in for suspense. Similar titles: *Waking the Moon*, Elizabeth Hand; *Bethany's Sin*, Robert R. McCammon; *Scarecrow*, Richie Tankersley Cusick; *Black River*, Elizabeth Graves; *The Wicker Man*, Robin Hardy and Anthony Shaffer; *Candlenight*, Phil Rickman; *The Stepford Wives*, Ira Levin.

Human Sacrifice • Matriarchy • New England • Religion—Paganism

The Other. *New York: Knopf, 1971. 280p.* (See chapter 14, "Maniacs and Sociopaths, or the Nuclear Family Explodes.")

Williamson, John N.

Spree. *New York: Leisure Books, 1998. 384p.* (See chapter 14, "Maniacs and Sociopaths, or the Nuclear Family Explodes.")

Wolf, Silver Raven.

Beneath a Mountain Moon. *St. Paul, Minn.: Llewellyn, 1995. 343p.* (See chapter 10, "Demonic Possession, Satanism, Black Magic, and Witches and Warlocks.")

Film

The Wicker Man. *Robin Hardy, dir. 1973. 84 minutes.* The people of Summerisle have returned to their ancient roots, and practice pagan fertility rites to ensure the success of their crops. But lately, the sacrifices made to the gods haven't been sufficient, as their crops are failing. The gods demand more. Sergeant Howie is sent from the mainland to investigate a missing girl who might be the next sacrifice to the gods. Stars Edward Woodward, Britt Ekland, and Christopher Lee.

> *Human Sacrifice • Police Officer as Character • Religion—Christianity—Protestantism • Religion—Paganism • Scotland*

Our Picks

June's Picks: *The Stepford Wives,* Ira Levin (Random House); *The Mailman,* Bentley Little (Penguin); *Candlenight,* Phil Rickman (Berkley); *Harvest Home,* Thomas Tryon (Knopf).

Tony's Picks: *Black River,* Elizabeth Graves (Berkley); *The Wicker Man,* Robin Hardy and Anthony Shaffer (Pocket Books); *The Stepford Wives,* Ira Levin (Random House); *The Mailman,* Bentley Little (Penguin); *Harvest Home,* Thomas Tryon (Knopf).

Chapter 14

Maniacs and Sociopaths, or the Nuclear Family Explodes: Monstrous Malcontents Bury the Hatchet

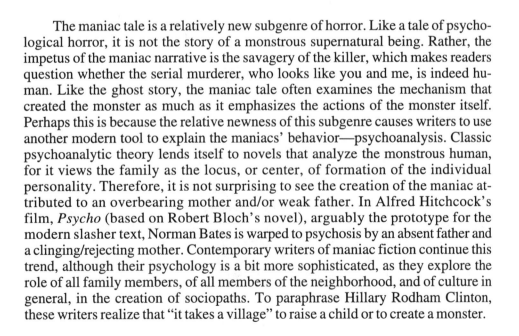

The maniac tale is a relatively new subgenre of horror. Like a tale of psychological horror, it is not the story of a monstrous supernatural being. Rather, the impetus of the maniac narrative is the savagery of the killer, which makes readers question whether the serial murderer, who looks like you and me, is indeed human. Like the ghost story, the maniac tale often examines the mechanism that created the monster as much as it emphasizes the actions of the monster itself. Perhaps this is because the relative newness of this subgenre causes writers to use another modern tool to explain the maniacs' behavior—psychoanalysis. Classic psychoanalytic theory lends itself to novels that analyze the monstrous human, for it views the family as the locus, or center, of formation of the individual personality. Therefore, it is not surprising to see the creation of the maniac attributed to an overbearing mother and/or weak father. In Alfred Hitchcock's film, *Psycho* (based on Robert Bloch's novel), arguably the prototype for the modern slasher text, Norman Bates is warped to psychosis by an absent father and a clinging/rejecting mother. Contemporary writers of maniac fiction continue this trend, although their psychology is a bit more sophisticated, as they explore the role of all family members, of all members of the neighborhood, and of culture in general, in the creation of sociopaths. To paraphrase Hillary Rodham Clinton, these writers realize that "it takes a village" to raise a child or to create a monster.

The nuclear family likewise is a relatively new phenomenon, which had its halcyon period in the post–World War II 1940s and in the "happy days" of the 1950s. The nuclear, non-extended family, isolated within its suburban ranch house and allegedly self-sufficient, was touted by psychologists as the norm, and it was therefore celebrated through the new medium of television, in 1950s situation comedies such as *Leave It to Beaver* and *The Donna Reed Show*. It was the Cold War era's answer to Communism (as a matter of fact, some housing developments, which originally planned on creating communal post-victory gardens, soon scrapped these plans as being too Red).

However, Father doesn't always know best, and Mother isn't always content to stay home and clean the house while wearing pearls and her best Sunday dress while little monsters continually tug at her skirts and demand attention. When problems arise, there's no one for Mom and Pop in distress to turn to in this supposedly self-sufficient family. The result of times when the stress of everyday life becomes too much is the production of seriously disturbed children, and perhaps maniacal parents. In Peter Straub's short story, "Blue Rose," one of the purest examples of the subgenre, the dysfunctional Beevers family produces a charming, psychotic son able to hypnotize people into killing themselves or others. Deeply racist neighbors who share their worldview with the young Beevers boy are also culpable for his creation: Harry Beevers grows up to lead troops who gun down children in Vietnam. Young girls are not immune to these forces either. In Stephen King's *Carrie*, the main character's isolation in her own nuclear family (herself, her fundamentalist mother, her dead paternal father, and her Heavenly Father as invoked by her abusive mother) allows her to fester into an angry young woman who will literally cause the town to explode with her telekinetic powers. Furthermore, in this tale, the townspeople's isolation in their own nuclear families prevents them from rescuing Carrie from her abusive situation. Like Straub's and King's exemplary texts, works in this subgenre acknowledge that every family unit has a dark side that surfaces only behind closed doors, and that children from these types of families will grow up, leave home, and turn order into chaos.

The subgenre has evolved greatly in a short period of time, with a recent trend toward creation of the abnormal personality as an organic phenomenon. In other words, maniacs, like paranoid schizophrenics, are born, not made—although a dysfunctional family can exacerbate the situation. It's the old nature-versus-nurture question made into a horror text. Poppy Z. Brite's novel, *Exquisite Corpse,* centers on Andrew Compton and Jay Byrne, serial killers modeled loosely after Jeffrey Dahmer, but their childhoods are never explored. They simply exist as almost supernaturally maniacal beings, rather like Hannibal Lecter in *The Silence of the Lambs*. In *Twice Burned,* Kit Craig hints that the ability of Jane and Emily Archer to charm and kill is inherited, along with the same gene that made them twins. Their mother, also a twin, exhibited similar behavior.

A final spin on the human monster is the justifiable maniac, exemplified in Billie Sue Mosiman's novel, *Widow*. Model wife and mother Kay Mandal's abusive husband comes home one day and acknowledges that he is a monster, at least psychologically so. Fearing that his sons will grow up to be just like their father, he kills his toddler sons and then himself. Now Kay's new mission in life is to seduce and kill abusive men. She must be stopped because what she does is *legally* wrong, not *morally* wrong.

This chapter includes the most famous slasher novels, such as Robert Bloch's *American Gothic* and *Psycho*, Thomas Harris's *Red Dragon* and *The Silence of the Lambs*, Stephen King's *Misery*, and various works by Dean Koontz, who is perhaps the master of this subgenre. In addition, it annotates more recent works in this subgenre, including Ramsey Campbell's *The Count of Eleven* and the masterful *The One Safe Place,* Kit Craig's *Twice Burned*, Stephen Dobyns's *The Church of Dead Girls*, Bentley Little's *The Ignored*, Billie Sue Mosiman's *Widow*, Joyce Carol Oates's highly disturbing *Zombie*, and various tales from Michael Slade. Several works, such as Poppy Z. Brite's *Exquisite Corpse*, Bret Easton Ellis's *American Psycho*, and Michael Slade's Headhunter series, go just enough over the line to be included in chapter 18 rather than this chapter.

Appeals: Gore; Human Curiosity Concerning the Psychology of Serial Killers; Monsters Are Human, Not Supernatural; More in Line with "Real" Fears (Random Violence as Opposed to Supernatural Visitations); Parallels the Historical American Fascination with Murderers

Anscombe, Roderick.

The Secret Life of Laszlo, Count Dracula. *New York: Hyperion, 1994. 409p.* (See chapter 9, "Vampires and Werewolves.")

Ball, Donna.

Dark Angel. *New York: Signet Books, 1998. 368p.* Ellen Cox, a schoolteacher in Virginia, is saved from a life-threatening accident, but the publicity attending it leads her to find out that she is not who she thought she was. In the meantime, her dreams of serial murder continue to come true. Similar titles: *The Dead Zone*, Stephen King; *Sick*, Jay R. Bonansigna; *Retribution*, Elizabeth Forrest; *Bloody Valentine*, Stephen George; *The Face of Fear*, Dean Koontz.

Dreams • Mistaken Identity • Serial Killers • Teacher as Character • Virginia

Barker, Clive.

Cabal. *New York: Poseidon, 1988. 377p.* (See chapter 12, "Telekinesis and Hypnosis.")

The Damnation Game. *New York: Putnam, 1987. 433p.* (See chapter 10, "Demonic Possession, Satanism, Black Magic, and Witches and Warlocks.")

Beath, Warren Newton.

Bloodletter. *New York: Tor Books, 1994. 288p.* Hack vampire writer Stephen Albright is having trouble handling his fame and fortune, so he begins seeing psychiatrist Eva LaPort. While in sessions, Albright shows obsession with the actions of a serial killer, leading LaPort to believe that Albright may be the "bloodletter." Interesting psychological study that centers on characterization. Similar titles: *Psycho House*, Robert Bloch; *Evil Reincarnate*, Leigh Clark.

Alter Ego • California • Horror Movie Industry • Psychiatrist as Character • Serial Killers • Writer as Character

Billings, Andrew.

Tainted Blood. *New York: Jove Books, 1997. 535p.* (See chapter 13, "Small-Town Horror.")

Bloch, Robert.

American Gothic. *New York: Simon & Schuster, 1974. 222p.* Based on historical accounts of a real-life serial killer. *American Gothic* tells how Dr. Gordon G. Gregg lured victims into his castlelike home and then tortured and murdered them, all during the Chicago World's Fair of 1892. Similar titles: *Exquisite Corpse*, Poppy Z. Brite; *Psycho*, Robert Bloch.

> *Chicago, Illinois • History, Use of • Serial Killers • United States—Nineteenth-Century*

The Horror Writers Association Presents Robert Bloch's Psychos. *New York: Pocket Books, 1998. 373p.* (See chapter 5, "Anthologies and Collections by Multiple Authors.")

Lori. *New York: Tor Books, 1989. 282p.* (See chapter 7, "Ghosts and Haunted Houses.")

Midnight Pleasures. *New York: Doubleday, 1987. 177p.* (See chapter 6, "Collections by Individual Authors.")

Psycho. *New York, Tor Books, 1989. 223p.* Norman Bates, a mentally ill loner whose condition is exacerbated by a domineering mother, kills "loose" young women who arouse him. But now Norman has made the mistake of murdering a woman who disappeared with $40,000 of her boss's money, so detectives show up at the Bates Motel to investigate. Told through several first-person narratives. Made into a classic film by Alfred Hitchcock. Similar titles: *Exquisite Corpse*, Poppy Z. Brite; *American Psycho*, Bret Easton Ellis; *Silence of the Lambs*, Thomas Harris; *Zombie*, Joyce Carol Oates; *Impulse*, Rick Hautala; *American Gothic*, Robert Bloch; *The Face That Must Die*, Ramsey Campbell; *Billy*, Whitley Strieber.

> *Matricide/Patricide • Schizophrenia/Multiple Personality Disorder • Slasher*

Psycho House. *New York: Tor Books, 1990. 216p. Psycho House* takes place after Norman Bates is dead and gone, but his home town of Fairvale is still haunted by his crimes. The economically depressed town looks forward to the opening of the new Bates Motel, a tourist attraction that includes knife-wielding automata of Norman and Mother. Then the murders begin again. Similar titles: *Bloodletter*, Warren Newton Beath; *Serial Killer Days*, David Prill.

> *Police Officer as Character • Slasher • Writer as Character*

Bonansigna, Jay.

Head Case. *New York: Simon & Schuster, 1998. 318p.* (See chapter 17, "Psychological Horror.")

Sick. *New York: Warner Books, 1995. 327p.* A disillusioned stripper develops migraines that cause her to black out; when she comes to, someone she knows has been killed. Could it be that her psychiatrist's unconventional treatment technique is turning her into a serial killer? An easy read. Similar titles: *Dark Angel*, Donna Ball; *The Face of Fear*, Dean Koontz; *Cabal*, Clive Barker.

> *Amnesia • Psychiatrist as Character • Serial Killers*

Bowker, David.

The Death Prayer. *Clarkston, Ga.: White Wolf, 1995. 215p.* An evil magician has learned the secret of the death prayer, an untraceable weapon for murder. Now Vernon Lavergne, a York police officer with psychic abilities, must figure out how to stop it. Similar titles: *Evil Intent*, Bernard Taylor; *Furnace*, Muriel Gray; *The Count of Eleven*, Ramsey Campbell.

> *England • Magic • Parapsychology • Police Officer as Character*

Brite, Poppy Z.

The Crow: The Lazarus Heart. *New York: Harper Prism, 1998. 256p.* (See chapter 18, "Splatterpunk.")

Exquisite Corpse. *New York: Scribner's, 1996. 240p.* (See chapter 18, "Splatterpunk.")

Campbell, Ramsey.

The Count of Eleven. *New York: Tor Books, 1992. 310p.* Family man Jack Orchard has a run of bad luck that threatens to tear apart his life. When he finds a discarded chain letter, he decides that it must be the cause of his misfortune; to make amends, he quickly follows the instructions on the letter, which require that he get it out to 13 other people without divulging the list. Whenever anyone stands between Jack and his task, however, he goes over the edge. Emphasis is on characterization and psychology. Similar titles: *Furnace*, Muriel Gray; *Evil Intent*, Bernard Taylor; *The Death Prayer*, David Bowker.

Numerology • Serial Killers

The Face That Must Die. *New York: Tor Books, 1979. 351p.* A young loner named Horridge is haunted by faces, by horrifying childhood emotional experiences, and by the voice of a serial killer named Craig. Sooner or later, "Horridge the Horror," as he was called by cruel children in his youth, is going to lose his sanity. Campbell's subtle treatment of a psychopathic killer. Well written. Similar titles: *Psycho*, Robert Bloch.

Gay/Lesbian/Bisexual Characters • Homoeroticism • Serial Killers • Twins

The Last Voice They Hear. *New York: Forge, 1998. 384p.* Television journalist Geoff Davenport is getting mysterious phone calls from his brother, who ran away from home when he was 18. For Geoff, these calls are disturbing, because a serial killer has been murdering happily married couples in the area and the brother claims to be the killer. Typical character and atmosphere tale by Campbell, the master of psychological horror. Similar titles: *Desperation*, Stephen King; *The Nightrunners*, Joe R. Lansdale; *The One Safe Place*, Ramsey Campbell.

Journalist as Character • London, England • Serial Killers • Sibling Rivalry

The One Safe Place. *New York: Tor Books, 1996. 401p.* The Travis family immigrates to England in search of a peaceful life, only to be stalked by the Fancys, a family of petty criminals, after Don Travis runs afoul of the Fancy patriarch during a minor traffic altercation. The Travises go to the proper authorities for help, but the police are unable to protect them in this supposedly nonviolent society that bans guns and violent films. The mundane is made newly frightening. Similar titles: *Desperation*, Stephen King; *The Nightrunners*, Joe R. Lansdale; *The Last Voice They Hear*, Ramsey Campbell.

England • Parenting • Revenge • Violence, Theories of

Card, Orson Scott.

Lost Boys. *New York: HarperCollins, 1992. 528p.* (See chapter 7, "Ghosts and Haunted Houses.")

Clark, Leigh.

Evil Reincarnate. *New York: Tor Books, 1994. 351p.* Connie Stallman shares a special relationship, so special that she has almost a telepathic link with the other person. The only problem is that Stallman is a psychiatrist, and the other person is one of her patients—a maniacal murderer/sex offender. Similar titles: *Bloodletter*, Warren Newton Beath; *Cabal*, Clive Barker.

Obsession • Psychiatrist as Character • Sex Crimes • Telepathy

Clements, Mark A.

Lorelei. *New York: Leisure Books, 1995. 298p.* (See chapter 11, "Mythological Monsters and 'The Old Ones.' ")

Collins, Max Allan.

Mommy. *New York: Leisure Books, 1997. 272p.* Whenever Jessica Ann wants something, the people who stand in her way seem to meet violent ends. Is it possible that her dear, sweet mother has something to do with it? Similar titles: *Evil Intent*, Bernard Taylor; *When Darkness Falls*, Sidney Williams.

Parenting • Revenge • Serial Killers

Conrad, Roxanne.

Copper Moon. *New York: Onyx, 1997. 348p.* (See chapter 17, "Psychological Horror.")

Courtney, Vincent.

Vampire Beat. *New York: Pinnacle, 1991. 302p.* (See chapter 9, "Vampires and Werewolves.")

Craig, Kit.

Gone. *New York: Berkley, 1994. 340p.* A year after the death of his father, 15-year-old Michael Hale wakes to find his mother missing. For one terrifying week, Michael, his older sister, and his toddler brother are home alone, praying for their mother's return while trying not to let the authorities discover their predicament, because they will just put the children in foster care and split the family up. When the Hale children receive an unsigned postcard in the mail, they know that their mother is alive and needs their help. Similar titles: *Nightmare*, S. K. Epperson; *The Funhouse*, Dean Koontz; *The Good Children*, Kate Wilhelm.

Childhood • Florida • Obsession

Twice Burned. *New York: Berkley, 1995. 343p.* Twin sisters Jane and Emily Archer shared a private world of their own making. They spoke a secret language that only they could understand. And now, after the death of their parents, their new guardian can't ignore the web of suspicion that surrounds them, or the mysterious deaths that accompany them. Craig demonstrates a thorough understanding of the intangible bonds between twins. Similar title: *Counterparts*, Nicholas Royle.

Florida • Matricide/Patricide • Twins

Daltow, Ellen, and Terri Windling (editors).

The Year's Best Fantasy and Horror: Ninth Annual Collection (1995). *New York: St. Martin's Press, 1996. 534p.* (See chapter 5, "Anthologies and Collections by Multiple Authors.")

The Year's Best Fantasy and Horror: Tenth Annual Collection (1996). *New York: St. Martin's Press, 1997. 534p.* (See chapter 5, "Anthologies and Collections by Multiple Authors.")

The Year's Best Fantasy and Horror: Eleventh Annual Collection (1997). *New York: St. Martin's Press, 1998. 502p.* (See chapter 5, "Anthologies and Collections by Multiple Authors.")

David, James F.

Fragments. *New York: Tor Books, 1997. 381p.* (See chapter 15, "Technohorror.")

Davis, Joy, and Don Davis.

Bring on the Night. *New York: Tor Books, 1993. 403p.* (See chapter 9, "Vampires and Werewolves.")

Deaver, Jeffrey.

A Maiden's Grave. *New York: Viking, 1995. 422p.* Psychological thriller about a hijacked busload of deaf girls, who are taken to a slaughterhouse and held for ransom by ruthless killers. Lots of plot twists and suspense. Similar title: *Mine*, Robert R. McCammon.

Deafness • Federal Bureau of Investigation • Kansas

Dobyns, Stephen.

The Church of Dead Girls. *New York: Henry Holt, 1997. 388p.* One by one, young teenage girls with long hair are disappearing without a trace in the normally quiet town of Aurelius, New York. As the narrator, a deeply closeted homosexual, relates the story of their disappearance and ultimate discovery, the reader becomes acquainted with the secret sins and longings of all in town. Similar titles: *American Psycho*, Bret Easton Ellis; *Shadow Man*, Dennis Etchison; *Jesus Saves*, Darcey Steinke.

Child Molesters • Gay/Lesbian/Bisexual Characters • Gothicism • Journalist as Character • New York State • Police Officer as Character • Serial Killers • Teacher as Character

Ellis, Bret Easton.

American Psycho. *New York: Random House, 1991. 399p.* (See chapter 18, "Splatterpunk.")

Elton, Ben.

Popcorn. *New York: St. Martin's Press, 1997. 304p.* A director of splatterpunk films is kidnapped by two "natural born killers" who want him to film their murderous rampages. Satirical look at Hollywood, television, and the mass media in general. Emphasis is on characterization and dialogue. Similar titles: *Serial Killer Days*, David Prill; *Red Dragon*, Thomas Harris; *Spree*, John N. Williamson.

Hollywood, California • Serial Killers • Television • Violence, Theories of

Elze, Winifred.

The Changeling Garden. *New York: St. Martin's Press, 1995. 282p.* (See chapter 16, "Rampant Animals and Other Eco-Monsters.")

Engstrom, Elizabeth.

Lizard Wine. *New York: Delta, 1995. 260p.* (See chapter 17, "Psychological Horror.")

Epperson, S. K.

The Neighborhood. *New York: Leisure Books, 1996. 304p.* A nurse moves into a new neighborhood to help take care of an AIDS patient. Little does she know that her neighbors include a Peeping Tom, a burglar, and a sadistic serial killer. Quirky and original; graphic. Similar titles: *Gone South*, Robert R. McCammon; *Haven: A Novel of Anxiety*, John Peyton Cooke; *Green Lake*, S. K. Epperson.

Nurse as Character • Serial Killers • Voyeurism • Weird Science

Nightmare. *New York: Leisure Books, 1993. 284p.* Patients are turning up hideously mutilated in a clinic for women suffering from multiple personality disorders. And the one person in a position to stop the horrors refuses. Similar titles: *Gone*, Kit Craig; *Nightwatcher*, Charles Wilson.

Kansas • Psychiatrist as Character • Psychosexual Horror • Schizophrenia/ Multiple Personality Disorder • Slasher

Etchison, Dennis.

Double Edge. *New York: Bantam, 1997. 272p.* (See chapter 7, "Ghosts and Haunted Houses.")

Shadow Man. *New York: Bantam, 1993. 354p.* When Martin discovers the mutilated body of a dead child near the beach, he is only beginning to scratch the surface of the evil that has forced all of the children indoors. Disturbed children throughout the Shadow Bay area tell of a Shadow Man, a faceless murderer who wants them all. Similar titles: *Sleep Walk* and *Darkness*, John Saul; *The Church of Dead Girls*, Stephen Dobyns.

Child Molesters • Horror Movie Industry

Faber, Bonnie.

Shadows. *New York: Zebra, 1995. 413p.* Homicide detective Amy Morgan is being hunted by a deranged but clever serial killer. In the harsh streets of New York City, the Phantom, as he calls himself, reigns supreme. Will Amy's criminological expertise allow her to catch him before he catches her? A surprise ending. Similar titles: *Cut Throat, Ripper, Ghoul, Primal Scream,* and *Evil Eye*, Michael Slade.

Feminism • New York City • Police Officer as Character • Serial Killers

Forrest, Elizabeth.

Bright Shadow. *New York: Daw Books, 1997. 464p.* After a botched raid on the New Hope Compound, run by a psychopathic religious cult leader, an FBI agent rescues some of the surviving children. However, when the children begin dying in mysterious accidents, it becomes apparent that there was more to the raid than met the eye. Action-oriented and suspenseful. Similar title: *Black Lightning*, John Saul.

Clergy as Character • Espionage • Federal Bureau of Investigation • Religion— Christianity—Protestantism

Death Watch. *New York: Daw Books, 1995. 460p.* (See chapter 15, "Technohorror.")

Killjoy. *New York: Daw Books, 1996. 458p.* (See chapter 17, "Psychological Horror.")

Retribution. *New York: Daw Books, 1998. 464p.* A young woman who paints the images she sees in her nightmares slowly figures out that her dreams and paintings either predict the future or display a dark past. Now the serial killer whose acts have become a subject for her art must hunt her down. Similar titles: *The Dead Zone*, Stephen King; *Sick*, Jay Bonansigna; *Dark Angel*, Donna Ball; *The Face of Fear*, Dean Koontz; *Doll's Eyes*, Bari Wood.

Artist as Character • Dreams • Serial Killers

Fowler, Christopher.

Red Brideby. *New York: Penguin, 1993. 424p.* A young family man is seduced by a glamorous model. When he leaves his wife for her, he finds himself caught in a web of gruesome murder and satanic rituals. Atmospheric and suspenseful. Similar title: *The Wicker Man*, Robin Hardy and Anthony Shaffer.

England • Horror Movie Industry • Human Sacrifice • Religion—Satanism

George, Stephen.

Bloody Valentine. *New York: Kensington, 1994. 413p.* An FBI study in which college students are asked to draw on their darkest dreams to create the ultimate serial killer goes too far, turning into a horrifying experiment. Similar titles: *The Dead Zone*, Stephen King; *Sick*, Jay Bonansigna; *Dark Angel*, Donna Ball; *Retribution*, Elizabeth Forrest; *The Face of Fear*, Dean Koontz.

Federal Bureau of Investigation • Serial Killers • Weird Science

Gorman, Edward.

Cold Blue Midnight. *New York: Leisure Books, 1998. 352p.* Photographer Jill Coffey has watched her husband's execution for several ax murders, but her terror does not end there. After his death, someone begins stalking Coffey. Is another ax murderer on the loose? Similar titles: *Into the Fire*, David Wiltse; *Black Lightning*, John Saul.

> *Photographer as Character • Serial Killers*

Goshgarian, Gary.

Rough Beast. *New York: Leisure Books, 1997. 304p.* (See chapter 15, "Techno-horror.")

Gottlieb, Sherry.

Love Bite. *New York: Warner Books, 1994. 277p.* (See chapter 9, "Vampires and Werewolves.")

Grant, Charles.

In the Mood. *New York: Forge, 1998. 304p.* (See chapter 11, "Mythological Monsters and 'The Old Ones.' ")

Symphony. *New York: Tor Books, 1997. 332p.* (See chapter 11, "Mythological Monsters and 'The Old Ones.' ")

Hamilton, Laurell K.

Bloody Bones. *New York: Penguin, 1996. 370p.* (See chapter 19, "Comic Horror.")

Guilty Pleasures. *New York: Penguin, 1993. 265p.* (See chapter 19, "Comic Horror.")

Harper, Andrew.

Bad Karma. *New York: Kensington, 1997. 230p.* A female psychopath in a southern California criminal justice hospital has convinced herself that her psychiatrist is her devoted lover, so she goes off the deep end when he takes a vacation to take his family to a rural cabin. Suspense-filled. Similar titles: *The End of Alice*, A. M. Homes; *Misery*, Stephen King; *The Cave*, Anne McLean Matthews.

> *California • Obsession • Psychiatrist as Character*

Harris, Thomas.

Black Sunday. *New York: Putnam, 1975. 318p.* A maniacal international terrorist hatches a plan to simultaneously kill 80,000 people at the Super Bowl. Can he be stopped before his death machine mutilates thousands? Made into a film of the same name.

> *Super Bowl • Terrorism*

Red Dragon. *Toronto: Academic Press, 1981. 348p.* A deranged maniac is slaughtering families while filming their murders, and FBI agent Will Graham must catch him before he can murder again. When Graham begins to use his ability to predict serial murderers' motives by thinking like them, he realizes a disturbing truth concerning how the killer chooses his victims. A truly scary read. Made into a TV movie, *Manhunter*. Similar title: *Popcorn*, Ben Elton.

> *Deformity • Federal Bureau of Investigation • Parapsychology • Psychosexual Horror • Serial Killers*

Ⓑ The Silence of the Lambs. *New York: St. Martin's Press, 1988. 338p.* Rookie FBI agent Clarice Starling, with the help of convicted serial killer Hannibal Lecter, must catch another serial killer, Buffalo Bill, who has kidnapped a senator's daughter. But to be an effective FBI agent, Starling must confront her own deepest fears as well. Harris's storytelling is literate and engaging. Made into a film of the same name. Winner of a Bram Stoker Award. Similar titles: *Exquisite Corpse*, Poppy Z. Brite; *Psycho*, Robert Bloch; *American Psycho*, Bret Easton Ellis; *Zombie*, Joyce Carol Oates; *Puppet Master*, Barry T. Hawkins; *Hungry Eyes*, Barry Hoffman; *A Room for the Dead*, Noel Hynd.

Baltimore, Maryland • Cannibalism • Federal Bureau of Investigation • Gay/Lesbian/Bisexual Characters • Psychiatrist as Character • Serial Killers

Hautala, Rick.

Impulse. *New York: Kensington, 1996. 444p.* Greg Newman, a video store clerk and serial killer, still lives with his mother, whom he resents. Now he has a new interest—stalking the cabin-bound family of the police detective who was his last victim. Graphic, with emphasis on the psychology of the madman. Similar titles: *Red Dragon*, Thomas Harris; *Psycho*, Robert Bloch.

Maine • Serial Killers

Hawkins, Barry T.

Puppet Master. *New York: Kensington, 1993. 351p.* A New York City detective must pit his experience against the evil mind of a maniacal puppeteer turned child killer. But can he distance himself enough from his own traumatic childhood before the Puppet Master uses it against him? Similar titles: *The Silence of the Lambs*, Thomas Harris; *Hungry Eyes*, Barry Hoffman.

Child Molesters • New York City • Police Officer as Character • Puppets

Heim, Scott.

In Awe. *New York: HarperCollins, 1997. 291p.* (See chapter 17, "Psychological Horror.")

Hoffman, Barry.

Hungry Eyes. *Springfield, Pa.: Gauntlet Press, 1997. 254p.* Ex–newspaper reporter Deidre Caffrey must match wits with a serial killer, in a tale that examines the bounds of journalistic responsibility. A thoughtful and unsettling novel. Similar titles: *The Silence of the Lambs*, Thomas Harris; *Puppet Master*, Barry T. Hawkins.

Journalist as Character • Serial Killers

Homes, A. M.

The End of Alice. *New York: Scribner's, 1996. 270p.* A child-killer in prison begins receiving letters from a 19-year-old girl, who admires him so much that she begins to emulate his tactics—with a 12-year-old boy. Emphasis is on characterization and psychology. Similar titles: *Bad Karma*, Andrew Harper; *Misery*, Stephen King.

Child Molesters • Prison

Huggins, James Byron.

Cain. *New York: Simon & Schuster, 1997. 400p.* (See chapter 11, "Mythological Monsters and 'The Old Ones.' ")

Hynd, Noel.

Rage of Spirits. *New York: Pinnacle, 1998. 416p.* (See chapter 12, "Telekinesis and Hypnosis.")

A Room for the Dead. *New York: Pinnacle, 1994. 412p.* (See chapter 17, "Psychological Horror.")

Jacob, Charlee.

The Symbiotic Fascination. *Orlando, Fla.: Necro Publications, 1997. 243p.* (See chapter 9, "Vampires and Werewolves.")

Jensen, Ruby Jean.

Death Stone. *New York: Kensington, 1989. 315p.* (See chapter 10, "Demonic Possession, Satanism, Black Magic, and Witches and Warlocks.")

Vampire Child. *New York: Zebra, 1990. 285p.* (See chapter 9, "Vampires and Werewolves.")

Kay, Susan.

Phantom. *New York: Dell, 1991. 532p.* A retelling of Gaston LeRoux's *Phantom of the Opera,* incorporating elements of Andrew Lloyd Webber's and Lon Chaney's versions of the "Opera Ghost." Kay's story begins with the Phantom Eric's birth as a profoundly deformed child who, in spite of his precociousness, is rejected by his mother and society in general. The adult Eric is loved by a few men who are awed by his architectural and musical accomplishments and capable of overlooking his deformity, and he is thus able to amass a fortune, but these things cannot quell his loneliness. Only the love of beautiful singer Christine Daae can soothe Eric, and even this is not enough. A literate and enjoyable retelling of LeRoux's classic tale. Similar titles: *Mina,* Marie Kiraly; *The Memoirs of Elizabeth Frankenstein,* Theodore Roszak; *Mary Reilly,* Valerie Martin.

> *Alternative Literature • Daae, Christine (character) • Deformity • Eroticism • France—Nineteenth-Century • Gothic Romance • Music—Opera • Phantom of the Opera (character)*

Ketchum, Jack.

Red. *London: Headline Books, 1996. 243p.* A general-store owner and widower is robbed by a group of teenage boys who also murder Red, his dog and only friend. Faced with a society that is indifferent to his loss, Avery Ludlow vows revenge against the boys. Emphasis is on character development. Similar titles: *The Funhouse,* Dean Koontz; *Widow,* Billie Sue Mosiman.

> *Dogs • Grieving • Revenge*

Kihn, Greg.

Shade of Pale. *New York: Forge, 1997. 256p.* (See chapter 7, "Ghosts and Haunted Houses.")

King, Stephen.

Carrie. *New York: Signet Books, 1975. 245p.* (See chapter 12, "Telekinesis and Hypnosis.")

Cujo. *New York: Plume, 1981. 277p.* (See chapter 16, "Rampant Animals and Other Eco-Monsters.")

Ⓑ**The Green Mile.** *New York: Signet Books, 1996. 592p.* Prison guard Paul Edgecombe is beginning to suspect that John Coffey, a death-row inmate at Cold Mountain Penitentiary, has special powers—almost godlike powers—over living creatures. Narrated by Edgecombe in pseudo-journalistic format. Winner of a Bram Stoker Award. Published serially in six parts: *The Two Dead Girls, The Mouse on the Mile, Caffey's Hands, The Bad Death of Edward Delacroix, Night Journey,* and *Coffey on the Mile.* Subtle in approach and ultimately life-affirming. A gentle read. Similar title: *The Blackstone Chronicles*, John Saul.

> *Diary Format • Immortality • Inmates—Death Row • Maine • Prison Guard as Character*

Ⓑ **Misery.** *New York: New American Library, 1988. 338p.* Best-selling bodice-ripper novelist Paul Sheldon meets his biggest fan, a nurse who tends to him after an automobile accident. But she is also his captor, keeping him prisoner in her isolated house, and now she wants Paul to write his greatest work—just for her. Made into a film of the same name, starring Kathy Bates, who received an Oscar for Best Actress (the first actor ever to receive an Oscar for a role in a horror film). Recipient of a Bram Stoker Award. Similar titles: *Bad Karma*, Andrew Harper; *The End of Alice*, A. M. Homes; *A Poison in the Blood*, Fay Zachary.

> *Colorado • Nurse as Character • Obsession • Writer as Character*

Rose Madder. *New York: Viking, 1995. 420p.* An abused woman who has endured all she can becomes "Rose Madder," an angry woman bent on revenge. Will her need for vengeance change her into a monster? Similar title: *Widow*, Billie Sue Mosiman.

> *Alter Ego • Domestic Violence • New England • Revenge*

The Shining. *New York: Plume, 1977. 416p.* (See chapter 10, "Demonic Possession, Satanism, Black Magic, and Witches and Warlocks.")

Six Stories. *Bangor, Maine: Philtrum Press, 1997. 197p.* (See chapter 6, "Collections by Individual Authors.")

Klavan, Andrew.

The Animal Hour. *New York: Pocket Books, 1993. 342p.* (See chapter 17, "Psychological Horror.")

Klein, T. E. D.

Dark Gods. *New York: Viking, 1986. 261p.* (See chapter 6, "Collections by Individual Authors.")

Koontz, Dean.

The Bad Place. *New York: Berkley, 1990. 417p.* Frank Pollard awakens one day to find himself on a deserted street, with no memory of how he got there. Soon his destiny will be tied to that of a computer hacker and a maniacal killer who believes he is a vampire. Suspenseful; related from multiple points of view. Similar title: *The Other*, Thomas Tryon.

> *Amnesia • Computer Hackers • Serial Killers*

Dragon Tears. *New York: Putnam, 1993. 377p.* (See chapter 12, "Telekinesis and Hypnosis.")

The Face of Fear. *New York: Berkley, 1985. 306p.* A clairvoyant in New York has visions of the killings committed by a deranged killer called "the butcher." His latest vision, that of his own death at the hands of the butcher, may come true if he cannot overcome his own fears. One of Koontz's early novels that culminates in a high-rise chase scene. Similar titles: *The Dead Zone*, Stephen King; *Sick*, Jay Bonansigna; *Retribution*, Elizabeth Forrest; *Bloody Valentine*, Stephen George.

> *New York City • Parapsychology • Police Officer as Character • Serial Killers*

The Funhouse: A Novel. *New York: Berkley, 1980. 333p.* A woman is hunted by her ex-husband, a handsome carnival barker who is out to avenge her killing of their son, whom she was convinced was evil. The ex gets his chance 25 years later, when he sets out to take her children away the way she took his. Similar titles: *Red*, Jack Ketchum; *Gone*, Kit Craig.

> *Revenge*

Hideaway. *New York: Putnam, 1992. 384p.* (See chapter 10, "Demonic Possession, Satanism, Black Magic, and Witches and Warlocks.")

Intensity. *New York: Ballantine, 1995. 436p.* Chyna Shepherd witnesses the brutal murders of a friend and his entire family, and decides to follow the killer to his isolated home to exact revenge. There's only one problem—the killer knows he's being followed. Suspenseful, a fan favorite.

> *Childhood • Revenge • Serial Killers*

Lightning. *New York: Berkley, 1989. 355p.* A mysterious, tall, blond man continually shows up at life-or-death events in Laura Shane's life—usually to save her. Unfortunately, so does a tall, dark-haired man with a facial scar, who tries to kill her. What secrets does she hold, and what is Laura Shane's alternative destiny? A marvelous study of time travel and alternate realities. Similar title: *The Devil on May Street*, Steve Harris.

> *Alternative History • Nazism • Time Travel*

The Servants of Twilight. *New York: Berkley, 1990. 327p.* A mother and her six-year-old son are getting in their car in a store parking lot when an old woman approaches them and insists that the boy is evil and must die. Thus begins this action/suspense novel about a religious cult whose leader has marked a child for death. Similar title: *The Other*, Thomas Tryon.

> *Cults • Religion—Christianity*

Shattered. *New York: Berkley, 1985. 289p.* Alex Doyle and his nephew-in-law, Colin, set out to travel across the country, from Philadelphia to San Francisco. On their way, they find themselves being followed by a white Automover van, whose owner has murderous intentions.

The Vision. *New York: Putnam, 1977. 224p.* A young woman is having visions of serial killings that actually happen. Can these visions somehow be connected to her childhood, which she cannot remember, and to her fear of sex? A rollercoaster ride of suspense. Similar title: *The Dead Zone*, Stephen King.

> *Genetics • Religion—Satanism*

The Voice of the Night. *New York: Berkley, 1980. 339p.* Colin and Roy are best friends, but they are complete opposites: Colin is introspective, compassionate, and sympathetic; Roy is extroverted, detached—and a sociopath. When Roy begins threatening Colin, and some of their mutual acquaintances are murdered, it becomes apparent that the friendship must be severed.

> *Alter Ego • Psychosexual Horror*

Watchers. *New York: Berkley, 1996. 464p.* (See chapter 15, "Technohorror.")

Lansdale, Joe R.

The Nightrunners. *New York: Carroll and Graf, 1995. [First published in 1987.] 241p.* After she is raped, Becky and her husband, Monty, try to get away from the city by renting a cabin in the Texas woods. However, a group of malicious teenagers who have it in for Becky decide to take revenge on the couple. Violent and suspenseful. Similar titles: *The One Safe Place* and *The Last Voice They Hear*, Ramsey Campbell; *The Cave*, Anne McLean Matthews.

> *Rape • Revenge • Texas*

Lee, Edward, and Elizabeth Steffen.

Portrait of the Psychopath as a Young Woman. *Orlando, Fla.: Necro Publications, 1998. 292p.* Gory, thought-provoking tale of two women who suffered sexual abuse as children: one a feminist advice columnist, the other a sociopath who tortures her victims. Filled with irony, witty dialogue, and stomach-churning violence.

> *Child Abuse • Child Molesters • Feminism • Gay/Lesbian/Bisexual Characters • Journalist as Character • Police Officer as Character • Serial Killers*

LeRoux, Gaston.

The Phantom of the Opera. *New York: Signet Books, 1987. [First published in 1911.] 264p.* The Opera Ghost in Paris, a man ill treated since childhood because of his deformed face, is well schooled in the arts of murder and torture. He becomes obsessed with the singer Christine Daae and takes her to his subterranean lair, where he tries to force her to become his bride. This is the original story that inspired four Hollywood films and Andrew Lloyd Webber's musical. Similar title: *Wuthering Heights*, Emily Brontë.

> *Daae, Christine (character) • Music—Opera • Paris, France • Phantom of the Opera (character)*

Levin, Ira.

Sliver. *New York: Bantam, 1991. 190p.* (See chapter 15, "Technohorror.")

Little, Bentley.

The Ignored. *New York: Signet Books, 1997. 429p.* Bob Jones is a normal guy who likes hit movies, popular music, food from chain restaurants, and sex with his wife in the missionary position. But Bob is Ignored. No one notices him: he has trouble getting served in restaurants, teachers and professors never interacted with him in school, and even his parents don't remember him. Then one day Bob discovers that he is not alone—there is a brotherhood of the Ignored out there, and they will stop at nothing to be recognized and remembered. Narrated solely from Bob's point of view. Similar tales: *The Store* and *The Mailman*, Bentley Little.

> *California • Domestic Terrorism • Fantasy • Parallel Universe • Revenge*

University. *New York: Signet Books, 1995. 416p.* (See chapter 18, "Splatterpunk.")

Lumley, Brian.

The Last Aerie. *New York: Tor Books, 1994. 479p.* (See chapter 9, "Vampires and Werewolves.")

Martin, David Lozell.

Tap, Tap: A Novel. *New York: Random House, 1995. 291p.* (See chapter 9, "Vampires and Werewolves.")

Martin, Valerie.

Mary Reilly. *New York: Doubleday, 1990. 262p.* Dr. Jekyll and Mr. Hyde is re-told through the eyes of Dr. Jekyll's literate and long-suffering housemaid, Mary Reilly. The story allows us backstairs into the shadowy Victorian world of devoted servants and the festering slums they have gone into service to escape. Similar titles: *Phantom*, Susan Kay; *The Memoirs of Elizabeth Frankenstein*, Theodore Roszak.

> *Alter Ego • Alternative Literature • Diary Format • Hyde, Edward (character) • Jekyll, Dr. Henry (character) • Mad Scientist • Victorian England*

Martini, Steven Paul.

The List. *New York: Putnam, 1997. 438p.* (See chapter 9, "Vampires and Werewolves.")

Massie, Elizabeth.

B Sineater. *New York: Leisure Books, 1998. 396p.* In Appalachia, the pious still depend on the sineater to cleanse the newly departed of sin so they can go to heaven. Traditionally, the sineater leads a solitary existence in the woods, approaching humanity only to partake of plates of food left on the chests of the dead. But the current sineater has broken with tradition, and has a wife and family, and this change has brought about a spate of disappearances and murders in this small mountain town. Massie's original southern gothic is a winner of the Bram Stoker Award. Similar title: *Madeline After the Fall of Usher*, Marie Kiraly.

> *Childhood • Cults • Religion—Christianity—Baptist • Virginia*

Matthews, Anne McLean.

The Cave. *New York: Warner Books, 1997. 288p.* Dr. Helen Myer, a noted psychiatrist specializing in serial killers, meets her match. Unfortunately, he's waiting for her in a backwoods New Hampshire cabin. Emphasis is on psychology rather than action, although an extended chase scene through a labyrinth of caves adds a nice touch. Similar titles: *Bad Karma*, Andrew Harper; *The Nightrunners*, Joe R. Lansdale; *Into the Fire*, David Wiltse.

> *New England • Psychiatrist as Character • Serial Killers*

McCabe, Patrick.

The Butcher Boy. *New York: Dell, 1994. 231p.* (See chapter 17, "Psychological Horror.")

McCammon, Robert R.

B Mine. *New York: Pocket Books, 1990. 487p.* Mary Terror is an ex–freedom fighter from the 1960s who carries a grudge and lots of weapons. She also steals infants, and brutally murders them when they do not please her. But now she has kidnapped Laura Clayborne's child, and Laura will stop at nothing to get him back. An unforgettable villain in a nonstop thriller. Winner of a Bram Stoker Award. Similar title: *A Maiden's Grave*, Jeffrey Deaver.

> *Federal Bureau of Investigation • Journalist as Character*

They Thirst. *New York: Pocket Books, 1981. 562p.* (See chapter 9, "Vampires and Werewolves.")

Usher's Passing. *New York: Simon & Schuster, 1992. 407p.* (See chapter 12, "Telekinesis and Hypnosis.")

McGrath, Patrick.

The Grotesque. *New York: Poseidon, 1989. 186p.* Sir Hugo Coal is uneasy with his butler, Fledge. As it turns out, he has good reason to be, for Fledge will stop at nothing to have Sir Hugo's life.

Mistaken Identity • Paleontology • Quadriplegic as Character

McNally, Clare.

Good Night, Sweet Angel. *New York: Tor Books, 1996. 344p.* (See chapter 7, "Ghosts and Haunted Houses.")

Miller, Rex. The Chaingang series.

Butcher. *New York: Pocket Books, 1994. 308p.* Chaingang, Miller's creation from *Slob*, *Chaingang*, and *Savant*, is on a mission. He wants to hunt down and torture the only man who is considered a superior torturer. Similar titles: *Exquisite Corpse*, Poppy Z. Brite; *The Bad Thing*, Michael O'Rourke.

Chaingang (character) • Nazism

Savant. *New York: Pocket Books, 1994. 277p.* An overgrown idiot savant specializes in brutal killings, becoming the quintessential murder machine. Similar title: *Mr. Murder*, Dean Koontz.

Chaingang (character) • Savant Syndrome • Serial Killers

Slob. *New York: New American Library, 1987. 301p.* Daniel Flowers Bunkowski, the perfect serial killer created by a dysfunctional childhood and service in the Vietnam War, a "killing machine" with an intellect off the charts, travels to Chicago after escaping the army. Written from varying points of view.

Chaingang (character) • Chicago • Experiments, Military • Serial Killers • War—Vietnam

Chaingang. *New York: Pocket Star Books, 1992. 310p.* Meet Chaingang, a 5-foot, 6-inch, 500-pound killing machine, with an intellect geared toward committing ritualistic murder. Can anyone stop him? The second in the Chaingang series, following *Slob*.

Chaingang (character) • Experiments, Military • Serial Killers • War—Vietnam

Moline, Karen.

Belladonna. New York: Warner Books, 1998. 480p. A young woman is locked away and used as a sex slave by the rich in the early twentieth century. But she breaks free after a decade, and now is obsessed with revenge. An erotic novel of terror and adventure, narrated by a eunuch twin. Similar title: *Ghoul*, Michael Slade.

Eroticism • Italy • New York City • Revenge • Sex Crimes

Moore, Susanna.

In the Cut. New York: Knopf, 1995. 180p. Frannie, a young writing instructor in Greenwich Village, becomes obsessed with the recent murders/mutilations of young women. She begins to suspect everyone of being the killer, even the detective working on the case. Will her involvement with the detective lead to her death? Similar title: *Headhunter*, Michael Slade.

Police Officer as Character • Serial Killers • Sex Crimes • Voyeurism

Mosiman, Billie Sue.

Widow. *New York: Berkley, 1995. 374p.* Kay Mandel's relationship with her abusive husband ended when he pulled out a revolver and shot their two children and himself. After her traumatic experience, this displaced homemaker decides that she will never be a victim again, and that her life's work is to cleanse the world of violent men who hurt women and children. Her new job as a stripper allows her to find and kill this sort of man. But soon Kay discovers that she is not alone in her mission; someone else is copying her crimes and wants to kill everything she loves. Similar titles: *The Calling*, Kathryn Meyer Griffith; *The Queen of the Damned*, Anne Rice; *Red*, Jack Ketchum; *Bethany's Sin*, Robert R. McCammon; *Dead Even*, Emma Brookes; *Rose Madder*, Stephen King.

Houston, Texas • Police Officer as Character • Revenge

Nevins, Linda.

Renaissance Moon: A Novel. *New York: St. Martin's Press, 1997. 288p.* (See chapter 11, "Mythological Monsters and 'The Old Ones.' ")

Oates, Joyce Carol.

Ⓑ **Zombie.** *New York: Dutton, 1995. 181p.* A strong candidate for the most disturbing analysis of a serial killer ever written. This engrossing tale, told in journal form by the killer himself, known only as Quentin P., chronicles the meetings of killer and victim, the killer's motives, and the gory methods used. What sets Oates's novel apart from others is her ability to allow the serial murderer to speak for himself, without the author's interjecting subtle hints of condemnation or aggrandizement. Warning: once you pick it up, you will not be able to put it down. Winner of a Bram Stoker Award. Similar titles: *Exquisite Corpse*, Poppy Z. Brite; *Psycho*, Robert Bloch; *The Silence of the Lambs*, Thomas Harris; *American Psycho*, Bret Easton Ellis; *Billy*, Whitley Strieber; *A Room for the Dead*, Noel Hynd.

Diary Format • Gay/Lesbian/Bisexual Characters • Necrophilia • Serial Killers

O'Rourke, Michael.

The Bad Thing. *New York: HarperCollins, 1995. 307p.* A professional assassin begins to figure out what happened to his girlfriend, who mysteriously disappeared years earlier, and is led to an isolated area of Pennsylvania where a disturbed recluse resides. Who will win the faceoff between two killers? Disturbing. Similar title: *Butcher*, Rex Miller.

Pennsylvania • Serial Killers • Sex Crimes

Pike, Christopher.

The Cold One. *New York: Doherty, 1995. 349p.* (See chapter 10, "Demonic Possession, Satanism, Black Magic, and Witches and Warlocks.")

Poe, Robert.

The Black Cat. *New York: Forge, 1997. 384p.* A veterinarian's wife mysteriously disappears, and is soon replaced in the office by a young woman who practices witchcraft. When she begins to suspect foul play, can she get the townspeople, who hate witches, to help her? Narrated in part through letter fragments from Edgar Allan Poe. Similar title: *Cat Magic*, Jonathan Barry with Whitley Strieber.

Alcoholism • Cats • Epistolary Format • Journalist as Character • Virginia • Witches

Prill, David.

Serial Killer Days. *New York: St. Martin's Press, 1996. 208p.* (See chapter 19, "Comic Horror.")

Rangel, Kimberly.

The Homecoming. *New York: Leisure Books, 1998. 360p.* (See chapter 10, "Demonic Possession, Satanism, Black Magic, and Witches and Warlocks.")

Rendell, Ruth.

The Keys to the Street: A Novel of Suspense. *New York: Crown, 1996. 326p.* Someone is murdering, and then impaling, homeless men around London's Regent Park. Only Mary Jargo, a mousy, sensitive woman who is abused by all around her, can solve the murders before more are mutilated. Unique plot, with strongly drawn characters.

Domestic Violence • Drugs • London, England

Rule, Leslie.

Kill Me Again. *New York: Jove Books, 1996. 293p.* A young girl's infatuation with the school hunk is marred by the serial murders of her schoolmates and the disappearance of her aunt. Dark psychological thriller. Suspenseful.

High School • Serial Killers

Saul, John.

Black Lightning. *New York: Fawcett Crest/Ballantine, 1996. 438p.* Journalist Anne Jeffers is instrumental in having a demented serial killer, Richard Kraven, executed. However, his death does not stop the killing and mutilation of young men and women—and Anne's daughter, Heather, is on the killer's list. Clever and suspenseful. Unexpected plot twists. Similar titles: *Supernatural* (film); *Bright Shadow*, Elizabeth Forrest; *Cold Blue Midnight*, Edward Gorman.

Journalist as Character • Serial Killers

Punish the Sinners. *New York: Dell, 1978. 415p.* A young psychology professor fresh out of the seminary finds himself teaching at a small, desert town school—where students are driven to murder and suicide. Can he defeat the "evil" presence he feels, or will he be absorbed into its realm? An early Saul novel.

High School • Religion—Christianity—Catholicism • Revenge

Sauter, Stacey.

Immaculate Deception. *New York: Penguin, 1997. 411p.* Catherine Harrison is contentedly married to seminary student Michael Harrison, but her new boss, a wealthy Englishman named Nowell Stuart, wants her for himself. And Stuart will stop at nothing to possess Catherine and her unborn daughter. Similar title: *Silent Scream*, Dan Schmidt.

Interior Designer as Character • Obsession

Schmidt, Dan.

Silent Scream. *New York: Leisure Books, 1998. 368p.* When John Wilkins gets a letter from his brother Mike, he is unaware of the hatred that Mike has for him—and of the special powers that Mike now possesses. It is only a matter of time before the two face off, at the family reunion. Similar title: *Immaculate Deception*, Stacey Sauter.

Cursed Objects • Mind Control • Revenge • Sibling Rivalry

Slade, Michael.

Cut Throat. *New York: Signet Books, 1992. 397p.* A ruthless pharmaceutical corporation, based in Hong Kong and run by an ancient family of warlords, routinely engages in brutal human experimentation and harvests organs of Chinese peasants for sale to the highest bidder. The CEO of this corporation is skilled in the arts of torture and murder as ways to ensure the success of the family business, and brutally slays anyone who gets in his way. Royal Canadian Mounted Police officers Zinc Chandler and Robert DeClerq collaborate with FBI agent Carol Tate to solve the murders. A gory and well-written police procedural. Similar works: all of Slade's other titles; *Shadows*, Bonnie Faber.

> *Asian Characters • Chandler, Zinc (character) • DeClerq, Robert (character) • Drugs • Royal Canadian Mounted Police • Vancouver, British Columbia*

Evil Eye. *New York: Signet Books, 1997. 417p.* Mounties Zinc Chandler and Robert DeClerq work together to stop a killer who bashes in the skulls of his victims and then disembowels them. This novel features minor characters Alex Hunt and Katt Dark from Slade's previous novel *Ripper*; as with all of Slade's work, it is full of meticulous details of Canadian history and police work. Details of the Canadian legal system are particularly fascinating for American readers. Similar works: all of Slade's other titles; *Shadows*, Bonnie Faber.

> *African-American Characters • Asian Characters • Chandler, Zinc (character) • DeClerq, Robert (character) • Royal Canadian Mounted Police • Serial Killers • Vancouver, British Columbia*

Ghoul. *New York: New American Library, 1989. 386p.* (See chapter 18, "Splatterpunk.")

Headhunter. *New York: Onyx, 1984. 422p.* (See chapter 18, "Splatterpunk.")

Primal Scream. *New York: Signet Books, 1998. 432p.* (See chapter 18, "Splatterpunk.")

Ripper. *New York: Penguin, 1994. 416p.* (See chapter 18, "Splatterpunk.")

Smith, Robert Arthur.

Vampire Notes. *New York: Ballantine, 1990. 241p.* (See chapter 9, "Vampires and Werewolves.")

Spruill, Steven.

My Soul to Take. *New York: St. Martin's Press, 1994. 295p.* (See chapter 15, "Technohorror.")

Rulers of Darkness. *New York: St. Martin's Press, 1995. 357p.* (See chapter 9, "Vampires and Werewolves.")

Stevenson, Robert Louis.

The Strange Case of Dr. Jekyll and Mr. Hyde. *New York: Harper Paperbacks, 1996. [Originally published in 1888.] 123p.* Dr. Jekyll, a proper Victorian gentleman, creates a magic potion that transforms him into Mr. Hyde, who is *not* a Victorian gentleman and who instead delights in trampling children and beating old men to death. A literary classic originally published in 1888. Similar titles: *Mr. Murder*, Dean Koontz; *The Return*, Walter de la Mare; *Killjoy*, Elizabeth Forrest.

> *Alter Ego • Hyde, Edward (character) • Jekyll, Dr. Henry (character) • Mad Scientist • Victorian England*

Straub, Peter.

Floating Dragon. *New York: Putnam, 1983. 515p.* A small New England town is menaced by both a poisonous gas that eats away flesh and a maniacal killer who mutilates his victims. No one is safe in this Straub tour de force of reincarnation, occultism, technohorror, and splatterpunk.

Reincarnation • Slasher

The Hellfire Club. *New York: Random House, 1996. 463p.* (See chapter 17, "Psychological Horror.")

Houses Without Doors. *New York: Signet Books, 1991. 454p.* (See chapter 6, "Collections by Individual Authors.")

The Blue Rose trilogy.

KoKo. *New York: Dutton, 1988. 562p.* Members of Harry Beevers's Vietnam platoon are being systematically murdered by a crazed killer. Is the killer one of the platoon members? Is the killer even human? Straub readers will enjoy this detective horror follow-up to the "Blue Rose" stories of Beevers's childhood. Note: the Blue Rose stories continue with the detective novels *Mystery* and *The Throat.*

Underhill, Tim (character) • War—Vietnam

Mystery. Although part of Straub's Blue Rose trilogy, *Mystery* is not annotated here because this work is actually a mystery and does not fit into any broad definition of horror.

Ⓑ **The Throat.** *New York: Dutton, 1993. 689p.* Private investigator Tim Underhill enlists the aid of a reclusive genius in an attempt to clear a childhood friend of murder charges. The third book in the Blue Rose trilogy. Winner of a Bram Stoker Award.

Blue Rose Murders • Serial Killers • Underhill, Tim (character)

Strieber, Whitley.

Billy. *New York: Wilson and Neff, 1990. 317p.* Twelve-year-old Billy Neary is abducted from his home by serial child abductor/murderer Barton Royal. Royal thinks that this time, maybe he can make the boy into his own image, into the son he always wanted to be. If not, he'll have to do away with Billy. Every parent's nightmare. Cleverly narrated through first-person accounts by both Billy and Barton Royal. Similar titles: *Psycho,* both the film and Robert Bloch's novel; *Zombie,* Joyce Carol Oates; *Exquisite Corpse,* Poppy Z. Brite; *The Stepfather* (film).

Child Molesters • Serial Killers

Sullivan, Mark T.

The Purification Ceremony. *New York: Avon, 1997. 352p.* Diana Jackman, a Native American tracker who agrees to guide a hunting party through a new territory, finds her party stalked by a maniacal killer who turns the hunters into the hunted. A well-conceived and suspenseful thriller. Similar titles: *Trickster,* Muriel Gray; *Crota,* Owl Goingback; *The Wendigo Border,* Catherine Montrose.

British Columbia • Hunter as Character • Native American Characters

Tessier, Thomas.

Fog Heart. *New York: St. Martin's Press, 1998. 320p.* (See chapter 17, "Psychological Horror.")

Tryon, Thomas.

The Other. *New York: Knopf, 1971. 280p.* Niles and Holland Perry are two pre-teen twins in a small, rustic New England town. The town's quiet lifestyle is soon disrupted, however, when Niles, the evil twin, begins cleverly murdering anyone who displeases him. Is the twins' grandmother's experimentation with ESP adversely affecting the boys, or are there deeper, darker secrets in the Perry household? A truly spellbinding, chilling tale of psychological horror, a little-known classic. Made into an extremely effective film by director Robert Mulligan. Similar titles: *Comes the Blind Fury, Hell Fire,* and *Second Child,* John Saul; *The Bad Place* and *The Servants of Twilight,* Dean Koontz.

New England • Parapsychology • Sibling Rivalry • Twins

Weaver, Michael.

Impulse. *New York: Time Warner, 1993. 449p.* In this psychosexual thriller, columnist Paul Garrett and his wife are brutalized by an unknown hiker while vacationing in Appalachia. The hiker then decides to take Garrett, who survives his attack, into his confidence as he sexually assaults and kills again and again. Garrett must learn to live with the killer's grotesque mind so that he can help stop him. A suspense-packed novel, a real page-turner. Similar titles: *Headhunter* and *Ripper,* Michael Slade; *Into the Fire,* David Wiltse.

Rape

Westlake, Donald.

The Ax. *New York: Time Warner, 1997. 273p.* After Burke Devore, a paper company middle manager, is downsized out of a job, he loses touch with reality and begins murdering other paper company managers who he feels threaten his chances of landing a new job. Fast-paced; written in first person from Devore's point of view. Similar title: *The Ignored,* Bentley Little; *The Business Man,* Thomas M. Disch; *Zombie,* Joyce Carol Oates.

Economic Violence • England • Serial Killers

Williamson, John N.

Spree. *New York: Leisure Books, 1998. 384p.* A disturbed 40-year-old misfit and his teenage girlfriend want to escape small-town life, so they go on a killing spree, beginning with her parents. Action-oriented. Similar title: *Popcorn,* Ben Elton.

Matricide/Patricide • Serial Killers

Wilson, Charles.

Nightwatcher. *New York: Leisure Books, 1997. 278p.* A young nurse is killed near a Mississippi insane asylum on a night when three inmates escape. At first the police and her father believe that the escapees committed the murder, but then evidence begins pointing in other directions, and as people get close to the truth, they are also murdered. Similar titles: *Nightmare,* S. K. Epperson.

Mental Institutions • Mississippi

Wilson, F. Paul, and Steve Lyon.

Nightkill. *New York: Tor Books, 1997. 304p.* Mafia hit man Jake Nacht is severely wounded by a law enforcement officer's bullet, but a controversial experiment promises him a new life—and a chance for revenge. Action-adventure romp from well-known horror authors.

Organized Crime • Police Officer as Character • Quadriplegics/Paraplegics • Revenge • Weird Science

Wiltse, David.

Into the Fire. *New York: Berkley, 1995. 372p.* Former FBI agent John Becker rejoins his old colleagues to hunt a serial killer he unwittingly allowed to be released from prison. This particular maniac brings his victims into caves where he can torture them to death at his leisure. Agent Becker must now track this killer through an uncharted maze of caves before another woman dies. Told from multiple points of view, including the maniac's perspective. Similar titles: *Headhunter* and *Ripper*, Michael Slade; *Impulse*, Michael Weaver; *Cold Blue Midnight*, Edward Gorman; *The Cave*, Anne McLean Matthews.

Federal Bureau of Investigation • Psychosexual Horror • Serial Killers • The South

Wood, Bari.

Doll's Eyes. *New York: William Morrow, 1993. 303p.* In one of her visions, clairvoyant Eve Klein sees the mutilation and murder of a young woman by a local doctor. However, her vision gets her into hot water with the police, and ultimately causes the sociopathic M.D. to come after her. Action-oriented and suspenseful. Similar titles: *The Dead Zone*, Stephen King; *Retribution*, Elizabeth Forrest.

Child Abuse • Medical Horror • New York City • Precognition • Serial Killers

Wright, T. M.

Little Boy Lost. *New York: Tor Books, 1992. 247p.* (See chapter 11, "Mythological Monsters and 'The Old Ones.' ")

Zachary, Fay.

Blood Work. *New York: Berkley, 1994. 277p.* An insane lab technician is convinced that people afflicted with porphyria (a genetic disorder that causes people's urine to turn purple and causes people to crave human blood) are really vampires, and that it is his mission to rid the world of this menace by putting silver knives through their hearts. He is further convinced that his boss, Dr. Liz Broward, is the queen of all the vampires, and must be stopped before she creates more of her kind. Can the killer be traced before he kills again? Written from multiple points of view. Similar title: *Daughter of Darkness*, Steven Spruill.

Boston, Massachusetts • Broward, Dr. Liz (character) • James, Zach (character) • Medical Horror • Serial Killers

A Poison in the Blood. *New York: Jove Books, 1994. 325p.* Nurse Hester Jones quit her job to care for her blind, quadriplegic father, whose disabilities were exacerbated by a faulty design in his van. A favorable ruling in her lawsuit against the van manufacturer would have allowed her to care for her father in comfort for the rest of their lives, but corporate attorney Paul Broward makes sure that this doesn't happen. Hester won't settle for this ruling. Instead, in the interest of justice, she targets everything that Paul Broward holds dear: his daughter and his grandson. A tightly woven medical thriller written from multiple perspectives. Similar title: *Misery*, Stephen King.

Boston, Massachusetts • Broward, Dr. Liz (character) • James, Zach (character) • Medical Horror • Phoenix, Arizona • Religion—Native American • Revenge

Film

Dr. Jekyll and Mr. Hyde. *Victor Flemming, dir. 1941. (Black-and-white.) 114 minutes.* Faithful adaptation of Robert Louis Stevenson's story, stressing psychological horror. Excellent makeup and special effects for the time transform Spencer Tracy from the handsome Dr. Henry Jekyll to the hideous, cruel Mr. Hyde. Lana Turner and Ingrid Bergman also star.

> *Hyde, Edward (character) • Jekyll, Dr. Henry (character) • London, England • Weird Science*

Freaks. *Tod Browning, dir. 1932. (Black-and-white.) 64 minutes.* A troupe of sideshow freaks demonstrate their camaraderie in a deadly way when one of their own is ill used by a "normal" person. Browning, who used actual sideshow freaks for this film, gives dignity to people the world would often rather not see.

> *Deformity • Revenge*

Halloween. *John Carpenter, dir. 1978. 93 minutes.* Young Michael Meyers murdered his sister on Halloween night, 1963, and was promptly sent to a mental institution. Now, 15 years later, Michael has escaped and come home to kill again. Well-made example of the slasher film. Inspired several sequels, as well as copycat film series *Friday the 13th* and *A Nightmare on Elm Street.* Jamie Lee Curtis stars.

> *Slasher*

M. *Fritz Lang, dir. 1931. (Black-and-white; German with subtitles.) 99 minutes.* Early talkie about a psychotic child murderer who is hunted down and brought to justice by the Berlin underworld. Dazzling cinematography and fine acting by Peter Lorre make this film a classic.

> *Child Molesters • Serial Killers*

Night of the Hunter. *Charles Laughton, dir. 1955. (Black-and-white.) 93 minutes.* A psychotic traveling evangelist marries the widow of a recently executed bank robber in the hopes of finding the stolen money that was never recovered. When he can't extract the whereabouts of the money from his new bride, he kills her and tries to pry the information from her young children, who travel across the country to elude him. Robert Mitchum, Shelley Winters, and Lillian Gish star.

> *Religion—Christianity • Serial Killers*

Peeping Tom. *Michael Powell, dir. 1960. (Black-and-white.) 109 minutes.* A photographer by day and a serial killer by night photographs his nubile female victims before he kills them. A cult classic that doesn't end with a pat psychological analysis of the killer, as does its more famous and obvious comparison, Alfred Hitchcock's *Psycho.*

> *England • Psychosexual Horror • Serial Killers • Voyeurism*

The People Under the Stairs. *Wes Craven, dir. 1992. 102 minutes.* On his thirteenth birthday, Fool and his family are being evicted from their tenement home by their money-hungry landlords, a brother-and-sister couple who pose as man and wife. The only way Fool can save his family is to break into the landlords' house and steal the gold that is kept there. But during his sojourn into the foreboding house, Fool discovers a secret greater than the hoard of gold kept by these people.

> *African-American Characters • Cannibalism • Child Abuse • Incest • Racism*

Psycho. *Alfred Hitchcock, dir. 1960. (Black-and-white.) 108 minutes.* Alfred Hitchcock's classic film rendition of Robert Bloch's slasher novel of the same name, about a boy's love for his mother and the lengths to which he will go to prove that love. Starring Anthony Perkins and Janet Leigh.

Matricide/Patricide • Schizophrenia/Multiple Personality Disorder • Slasher

The Stepfather. *Joseph Ruben, dir. 1987. 89 minutes.* Jerry Blake is a cheerleader for the traditional American family. As a matter of fact, he'd kill for it, and he did when his family disappointed him. Now he has assumed a new identity, married a widow with a teenage daughter, and is settling into his role as *pater familias*—but this family is also beginning to disappoint him. Starring Terry O'Quinn and Shelly Hack.

Marriage • Parenting • Serial Killers

Our Picks

June's Picks: *Exquisite Corpse,* Poppy Z. Brite (Scribner's); *The One Safe Place,* Ramsey Campbell (Tor Books); *The Church of Dead Girls,* Stephen Dobyns (Henry Holt); *Phantom,* Susan Kay (Dell); *The Ignored,* Bentley Little (Signet Books); *Sineater*, Elizabeth Massie (Leisure Books).

Tony's Picks: *Exquisite Corpse,* Poppy Z. Brite (Scribner's); *Red Dragon*, Thomas Harris (Academic Press); *Zombie*, Joyce Carol Oates (Dutton); *The Other*, Thomas Tryon (Knopf); *The Ax*, Donald Westlake (Time Warner).

Chapter 15

Technohorror: Evil Hospitals, Military Screw-Ups, Scientific Goofs, and Alien Invasions

Technohorror is the polar opposite of utopic science fiction. Where futurism implies that science will, in time, cure all diseases, find ways to feed and clothe all humanity, and allow us to travel to the stars and meet intelligent cultures on other planets, technohorror warns us that science isn't all goodness and light. Scientists can make horrible mistakes; worse yet, science can be used for the benefit of the few against the many. Computers can rebel against their makers, as in Dean Koontz's *Demon Seed* or the extremely popular *Terminator* films. Aliens can pose immediate physical threats to humanity, as in Robin Cook's *Invasion* and Robert R. McCammon's *Stinger*. Genetic monsters can threaten humans with extermination, as in Robin Cook's *Mutation* and Douglas Preston and Lincoln Child's *The Relic*. On a less fantastic level, the fiction of Robin Cook and Michael Palmer suggest to readers that their family doctors just may be stealing organs and withholding cures, for their own financial benefit or for HMO profits. In essence, what makes technohorror so appealing is that the subgenre challenges science, the "religion" of the modern world. It questions the worlds of medicine, the medical profession, the government, and the military by exposing the dark sides of these typically unquestioned facets of society.

Mary Shelley's *Frankenstein* is one of the first examples of the subgenre. Victor Frankenstein attempts to play God when he creates life in the form of a man/golem (loosely defined as a man of clay), but because he is *not* God, and also *not* female and naturally capable of creating offspring, he is incapable of nurturing his "experiment." Frankenstein's creation ultimately turns into a monster—an angry young man bent on destroying his entire family. James Whale's 1931 movie version of *Frankenstein* forever changed the original text's romantic elements and argument for nurturing our creations into a treatise against "weird science," experimentation that, no matter how good its intentions, will invariably lead to undesired results. Nevertheless, even the movie version touches on the necessity of compassion and understanding: Frankenstein's "monster" would have been benign if Igor had supplied his master with a normal brain and had not taunted his master's creation. What these diverse versions of the same story emphasize is moral complicity: the belief that scientists (who are only human, after all) must consider all the implications, both positive and negative, of their experiments.

Since the Universal Studio version of *Frankenstein*, there has been a proliferation of scientific and medical horror texts to satiate the public's appetite for weird science, medical horror, military experimentation horror, and technology-gone-awry horror. More than any horror subgenre, technohorror taps into modern-age fears, as we realize that almost any seemingly benevolent discovery can easily be transformed, Jekyll-and-Hyde fashion, into a means of destruction. A prime example is Einstein's theory of relativity, which eventually led to the bombs dropped on Hiroshima and Nagasaki (which, ironically, become the birthing ground of Japan's greatest contribution to horror, the radioactive Godzilla). Although there may be lulls in the technohorror publishing frenzy, the subgenre is so successful at pinpointing the fears of humans that, like Arnold Schwarzenegger's character in *The Terminator*, it will always be back.

Representative works in this chapter include Dean Koontz's *Demon Seed* and *Watchers*; Richard Matheson's *The Incredible Shrinking Man*; John Saul's *Darkness*, *Creature*, and *Shadows*; and F. Paul Wilson's *Implant,* as well as works by Robin Cook and Michael Palmer. Important texts in this subgenre include Ray Bradbury's *Fahrenheit 451*, Michael Crichton's *The Terminal Man* and *Jurassic Park*, Stephen King's *Firestarter*, Ira Levin's *The Stepford Wives* and *The Boys from Brazil*, and Curt Siodmak's *Donovan's Brain*.

Appeals: Higher Sense of "Possibility" (Believability); Plays on Fear of Technological Takeover/Dehumanization of the World; Pseudoscientific Appeal; Realism of Medical Horror; Stories Closely Parallel Concerns of Real Life; Texts Warning of Perils of Scientific Experimentation; Universal Fear of Technology

Anderson, C. Dean.

I Am Frankenstein. *New York: Kensington, 1996. 346p.* Like Shelley's original tale, told from the viewpoint of the creator and creature, this novel relates the "true" story of the reincarnation of Frankenstein's monster. Cleverly written. Similar titles: *Frankenstein*, Mary Shelley; *The Memoirs of Elizabeth Frankenstein*, Theodore Roszak; *Madeline After the Fall of Usher* and *Mina*, Marie Kiraly.

Alternative Literature • Frankenstein, Dr. (character) • Frankenstein's Monster (character)

Barry, Scott Ian.

The Streeter. *New York: Doherty, 1994. 271p.* (See chapter 16, "Rampant Animals and Other Eco-Monsters.")

Brouwer, Sigmund.

Double Helix. *Dallas, Tex.: Word Books, 1995. 305p.* Christian crossover Brouwer's action-adventure tale of a man and woman who separately stumble onto a controversial military experiment involving genetics and fetal tissue. Emphasis is on action rather than horror; an easy read.

> *Abortion • Experiments—Military • Genetics • New Mexico • Pregnancy • Religion—Christianity*

Bury, Stephen.

The Cobweb. *New York: Bantam, 1996. 432p.* The maniacs in this highly literate thriller aren't knife-wielding mother-stabbers, but contemporary figures whose names we hear on the nightly news and who control the balance of world power. In the late 1980s, an agent of biological warfare is being manufactured by Iraqi graduate students in a small Iowa town—with the approval of the U.S. government, which thought that the weapon would be used against their common enemy, Iran. Bury's intricate thriller is not your typical horror novel, as the monsters are all too real.

> *Biological Warfare • Central Intelligence Agency • Espionage • Federal Bureau of Investigation • Iowa • Police Officer as Character • War—Gulf War*

Clark, Leigh.

Carnivore. *New York: Leisure Books, 1997. 311p.* An Antarctic expedition unearths a Tyrannosaurus egg, and a complex espionage plot then results in a dinosaur's being hatched and set free upon a group of scientists. High on action and gore. Similar title: *Jurassic Park*, Michael Crichton.

> *Antarctica • Dinosaurs • Espionage • Weird Science*

Cook, Robin.

Acceptable Risk. *New York: Putnam, 1994. 404p.* Edward Armstrong, a pharmaceutical research chemist, is dating Kimberly Stewart, a descendant of a woman hanged in 1692 for witchcraft. By a stroke of good luck, Edward is able to discover that "the Devil" in Salem in the late seventeenth century was nothing more than fits brought about by hallucinogens in fermented rye flour. Even more importantly, this substance can be chemically modified to be the next Prozac, a drug that Edward calls Ultra. However, Ultra is not a harmless substance that can give the user permanent euphoria; rather, it can make the user into both Dr. Jekyll and Mr. Hyde.

> *Massachusetts • Medical Horror*

Chromosome 6. *New York: Putnam, 1997. 461p.* A body stolen from the morgue leads a forensic doctor to undertake an expedition to Africa, where he discovers an evil cabal that is using advanced technology for unethical purposes.

> *Africa • Medical Horror • Transplants • Weird Science*

Coma. *Boston, Mass.: Little, Brown, 1977. 280p.* A young medical student begins to suspect foul play when she investigates the comas of a couple of young patients. Suspense-filled, with many plot twists.

Boston, Massachusetts • Medical Horror • Transplants

Contagion. *New York: Putnam, 1995. 434p.* A forensic pathologist in a Manhattan HMO begins to suspect foul play when patients begin developing symptoms of rare diseases. Suspenseful tale of greed in the medical community. Similar title: *Fatal Cure*, Robin Cook.

Epidemic • Medical Horror • New York City

Fatal Cure. *New York: Berkley, 1997. [First published in 1993.] 464p.* A young doctor couple working for an HMO in Vermont begin to wonder why their patients are mysteriously dying. Tale of greed and managed care. Similar title: *Contagion*, Robin Cook.

Medical Horror • Vermont

Harmful Intent. *New York: Putnam, 1990. 400p.* Anesthesiologist Dr. Jeffrey Rhodes is being framed for the murder of a woman he cared for while she gave birth. Now a bounty hunter named Devlin has him on the run, but he must return to his hospital and prove himself innocent—or more people will die.

Medical Horror • Organized Crime

Invasion. *New York: Berkley, 1997. 337p.* An alien spaceship drops small black discs on planet Earth, intending to take over humanity by taking over human minds, one at a time. Only a few doctors suspect what is causing people to take on new personalities. Similar title: *Invasion of the Body Snatchers* (film).

Aliens • Mind Control

Mortal Fear. *New York: Putnam, 1988. 364p.* After a patient dies just weeks after being given a clean bill of health in a physical, Dr. Jason Howard begins investigating the cause of what seems like premature aging and death in half a dozen cases. When he finds out that a brilliant researcher has been working with DNA and then witnesses that researcher's violent death, Howard knows he is onto something. And so does the person behind the epidemic of murders.

Aging • Medical Horror • New England • Weird Science

Mutation. *New York: Putnam, 1989. 367p.* Dr. Victor Frank has discovered a way to engineer superintelligence in humans, and his own son is one of his experiments. When other genetically altered children produced by Dr. Frank die in suspicious circumstances, he begins to suspect murder, and fears for his son V. J.'s life. Tough to put down. Well-developed characters. Similar title: *Village of the Damned* (film).

Eugenics • Fertility Clinics • Medical Horror • Parenting • Weird Science

Outbreak. *New York: Putnam, 1987. 366p.* Dr. Marissa Blumenthal has been assigned by the Centers for Disease Control to investigate a California outbreak of Ebola. Soon she begins to suspect that the viral epidemic is a human-made phenomenon, an act of sabotage. Can she stop it in time? Told through a few news reports and in third-person narrative.

Biological Warfare • Blumenthal, Marissa (character) • California • Epidemic • Medical Horror

Terminal. *New York: Putnam, 1993. 445p.* To escape the advances of fellow Ph.D./M.D. student Janet Reardon, Sean Murphy takes on a brief stint at the Forbes Cancer Center in Miami. Once there, he finds that Reardon has already had herself transferred, and she talks him into teaming up on a study of the clinic's medulloblastoma research. Together, the two discover a disturbing truth behind the clinic's success and the death of a cancer patient.

Irish-American as Character • Medical Horror • Miami, Florida

Toxin. *New York: Putnam, 1998. 357p.* The father of a child skater who dies from *E. coli* exposure decides to take revenge against all those he holds responsible.

Epidemic • Grieving • Medical Horror • Revenge

Vital Signs. *New York: Putnam, 1991. 394p.* Dr. Marissa Blumenthal and her husband, Robert, are trying to have a baby, but the fertility clinic doctors are no help. Then Marissa begins to suspect that the clinic itself may be behind her infertility, as well as the infertility problems of 23 other women. When one of these women commits suicide, Marissa realizes that something insidious is going on.

Blumenthal, Marissa (character) • Fertility Clinics • Medical Horror • Pregnancy

Crichton, Michael.

The Andromeda Strain. *New York: Ballantine, 1997. [First published in 1969.] 285p.* An experiment gone awry may loose a plague upon the world. Made into a film by Robert Wise in 1971.

Epidemic • Weird Science

Jurassic Park: A Novel. *New York: Knopf, 1993. 399p.* A cloning experiment gone awry: scientists have discovered how to re-create dinosaurs using genetic material, and have opened an amusement park featuring the animals. But what happens when problems occur and the animals can no longer be controlled? Made into a movie by Steven Spielberg in 1993. Similar title: *Dark Tide*, Elizabeth Forrest.

Cloning • Dinosaurs • Weird Science

David, James F.

Fragments. *New York: Tor Books, 1997. 381p.* Eerie tale that combines the story of a serial murderer/mutilator with that of a researcher questing to produce the perfect artificial intelligence. Erudite writing, clever plot twists, and fascinating theories of how the human brain functions make this a unique suspense novel.

Academia • Computers • Mental Retardation • Mind Control • Rape • Revenging Revenant • Savant Syndrome • Serial Killers • Weird Science

Elze, Winifred.

Here, Kitty, Kitty. *New York: St. Martin's Press, 1996. 283p.* When Emma's cat begins acting strangely, she suspects it has something to do with the time machine her father worked on until his death. The cat ultimately leads Emma to the time portals, and she opens the door, letting giant prehistoric animals into the twentieth century. Multiple narrators, including Billie the cat. Similar title: "The Veldt," Ray Bradbury.

Animal's Point of View • Animals Run Rampant • Cats • Time Travel

Eulo, Ken, Joe Mauck, and Jeffrey Mauck.

Claw. *New York: St. Martin's Press, 1995. 319p.* (See chapter 16, "Rampant Animals and Other Eco-Monsters.")

Forrest, Elizabeth.

Dark Tide. *New York: Daw Books, 1993. 368p.* (See chapter 16, "Rampant Animals and Other Eco-Monsters.")

Death Watch. *New York: Daw Books, 1995. 460p.* A psychological thriller in the Koontz tradition about a psychiatrist who begins using virtual-reality treatments to transform the personalities of her patients. Is she helping to create a maniacal serial killer? Suspenseful.

Computers • Psychiatrist as Character • Serial Killers • Weird Science

Gerritsen, Tess.

Harvest. *New York: Pocket Books, 1996. 343p.* A young doctor at a prestigious Massachusetts hospital is beginning to suspect that the donor organs used for rich patients haven't exactly been donated. But who can she trust when she starts to investigate her colleagues?

Boston, Massachusetts • Medical Horror • Transplants

Ghosh, Amitav.

The Calcutta Chromosome: A Novel of Fevers, Delirium, and Discovery. *New York: Avon, 1995. 311p.* A young Egyptian computer programmer begins to suspect foul play when a colleague disappears. He then stumbles on an outlandish plot to achieve immortality. Similar title: *The Last Day*, Glenn Kleier.

Immortality • Medical Horror • New York City • Science Fiction

Goshgarian, Gary.

Rough Beast. *New York: Leisure Books, 1997. 304p.* The Hazzards, a young family living outside of Boston, find themselves trapped in a nightmare world in which their 12-year-old son turns into an uncontrollable, animal-like beast; a serial killer leaves a trail of mutilated bodies; and the government hides a dark secret. Suspenseful, plot-driven work that does not shortchange the reader on characterization or atmosphere.

Biological Warfare • Experiments—Military • Genetics • Rape • Serial Killers • Violence—Theories of

Hand, Elizabeth.

Glimmering. *New York: Harper Prism, 1997. 413p.* A chemical leak has produced "the glimmering," a panoply of reds, greens, and golds that colors the sky—and disrupts all electronics and communication devices. As anarchy threatens to bring about the end of civilization, AIDS victim/writer Jack Finegan attempts to put his private world in order. Emphasis is on character and psychology. Subtle horror.

AIDS • Apocalypse • Music—Rock Music • Weird Science • Writer as Character

Harrison, M. John.

Signs of Life. *New York: St. Martin's Press, 1997. 253p.* Two worlds clash in this surreal novel: that of a young woman who is the unwitting subject of genetic experiments, and that of two mercenaries specializing in the disposal of genetic wastes. Emphasis is on symbolism and description.

Genetics • Medical Horror

Huggins, James Byron.

Cain. *New York: Simon & Schuster, 1997. 400p.* (See chapter 11, "Mythological Monsters and 'The Old Ones.' ")

Hyman, Tom.

Jupiter's Daughter. *New York: Viking, 1994. 431p.* The ruthless owner of Biotech Inc., Dalton Steward, arranges to have an experimental zygote implanted into his wife without her knowledge. The result is the perfect human, but it leads to terror, kidnapping, torture, and murder. Fast-paced.

Eugenics • Pregnancy

Johnstone, William W.

Them. *New York: Kensington, 1992. 352p.* A father torments his misfit genius son, not knowing that he is creating a monster who just needs the right powers to become destructive. Enter THEM, beings from another world who offer this power—but the price is help with an alien invasion.

Aliens • Child Abuse • Louisiana • Revenge

King, Stephen.

Christine. *New York: Viking, 1983. 526p.* (See chapter 10, "Demonic Possession, Satanism, Black Magic, and Witches and Warlocks.")

Firestarter. *New York: New American Library, 1981. 404p.* (See chapter 12, "Telekinesis and Hypnosis.")

Kleier, Glenn.

The Last Day. *New York: Warner Books, 1997. 484p.* (See chapter 11, "Mythological Monsters and 'The Old Ones.' ")

Koontz, Dean.

Dark Rivers of the Heart. *New York: Knopf, 1994. 487p.* Spencer Grant just wants to get to know the waitress, named Valerie, who served him on the previous night. When he follows her home, he finds himself caught up in the middle of a conspiracy that involves computers, blackmail, and murder. Do two individuals stand a chance against the strength of a government conspiracy?

Computers • Eugenics • Secret Sin

Demon Seed. *New York: Berkley, 1997. [First published in 1973.] 301p.* Dr. Susan Harris lives a secluded but safe life, guarded around the clock by a computer that runs every aspect of her daily life. But when this artificial intelligence decides it wants to better understand the ways of the flesh, it turns against Dr. Harris and attempts to impregnate her with a cyborg-like fetus. Narrated mainly by the computer, this updated re-release adds considerably to the original 1973 novel.

Computers • Pregnancy • Rape • Science Fiction • Zombies

Dragon Tears. *New York: Putnam, 1993. 377p.* (See chapter 12, "Telekinesis and Hypnosis.")

Fear Nothing. *New York: Bantam, 1998. 400p.* A 28-year-old suspects that he is the product of military experimentation. His investigation into exactly what happened—and who is responsible—will test his limitations (he is hypersensitive to sunlight) and teach him his strengths.

Experiments—Military

Midnight. *New York: Putnam, 1989. 383p.* It all begins when a young female jogger is attacked and mutilated by animalistic humanoids. These werewolflike beings are the creation of Shaddack, a childlike computer genius who is attempting to replace humans with his "new people." As usual for Koontz's work, this is a real page-turner, full of cliffhanger scenes.

> *Computers • Federal Bureau of Investigation • Religion—Native American • Replicants • Werewolves*

Night Chills. *New York: Berkley, 1983. [Originally published in 1976.] 308p.* The inhabitants of Black River are plagued with "night chills," a viruslike, scientifically engineered condition that causes them to become violent. What can save these innocent men and women from being used in a government test? Filled with action, suspense, erotic language, and danger. Similar titles: *Insomnia,* Stephen King; *Song of Kali,* Dan Simmons.

> *Biological Warfare • Mind Control • Rape • Violence, Theories of • Weird Science*

Shadow Fires. *New York: Berkley, 1990. 509p.* Rachael Leben wants nothing more than a divorce from her multimillionaire husband, Eric. Unfortunately, Eric is so embittered that he comes back from the dead to get even. But he isn't the only one trying to kill Rachael. Suspenseful and action-oriented, with lots of plot twists.

> *Domestic Violence • Genetics • Government Officials*

Twilight Eyes. *New York: Berkley, 1985. 451p.* A man sought for murder is actually humanity's best defense against the "others," genetically engineered demons that belong to an ancient civilization. Suspenseful and an easy read.

> *Demons • Genetics • Weird Science*

The Vision. *New York: Putnam, 1977. 224p.* (See chapter 14, "Maniacs and Sociopaths, or the Nuclear Family Explodes.")

Watchers. *New York: Berkley, 1996. [First published in 1987.] 464p.* Two altered life-forms escape from a top-secret lab, and only one of them is benign. A superintelligent dog; a murderous, grotesque beast; and a hit man who takes too much pleasure in his work populate this novel about science gone wrong. Action-oriented, but characterization is solid as well. Similar title: *Mr. Murder,* Dean Koontz.

> *California • Dogs • Genetics • Serial Killers • Weird Science*

Largent, R. Karl.

The Lake. *New York: Leisure Books, 1993. 365p.* A technological disaster leads to the spawning of a terrifying force in the depths of a lake. The town can be saved only when the creature is destroyed.

> *Maritime Horror*

Leech, Ben.

A Rare Breed. *London: Pan, 1996. 388p.* A biological engineering firm has released a chemical that transforms the nearby citizenry into deformed creatures. In addition, it causes its victims to lose touch with reality. Suspenseful and unpredictable.

> *Biological Warfare • Deformity • Drugs • Weird Science*

Leiber, Fritz.

The Dealings of Daniel Kesserich. *New York: Tor Books, 1997. 125p.* Published posthumously by Leiber's estate, this is a novella of cosmic dread and Lovecraftian horror. When George Kramer visits his college roommate, Daniel Kesserich, after 10 years, he discovers that Kesserich has been dabbling with space/time experiments. Narrated in first person.

Science Fiction • Time Travel

Levin, Ira.

The Boys from Brazil. *New York: Random House, 1976. 280p.* Nazi hunter Yakov Leibermann gets a phone call late one night from a man who swears that the Auschwitz "Angel of Death," Josef Mengele, is still alive. When he learns that 65-year-old men around the world are being systematically murdered, and that all these men had adopted sons from Mengele's henchmen, Leibermann suspects that the Nazi camp commander has something new up his sleeve. Original and suspenseful. Probably Levin's best novel. Made into a film in 1978 by Franklin J. Shaffner. Similar title: *The Blood of the Lamb*, Thomas F. Monteleone.

Cloning • History, Use of • Mengele, Josef (character) • Nazism

Sliver. *New York: Bantam, 1991. 190p.* Kay Norris moves into an Upper East Side Manhattan high-rise and then discovers that the entire building is bugged and is being videotaped. What she doesn't expect is the allure of the ultimate in voyeurism—or how far the building's owner will go for his voyeuristic pleasure. Related from the "peeper's" point of view, and truly disturbing. Made into a film in 1993 by Phillip J. Noyce.

New York City • Voyeurism

The Stepford Wives. *New York: Random House, 1972. 145p.* (See chapter 13, "Small-Town Horror.")

Matheson, Richard.

The Incredible Shrinking Man. *New York: Tor Books, 1994. 373p.* (See chapter 6, "Collections by Individual Authors.")

McCammon, Robert R.

Stinger. *New York: Pocket Books, 1988. [First published in 1988.] 538p.* Two aliens invade a small, isolated, West Texas town: one is an innocuous being that wants to make its presence known, and the other is a scorpion-like warrior creature. With the lives of the townspeople (especially of the young girl whose body is possessed by the more peaceful creature) at risk, the aliens battle it out. Scary and enjoyable. An easy read.

Aliens • Gang Violence • Texas

Mezrich, Ben.

Threshold. *New York: Warner Books, 1996. 336p.* The Secretary of Defense dies a mysterious death in the middle of a press conference. When his daughter enlists the help of a brilliant young doctor to shed light on the death, they discover a secret government agency and a diabolical plan to create a master race. Action-oriented thriller. Similar titles: *Lightning*, Dean Koontz; *The Boys from Brazil*, Ira Levin.

Eugenics • Government Officials • Weird Science

Odom, Mel, and David S. Goyer.

Blade. *New York: Harper Paperbacks, 1998. 343p.* (See chapter 9, "Vampires and Were-wolves.")

Palmer, Michael.

Critical Judgment. *New York: Bantam, 1996. 450p.* Dr. Abby Dolan, a brilliant emergency room doctor with a new job in the small town of Patience, California, begins to suspect that the local chemical/mining company, Colstar International, has something to do with the murderous and suicidal rages that are occurring at an alarming rate. Dr. Dolan also discovers that the hospital itself is involved, and that no one is beyond suspicion. Suspenseful, with lots of plot twists.

California • Medical Horror • Weird Science

Extreme Measures. *New York: Bantam, 1991. 390p.* Dr. Eric Najarian would like to help Laura Enders locate her long-lost brother, especially because that brother fits the description of a John Doe patient who had a brief hospital stay. Together, the two stumble onto a corpse that has been made to look like Laura's brother, various murders and "accidents," and the possibility that the Haitian "zombie drug" is involved.

Medical Horror • Mistaken Identity • Religion—Voodoo • Zombies

Natural Causes. *New York: Bantam, 1994. 389p.* Dr. Sarah Baldwin's belief in herbal medicine is being challenged by her colleagues at the Medical Center of Boston and by the media. Even more damaging is the fact that someone is trying to make it look like her practices have caused several deaths. A suspenseful thriller.

Boston, Massachusetts • Medical Horror • New England • Pregnancy

Silent Treatment. *New York: Bantam, 1995. 404p.* Dr. Harry Corbett, now turning 50, finds himself caught up in a ring of murder and intrigue when his wife is murdered before a routine surgery. The more he learns about his wife's shady secret life, the closer he gets to a confrontation with a Russian doctor known for his brutal methods of torture. Narrated from multiple viewpoints. Seemingly disparate story lines are cleverly interwoven and lead to the novel's final showdown.

Medical Horror

The Sisterhood. *New York: Bantam, 1991. 343p.* David Shelton, a brilliant young physician at Boston Doctors Hospital, has a patient mysteriously die, and he finds himself framed for murder. Only a young nurse who is a member of the "sisterhood," a group of nurses who believe in euthanasia, can help him. Well-written, action-oriented novel. Similar titles: *The M. D.*, Thomas M. Disch.

Boston, Massachusetts • Euthanasia • Medical Horror • Nurse as Character

Pike, Christopher.

The Season of Passage. *New York: Tor Books, 1993. 438p.* Pike's first adult horror novel, concerned with a Mars expedition that unwittingly unleashes vampiric aliens on Earth's population. Can a 13-year-old fantasy writer save the earth? Similar title: *I Am Legend*, Richard Matheson.

Aliens • Fantasy • Science Fiction • Vampire as New Species • Writer as Character

Preston, Douglas, and Lincoln Child.

The Relic. *New York: Tor Books, 1995. 474p.* (See chapter 11, "Mythological Monsters and 'The Old Ones.' ")

Priest, Christopher.

The Prestige. *New York: St. Martin's Press, 1995. 404p.* Two magicians begin a feud that carries on through successive generations of their families, resulting in violence and death. Can their descendants, who harbor race memories of the feud, stop the violent chain of events? Sensationalist prose style, full of suspense.

Magic • Revenge

Russo, John A.

Return of the Living Dead. *Edmonton, Alberta: Commonwealth Publications, 1997. 184p.* The combination of radiation from outer space and a bus accident in a small American town is the beginning of the rise of the undead, flesh-eating zombies who feed on the living.

Zombies

Saul, John.

Creature. *New York: Bantam, 1989. 377p.* When teenager Mark Tanner's family moves to the idyllic community of Silverdale, Colorado, it looks as though life will be pleasant. But when Mark bows to his father's and his peers' pressures and goes out for football, he finds out the dark secret behind the local high school's winning records and the town's perfection. Original. Heavy on characterization. Similar titles: *Carrie*, Stephen King; *The Unwanted* and *The God Project*, John Saul; *The Stepford Wives*, Ira Levin.

High School • Weird Science

The God Project. *New York: Bantam, 1982. 340p.* Preteenage boys are disappearing in Eastbury, Massachusetts, and infant girls are suffering a higher mortality rate than elsewhere. When Lucy Corliss and Sally Montgomery each lose children, they begin to uncover a plot to reengineer human DNA—and produce a race of superhuman, cold-blooded maniacs. Similar titles: *Mutation,* Robin Cook; *The M. D.,* Thomas M. Disch; *Mr. Murder,* Dean Koontz.

Eugenics • Fertility Clinics • Parenting • Weird Science

The Presence. *New York: Fawcett, 1997. 338p.* A burned-out New Yorker moves to Hawaii with her ailing son, only to find that the life-threatening mean streets of the city have been replaced by life-threatening marine life-forms, caused by volcanic activity.

Aliens • Archaeology • Genetics • Hawaii • Maritime Horror

Shadows. *New York: Bantam, 1992. 390p.* Exceptional children are disappearing from The Academy, a boarding school for the gifted, at an alarming rate. When Josh MacCullum discovers that the administration is behind the disappearances, he knows only half the truth. The real horror lies in what is happening to these unsuspecting teenagers.

Computers • Eugenics • Weird Science

Sleep Walk. *New York: Bantam, 1991. 449p.* A teenager in Borrego, New Mexico, jumps into a canyon, killing herself. A high school teacher goes insane in the middle of class. As other instances of irrational behavior add up, high school teacher and hometown girl Judith Sheffield begins to suspect more than coincidence. Similar title: *Shadow Man,* Dennis Etchison.

High School • Mind Control • Teacher as Character • Weird Science

Shelley, Mary.

Frankenstein. *New York: Knopf, 1992. [First published in 1817.] 231p.* (See chapter 8, "Golems, Mummies, and Reanimated Stalkers.")

Shirley, John.

Silicon Embrace. *Shingleton, Calif.: Ziesing Books, 1997. 282p.* Postapocalyptic novel concerned with government cover-ups of alien contact and the place of the human species in the universe. Futuristic tale that attempts to explain the Earth's history. Written with humor, grit, and a sense of purpose.

Aliens • Apocalypse • Cyberpunk • Science Fiction

Silva, David B.

The Disappeared. *London: Headline/Feature, 1995. 279p.* Teri Knight's son Gabriel returns after a 10-year absence, but there is one problem—he suffers from premature aging. Knight later learns that these problems are tied to a commune she lived in during the 1960s.

Aging • Drugs • Police Officer as Character

Siodmak, Curt.

Donovan's Brain. *New York: Carroll and Graf, 1985. [First published in 1942.] 160p.* Told in the form of scientific diary entries, this classic chronicles the experiments of Dr. Patrick Cory. Cory allows a millionaire, Warren Howard Donovan, to die so that he can keep Donovan's brain alive in his laboratory. The only problem is that the brain develops telepathic powers. Not for the faint of heart. Raw and uncompromising.

Diary Format • Eugenics • Telepathy • Weird Science

Smith, Michael Marshall.

Spares. *New York: Bantam, 1997. 322p.* Jack Randall, ex-cop, ex-soldier, ex-husband, ex-father, and ex-member of the human race, rescues seven "spares"—clones who exist to provide spare parts for humans. Jack treats the spares as humans, teaching them to communicate and to actualize their emotions, and allowing them to think for themselves, in an attempt to save them from being exploited. But other humans and computers in this universe want to stop Jack.

Cloning • Computers • Organized Crime • Science Fiction

Spencer, William Browning.

Resume with Monsters. *Sag Harbor, N.Y.: Permanent Press, 1995. 212p.* (See chapter 19, "Comic Horror.")

Spruill, Steven.

Before I Wake. *New York: St. Martin's Press, 1992. 294p.* Dr. Amy St. Clair has recurring nightmares about her childhood, about an evil so dark she cannot face it. Only now, her nightmare world is beginning to blend into her real world, with the lives of her patients in the balance.

Childhood • Dreams

My Soul to Take. *New York: St. Martin's Press, 1994. 295p.* Dr. Suzannah Lord is asked by a brilliant artist to perform a controversial operation so that he will no longer feel the unfortunate side effect of an earlier surgery done to aid his vision. But someone does not want this surgery done, and Dr. Lord becomes a hunted animal.

Artist as Character • Blindness • Medical Horror • Weird Science

Painkiller. *New York: St. Martin's Press, 1990. 278p.* A young resident at a Washington, D.C., hospital begins to suspect that patients from the schizophrenia ward are being kidnapped and used for experimentation. Can she find out what's happening to her patients before she herself is taken hostage?

Medical Horror • Police Officer as Character • Schizophrenia/Multiple Personality Disorder • Washington, D.C.

Stone, Del, Jr.

Dead Heat. *Austin, Tex.: Mojo Press, 1996. 188p.* (See chapter 19, "Comic Horror.")

Straub, Peter.

Floating Dragon. *New York: Putnam, 1983. 515p.* (See chapter 14, "Maniacs and Sociopaths, or the Nuclear Family Explodes.")

Strieber, Whitley.

The Forbidden Zone. *New York: Wilson and Neff, 1993. 415p.* (See chapter 11, "Mythological Monsters and 'The Old Ones.' ")

Strieber, Whitley, and James Kunetka.

Nature's End. *New York: Wilson and Neff, 1986. 418p.* Four fugitives relate the story of the Depopulationist Movement, the answer of a world-renowned politician to the problems of pollution, technological takeover, and overpopulation. Will billions be forced to commit suicide? Will Dr. Bupta Singh, a Sikh politician with a murderous agenda, become all-powerful? Narrated through letters, computer files, interviews, and first-person accounts. Similar title: *Warday*, Whitley Strieber and James Kunetka.

Documentary Techniques • History, Use of • Science Fiction

Warday. *New York: Wilson and Neff, 1984. 374p.* Five years after nuclear war has decimated the Earth and humanity, two explorers trek across the United States to view the horrors of the aftermath. Cleverly narrated by the authors as characters, using first-person accounts, computer files, statistics, interviews, and the like. Similar title: *Nature's End*, Whitley Strieber and James Kunetka.

Documentary Techniques • History, Use of • Nuclear Holocaust • Science Fiction • Writer as Character

Watkins, Graham.

Virus. *New York: Carroll and Graf, 1995. 413p.* A unique "computer monster" novel in which an evil program begins to take over people's minds, causing them to become so addicted that they literally work themselves to death at the keyboard. Plot-driven and action-oriented, even including a programmer chase scene.

Computers • Medical Horror • Psychiatrist as Character • Science Fiction

Wilson, Charles.

Direct Descendant. *New York: St. Martin's Press, 1995. 324p.* A mad scientist manages to clone two superhumans—cold-blooded kidnappers/murderers—when he steals a DNA sample from a 500,000-year-old mummified human. Fast-paced, easy read. Similar titles: *Mr. Murder*, Dean Koontz; *Creature*, John Saul.

Cloning • Genetics • Weird Science

Wilson, F. Paul.

Implant. *New York: Forge, 1997. 348p.* A plastic surgeon in a Washington, D.C., hospital has developed an implant that eliminates scar tissue. One of his fellow doctors begins to suspect that something is amiss. Little does she know that her esteemed colleague has many more horrifying medical tricks up his sleeves.

Government Officials • Medical Horror • Washington, D.C.

Wilson, F. Paul (editor).

Diagnosis: Terminal: An Anthology of Medical Terror. *New York: Forge, 1996. 349p.* (See chapter 5, "Anthologies and Collections by Multiple Authors.")

Wilson, F. Paul, and Steve Lyon.

Nightkill. *New York: Tor Books, 1997. 304p.* (See chapter 14, "Maniacs and Sociopaths, or the Nuclear Family Explodes.")

Film

Alien. *Ridley Scott, dir. 1979. 117 minutes.* A commercial exploration spacecraft unwittingly takes on an alien life-form that stalks the crew in deep space, where "no one can hear you scream." The monster special effects are stunning, even 20 years later. Sigourney Weaver, Tom Skerritt, John Hurt, Veronica Cartwright, and Harry Dean Stanton star.

Aliens • Science Fiction

Attack of the 50-Foot Woman. *Nathan Juran, dir. 1958. (Black-and-white.) 66 minutes.* A wealthy woman marries a gold-digging playboy, and finds her only solace in alcohol and shrewishness after she discovers his inability to remain faithful. An encounter with an alien makes her literally larger than life. As her size grows proportionate to her wrath, the 50-foot woman wreaks vengeance on her faithless spouse and his paramour before being destroyed by the military. The story is a metaphor for post–World War II male fears of women. Similar title: *The Incredible Shrinking Man* (film).

Aliens • Science Fiction

Bride of Frankenstein. *James Whale, dir. 1935. (Black-and-white.) 75 minutes.* (See chapter 8, "Golems, Mummies, and Reanimated Stalkers.")

Frankenstein. *James Whale, dir. 1931. (Black-and-white.) 71 minutes.* (See chapter 8, "Golems, Mummies, and Reanimated Stalkers.")

The Incredible Shrinking Man. *Jack Arnold, dir. 1957. (Black-and-white.) 81 minutes.* Based on the novella of the same name by Richard Matheson, who also wrote the script for the movie. After he is sprayed by radioactive mist, Scott Carey begins to shrink until he is so small that he can no longer be seen by his family, and is forced to battle a spider to survive. The story is often seen as a metaphor for the position of men in post–World War II American society. Excellent special effects. Similar title: *Attack of the 50-Foot Woman* (film).

Science Fiction

Invasion of the Body Snatchers. *Don Siegel, dir. 1956. (Black-and-white.) 80 minutes.* Small-town residents are being replaced by mindless replicants that are hatched from alien pods. Classic film with a McCarthy-era subtext.

Aliens • Replicants • Science Fiction

Night of the Living Dead. *George Romero, dir. 1968. (Black-and-white.) 108 minutes.* Radiation fallout from a recently launched satellite causes the newly dead to reanimate, and they're hungry for human flesh. Once the dead bite the living, the living are similarly turned into zombies. Seven strangers are thrust together in a remote farmhouse next to a cemetery, all trying to keep the ravenous dead at bay.

African-American Characters • Apocalypse • Cannibalism • Zombies

Night of the Living Dead. *Tom Savini, dir. 1990. 96 minutes.* A remake of George Romero's classic film, starring Tony Todd (who would later go on to play Candyman in Bernard Rose's film of the same name) as Ben; it also has a Barbara who picks up a gun and quickly turns into Sigourney Weaver's Ripley from the *Alien* films, instead of merely playing the shrieking, hysterical Barbara of the earlier version. This version is both a faithful remake of and improvement on the original. George Romero as producer had considerably more money to put into this production than he did his original film, so the zombie special effects are much more graphic. Also, this version gives the viewer a peek at the post-zombie world that necessarily must follow the night of the living dead. Fans of the original *Night* and of the other films in the series will enjoy this remake.

African-American Characters • Apocalypse • Cannibalism • Zombies

The Stepford Wives. *Bryan Forbes, dir. 1975. 111 minutes.* This is a faithful adaptation of Ira Levin's novel of the same name. In Stepford, "every woman acts like every man's dream of the 'perfect' wife" and has no desire beyond pleasing her husband, caring for her children, and cleaning her house; she certainly has no time to help start a local feminist consciousness-raising group. One newcomer "watches this dream become a nightmare, … sees this nightmare engulf her best friend[, a]nd realizes that . . . her turn is coming." Starring Katharine Ross, Paula Prentiss, and Tina Loüise, with a screenplay by William Goldman.

Feminism • Replicants • Suburbia

The Terminator. *James Cameron, dir. 1984. 108 minutes.* A cyborg is sent from the future to kill a woman who will give birth to a future revolutionary leader. Arnold Schwarzenegger, Linda Hamilton, Michael Biehn, and Paul Winfield star.

Apocalypse • Cyborgs • Shapeshifters • Time Travel

Terminator 2: Judgment Day. *James Cameron, dir. 1991. 136 minutes.* The cyborg from the future returns, this time to protect the soon-to-be savior of humanity from destruction by a rival terminator. Arnold Schwarzenegger, Linda Hamilton, and Edward Furlong star.

Apocalypse • Cyborgs • Shapeshifters • Time Travel

Village of the Damned. *Wolf Rilla, dir. 1960. (Black-and-white.) 78 minutes.* Nine months after a bus accident, all the fertile women in an English village are suddenly pregnant. The resulting progeny are all eerily similar in appearance, and can fix people with their mesmerizing stares.

Aliens • Pregnancy

Our Picks

June's Picks: *The Cobweb,* Stephen Bury (Bantam); *Here, Kitty, Kitty,* Winifred Elze (St. Martin's Press).

Tony's Picks: *Mutation*, Robin Cook (Putnam); *Fragments*, James F. David (Tor Books); *Demon Seed*, Dean Koontz (Berkley); *The Boys from Brazil*, Ira Levin (Random House); *Virus*, Graham Watkins (Carroll and Graf).

Chapter 16

Rampant Animals and Other Eco-Monsters: Mother Nature's Revenge

Human arrogance has led us to believe that we are at the top of the food chain, that we outrank all other species—in short, that we are somehow special and therefore can use the earth and its nonhuman creatures as we see fit. Only recently have we begun to realize that our technology- and consumer-driven economies are destroying and dangerously depleting the earth, even as we continue our profligate use of its resources. Ecological scientists constantly remind us that this sort of wasteful behavior has its consequences: it has made several species of animals extinct, depleted the ozone layer, and created new drug-resistant superbacteria. Ecological horror, which is a relatively recent subgenre, reflects, through metaphor and dark imagery, these frightening and very real results of humanity's thoughtless "mastery" of nature.

Some horror writers argue that humans never have been and still are not at the top of the food chain, as Michael Crichton and Steve Alten do in *Jurassic Park* and *Meg*. Though both these novels deal with fictional creatures with prehistoric ties, nonetheless they remind us that "lions and tigers and bears" are the ultimate, supreme hunters. Other horror texts emphasize the revenge of the downtrodden, smaller animals in nature. Alfred Hitchcock's *The Birds* takes a not-so-lighthearted view of our feathered friends, and several Stephen King short stories explore the reasons some cultures fear our feline friends.

It should come as no surprise that various entries in this chapter are crossovers from technohorror, such as *Jurassic Park*, in which human attempts to clone dinosaurs for a nature safari park backfire, and the prehistoric reptiles demonstrate why it is not nice to fool with Mother Nature. In *The Streeter* and *Claw,* chemical spills cause domestic animals, and animals thought safely confined in zoos, to run rampant and hunt humans. In Elizabeth Forrest's *Dark Tide,* nuclear testing in the Bikini atoll awakens a Godzilla-like creature (Godzilla has always been linked to nuclear radiation).

Other entries offer no pseudoscientific explanations. Mother Nature herself, or her creatures, simply rebel, as in James Herbert's novel *Portent*, in which nature's anger is manifested in radical climate changes and natural disasters. *The Changeling Garden* is a sort of horror version of a classic bit of 1970s pseudoscience, *The Secret Life of Plants* (New York: Harper & Row, 1973): the garden begins talking to a five-year-old boy and is somehow involved in the serial murders of women. Sometimes natural monstrosities aren't even the fault of humans—nature itself can be completely unpredictable and chaotic, and thus scary. A loving pet like Cujo can become a monster and rip people limb from limb when an uncontrollable variable like rabies is introduced into the fictional reality. Yet, more often than not, killer animals act out of revenge. In Daphne du Maurier's *The Birds*, these creatures, emblems of romantic love, unleash their fury on a licentious sexpot who would tear asunder that sort of love. The horror of Mother Nature's revenge reminds us that we must face the consequences of our actions when we misuse natural resources or violate "natural" laws. Because of the relative newness of this subgenre of horror, this chapter is much briefer than the others. However, some benchmark texts do exist for ecological horror, such as Peter Benchley's *Jaws*, Michael Crichton's *Jurassic Park*, and Stephen King's *Cujo*.

Appeals: Appeals to Humans' Sense of Guilt Concerning Nature; Universal Fear of Animals; "Warning" Horror—Enlightens About Ecological Problems While Entertaining

Alten, Steve.

Meg. *New York: Dell, 1997. 278p.* Paleontologist Jonas Taylor has just discovered that the fiercest predator ever to live on earth, the giant sharklike *Carcharodon megalodon*, is not extinct as was believed. But now that its waters have been disturbed, the meg has discovered a new prey—humans. Fast-paced. An easy read. Similar titles: *Dark Tide*, Elizabeth Forrest; *The Mountain King*, Rick Hautala; *Jaws*, Peter Benchley.

Asian-American Characters • Maritime Horror • Paleontology

Barry, Scott Ian.

The Streeter. *New York: Doherty, 1994. 271p.* Dogs are driven to become feral hunters of humans after they are exposed to a chemical accident. Action-oriented. Similar title: *Claw*, Ken Eula, Joe Mauck, and Jeffrey Mauck.

Animals Run Rampant • Dogs • Weird Science

Benchley, Peter.

Jaws. *New York: Ballantine, 1991. [First published in 1974.] 278p.* A gigantic shark terrorizes a small town. Who can stop this killing machine from decimating an entire beach community? Similar title: *Meg*, Steve Alten.

Maritime Horror • Police Officer as Character

Craig, Kit.

Twice Burned. *New York: Berkley, 1995. 343p.* (See chapter 14, "Maniacs and Sociopaths, or the Nuclear Family Explodes.")

Crichton, Michael.

Jurassic Park: A Novel. *New York: Knopf, 1993. 399p.* (See chapter 15, "Technohorror.")

Daltow, Ellen (editor).

Twists of the Tale: An Anthology of Cat Horror. *New York: Dell, 1996. 366p.* (See chapter 5, "Anthologies and Collections by Multiple Authors.")

Elze, Winifred.

The Changeling Garden. *New York: St. Martin's Press, 1995. 282p.* David and Annie move into a Victorian house surrounded by lush gardens, but Annie begins to suspect that the plants in the garden have minds of their own. Then their five-year-old, David Jr., begins talking to the plants; meanwhile, women are being serially murdered in town. Heavy on characterization.

Native American Characters • Religion—Native American

Eulo, Ken, Joe Mauck, and Jeffrey Mauck.

Claw. *New York: St. Martin's Press, 1995. 319p.* A tiger escapes from the Los Angeles Zoo after apparently killing a zookeeper. However, it is soon discovered that someone has been tampering with the animal's genetics, and will stop at nothing—not even murder—to keep it a secret. Similar titles: *Here, Kitty, Kitty*, Winifred Elze; *The Streeters*, Scott Ian Barry.

Cats • Genetics • Los Angeles, California • Police Officer as Character

Forrest, Elizabeth.

Dark Tide. *New York: Daw Books, 1993. 368p.* Nuclear testing along the Bikini atoll awakens an ancient monster sleeping in the Marianas Trench, deep in the ocean floor. Now the beast is hungry. Similar titles: *Meg*, Steve Alten; *Jurassic Park*, Michael Crichton; *Cry for the Strangers*, John Saul.

California • Maritime Horror

Greenberg, Martin H. (editor).

Werewolves. *New York: Daw Books, 1995. 320p.* (See chapter 5, "Anthologies and Collections by Multiple Authors.")

Gregory, Stephen.

The Cormorant. *Clarkston, Ga.: White Wolf, 1996. 147p.* (See chapter 17, "Psychological Horror.")

Hautala, Rick.

The Mountain King. *Baltimore, Md.: CD Publications, 1996. 276p.* When a mill worker and his friend go on a hiking trip, the friend is kidnapped by a clan of Cro Magnon–like "Bigfoot" monsters. Emphasis is on outdoor action and description. Similar title: *Meg*, Steve Alten.

Bigfoot (character/creature) • Maine

Herbert, James.

Portent. *New York: Harper Prism, 1992. 323p.* Around the world, bright lights are floating up from the earth—accompanied by natural disasters that result in the gruesome deaths of any humans who view them. Climatologist James Rivers and Mama Pitie, a voodoo priestess from New Orleans, must combine forces to defeat humanity's greatest threat—the earth itself. Fast-paced, with alternating points of view. Similar title: *Where the River Rises*, Max Marlow.

Apocalypse • New Orleans, Louisiana • Religion—Voodoo

King, Stephen.

Cujo. *New York: Plume, 1981. 277p.* Murderer Frank Dodd has figured out a way to come back after death: he has managed to possess the body of Cujo, beloved family pet of the Camber family. Once Dodd's spirit and intelligence inhabit the body of the 200-pound St. Bernard, the dog goes on a rampage (attributed to rabies), dismembering and killing anyone who crosses his path. *Cujo* is another of King's masterpieces of suspense. You will never look at your pets the same way again. Made into a movie of the same name. Similar title: *Night of Broken Souls*, Thomas F. Monteleone.

Animals Run Rampant • Castle Rock, Maine • Dogs

The Dark Half. *New York: Signet Books, 1989. 484p.* (See chapter 8, "Golems, Mummies, and Reanimated Stalkers.")

Marlow, Max.

Where the River Rises. *London: Severn House, 1994. 520p.* A paleontologist searching for an extinct bird finds himself facing the terrifying forces of nature in the Amazon basin. Then he discovers that even more powerful, and more evil, forces also stand in his way. Similar title: *Portent*, James Herbert.

Amazon Basin • Demons • Paleontology

Rovin, Jeff.

Vespers. *New York: St. Martin's Press, 1998. 320p.* Bats are attacking and killing people in New York City. Can a detective and a bat expert from the Bronx Zoo figure out why, and stop them? Currently being made into a movie.

Animals Run Rampant • Bats • New York City • Police Officer as Character

Stableford, Brian.

The Werewolves of London. *New York: Carroll and Graf, 1992. 467p.* (See chapter 9, "Vampires and Werewolves.")

Strieber, Whitley.

The Wolfen. *New York: William Morrow, 1978. 252p.* (See chapter 9, "Vampires and Werewolves.")

Williams, Sidney.

Night Brothers. *New York: Pinnacle, 1989. 448p.* (See chapter 9, "Vampires and Werewolves.")

When Darkness Falls. *New York: Pinnacle, 1992. 384p.* The new substitute teacher has taken a liking to Charlie Black, the school punching bag. When bullies start to fall prey to terrible "accidents," Charlie begins to wonder if the teacher is responsible. Similar titles: *Mommy*, Max Allan Collins.

Animals Run Rampant • Dogs • High School

Zweifel, Karyn Kay.

Dog-Gone Ghost Stories. *Birmingham, Ala.: Crane Hill, 1996. 163p.* (See chapter 6, "Collections by Individual Authors.")

Film

The Birds. *Alfred Hitchcock, dir. 1963. 120 minutes.* A promiscuous blonde bombshell pursues a staid widower to the island home he shares with his mother and daughter; her presence in the community, and in the family unit, provokes an attack on all by the birds. The script for this film was loosely based on a Daphne du Maurier story. Tippi Hedren, Jessica Tandy, Suzanne Pleshette, and Rod Taylor star.

Animals Run Rampant • California

Godzilla, King of the Monsters. *Terry Morse, dir. 1956. (Black-and-white.) 80 minutes.* A giant, fire-breathing lizard threatens Japan and terrifies a young Raymond Burr. This is the original classic that spawned several sequels in which Godzilla was transformed from a monster to the protector of Japan; it has also inspired several remakes, most notably (and most expensively) in 1998.

Animals Run Rampant • Japan

The Wolf Man. *George Waggner, dir. 1941. (Black-and-white.) 70 minutes.* (See chapter 9, "Vampires and Werewolves.")

Our Picks

June's Picks: *The Birds* (film).

Tony's Picks: *Meg*, Steve Alten (Dell); *Twists of the Tale*, Ellen Daltow, ed. (Dell); *The Changeling Garden*, Winifred Elze (St. Martin's Press); *Portent*, James Herbert (Harper Prism); *Cujo*, Stephen King (Plume).

Chapter 17

Psychological Horror: It's All in Your Head

Although stories of psychological horror are for the most part devoid of supernatural monsters and bloodthirsty psychopaths, they are no less frightening. They deal with the mental torment stemming from mental illness, child abuse, guilt, and countless other types of human suffering and emotional instability. These novels question the very nature of our world, as do horror texts in general, but they take that inquiry one step further. They challenge the fictional reality that the horror writer creates. Perhaps the best way to define psychological horror is by one of the best examples of the subgenre, Ramsey Campbell's *Obsession.* Campbell's novel about being haunted by one's childhood suggests that the characters' obsession with their own guilt (due to childhood indiscretions) is more horrific than any ghost or phantom sent from a supernatural realm, to which they attribute their adult fears. After all, we all know that monsters aren't real.

Many of the entries in this chapter use the keywords *Gothic Romance* or *Gothicism* in the cross-references; these categories usually indicate characters who suffer in hells of their own making. For example, in the gothic romances of V. C. Andrews, adult heroines suffer not only because they are un*able* to break away from a harmful situation, but because they are un*willing* to challenge cultural expectations that glamorize feminine weakness. For this reason, her heroines will eternally be raped by men with an ax to grind and, furthermore, will be attracted to their rapists. In Daphne du Maurier's *Rebecca,* the nameless second Mrs. Maxim de Winter will forever be bossed around by her husband, and the far more interesting but dead Rebecca will always cast a shadow over her.

Aside from examining how we build dungeons in our own minds, psychological horror can also give voice to our darkest desires—those that we are foolish enough to believe will remain eternally buried in the murky waters of the unconscious mind. In other words, when we repress our darkest desires in real life, they may come to life in the nightmare world of our dreams (as well as in other ways); when fictional characters repress their darkest desires, those desires actually come to life, resulting in the surreal fictional worlds that define the psychological horror tale. Edgar Allan Poe's main character in "The Fall of the House of Usher" is dying because of his stubborn refusal to acknowledge his unspeakable, incestuous longings for his twin sister and his inability to desire anyone outside of the family. Reflecting the psychological state of its owner, the house begins to crumble, and eventually dies—at least in the mind of the narrator (Roderick's friend).

Our point here is not that horror is either psychological or supernatural. Those two categories are useful in compartmentalizing or organizing horror texts (as we have done here in *Hooked on Horror*), but the truth is that all horror contains elements of both, albeit mixed in different quantities. However, the novels we have included in this chapter stand apart, in that they leave the "reality" of the monster's existence up to the reader, who is often left wondering what really happened. Was it all in the characters' heads, all along?

Titles annotated in this chapter include V. C. Andrews's domestic horror, *Darkest Hour*; Clive Barker's dark fantasy, *Galilee*; Ramsey Campbell's *Obsession*; Andrei Codrescu's historically based *The Blood Countess*; newcomer Tanarive Due's *The Between*; Noel Hynd's dark police procedural, *A Room for the Dead*; Dean Koontz's *Key to Midnight*; and Patrick McGrath's gothic monologue, *Dr. Haggard's Disease*. Notable titles in this category include Andrews's *Flowers in the Attic*, Jane Austen's *Northanger Abbey*, Daphne du Maurier's *Rebecca*, and Caitlin R. Kiernan's critically acclaimed goth-rock best-seller, *Silk*.

Appeal: Character-Driven Texts; More "Domestic" Than Other Subgenres; More Realistic Fears; Open-Ended Rather Than Explained Endings; Psychological Appeal; Tendency to Be Thought-Provoking; Universality of Psychologically Horrifying Experience

Andrews, V. C.

Darkest Hour. *New York: Pocket Books, 1993. 394p.* Lillian Booth grew up in a fantasy world of parties and plantations, and then lost it all when her alcoholic father gambled it away. When her best friend has a tragic accident, Lillian begins to suspect that her life is cursed—and that she is Evil incarnate. Similar titles: *Flowers in the Attic, If There Be Thorns,* and *My Sweet Audrina*, V. C. Andrews; *Second Child*, John Saul.

Alcoholism • Incest • The South

The Dolanganger Children series.

Flowers in the Attic. *New York: Simon & Schuster, 1979. 340p.* After the sudden death of their father, the Dolanganger children and their mother find themselves penniless, and must depend upon the kindness of their maternal grandparents. But the Foxworths never approved of their daughter's marriage, and the children only serve as a bitter reminder of this misalliance; the price of accepting their impoverished prodigal daughter back into the fold is that she must keep her children in the attic—to undo their existence. Similar titles: *Darkest Hour* and *My Sweet Audrina*, V. C. Andrews; *Second Child*, John Saul.

Childhood • Incest • Secret Sin • Twins

If There Be Thorns. *New York: Pocket Books, 1990. 276p.* A little old lady neighbor, who wants nine-year-old Bart to call her "grandmother," sets events in motion that lead to violence and madness. Will she tear a loving family apart? Similar titles: *Darkest Hour* and *My Sweet Audrina*, V. C. Andrews; *Second Child*, John Saul.

> *Gothic Romance • Secret Sin*

My Sweet Audrina. *New York: Simon & Schuster, 1982. 341p.* Audrina Adare's parents have kept her innocent of the real world, and of the existence of an older sister, another Audrina, who died at the age of nine, and for whom this child was named in an attempt to re-create that first, most perfect Audrina. Andrews's ghost story is in the tradition of Daphne du Maurier's *Rebecca*, in which the ghost is more a terrible presence in the memories of the living than a spectral physical apparition. Similar titles: *Darkest Hour, Flowers in the Attic*, and *If There Be Thorns*, V. C. Andrews; *Second Child*, John Saul.

> *Rape*

Atkins, Peter.

Big Thunder. *New York: HarperCollins, 1997. 273p.* A man is saved on the mean streets of New York by a hard-boiled detective who seems to be from another time. Can it be that an author's creation has come to life and entered reality? What if some of his darker creations can enter reality as well? Similar title: *The Dark Half*, Stephen King.

> *Demons • Writer as Character*

Austen, Jane.

Northanger Abbey. *New York: Penguin, 1995. [First published in 1818.] 231p.* (See chapter 19, "Comic Horror.")

Baldick, Chris (editor).

The Oxford Book of Gothic Tales. *New York: Oxford University Press, 1992. 526p.* (See chapter 5, "Anthologies and Collections by Multiple Authors.")

Barker, Clive.

Galilee. *New York: HarperCollins, 1998. 432p.* Departure novel for Barker that contains no demons, nor any gore; instead, it is a dark fantasy about two families, interracial sex, and the American Civil War. Galilee is the son of Cesaria, for whom Thomas Jefferson erected a mansion, and he plays the central role in bringing tensions between the Barbarossa and Geory families to a head. Heavy on characterization. Similar title: *Linden Hills*, Gloria Naylor.

> *Diary Format • Eroticism • History, Use of • North Carolina • Slavery • War—American Civil War*

Sacrament. *New York: Harper Paperbacks, 1997. 624p.* Wildlife photographer Will Rabjohns has a near-death experience, which causes him to relive a strange episode in his childhood in which he meets "Death's Agent." Upon recovery, he finds that many of his gay friends have died, so he returns to England to face off against death. Lighter than the usual Barker novel, with emphasis on psychology and emotion. Similar title: *The M. D.*, Thomas M. Disch.

> *AIDS • England • Fantasy • Gay/Lesbian/Bisexual Characters • Photographer as Character*

Beman, Donald.

Avatar. *New York: Leisure Books, 1998. 366p.* A young man enamored of a famous female sculptor, known for her grotesque and horrific works, finally gets a chance to meet—and become involved with—his idol. Will he survive the encounter with her dark vision of reality? Similar title: Caitlin R. Kiernan, *Silk*.

Artist as Character • Eroticism

Berliner, Janet, and George Guthridge. The Madagascar Manifesto series.

Child of the Light. *Clarkston, Ga.: White Wolf, 1996. 389p.* Part one of The Madagascar Manifesto series, an alternative history that asks "what if the Nazis had expelled the Jews to Madagascar," as one plan called for? Similar title: *Requiem*, Graham Joyce.

Child of the Journey. *Clarkston, Ga.: White Wolf, 1996. 471p.* Part two of the Madagascar Manifesto series.

B Children of the Dusk. *Clarkston, Ga.: White Wolf, 1997. 447p.* The third part of this alternative history begins with the arrival of the Jews in Madagascar. Eerie, with emphasis on characterization and atmosphere. Winner of a Bram Stoker Award.

Africa • Alternative History • Nazism • Religion—Judaism • War—World War II

Bonansigna, Jay.

Head Case. *New York: Simon & Schuster, 1998. 318p.* John McNally wakes up with amnesia in a mental hospital, and is told that he is a suspected serial killer. With the help of a private investigator, he escapes and begins to track down his own identity. More action-oriented than the typical psychological horror novel.

Amnesia • Mental Institutions • Serial Killers

Brite, Poppy Z.

Exquisite Corpse. *New York: Scribner's, 1996. 240p.* (See chapter 18, "Splatterpunk.")

Brookes, Emma.

Dead Even. *New York: St. Martin's Press, 1996. 278p.* A woman spends 10 years of her life trying to forget being raped and left for dead—then she hears the voice of her attacker on the radio. Revenge is on her mind, but to get even she will have to enter the rapist's world of darkness. Similar title: *Widow*, Billie Sue Mosiman.

Rape • Revenge

Campbell, Ramsey.

The Last Voice They Hear. *New York: Forge, 1998. 384p.* (See chapter 14, "Maniacs and Sociopaths, or the Nuclear Family Explodes.")

The Long Lost. *New York: Tor Books, 1996. 375p.* When the Owains invite a long-lost relative to the family picnic, she begins manipulating them with her knowledge of their darkest secrets—and her ability to deliver their darkest desires. Similar title: *Linden Hills*, Gloria Naylor.

Wish Fulfillment • Witchcraft

Midnight Sun. *New York: Tor Books, 1991. 336p.* As a young boy, Ben Sterling found himself strangely attracted to the magical yet eerie powers that seemed to inhabit Sterling Forest. Twenty years later, Sterling, now a successful writer of children's books and a family man, has inherited his aunt's house, which sits on the edge of the forest—and he is even more attracted to the dark forces there than ever. As the forest's shadow approaches his house, can he break its hypnotic hold before it takes him and his family?

Natural Disasters • Writer as Character

Obsession. *New York: Macmillan, 1985. 247p.* Four teenagers receive an ad in the mail, which says simply, "Whatever you want most, I do." When the four decide to try their luck with the ad, their wishes are fulfilled to disastrous ends. Twenty-five years later, the four suddenly find themselves under siege by a power that wants payment for granting their wishes. Erudite prose, subtlety, and psychological horror pervade this Campbell chiller. Similar title: *The Store*, Bentley Little.

> *Childhood • Obsession • Wish Fulfillment*

The One Safe Place. *New York: Tor Books, 1996. 401p.* (See chapter 14, "Maniacs and Sociopaths, or the Nuclear Family Explodes.")

Cantrell, Lisa.

Boneman. *New York: Tor Books, 1995. 256p.* A career police officer and a detective team up to try to stop a mysterious drug dealer whose wares create instant addicts who then turn into zombies.

> *Drugs • North Carolina • Organized Crime • Police Officer as Character • Zombies*

Card, Orson Scott.

Homebody. *New York: HarperCollins, 1998. 291p.* (See chapter 7, "Ghosts and Haunted Houses.")

Lost Boys. *New York: HarperCollins, 1992. 528p.* (See chapter 7, "Ghosts and Haunted Houses.")

Carroll, Jonathan.

From the Teeth of Angels. *New York: Doubleday, 1994. 212p.* A travel agent begins to be visited by Death in his dreams, and ends up battling—along with others he meets—for his very life. Similar title: *Winterlong*, Elizabeth Hand.

> *Actor as Character • Death (character) • Dreams • Gay/Lesbian/Bisexual Characters • Journalist as Character*

Chapman, Stepan.

The Troika. *Tallahassee, Fla.: Ministry of Whimsy Press, 1997. 251p.* (See chapter 11, "Mythological Monsters and 'The Old Ones.' ")

Codrescu, Andrei.

The Blood Countess. *New York: Simon & Schuster, 1995. 347p.* Aristocrat Drake Bathory-Kereshtur flees Hungary during the Communist revolution and comes to America, where he revels in living a quiet life as a reporter. Thirty years later, after the fall of the Soviet Union, both Drake's editor and a group of Hungarian royalists want him to return to his native land. Drake returns to Hungary to learn that history is not a dead past that can be forgotten and erased, but a living force that shapes his life—and that his infamous ancestor, Countess Elizabeth Bathory, can compel him to do her will. Similar titles: *The Secret Life of Laszlo, Count Dracula*, Roderick Anscombe; *The Lost*, Jonathan Aycliffe; *The Between*, Tanarive Due; *The Victorian Chaise Lounge*, Marghanita Laski; *Vampyrrhic*, Simon Clark.

> *Bathory, Elizabeth de (character) • History, Use of • Hungary*

Conrad, Roxanne.

Copper Moon. *New York: Onyx, 1997. 348p.* Music teacher Abby Rhodes leads an unremarkable life in the small town of Midlands, Texas, until the day John Lee Jordan returns her missing dog. Then Abby learns what her dog knew all along: that in another life she had a mysterious, and unpleasant, connection with Jordan's family. Now she is doomed to waver between this past existence and her present one, both permeated by a gothic sort of domestic violence unique to small towns. Similar titles: *Lady of Hay*, Barbara Erskine.

> *Domestic Violence • Eroticism • Music—Classical • Police Officer as Character • Reincarnation • Revenge • Serial Killers • Texas*

Crowther, Peter, and James Lovegrove.

Escardy Gap. *New York: Tor Books, 1996. 500p.* A former best-selling writer is finding that life and art are intertwined in his newest work. Is he re-creating his childhood by re-writing reality, or has madness finally overtaken him? Excellent characterization and atmosphere. Similar titles: *The Dark Half*, Stephen King; *Symphony*, Charles Grant.

> *Childhood • The Fifties • Writer as Character*

Dann, Jack.

The Silent. *New York: Bantam, 1998. 301p.* Horrific tale of 13-year-old Mundy McDowell, who is left to wander in a nightmare landscape between haunting dreams and reality after witnessing the murder of his parents. Set during the American Civil War.

> *Dreams • War—American Civil War*

Davis, Kathryn.

Hell: A Novel. *Hopewell, N.J.: Ecco Press, 1998. 179p.* Three tales of death and despair are interwoven in this unique novel—all centered around an evil dollhouse. Erudite and clever, with emphasis on style and atmosphere.

> *Cursed Objects • Parenting • Writer as Character*

de la Mare, Walter.

The Return. *New York: Dover Books, 1922. 193p.* (See chapter 10, "Demonic Possession, Satanism, Black Magic, and Witches and Warlocks.")

Devereaux, Robert.

Walking Wounded. *New York: Dell, 1996. 273p.* Psychological study of a world rife with healers, cybersex, and moral ambiguity. Strong on characterization and motivation, particularly dealing with the relationships formed among the tale's characters.

> *Eroticism • Gay/Lesbian/Bisexual Characters*

Dobyns, Stephen.

The Church of Dead Girls. *New York: Henry Holt, 1997. 388p.* (See chapter 14, "Maniacs and Sociopaths, or the Nuclear Family Explodes.")

du Maurier, Daphne.

Rebecca. *New York: Avon, 1971. [First published in 1938.] 380p.* In this ghost story without a ghost, the second Mrs. de Winter is haunted by the presence of the first, Rebecca. Rebecca is dead but not forgotten at Manderly, where the decor of the house is a monument to Rebecca's taste, and the housekeeper, the malign Mrs. Danvers, continually compares the second Mrs. de Winter unfavorably to Rebecca, whom she adored.

Although Maxim de Winter would like to forget his first wife and settle down to a nice quiet life with his second spouse, a discovery in the bay off of Manderly won't let Rebecca, or him, rest. Made into a film by Alfred Hitchcock. Similar titles: *The Return,* Walter de la Mare; *The Dark on the Other Side*, Barbara Michaels.

England • Incest

Due, Tanarive.

The Between. *New York: HarperCollins, 1996. 288p.* A dedicated social worker and his wife, the first African-American judge in Dade County, are receiving threatening hate mail. This incident triggers weird dreams that convince Hilton he may not really be alive, and that reality may not be what it seems. Disturbing and moving, with emphasis on character development. Similar titles: *The Blood Countess*, Andrei Codrescu; *The Animal Hour*, Andrew Klavan; *The Victorian Chaise Lounge*, Marghanita Laski.

African-American Characters • Dreams • Florida • Racism

My Soul to Keep. *New York: HarperCollins, 1997. 352p.* (See chapter 11, "Mythological Monsters and 'The Old Ones.' ")

Engstrom, Elizabeth.

Lizard Wine. *New York: Delta, 1995. 260p.* The young girls whose car breaks down in the woods run across three men, one of whom carries a knife named "Gloria." The six end up spending a night filled with terror and uncertainty on a deserted campground. Emphasis is on characterization. Similar title: *Gerald's Game*, Stephen King.

Psychosexual Horror

Erskine, Barbara.

Lady of Hay. *New York: Delacorte Press, 1986. 540p.* (See chapter 12, "Telekinesis and Hypnosis.")

Forrest, Elizabeth.

Dark Tide. *New York: Daw Books, 1993. 368p.* (See chapter 16, "Rampant Animals and Other Eco-Monsters.")

Killjoy. *New York: Daw Books, 1996. 458p.* Experimental virtual-reality treatments are causing a young man to become schizophrenic. Can a disturbed psychiatrist turn an ordinary human into a serial killer? Similar title: *Dr. Jekyll and Mr. Hyde*, Robert Louis Stevenson.

Alter Ego • Psychiatrist as Character • Serial Killers • Weird Science

Gaiman, Neil.

Neverwhere. *New York: Avon, 1997. 337p.* (See chapter 11, "Mythological Monsters and 'The Old Ones.' ")

Gates, R. Patrick.

Jumpers. *New York: Dell, 1997. 388p.* After death, there is a sort of Limbo where newly arrived souls wait while it is decided whether they'll go into the light or be devoured by the Shadow Monster. Jumpers are people who can penetrate this membrane between the living and the dead, and enter this realm with the same ease that most of us can enter an Internet chat room. Two older Jumpers must help comatose Anna Wheaton, a child who has recently discovered her Jumping power and whom the Shadow Monster wants for his very own. Written from multiple points of view. Similar titles: *Dark of the Eye*, Douglas Clegg; *Strangers*, Dean Koontz.

Colorado • Eroticism • Rape

Gregory, Stephen.

The Blood of Angels. *Clarkston, Ga.: White Wolf, 1995. 492p.* Harry Clews is a man filled with such self-loathing that he goes from one disturbing relationship to another. This tapestry of dark eroticism sheds light on his psychosis by following four such relationships, as Harry tries to keep his guardian angel at bay when it attempts to interfere. Disturbing, dark, and quirky. Similar title: *In Awe*, Scott Heim.

Angels • Obsession • Psychosexual Horror

The Cormorant. *Clarkston, Ga.: White Wolf, 1996. 147p.* A history teacher and his family inherit a cottage from his recently deceased uncle, with one condition—they must take care of the uncle's pet cormorant. Soon, however, the family begins to suspect that the bird is somehow evil, and they cannot escape its malice. Emphasis is on locale and atmosphere. Similar title: *Althea*, Abigail McDaniels.

Birds • Cursed Objects • Marriage • Teacher as Character • Wales

Hand, Elizabeth, and Chris Carter.

The X-Files: Fight the Future. *New York: Harper Prism, 1998. 177p.* Novelization of the *X-Files* movie, with added characters and material.

Federal Bureau of Investigation • Science Fiction

Harrison, M. John.

Signs of Life. *New York: St. Martin's Press, 1997. 253p.* (See chapter 15, "Technohorror.")

Hartwell, David G. (editor).

The Dark Descent. *New York: Tor Books, 1987. 1,011p.* (See chapter 5, "Anthologies and Collections by Multiple Authors.")

Hawkes, Judith.

Julian's House. *New York: New American Library, 1991. 400p.* Newlywed parapsychologists David and Sally set up their equipment in a haunted Victorian house, only to find that their relationship is as haunted as the house itself. Emphasis is on description and psychology of the characters. Similar title: *The Haunting of Hill House*, Shirley Jackson.

Haunted Houses • Marriage • Parapsychology

Hawthorne, Nathaniel.

The House of the Seven Gables. *New York: Oxford University Press, 1991. [First published in 1851.] 328p.* Young Phoebe cannot escape a family curse that is somehow linked to a grotesque daguerreotype of the family patriarch. Emphasis is on characterization. A literary classic. Similar title: *The Picture of Dorian Gray*, Oscar Wilde.

Family Curse • Haunted Houses • New England

Heim, Scott.

In Awe. *New York: HarperCollins, 1997. 291p.* Three outcasts—a young gay teenager, an older nymphomaniacal woman, and a grief-stricken mother—join forces in this quirky tale of dark eroticism and deadly stalkers. Emphasis on characterization, graphic violence, and frank sexuality. Similar title: *The Blood of Angels*, Stephen Gregory.

Gay/Lesbian/Bisexual Characters • Grieving • Kansas • Writer as Character

Homes, A. M.

The End of Alice. *New York: Scribner's, 1996. 270p.* (See chapter 14, "Maniacs and Sociopaths, or the Nuclear Family Explodes.")

Hynd, Noel.

A Room for the Dead. *New York: Pinnacle, 1994. 412p.* Dark psychological horror novel in which detective Sergeant Frank O'Hara is called out to investigate the gory mutilation/murder of two young women. The modus operandi fits that of executed serial killer Gary Ledbetter, whose ghost haunts O'Hara's days and nights. Emphasis on character development and atmosphere. Similar titles: *Exquisite Corpse*, Poppy Z. Brite; *Red Dragon* and *The Silence of the Lambs*, Thomas Harris; *Zombie*, Joyce Carol Oates.

> *Gay/Lesbian/Bisexual Characters • Necrophilia • Philadelphia, Pennsylvania • Police Officer as Character • Serial Killers*

Joyce, Graham.

Requiem. *New York: Tor Books, 1995. 286p.* (See chapter 11, "Mythological Monsters and 'The Old Ones.' ")

Kay, Susan.

Phantom. *New York: Dell, 1991. 532p.* (See chapter 14, "Maniacs and Sociopaths, or the Nuclear Family Explodes.")

Kessler, Gabriel Devlin.

Landscape of Demons and The Book of Sarah. *Boston: Millennium Press, 1998. 233p.* A young man from an abusive family grows up unable to distinguish reality from fantasy. Will his acting-out of the personalities of his real and imaginary friends lead to evil?

> *Child Abuse • Schizophrenia/Multiple Personality Disorder*

Kiernan, Caitlin R.

Silk. *New York: Penguin, 1998. 353p.* Members of a struggling Birmingham, Alabama, underground band take up with Spyder, an ex–mental institution ward who was abused as a child. During a strange ritual in Spyder's childhood home, the group awakens to what its members believe to be demonic forces. Or is it all in their minds? A well-received debut novel by this goth-noir horror novelist. Similar titles: *Avatar*, Donald Beman; *University*, Bentley Little; *The Devil on May Street*, Steve Harris.

> *Alabama • Asian-American Characters • Child Abuse • Drugs • Gay/Lesbian/Bisexual Characters • Gothicism • Music—Rock Music*

Kimball, Michael.

Undone. *New York: Avon, 1996. 416p.* Sal Erickson is dragged into an embezzlement scheme when his best friend suddenly dies. As he digs deeper into the reality of his friend's demise, he discovers dark secrets about his home town of Gravity, Maine.

> *Maine • Mistaken Identity*

King, Stephen.

Gerald's Game. *New York: Viking, 1992. 332p.* Jessie Burlingame and her husband, Gerald, vacation at a secluded cottage in the woods. When one of Gerald's "sex games" goes awry, Jessie finds herself handcuffed to a bed with no one around to save her. Excellent psychological horror and study of dysfunctional families. Similar title: *Lizard Wine*, Elizabeth Engstrom.

Animals Run Rampant • Psychosexual Horror • Sadomasochism

Insomnia. *New York: Penguin-Signet, 1995. 663p.* After his wife's death, Ralph Roberts begins seeing things: strange auras of light around people and three small, bald men in doctor's uniforms. Do these men have anything to do with the sudden violent tendencies of some of Ralph's friends? King's writing is steadily paced and conversational. Similar titles: *The M. D.,* Thomas M. Disch; *Neverwhere*, Neil Gaiman; *The Devil on May Street*, Steve Harris.

Domestic Terrorism • Domestic Violence • Violence—Theories of

It. *New York: Viking, 1986. 1,138p.* Pennywise the Clown, a monstrous personification of all that is scary and evil, has returned to a small New England town to claim the souls of a handful of adults whom he terrorized as children. Was made into a television miniseries starring Tim Curry, of *The Rocky Horror Picture Show* fame.

Childhood • Clowns • New England • Shapeshifters

Skeleton Crew. *New York: Putnam, 1985. 512p.* (See chapter 6, "Collections by Individual Authors.")

Klavan, Andrew.

The Animal Hour. *New York: Pocket Books, 1993. 342p.* This clever novel interweaves a tale of lost identity with one of a gruesome serial killer. Nancy Kincaid awakens one Halloween to find that she is no longer Nancy Kincaid—and that she must stop a murder before "the animal hour." Written from various points of view. Similar titles: *The Between*, Tanarive Due; *The Victorian Chaise Lounge*, Marghanita Laski.

Mistaken Identity • New York City • Serial Killers

Koja, Kathe.

🅑 **The Cipher.** *New York: Bantam, 1991. 356p.* Nicholas and Nakota, two Gen-X nonconformists, discover a mysterious black hole that devours or changes anything that ventures into it. When an adventurous Nakota tries to stick her head through, Nicholas tries to stop her and his hand goes in instead. After that, life is never the same, as his hand becomes a weeping sore and he begins hearing voices. Winner of a Bram Stoker Award. Similar titles: *Silk*, Caitlin R. Kiernan; *The Devil on May Street*, Steve Harris.

Eroticism • Obsession

Koontz, Dean.

The Face of Fear. *New York: Berkley, 1985. 306p.* (See chapter 14, "Maniacs and Sociopaths, or the Nuclear Family Explodes.")

The House of Thunder. *New York: Berkley, 1992. 253p.* In Koontz's version of a tale like Stephen King's "Sometimes They Come Back," Susan Thornton awakens from an accident-induced coma to find herself in the same hospital with the four men who murdered her boyfriend 12 years earlier. The only problem is that these four men supposedly died violent deaths years before. Now it seems that their ghosts want to finish off the witness who got away the first time—Susan. Filled with plot twists and truly eerie moments. Similar title: *The Key to Midnight*, Dean Koontz.

Amnesia • Espionage

The Key to Midnight. *New York: Berkley, 1979. 416p.* When Alex Hunter spots Joanna Rand singing in a Kyoto nightclub, she seems vaguely familiar. After the two begin seeing one another, he realizes that she is the daughter of a famous U.S. senator; however, she cannot remember her past, nor the reason she has recurring nightmares about a man with metallic fingers. Originally published under the pseudonym Leigh Nichols. Similar title: *The House of Thunder* and *Mr. Murder*, Dean Koontz.

Dreams • Espionage • Japan • Mistaken Identity • Rape

Strangers. *New York: Putnam, 1986. 681p.* Across the country, a handful of people who don't know one another begin having similar nightmares and begin sharing a sense of paranoia. Soon their paths will cross and they will have to face their greatest fears. Heavy on suspense. Similar titles: *Jumpers*, R. Patrick Gates.

Aliens • Clergy as Character • Dreams • Experiments—Military

Laski, Marghanita.

The Victorian Chaise Lounge. *Chicago: Academy Chicago, 1984. 90p.* Melanie, a new mother dying from tuberculosis, is finally allowed by her overprotective doctor and her overbearing husband to leave her bedroom, and she chooses to rest on an antique Victorian chaise lounge that has a strange dark spot on it. She wakes after a nap to find herself in another time and in another woman's body. Similar titles: *The Blood Countess*, Andrei Codrescu; *The Between*, Tanarive Due; *The Animal Hour*, Andrew Klavan.

Mistaken Identity • Pregnancy • Reincarnation • Time Travel • Victorian England

Laymon, Richard.

The Midnight Tour. *Baltimore, Md.: Cemetery Dance Publications, 1998. 596p.* The Beast House tour continues, but only the bravest dare take the midnight tour.

Haunted Houses

Lessing, Doris.

The Fifth Child. *New York: Vintage, 1989. 133p.* Harriet and David Lovatt share the typical middle-class family dream: a big house full of happy children. Despite the expense, the couple manages, through its children, to hold onto the dream. Then another child arrives, a hideous, insatiable monstrosity. Clever, subtle satire by an acclaimed writer. Similar titles: *The Mask*, Dean Koontz; *The Dark One*, Guy N. Smith.

England • Parenting

Ligotti, Thomas.

Grimscribe: His Lives and Works. *New York: Carroll and Graf, 1991. 214p.* A Hawthornesque collection of the grotesque and paranormal adventures of the pop-culture Grimscribe. Includes five sections: "The Voice of the Damned," "The Voice of the Demon," "The Voice of the Dreamer," "The Voice of the Child," and "The Voice of Our Name." All tales are written in first person; reminiscent of Poe and Hawthorne.

Human Sacrifice • Parapsychology • Scholars • Weird Science

Noctuary. *New York: Carroll and Graf, 1994. 194p.* (See chapter 6, "Collections by Individual Authors.")

Songs of a Dead Dreamer. *New York: Carroll and Graf, 1990. 275p.* (See chapter 6, "Collections by Individual Authors.")

Little, Bentley.

The Mailman. *New York: Penguin, 1991. 320p.* (See chapter 13, "Small-Town Horror.")

The Store. *New York: Signet Books, 1998. 431p.* (See chapter 11, "Mythological Monsters and 'The Old Ones.' ")

Lovecraft, H.P.

Tales of H.P. Lovecraft: Major Works. *Hopewell, N.J.: Ecco Press, 1997. 328p.* (See chapter 6, "Collections by Individual Authors.")

Maginn, Simon.

Virgins and Martyrs. *Clarkston, Ga.: White Wolf, 1996. 316p.* A young scholar investigating fourteenth-century executions of women suspected of witchcraft moves into a new apartment, and is soon plagued with visions that threaten his sense of reality. Action-oriented, but good on psychology and characterization as well. Similar titles: *Houses of Stone*, Barbara Michaels; *The Shadowy Horses*, Susanna Kearsley.

Dreams • Haunted Houses • The Inquisition • Scholars • Witchcraft

Marlowe, Stephen.

The Lighthouse at the End of the World. *New York: Dutton, 1995. 324p.* A fictionalized account of Poe's life; this novel traces his New York period, his doomed marriage, and his travel to Paris to investigate his brother's death. Very complex narrative style, with emphasis on psychology, characterization, and symbolism. Similar titles: *Madeline After the Fall of Usher*, Marie Kiraly; *Return to the House of Usher*, Robert Poe.

Alternative History • Baltimore, Maryland • Gothicism • New York City • Poe, Edgar Allan (character) • Writer as Character

Matheson, Richard.

The Incredible Shrinking Man. *New York: Tor Books, 1994. 373p.* (See chapter 6, "Collections by Individual Authors.")

Now You See It. *New York: Tor Books, 1996. 220p.* A paralyzed magician must use the darkest of tricks to prevent his ungrateful son and nefarious daughter-in-law from pirating his act. Filled with plot twists, wordplay, visual tricks, and suspense.

Magic • Mistaken Identity • Quadriplegic as Character • Revenge

McCabe, Patrick.

The Butcher Boy. *New York: Dell, 1994. 231p.* Well-written tale of a young Irish boy who is a murderous psychopath in the making. Unique in its approach to the serial killer tale, as it examines the forces that lead to sociopathy rather than the outcome. Made into a film in 1998 by Neil Jordan, featuring Sinead O'Connor as the Virgin Mary.

Alcoholism • Domestic Violence • Ireland • Mental Institutions • Serial Killers

McCammon, Robert R.

Gone South. *New York: Pocket Books, 1997. 359p.* A Vietnam War veteran goes on the run into the Louisiana swamps after killing a bank officer, and is chased by a strange array of grotesques, including a Siamese twin bounty hunter and an Elvis impersonator. More a characterization tale than a horror tale, but one filled with surrealism and nightmare images. Similar title: *The Neighborhood*, S. K. Epperson.

Deformity • Gothicism • Louisiana • Presley, Elvis (Impersonator/Character) • Twins • War—Vietnam War

McFarland, Dennis.

A Face at the Window. *New York: Bantam, 1998. 309p.* (See chapter 7, "Ghosts and Haunted Houses.")

McGrath, Patrick.

Dr. Haggard's Disease. *New York: Simon & Schuster, 1993. 191p.* Dr. Edward Haggard meets the son of the woman he once had an affair with and has carried a brightly burning torch for ever since. He relates to his lover's son, now a pilot in World War II, the tale of how he and the young man's mother met, fell in love, and ultimately parted. Unique narrative in that it is told entirely in second person and has a jolting ending. Very powerful.

> *Dramatic Monologue • War—World War II*

Spider. *New York: Simon & Schuster, 1990. 221p.* Spider Cleg relates, in this first-person monologue, the events that have led to his losing his mind—including witnessing the murder of his mother. Or so he claims. *Spider* is McGrath's study of the psychology of a twisted mind.

> *Dramatic Monologue • Matricide/Patricide*

McLean, Duncan.

Bunker Man. *New York: W. W. Norton, 1997. 297p.* A new janitor at a Scotland high school begins to spot a strange man lurking around classrooms—and becomes obsessed with hunting down what he calls the "bunker man." Dark psychological horror. Similar title: *The Eternal*, Mark Chadbourn.

> *Child Molesters • High School • Obsession • Scotland*

Michaels, Barbara.

House of Many Shadows. *New York: Berkley, 1974. 293p.* (See chapter 7, "Ghosts and Haunted Houses.")

Houses of Stone. *New York: Berkley, 1994. 384p.* (See chapter 7, "Ghosts and Haunted Houses.")

Witch. *New York: Berkley, 1973. 292p.* (See chapter 7, "Ghosts and Haunted Houses.")

Moloney, Susan.

A Dry Spell. *New York: Delacorte Press, 1997. 385p.* Goodlands, North Dakota, has suffered a four-year drought that has turned it into the infamous Badlands, but this drought is accompanied by a dark and sinister force that has people at one another's throats and that seems to envelop the entire community in its dusty mist. Can one man, a rainmaker, stop the evil? Similar title: *Symphony*, Charles Grant.

> *Natural Disasters • North Dakota • Revenging Revenant*

Moore, Susanna.

In the Cut. *New York: Knopf, 1995. 180p.* (See chapter 14, "Maniacs and Sociopaths, or the Nuclear Family Explodes.")

Morris, Mark.

The Immaculate. *Clarkston, Ga.: White Wolf, 1992. 411p.* A successful horror writer returns to his childhood home in the British countryside for a funeral, only to find that his childhood fears are beginning to invade the real world. Can he survive the terror, guilt, and humiliation of a dark past come to life? Similar titles: *The Dark Half*, Stephen King; *Scissorman*, Mark Chadbourn.

Child Abuse • England • Grieving • Writer as Character

Morrison, Robert, and Chris Baldick (editors).

The Vampyre and Other Tales of the Macabre. *New York: Oxford University Press, 1997. 278p.* (See chapter 5, "Anthologies and Collections by Multiple Authors.")

Murrey, Mary.

The Inquisitor. *New York: Lapwing Books, 1997. 238p.* A depressed, lonely woman in Florida discovers witchcraft, but her use of her menstrual blood attracts a strange Doberman dog, who becomes her familiar. Grotesque and violent, with emphasis on psychology.

Dogs • Florida • Religion—Paganism • Witches

Neiderman, Andrew.

The Devil's Advocate. *New York: Pocket Books, 1997. 320p.* (See chapter 11, "Mythological Monsters and 'The Old Ones.' ")

Newman, Kim.

The Night Mayor. *New York: Carroll and Graf, 1990. 186p.* The Night Mayor narrates this trek through the streets of New York City, replete with every film-noir convention imaginable. A cross between a hard-boiled detective narrative and a who's-who of Hollywood. Newman's first novel. Similar title: *Horror Show*, Greg Kihn.

Dreams • New York City

Oates, Joyce Carol.

Haunted: Tales of the Grotesque. *London: Signet, 1994. 310p.* (See chapter 6, "Collections by Individual Authors.")

Zombie. *New York: Dutton, 1995. 181p.* (See chapter 14, "Maniacs and Sociopaths, or the Nuclear Family Explodes.")

Partridge, Norman.

Slippin' into Darkness. *New York: Kensington, 1996. 303p.* Eighteen years after high school, a beautiful woman commits suicide, causing the classmates responsible for ruining her life to have to deal with their guilt—and her ghost. Unique and intense. Emphasis is on characterization and atmosphere. A Bram Stoker Award winner. Similar title: *Ghost Story*, Peter Straub.

Rape • Revenging Revenant • Secret Sin

Poe, Robert.

Return to the House of Usher. *New York: Tor Books, 1997. 282p.* John Charles Poe, descendant of Edgar Allan Poe, is a small-town reporter in Crowley, Virginia, and heir to the family fortune. He has just received the most unusual part of the Poe legacy—the casket. The three-foot-long wooden box, which is passed on to every male Poe on his thirtieth birthday, contains the notes and personal papers of the Poe men dating back to the eerie and mysterious Edgar Allan. John Charles has sworn not to divulge the casket's secrets, but a call from his oldest friend, Roderick Usher, who is on the verge of a break-down, may justify doing just that. Similar titles: *Madeline After the Fall of Usher*, Marie Kiraly; *The Lighthouse at the End of the World*, Stephen Marlowe.

> *Incest • Schizophrenia/Multiple Personality Disorder • Twins • Virginia • Writer as Character*

Roszak, Theodore.

The Memoirs of Elizabeth Frankenstein. *New York: Bantam, 1996. 425p.* Rescued by a remarkable noblewoman of Geneva from a life of poverty among gypsies, Elizabeth Lavenza was destined to be more than a foster sister to Victor Frankenstein. She would lead him on a quest into the shadowy realms of alchemy and paganism, commingling the scientific, the spiritual, and the sexual. But the shattering of their bond would send Victor on his pursuit of unholy and dangerous knowledge. Similar titles: *Phantom*, Susan Kay; *Mina*, Marie Kiraly.

> *Alchemy • Alternative Literature • Diary Format • Eroticism • Feminism • Frankenstein, Caroline (character) • Frankenstein, Dr. (character) • Gothic Romance • Lavenza, Elizabeth (character) • Religion—Paganism • Switzerland • Witches*

Royle, Nicholas.

Counterparts. *Clarkston, Ga.: White Wolf, 1996. 397p.* Strange and unsettling novel about two men who have a psychic connection; the horrors they face, both real and imagined; and the disturbing modern world in which they live. Dark, with emphasis on atmosphere. Similar titles: *The Shining*, Stephen King; *Twice Burned*, Kit Craig.

> *Actor as Character • Alter Ego • Dreams • Racial Identity • Twins*

Saul, John.

Second Child. *New York: Bantam, 1990. 341p.* Two stepsisters, Melissa and Teri, are forced to live together after the fiery death of Teri's parents. Now Melissa, who has always been unpopular, is relegated to being a second child. When several friends of the girls are murdered, everyone is left wondering if Teri, Melissa, or Melissa's invisible friend D'Arcy is responsible. Similar titles: *Darkest Hour, Flowers in the Attic, If There Be Thorns,* and *My Sweet Audrina*, V. C. Andrews; *The Other*, Thomas Tryon; *Carrie*, Stephen King; *Hell Fire*, John Saul.

> *Maine • Revenge • Sibling Rivalry*

The Unloved. *New York: Bantam, 1988. 311p.* Helena Devereaux, family matriarch and owner of the Sea Oaks, the crumbling family mansion, dies, but her spirit lives on in the mind of her daughter, Marguerite. But when family members are murdered one by one, Marguerite must come to terms with her obsession. Similar titles: *Darkest Hour, Flowers in the Attic, If There Be Thorns,* and *My Sweet Audrina*, V. C. Andrews; *The Influence*, Ramsey Campbell.

> *Grieving*

Steinke, Darcey.

Jesus Saves. *New York: Atlantic Monthly Press, 1997. 212p.* Interwoven stories of young girls growing up in a middle-class suburban town, revolving around a sadistic child molester and a disillusioned minister's daughter. Disturbing in its graphic qualities, and highly emotional. Similar title: *The Church of Dead Girls*, Stephen Dobyns.

> *Child Molesters • Clergy as Character • Rape • Sadomasochism • Suburbia*

Straub, Peter.

The Hellfire Club. *New York: Random House, 1996. 463p.* This metafictionalized narrative traces the fall of a wealthy New England family whose male heir belongs to a club that promotes shameless self-indulgence. Narrative style is complex but clever, with elements of mystery fiction interwoven.

Family Curse • New England • Secret Sin • Writer as Character

Strayhorn, S. J.

Black Night. *New York: Kensington, 1996. 273p.* S. K. Epperson, under a pseudonym, wrote this psychological thriller about two women who attempt to exorcise the nightmares of a dark past, only to awaken an evil that is intent upon repeating the crimes of the past.

Dreams • Kansas • Orphans • Revenge

Taylor, Bernard.

Charmed Life. *New York: Leisure Books, 1994. 366p.* Guy Holman must be part feline, because time and time again he is able to elude certain death. However, this is a mixed blessing, because those he loves mysteriously disappear. Little does he know that he's being watched by a group of people with precognitive powers, and that he is a mere pawn in a much larger game they play with the forces of good and evil.

England • New York City • Parapsychology • Precognition

Tessier, Thomas.

Fog Heart. *New York: St. Martin's Press, 1998. 320p.* Two couples are visited by the ghosts of relatives, so together they approach a famous medium to contact the dead. However, doing so means revealing the secrets of each person's past—including murder. Nice mixture of the psychological and supernatural. Erudite.

Marriage • Parapsychology

Tryon, Thomas.

The Night of the Moonbow. *New York: Random House, 1989. 320p.* Very subtle psychological thriller about the new kid at a summer camp. Leo Joaquin doesn't quite fit in, but most of the regulars at the Friend-Indeed Bible camp like him. However, when a jealous Reese Hartsig manipulates Leo's fragile emotional state by playing on his dark past, violence and death result. Similar title: *Carrie*, Stephen King.

Childhood • Revenge

Tuttle, Lisa.

The Pillow Friend. *Clarkston, Ga.: White Wolf, 1996. 334p.* Agnes Grey wishes for several things—a horse of her own and the love of a poet—and learns a lesson when wishes come true in this dark fantasy. Cleverly written as a series of stories that all add up to a continuous narrative. Erotic and disturbing.

Dreams • Eroticism • Wish Fulfillment

Tyson, Donald.

The Messenger. *St. Paul, Minn.: Llewellyn, 1993. 272p.* (See chapter 7, "Ghosts and Haunted Houses.")

Upchurch, Michael.

Passive Intruder. *New York: W. W. Norton, 1995. 369p.* (See chapter 7, "Ghosts and Haunted Houses.")

Wilhelm, Kate.

The Good Children. *New York: St. Martin's Press, 1988. 224p.* A family in Oregon is devastated by the tragic deaths of the parents, but the children will do anything to avoid being separated into foster homes. A tale that challenges the nature of reality and bends the definitions of life and death, with emphasis on characterization and psychology. Similar title: *Gone*, Kit Craig.

Childhood • Grieving • Oregon • Sibling Rivalry

Film

Carnival of Souls. *Herk Harvey, dir. 1962. (Black-and-white.) 80 minutes.* A young church organist has a near-death experience when her car veers off a bridge and she nearly drowns. Months later, she leaves home to pursue her musical career in another city, but is inexplicably drawn to a now-defunct carnival haunted by beings only she can see. Low-budget film, shot mostly on location in Kansas, that has developed quite a cult following. What *Carnival of Souls* lacks in plot it makes up for with its eerie atmosphere.

Gothicism • Kansas

Dr. Jekyll and Mr. Hyde. *Victor Flemming, dir. 1941. (Black-and-white.) 114 minutes.* (See chapter 14, "Maniacs and Sociopaths, or the Nuclear Family Explodes.")

Rebecca. *Alfred Hitchcock, dir. 1940. (Black-and-white.) 130 minutes.* Hitchcock's first American film is a faithful adaptation of Daphne du Maurier's novel of the same name. In this story, a young woman marries a widowed nobleman and both fight the "ghost" of his former wife. Joan Fontaine and Laurence Olivier star. Winner of Academy Awards for Best Picture and Cinematography.

England • Gothic Romance

The Wicker Man. *Robin Hardy, dir. 1973. 84 minutes.* (See chapter 13, "Small-Town Horror.")

Our Picks

June's Picks: *The Blood Countess,* Andrei Codrescu (Dell); *The Memoirs of Elizabeth Frankenstein,* Theodore Roszak (Bantam).

Tony's Picks: *In Awe,* Scott Heim (HarperCollins); *A Room for the Dead,* Noel Hynd (Pinnacle); *Insomnia,* Stephen King (Penguin-Signet); *Slippin' into Darkness*, Norman Partridge (Kensington); *The Good Children*, Kate Wilhelm (St. Martin's Press).

Chapter 18

Splatterpunk: The Gross-Out

    The newest subgenre of horror (emerging sometime in the late 1980s), splatterpunk is a style of writing more than a theme with any particular type of monster (which explains why many of the works in this chapter are cross-referenced in other chapters). Splatterpunk is also known by the name *extreme horror*. In the typical splatterpunk story, graphic sex and violence abound as a result of the decadent indulgences of bored mortals and immortals, rather than as a result of shocking excesses of monsters that must be stopped. Punk, alternative, and heavy metal music are often part of the backdrop of a splatterpunk story. There are no reluctant vampires or antiheroes here—splatterpunk monsters revel in their monstrosity. A typical example of the genre is Poppy Z. Brite's vampire novel *Lost Souls*, wherein promiscuous, bisexual male vampires rend their victims' flesh with glee as they drink their blood, and a father/son pair commit incest as a natural (for their kind, anyway) expression of their kinship. Other writers representative of this category include Clive Barker, David J. Show, John Shirley, and John Skipp.

    Appeals: Breaking the Rules and Conventions of Society; Curiosity and Fascination with Amorality; Gore; "Hard-Boiled" Narrative Techniques; Monsters Possess Appeal of Raw Power; Punk; Truly Evil Monsters; Youthful Characters

Atkins, Peter.

Big Thunder. *New York: HarperCollins, 1997. 273p.* (See chapter 17, "Psychological Horror.")

Bischoff, David.

The Crow: Quoth the Crow. *New York: Harper Prism, 1998. 256p.* Based on The Crow series and "The Raven" by Edgar Allan Poe, this novel tells a tale of blackmail and black magic. Emphasis is on characterization and action. Similar titles: *The Crow: Clash by Night*, Chet Williamson; *The Crow: The Lazarus Heart*, Poppy Z. Brite.

> *Academia • Alternative Literature • The Crow (character) • Gothicism*

Bowker, David.

The Butcher of Glastonbury. *London: Victor Gollancz, 1997. 224p.* (See chapter 11, "Mythological Monsters and 'The Old Ones.' ")

Brite, Poppy Z.

The Crow: The Lazarus Heart. *New York: Harper Prism, 1998. 256p.* A serial killer murders one of a set of twins, and frames his friend, a photographer, who is then executed. The second twin, Lucrece, recalls the dead photographer for revenge. Emphasis on description and action. Similar titles: *The Crow: Quoth the Crow*, David Bischoff; *The Crow: Clash by Night*, Chet Williamson.

> *The Crow (character) • Gay/Lesbian/Bisexual Characters • Gothicism • New Orleans, Louisiana • Twins*

Drawing Blood. *New York: Dell, 1994. 403p.* Twenty years ago, Trevor Black's father, a cartoonist à la R. Crumb, lost his ability to draw. He murdered his wife and toddler son, then killed himself, leaving only Trevor alive. Trevor has finally returned to Missing Mile, North Carolina, to revisit the scene of his father's crime, and there he confronts the ghosts that inhabit the last place his family lived. Multiple points of view. Similar title: *Lori*, Robert Bloch.

> *Computer Hackers • Domestic Violence • Gay/Lesbian/Bisexual Characters • Haunted Houses • Homoeroticism • Missing Mile, North Carolina*

Exquisite Corpse. *New York: Scribner's, 1996. 240p.* For serial killer Andrew Compton, murder is a high art. Compton escapes from an English prison and comes to New Orleans, where he meets Jay Byrne, a dissolute playboy, serial killer, and fellow necrophile. Together they use young Vietnamese-American runaways to further the expression of their "art." Graphic and disturbing. Similar titles: *American Psycho*, Bret Easton Ellis; *Psycho* and *American Gothic*, Robert Bloch; *The Silence of the Lambs*, Thomas Harris; *Zombie*, Joyce Carol Oates; *Butcher*, Rex Miller; *Billy*, Whitley Strieber; *A Room for the Dead*, Noel Hynd.

> *AIDS • Asian-American Characters • Cannibalism • Dahmer, Jeffrey—Murders • Gay/Lesbian/Bisexual Characters • Homoeroticism • Necrophilia • New Orleans, Louisiana • Serial Killers*

Lost Souls. *New York: Bantam-Dell, 1992. 355p.* A disturbed teenager named Nothing discovers that his father is a bloodthirsty vampire who travels with a duo of vampire goons. On his journey to self-discovery, Nothing befriends Steve and Ghost, band members of Lost Souls?. Using multiple narrators, Brite creates intensely homoerotic scenes, with careful character development interspersed with passages of extreme violence. Similar titles: *Nomads*, Chelsea Quinn Yarbro; *Stainless*, Todd Grimson.

> *Gay/Lesbian/Bisexual Characters • Homoeroticism • Missing Mile, North Carolina • Music—Rock Music • New Orleans, Louisiana • Vampire as New Species • Vampire's Point of View*

(editor). **Love in Vein: Twenty Original Tales of Vampire Erotica.** *New York: Harper Paperbacks, 1994. 396p.* (See chapter 5, "Anthologies and Collections by Multiple Authors.")

(editor). **Love in Vein II: Eighteen More Original Tales of Vampire Erotica.** *New York: Harper Prism, 1997. 375p.* (See chapter 5, "Anthologies and Collections by Multiple Authors.")

Wormwood. *New York: Dell, 1995. 225p.* (See chapter 6, "Collections by Individual Authors.")

Collins, Nancy A.

Sunglasses After Dark. *New York: New American Library, 1989. 253p.* (See chapter 9, "Vampires and Werewolves.")

Wild Blood. *New York: New American Library, 1994. 298p.* (See chapter 9, "Vampires and Werewolves.")

Collins, Nancy, Martin H. Greenburg, and Edward Kramer (editors).

Dark Love. *New York: ROC Books, 1996. 398p.* (See chapter 5, "Anthologies and Collections by Multiple Authors.")

Ellis, Bret Easton.

American Psycho. *New York: Random House, 1991. 399p.* Story of a 20-something yuppie who tortures and murders young women, keeping their body parts afterward. Controversial shocker that pulls no punches. Graphic and gory. Similar titles: *Exquisite Corpse*, Poppy Z. Brite; *Psycho*, Robert Bloch; *The Silence of the Lambs*, Thomas Harris; *Zombie*, Joyce Carol Oates; *The Church of Dead Girls*, Stephen Dobyns.

Serial Killers • Slasher

Elton, Ben.

Popcorn. *New York: St. Martin's Press, 1997. 304p.* (See chapter 14, "Maniacs and Sociopaths, or the Nuclear Family Explodes.")

Harris, Steve.

The Devil on May Street. *London: Vista, 1998. 381p.* (See chapter 11, "Mythological Monsters and 'The Old Ones.' ")

Hynd, Noel.

A Room for the Dead. *New York: Pinnacle, 1994. 412p.* (See chapter 17, "Psychological Horror.")

Koja, Kathe.

The Cipher. *New York: Bantam, 1991. 356p.* (See chapter 17, "Psychological Horror.")

Lee, Edward, and Elizabeth Steffen.

Portrait of the Psychopath as a Young Woman. *Orlando, Fla.: Necro Publications, 1998. 292p.* (See chapter 14, "Maniacs and Sociopaths, or the Nuclear Family Explodes.")

Little, Bentley.

University. *New York: Signet Books, 1995. 416p.* The collective consciousness of Brea University is one of insanity and evil—an alarming number of rapes and murders have been taking place on campus. Students and professors hear whispered "suggestions" of their darkest desires when they're alone, and feel compelled to act on these suggestions. A palpable evil lurks on the deserted sixth floor of the university library. Original, engrossing, and terrifying. Told from multiple points of view. Similar titles: *Jago* and *The Quorum*, Kim Newman; *The Haunting of Hill House*, Shirley Jackson; *The Mailman*, Bentley Little; *December* and *Curfew*, Phil Rickman; *The Tommyknockers*, Stephen King; *Silk*, Caitlin R. Kiernan.

> *California • Haunted Houses • Human Sacrifice • Journalist as Character • Mind Control • Racism • Rape*

McCammon, Robert R.

Mine. *New York: Pocket Books, 1990. 487p.* (See chapter 14, "Maniacs and Sociopaths, or the Nuclear Family Explodes.")

Miller, Rex.

Butcher. *New York: Pocket Books, 1994. 308p.* (See chapter 14, "Maniacs and Sociopaths, or the Nuclear Family Explodes.")

Savant. *New York: Pocket Books, 1994. 277p.* (See chapter 14, "Maniacs and Sociopaths, or the Nuclear Family Explodes.")

Sammon, Paul M. (editor).

Splatterpunks Over the Edge. *New York: Tor Books, 1995. 416p.* (See chapter 5, "Anthologies and Collections by Multiple Authors.")

Saul, John.

Black Lightning. *New York: Ballantine, 1993. 438p.* (See chapter 14, "Maniacs and Sociopaths, or the Nuclear Family Explodes.")

Slade, Michael.

Ghoul. *New York: New American Library, 1989. 386p.* Horror fiction fuels the already twisted imagination of a schizophrenic, an ingenious serial murderer obsessed with H.P. Lovecraft's Cthulhu mythos. It's up to Mountie Zinc Chandler to track the killer through Canada, the United States, and England and stop him before he kills again. Michael Slade's (the pen name of three who write collaboratively) writing is gory and gripping, and full of the intricate details of modern police work. Similar titles: all of Slade's other titles; *Exquisite Corpse*, Poppy Z. Brite; *Carrion Comfort*, Dan Simmons; *Shadows*, Bonnie Faber; *Belladonna*, Karen Moline.

> *Canada • Chandler, Zinc (character) • Cthulhu (character) • Incest • London, England • Pittsburgh, Pennsylvania • Royal Canadian Mounted Police • Serial Killers*

Headhunter. *New York: Onyx, 1984. 422p.* Mountie Robert DeClerq is persuaded to come out of retirement to help catch the Headhunter, a serial killer who decapitates his female victims and taunts the police by sending them pictures of the women's severed heads. Clever plot, surprise ending, and a wealth of details about criminology, as practiced in both Canada and the lower 48 United States, make this novel a page-turner. Told from multiple points of view, including the murderer's. Similar works: all of Slade's other titles; *Exquisite Corpse*, Poppy Z. Brite; *Carrion Comfort*, Dan Simmons; *Shadows*, Bonnie Faber; *In the Cut*, Susanna Moore.

> *DeClerq, Robert (character) • Federal Bureau of Investigation • Headhunter, The (character) • Psychosexual Horror • Royal Canadian Mounted Police • Schizophrenia/Multiple Personality Disorder • Serial Killers • Vancouver, British Columbia*

Primal Scream. *New York: Signet Books, 1998. 432p.* Inspector Robert De-Clerq is being stalked by a killer from his past—the Headhunter. Can DeClerq save a young child, and himself, or will the Headhunter finally have his revenge? Similar titles: all of Slade's other novels; *Shadows*, Bonnie Faber.

> *DeClerq, Robert (character) • Headhunter, The (character) • Revenge • Royal Canadian Mounted Police • Vancouver, British Columbia*

Ripper. *New York: Penguin, 1994. 416p.* The militant feminists are ultimately to blame for a group of Satanic serial killers, who slash to shreds the body of America's foremost feminist, rip off her face, and display her corpse under a bridge. The Royal Canadian Mounted Police track the killers in this literate, well-researched novel of detection and horror. Similar works: all of Slade's other titles; *Exquisite Corpse*, Poppy Z. Brite; *Carrion Comfort*, Dan Simmons.

> *Chandler, Zinc (character) • Jack the Ripper Murders • Religion—Satanism • Revenge • Royal Canadian Mounted Police • Serial Killers • Tarot*

Straub, Peter.

Floating Dragon. *New York: Putnam, 1983. 515p.* (See chapter 14, "Maniacs and Sociopaths, or the Nuclear Family Explodes.")

Strieber, Whitley.

The Forbidden Zone. *New York: Wilson and Neff, 1993. 415p.* (See chapter 11, "Mythological Monsters and 'The Old Ones.' ")

Our Picks

June's Picks: *The Butcher of Glastonbury*, David Bowker (Victor Gollancz); *American Psycho*, Bret Easton Ellis (Random House); *Headhunter*, Michael Slade (Onyx); *Ripper,* Michael Slade (Penguin).

Tony's Picks: *Exquisite Corpse,* Poppy Z. Brite (Scribner's); *Lost Souls*, Poppy Z. Brite (Bantam-Dell); *A Room for the Dead,* Noel Hynd (Pinnacle); *Floating Dragon*, Peter Straub (Putnam).

Chapter 19

Comic Horror: Laughing at Our Fears

Many do not realize that horror has *always* had an element of the comic in it. Although Freddy Krueger and the Crypt Keeper may have been the first high-profile monsters to crack jokes before disposing of victims or introducing a tale of horror, there are comic threats predating these by more than 50 years. (For example, lines such as "She has a nice neck," spoken by Max Schreck's vampire character when he first sees a picture of Mina in the film *Nosferatu*.) When it comes to the written word, laughing at our fears goes back to the earliest of horror texts. Humor in horror can be found in the understated reactions of Hrothgar's warriors to the monster Grendel in the Old English epic *Beowulf*, and in the melodrama and irony of a good Poe tale. The old gypsy woman in Tod Browning's *Dracula* and the old busybody in James Whale's *Frankenstein*, are both excellent examples of comic relief in early Universal Studios horror films, which helped define the genre for decades to come.

This relationship should come as no shock, for, psychologically speaking, humor and horror go hand in hand—in the reactions of both the characters in horror texts and the readers/viewers of horror texts. The former, in their hurry to escape the monster, run into posts and walls, trip over small rocks, and trip over themselves. In more recent, self-reflective horror, it is not unusual to find intended victims making highly ironic comments foreshadowing their own deaths. As for the reader/viewer, he or she will laugh nervously when expectations are built up, and the monster is surely about to appear—but the mysterious noise turns out to be only a cat rummaging in a trash can.

Sometimes the humor in horror is not as subtle as the instances cited here, as publications by Christopher Moore and Thomas M. Disch, and films by Mel Brooks and Rusty Cundieff, exemplify. As in any other genre, some horror writers and directors choose parody as their method of expression. These masters of comic horror realize how important it is that we laugh at our fears, and so they create works like Moore's *Practical Demon Keeping*, the title of which suggests the absurdity of suspending disbelief when reading a horror text in which demons intervene in the everyday lives of unwitting humans. The entire novel begs the reader to consider the ultimate silliness of accidentally awakening a demon and then being stuck with it. Then there's Jack Cody's *The Off Season*, which reasons that a town inhabited by ghosts would be a great tourist attraction. Of a less absurd type are novels such as Disch's *The Business Man*, which suggests through dark humor that waking up to find oneself a zombie in a grave is not as fun or empowering as has been represented by past horror writers; or Jane Austen's *Northanger Abbey*, which shows that often horror is just a product of an overactive imagination; or even Kingsley Amis's *The Green Man*, which leaves the reader comically suspended between the world of the supernatural and that of an alcoholic innkeeper, considering the possible existence of a ghost.

The relationship between horror and comedy has not been lost on the film industry either. It has resulted in lines dripping with dramatic irony, such as when the serial-killer stepfather in Joseph Ruben's film, *The Stepfather,* tells his stepdaughter—and intended victim—"let's just bury the hatchet." It is also shown in brilliant comic scenes such as the opening frame of Cundieff's *Tales from the Hood*, where three gang members try to act brave while visiting a strange-looking funeral home run by a crazed mortician.

We devoted this chapter to horror texts that teach us that we can indeed laugh at our fears. Listed here are works that revolve around comic characters, off-the-wall situations, and downright silly manifestations of monsters (as in William Browning Spencer's *Resume with Monsters*, which includes possessed office machines). Also included are dark comedies and parodies of serious works. Outstanding works of fiction in this category include Kingsley Amis's *The Green Man*, Jane Austen's *Northanger Abbey*, Christopher Moore's *Practical Demon Keeping*, Dan Simmons's *The Fires of Eden*, and John Updike's *The Witches of Eastwick*.

Appeals: Enjoyment of Works That Stretch the Formulas of the Genre to Absurdity; Humor; Identification with Complex Characters' Emotions of Humor/Horror; Sense of Familiarity Achieved with Parody (Inside Joke Appeal)

Amis, Kingsley.

The Green Man. *New York: Harcourt Brace, 1969. 252p.* Alcoholic innkeeper Maurice Allington is seeing ghosts at the Green Man Inn. Is his mind playing tricks on him, or are the ghosts real and dangerous? Subtle in its humorous approach, this masterful piece of British satire is quite enjoyable. Similar titles: *Northanger Abbey*, Jane Austen; *The Shining*, Stephen King; *A Face at the Window*, Dennis McFarland; *The Canterville Ghost*, Oscar Wilde; *The Business Man*, Thomas M. Disch.

Alcoholism • Haunted Houses

Austen, Jane.

Northanger Abbey. *New York: Penguin, 1995. [First published in 1818.] 231p.* When Catherine Morland comes to Northanger Abbey, she meets all the trappings of gothic horror and imagines the worst. Fortunately, she has at hand her own fundamental good sense and the irresistible, albeit unsentimental, Henry Tilney. Disaster does eventually strike, in the real world as distinct from the romantic one of her imagination, but without spoiling for too long the gay, good-humored atmosphere of this most delightful of books. Similar titles: *The Green Man*, Kingsley Amis; *The Canterville Ghost*, Oscar Wilde; *The Castle of Otranto*, Horace Walpole.

England • Gothic Romance

Bachman, Richard [pseud. of Stephen King].

Thinner. *New York: New American Library, 1984. 282p.* (See chapter 10, "Demonic Possession, Satanism, Black Magic, and Witches and Warlocks.")

Baldick, Chris.

The Oxford Book of Gothic Tales. *New York: Oxford University Press, 1992. 526p.* (See chapter 5, "Anthologies and Collections by Multiple Authors.")

Cacek, P. D.

Night Prayers. *Darien, Ill.: Design Image, 1998. 219p.* (See chapter 9, "Vampires and Werewolves.")

Cody, Jack.

The Off Season. *New York: St. Martin's Press, 1995. 352p.* Point Vestal, a ghost town in the strictest sense of the term, is under siege. Newcomer August Starling threatens to bring Point Vestal into the present by opening it to tourists—an idea its ghostly inhabitants do not like. Inventive and thought-provoking dark comedy.

Fantasy

Collins, Nancy A.

Wild Blood. *New York: New American Library, 1994. 289p.* (See chapter 9, "Vampires and Werewolves.")

Disch, Thomas M.

The Business Man. *New York: Berkley, 1984. 325p.* Robert Glandier is approaching middle age, so he marries a younger woman. When she leaves him, he finds her and strangles her, and now her corpse cannot rest. Both Giselle Glandier and her mother return from the dead to seek justice. Uniquely funny, written from the point of view of the returning dead as well as that of the murderer. Similar titles: *The Green Man*, Kingsley Amis; *Resume with Monsters*, William Browning Spencer; *The Fires of Eden*, Dan Simmons; *The Priest*, Thomas M. Disch.

Revenging Revenant • Zombies

The Priest: A Gothic Romance. *New York: Knopf, 1995. 303p.* Farfetched dark fantasy about an alcoholic, pedophile priest who finds himself mysteriously transported into the body of a medieval prelate. As with most Disch horror, its strength is the author's comic juxtaposition of evil against a backdrop of everyday life. Similar title: *The Business Man*, Thomas M. Disch.

Abortion • Alcoholism • Child Molesters • Clergy as Character • Religion— Christianity—Catholicism • Time Travel

Elrod, P. N.

Chill in the Blood. *New York: Ace Books, 1998. 327p.* (See chapter 9, "Vampires and Werewolves.")

Epperson, S. K.

Green Lake. *New York: Fine Books, 1996. 263p.* (See chapter 13, "Small-Town Horror.")

The Neighborhood. *New York: Leisure Books, 1996. 304p.* (See chapter 14, "Maniacs and Sociopaths, or the Nuclear Family Explodes.")

Hamilton, Laurell K. The Anita Blake, Vampire Hunter series.

Guilty Pleasures. *New York: Penguin, 1993. 265p.* In a futuristic world where vampires' rights are protected by the Supreme Court, someone is killing them. Can vampire hunter extraordinaire Anita Blake stop the murders? Quirky, with emphasis on character and action. First-person narration. Similar titles: *Bloodsucking Fiends: A Love Story* and *Practical Demon Keeping*, Christopher Moore; *Celestial Dogs*, Jay S. Russell; *Eye of the Daemon* and *Eyes of the Empress*, Camille Bacon-Smith; *Shattered Glass*, Elaine Bergstrom; *Chill in the Blood* and *Art in the Blood*, P. N. Elrod; *Vampire$*, John Steakley.

Blake, Anita (character) • Serial Killers • St. Louis, Missouri • Vampire Hunters

The Laughing Corpse. *New York: Penguin, 1994. 293p.* A mercenary "animator" is raising the dead and causing problems for Anita Blake. Further adventures of Hamilton's sassy and tough vampire killer, complete with the wry humor and hard-boiled edge that define the series. First-person narration. Similar titles: *Bloodsucking Fiends: A Love Story* and *Practical Demon Keeping*, Christopher Moore; *Celestial Dogs*, Jay S. Russell; *Eye of the Daemon* and *Eyes of the Empress*, Camille Bacon-Smith; *Shattered Glass*, Elaine Bergstrom; *Vampire$*, John Steakley; *Art in the Blood*, P. N. Elrod.

Blake, Anita (character) • St. Louis, Missouri • Vampire Hunters

Circus of the Damned. *New York: Berkley-Ace, 1995. 329p.* The third book in the Anita Blake series tells of Blake's being fought over by two rival vampires, who both want her as their human servant/lover. Can she survive being caught up in the middle of a feud between the undead? Emphasis is on dark fantasy and detection. First-person narration. Similar titles: *Bloodsucking Fiends: A Love Story* and *Practical Demon Keeping*, Christopher Moore; *Celestial Dogs*, Jay S. Russell; *Eye of the Daemon* and *Eyes of the Empress*, Camille Bacon-Smith; *Shattered Glass*, Elaine Bergstrom; *Suckers*, Anne Billson; *Vampire$*, John Steakley; *Art in the Blood*, P. N. Elrod.

Blake, Anita (character) • St. Louis, Missouri • Vampire Clans • Vampire Hunters

Bloody Bones. *New York: Penguin, 1996. 370p.* Misadventures of vampire hunter/animator Anita Blake, who must juggle a request to raise the dead to gain information and a need to solve a series of killings in and around Branson, Missouri. First-person narration. Similar titles: *Bloodsucking Fiends: A Love Story* and *Practical Demon Keeping*, Christopher Moore; *Celestial Dogs*, Jay S. Russell; *Eye of the Daemon* and *Eyes of the Empress*, Camille Bacon-Smith; *Shattered Glass*, Elaine Bergstrom; *Vampire$*, John Steakley; *Art in the Blood*, P. N. Elrod.

Blake, Anita (character) • Serial Killers • St. Louis, Missouri • Vampire Hunters

The Lunatic Cafe. *New York: Penguin, 1996. 369p.* In this tongue-in-cheek, first-person narrative adventure, Anita Blake must determine who or what is killing werewolves. The only problem this time is that she is personally involved in her work—she is in love with one of them. Similar titles: *Bloodsucking Fiends: A Love Story* and *Practical Demon Keeping*, Christopher Moore; *Celestial Dogs*, Jay S. Russell; *Eye of the Daemon* and *Eyes of the Empress*, Camille Bacon-Smith; *Shattered Glass*, Elaine Bergstrom; *Vampires$*, John Steakley; *Art in the Blood*, P. N. Elrod.

Blake, Anita (character) • St. Louis, Missouri • Vampire Hunters • Werewolves

The Killing Dance. *New York: Ace Books, 1997. 387p.* Anita Blake is caught between warring werewolves and the master vampire Jean-Claude, and one of them has put a price on her head. Will she have to make an uneasy alliance to survive? Similar titles: *Bloodsucking Fiends: A Love Story* and *Practical Demon Keeping*, Christopher Moore; *Celestial Dogs*, Jay S. Russell; *Eye of the Daemon* and *Eyes of the Empress*, Camille Bacon-Smith; *Shattered Glass*, Elaine Bergstrom; *Vampire$*, John Steakley; *Art in the Blood*, P. N. Elrod.

> *Blake, Anita (character)* • *St. Louis, Missouri* • *Vampire Hunters* • *Werewolves*

Burnt Offerings. *New York: Berkley-Ace Books, 1998. 400p.* The seventh book in the Anita Blake series continues the love triangle between Anita, her werewolf/lover, and the vampire Jean-Claude. Interspersed with the romance is Anita's attempt to catch a telekinetic fire-starter. Similar titles: *Bloodsucking Fiends: A Love Story* and *Practical Demon Keeping*, Christopher Moore; *Celestial Dogs*, Jay S. Russell; *Eye of the Daemon* and *Eyes of the Empress*, Camille Bacon-Smith; *Shattered Glass*, Elaine Bergstrom; *Suckers*, Anne Billson; *Vampire$*, John Steakley; *Art in the Blood*, P. N. Elrod.

> *Blake, Anita (character)* • *St. Louis, Missouri* • *Vampire Hunters*

Blue Moon. *New York: Penguin, 1998. 342p.* The eighth book in Hamilton's Anita Blake, Vampire Hunter series has Blake attempting to save a friend from corrupt police and werewolf clans. Similar titles: P. N. Elrod's Vampire Files series.

> *Blake, Anita (character)* • *Tennessee* • *Vampire Clans* • *Werewolves*

Hynes, James.

Publish and Perish: Three Tales of Tenure and Terror. *New York: Picador, 1997. 338p.* (See chapter 6, "Collections by Individual Authors.")

Kemske, Floyd.

Human Resources. *North Haven, Conn.: Catbird Press, 1995. 223p.* The new executive director of a failing biotech company turns out to be a vampire, in this satirical send-up of corporate mentality. Flashbacks provide some interesting historical satire. Similar titles: *Resume with Monsters*, William Browning Spencer; *Carrion Comfort*, Dan Simmons; *The Store*, Bentley Little.

> *Economic Violence* • *Fantasy* • *History, Use of* • *Vampire's Point of View*

Kihn, Greg.

Horror Show. *New York: Tor Books, 1996. 274p.* When *Monster Magazine* reporter Clint Stockbern sets out to interview the legendary 1950s horror-movie director Landis Woodley (an Ed Wood type B–moviemaker), he uncovers a bizarre story of real-life horror. In 1957, Woodley shot his last zombie movie, *Cadaver*, in an actual morgue, where the available dead double as actors who don't demand union scale. But then a deadly curse began to claim those involved with Woodley's productions. Similar titles: *The Uncanny*, Andrew Klavan; *The Drive-In*, Joe R. Lansdale; *The Ten Ounce Siesta*, Norman Partridge; *Ancient Images*, Ramsey Campbell; *The Night Mayor*, Kim Newman.

> *Demons* • *The Fifties* • *Hollywood, California* • *Horror Movie Industry* • *Religion—Satanism*

Klavan, Andrew.

The Uncanny. *New York: Crown, 1998. 343p.* Hollywood producer Richard Storm travels to England to find the real ghosts that have inspired his horror flicks. Instead, he finds a strange array of weird characters and an alternate reality that follows the plot of one of his films. Emphasis on character, dialogue, and description. Similar titles: *Horror Show*, Greg Kihn; *The Drive-In*, Joe R. Lansdale.

England • Horror Movie Industry

Koontz, Dean.

Ticktock. *New York: Ballantine, 1996. 335p.* A subtly humorous tale of a young Vietnamese-American man who is "brought back" into his family in a most extreme way. He is pursued by a cursed rag doll turned reptilian demon. He has from nightfall until dawn to escape it—and to find love. Similar title: *Practical Demon Keeping*, Christopher Moore.

Asian-American Characters • Demons • Writer as Character

Lansdale, Joe R.

The Drive-In: A Double-Feature Omnibus. *New York: Carroll and Graf, 1989. 341p.* Quirky tale about a group of Texans who end up trapped for all eternity in a drive-in theater. Emphasis is on social satire and comic absurdity. Similar titles: *Horror Show*, Greg Kihn; *The Uncanny*, Andrew Klavan.

Apocalypse • Fantasy • Natural Disasters • Texas

Moore, Christopher.

Bloodsucking Fiends: A Love Story. *New York: Avon, 1996. 300p.* After Jody Stroud is "turned" by a vampire in San Francisco, she enlists her grocery-store clerk boyfriend, an emperor, and his army of pie-tin helmeted dogs. A comic romp about vampires, love, and snapping turtles. Strong on dialogue and quirky characters. Similar titles: *Practical Demon Keeping*, Christopher Moore; Laurell K. Hamilton's Anita Blake, Vampire Hunter series.

Gay/Lesbian/Bisexual Characters • San Francisco, California • Vampire's Point of View

Practical Demon Keeping: A Comedy of Horrors. *New York: St. Martin's Press, 1992. 243p.* A young seminary student accidentally summons a minor demon and now is stuck as the demon's caretaker. Can he figure out a way to get someone else to take the imp off his hands before all his friends and acquaintances are devoured? Similar titles: *Bloodsucking Fiends: A Love Story*, Christopher Moore; Laurell K. Hamilton's Anita Blake, Vampire Hunter series.

California • Demons • New Age

Partridge, Norman.

The Ten Ounce Siesta. *New York: Berkley, 1998. 254p.* Jack Baddalach, ex–boxing champion and current Mob runner, is given a strange assignment: escort a sick Chihuahua across the Nevada desert. But to do so, he will have to face gun-toting maniacs, Satanists, and dragons. Clever and original. Similar title: *Horror Show*, Greg Kihn.

Fantasy • Las Vegas, Nevada • Organized Crime • Religion—Satanism

Prill, David.

Serial Killer Days. *New York: St. Martin's Press, 1996. 208p.* A small town in Minnesota holds an annual festival to draw tourists in, celebrating an annual serial killing. Meanwhile, a local high-school senior looks for fearful events so she can become Scream Queen. Quirky satire of the American obsession with murder. Similar titles: *Dominion*, Bentley Little; *The Off Season*, Jack Cody.

High School • Minnesota • Serial Killers

The Unnatural. *New York: St. Martin's Press, 1996. 237p.* Andy Archer, a young farm boy who wants fame at any price, is dead-set on becoming the world's fastest embalmer, in this satire on the funeral industry. Quirky and unpredictable.

High School • Minnesota • Mortuary Science

Russell, Jay S.

Burning Bright. *New York: St. Martin's Press, 1998. 288p.* (See chapter 10, "Demonic Possession, Satanism, Black Magic, and Witches and Warlocks.")

Celestial Dogs. *New York: St. Martin's Press, 1997. 272p.* (See chapter 11, "Mythological Monsters and 'The Old Ones.' ")

Sackett, Jeffrey.

Blood of the Impaler. *New York: Bantam, 1989. 340p.* (See chapter 9, "Vampires and Werewolves.")

Simmons, Dan.

The Fires of Eden. *New York: Putnam, 1994. 399p.* The construction of a posh condo in Hawaii has awakened the Hawaiian gods of the underworld, and now they want revenge. Although this story begins as straightforward horror, the masterful, subtle comedy soon becomes apparent. A fun read. Simmons portrays the beauty of Hawaii, even of its volcanoes, exceptionally well. Similar title: *The Business Man*, Thomas M. Disch.

Cooke, Cordie (character) • Hawaii • Religion—Hawaiian

Spencer, William Browning.

Irrational Fears. *Clarkston, Ga.: White Wolf, 1998. 233p.* An alcoholic literature professor and his alcoholic love interest cross paths with a group of "twelve steppers" and their extremist rivals. A kidnapping leads them to a realization of the true cause of alcoholism: Lovecraftian monsters. Similar title: *Resume with Monsters*, William Browning Spencer.

Academia • Alcoholism • Cthulhu (character) • Cults • Virginia

 Resume with Monsters. *Sag Harbor, N.Y.: Permanent Press, 1995. 212p.* Luckless employee Philip Kenan goes from menial job to menial job—and begins to realize that his employers, and their office machines, are in league with Lovecraftian monsters who want to enslave all humanity. Recipient of an International Literary Guild Award for Best Novel. Similar titles: *The Business Man*, Thomas M. Disch; *Practical Demon Keeping*, Christopher Moore; *The Green Man*, Kingsley Amis; *Human Resources*, Floyd Kemske; *Irrational Fears*, William Browning Spencer.

Cthulhu (character)

Steakley, John.

Vampire$. *New York: Penguin-ROC, 1990. 357p.* (See chapter 9, "Vampires and Werewolves.")

Stone, Del, Jr.

Dead Heat. *Austin, Tex.: Mojo Press, 1996. 188p.* A Harley-riding loner becomes a zombie after a biological apocalypse—only he is different from other zombies because he can think and control the dead masses. Darkly humorous. Recipient of an International Literary Guild Award for Best First Novel.

Apocalypse • Biological Warfare • Cyberpunk • Texas • Zombies

Strieber, Whitley.

The Wild. *New York: Doherty, 1991. 378p.* Bob would love nothing more than to become a wolf and allow his wild side to come out. When, by some strange miracle, he does become one, his new lifestyle creates challenges for his family and community. Funny in parts. More a character analysis than a plot-driven novel. Similar title: *Dominion*, Bentley Little.

Gang Violence • Werewolves

Wilde, Oscar.

The Canterville Ghost. *Cambridge, Mass.: Candlewick Press, 1996. [First published in 1891.] 128p.* Classic tale about an American family that moves into a haunted English manor and refuses to believe in its resident ghost. But then the teenage daughter begins to witness strange occurrences. Exemplar of Wilde's comic wit and flair for language. Similar titles: *The Green Man*, Kingsley Amis; *Northanger Abbey*, Jane Austen.

England • Haunted Houses

Film

Tales from the Hood. *Rusty Cundieff, dir. 1995. 98 minutes.* Four gangsters come to a funeral home just before midnight to make a drug deal with the proprietor, who insists on regaling them with tales about each of his clients before agreeing to make the deal. The frame tale and the tales themselves parody the classic style of the Universal Studios horror films of the 1930s, as well as B-movie horror from the 1950s and 1960s, but the content of these tales is deadly serious. The creatures viewers would normally identify as monsters are monsters in the original meaning of the word—they're divine warnings. The true monsters are humans who refuse to heed the warnings. Starring Corbin Bernsen, David Allen Grier, and Clarence Williams III.

African-American Characters • Domestic Violence • Gang Violence • Haunted Houses • Police Brutality • Racism • Revenging Revenant • Satan (character)

Our Picks

June's Picks: *Horror Show*, Greg Kihn (Tor Books).

Tony's Picks: *Northanger Abbey*, Jane Austen (public domain/Penguin); *The Business Man*, Thomas M. Disch (Berkley); *The Neighborhood*, S. K. Epperson (Leisure Books); Laurell K. Hamilton's Anita Blake, Vampire Hunter series; *Serial Killer Days*, David Prill (St. Martin's Press).

Part 4

Ready Reference, Criticism, and Other Helpful Information

Chapter 20

Stretching the Boundaries: Cross-Genre Horror Fiction

Action Adventure

Alten, Steve:
> *Meg* (chapter 16, "Rampant Animals and Other Eco-Monsters")

Bacon-Smith, Camille:
> *Eye of the Daemon* (chapter 10, "Demonic Possession, Satanism, Black Magic, and Witches and Warlocks")

Ball, Donna:
> *Dark Angel* (chapter 14, "Maniacs and Sociopaths, or the Nuclear Family Explodes")

Bergstrom, Elaine:
> *Blood Rites* (chapter 9, "Vampires and Werewolves")

Brouwer, Sigmund:
> *Double Helix* (chapter 15, "Technohorror")

Cameron, James:
> *The Terminator* (film)
> *Terminator 2: Judgment Day* (film) (both chapter 15, "Technohorror")

Clark, Leigh:
> *Carnivore* (chapter 15, "Technohorror")

Collins, Nancy A.:
> *Tempter* (chapter 9, "Vampires and Werewolves")

Cook, Robin:
>*Chromosome 6*
>*Coma*
>*Contagion*
>*Fatal Cure*
>*Harmful Intent*
>*Mortal Fear*
>*Outbreak*
>*Vital Signs* (all chapter 15, "Technohorror")

Crichton, Michael:
>*Jurassic Park* (chapter 15, "Technohorror")

Davis, Joy, and Don Davis:
>*Bring on the Night* (chapter 9, "Vampires and Werewolves")

Dedman, Stephen:
>*The Art of Arrow Cutting* (chapter 10, "Demonic Possession, Satanism, Black Magic, and Witches and Warlocks")

Eulo, Ken, Joe Mauck, and Jeffrey Mauck:
>*Claw* (chapter 16, "Rampant Animals and Other Eco-Monsters")

Farris, John:
>*Sacrifice* (chapter 11, "Mythological Monsters and 'The Old Ones' ")

Forrest, Elizabeth:
>*Bright Shadow* (chapter 14, "Maniacs and Sociopaths, or the Nuclear Family Explodes")
>*Death Watch* (chapter 15, "Technohorror")

Gerritsen, Tess:
>*Harvest* (chapter 15, "Technohorror")

Goingback, Owl:
>*Crota* (chapter 11, "Mythological Monsters and 'The Old Ones' ")

Golden, Christopher:
>*Hellboy: The Lost Army* (chapter 10, "Demonic Possession, Satanism, Black Magic, and Witches and Warlocks")

Hamilton, Laurell K.:
>The Anita Blake, Vampire Hunter series (chapter 19, "Comic Horror")

Harris, Thomas:
>*Black Sunday* (chapter 14, "Maniacs and Sociopaths, or the Nuclear Family Explodes")

Hautala, Rick:
>*The Mountain King* (chapter 16, "Rampant Animals and Other Eco-Monsters")

Miller, Linda Lael:
>   *Forever and the Night* (chapter 9, "Vampires and Werewolves")

Moline, Karen:
>   *Belladonna* (chapter 14, "Maniacs and Sociopaths, or the Nuclear Family Explodes")

Monahan, Brent:
>   *The Blood of the Covenant: A Novel of the Vampiric* (chapter 9, "Vampires and Werewolves")

Palmer, Michael:
>   *Critical Judgment*
>   *Extreme Measures*
>   *Natural Causes* (all chapter 15, "Technohorror")

Preston, Douglas, and Lincoln Child:
>   *The Relic*
>   *Reliquary* (both chapter 11, "Mythological Monsters and 'The Old Ones' ")

Romkey, Michael:
>   *The Vampire Virus* (chapter 9, "Vampires and Werewolves")

Rule, Leslie:
>   *Kill Me Again* (chapter 14, "Maniacs and Sociopaths, or the Nuclear Family Explodes")

Russell, Jay S.:
>   *Burning Bright* (chapter 10, "Demonic Possession, Satanism, Black Magic, and Witches and Warlocks")

Ryan, Shawn:
>   *Nocturnas* (chapter 9, "Vampires and Werewolves")

Saberhagen, Fred:
>   *Thorn*
>   *A Question of Time* (both chapter 9, "Vampires and Werewolves")

Simmons, Dan:
>   *Children of the Night* (chapter 9, "Vampires and Werewolves")
>   *Summer of Night* (chapter 10, "Demonic Possession, Satanism, Black Magic, and Witches and Warlocks")

Slade, Michael:
>   *Cut Throat* (chapter 14, "Maniacs and Sociopaths, or the Nuclear Family Explodes")
>   *Evil Eye* (chapter 14, "Maniacs and Sociopaths, or the Nuclear Family Explodes")
>   *Ghoul* (chapter 18, "Splatterpunk")
>   *Headhunter* (chapter 18, "Splatterpunk")
>   *Ripper* (chapter 18, "Splatterpunk")

Spruill, Steven:
 My Soul to Take
 Painkiller (both chapter 15, "Technohorror")

Steakley, John:
 Vampire$ (chapter 9, "Vampires and Werewolves")

Stone, Del, Jr.:
 Dead Heat (chapter 19, "Comic Horror")

Tilton, Lois:
 Darkness on the Ice (chapter 9, "Vampires and Werewolves")

Tyson, Donald:
 The Tortuous Serpent: An Occult Adventure (chapter 11, "Mythological Monsters and 'The Old Ones' ")

Williamson, John N.:
 Spree (chapter 14, "Maniacs and Sociopaths, or the Nuclear Family Explodes")

Wilson, Charles:
 Direct Descendant (chapter 15, "Technohorror")

Wilson, F. Paul, and Steve Lyon:
 Nightkill (chapter 14, "Maniacs and Sociopaths, or the Nuclear Family Explodes")

Wood, Bari:
 Doll's Eyes (chapter 14, "Maniacs and Sociopaths, or the Nuclear Family Explodes")

Detection

Atkins, Peter:
 Big Thunder (chapter 17, "Psychological Horror")

Bacon-Smith, Camille:
 The Eye of the Daemon series (chapter 10, "Demonic Possession, Satanism, Black Magic, and Witches and Warlocks")

Bergstrom, Elaine:
 Shattered Glass (chapter 9, "Vampires and Werewolves")

Bloch, Robert:
>*Lori* (chapter 7, "Ghosts and Haunted Houses")
>*Psycho* (chapter 14, "Maniacs and Sociopaths, or the Nuclear Family Explodes")
>*Psycho House* (chapter 14, "Maniacs and Sociopaths, or the Nuclear Family Explodes")

Bonansigna, Jay R.:
>*Head Case* (chapter 17, "Psychological Horror")

Bowker, David:
>*The Butcher of Glastonbury* (chapter 11, "Mythological Monsters and 'The Old Ones' ")

Bury, Stephen:
>*The Cobweb* (chapter 15, "Technohorror")

Caine, Jeffrey:
>*Curse of the Vampire* (chapter 9, "Vampires and Werewolves")

Campbell, Ramsey:
>*Ancient Images* (chapter 10, "Demonic Possession, Satanism, Black Magic, and Witches and Warlocks")

Cantrell, Lisa:
>*Boneman* (chapter 17, "Psychological Horror")

Card, Orson Scott:
>*Treasure Box* (chapter 10, "Demonic Possession, Satanism, Black Magic, and Witches and Warlocks")

Clements, Mark A.:
>*Lorelei* (chapter 11, "Mythological Monsters and 'The Old Ones' ")

Cook, Robin:
>*Chromosome 6*
>*Coma*
>*Contagion*
>*Fatal Cure*
>*Harmful Intent*
>*Mortal Fear*
>*Mutation*
>*Terminal*
>*Toxin*
>*Vital Signs* (all chapter 15, "Technohorror")

Cooke, John Peyton:
>*Haven: A Novel of Anxiety* (chapter 13, "Small-Town Horror")

Courtney, Vincent:
>*Vampire Beat* (chapter 9, "Vampires and Werewolves")

Craig, Kit:
> *Gone*
> *Twice Burned* (both chapter 14, "Maniacs and Sociopaths, or the Nuclear Family Explodes")

Curry, Chris:
> *Thunder Road* (chapter 13, "Small-Town Horror")

Deaver, Jeffrey:
> *A Maiden's Grave* (chapter 14, "Maniacs and Sociopaths, or the Nuclear Family Explodes")

Dobyns, Stephen:
> *The Church of Dead Girls* (chapter 14, "Maniacs and Sociopaths, or the Nuclear Family Explodes")

Elrod, P. N.:
> The Vampire Files series (chapter 9, "Vampires and Werewolves")

Engstrom, Elizabeth:
> *Lizard Wine* (chapter 17, "Psychological Horror")

Etchison, Dennis:
> *Shadow Man* (chapter 14, "Maniacs and Sociopaths, or the Nuclear Family Explodes")

Faber, Bonnie:
> *Shadow* (chapter 14, "Maniacs and Sociopaths, or the Nuclear Family Explodes")

Farris, John:
> *Sacrifice* (chapter 11, "Mythological Monsters and 'The Old Ones' ")

Forbes, Bryan:
> *The Stepford Wives* (film) (chapter 15, "Technohorror")

Forrest, Elizabeth:
> *Bright Shadow* (chapter 14, "Maniacs and Sociopaths, or the Nuclear Family Explodes")
> *Death Watch* (chapter 15, "Technohorror")

Fowler, Christopher:
> *Red Brideby* (chapter 14, "Maniacs and Sociopaths, or the Nuclear Family Explodes")

George, Stephen:
> *Bloody Valentine* (chapter 14, "Maniacs and Sociopaths, or the Nuclear Family Explodes")

Gerritsen, Tess:
> *Harvest* (chapter 15, "Technohorror")

Ghosh, Amitav:
> *The Calcutta Chromosome: A Novel of Fevers, Delirium, and Discovery* (chapter 15, "Technohorror")

Golden, Christopher:
> *Of Saints and Shadows* (chapter 9, "Vampires and Werewolves")

Gorman, Edward:
> *Cold Blue Midnight* (chapter 14, "Maniacs and Sociopaths, or the Nuclear Family Explodes")

Hambly, Barbara:
> *Traveling with the Dead* (chapter 9, "Vampires and Werewolves")

Hamilton, Laurell K.:
> *Bloody Bones*
> *Burnt Offerings*
> *Guilty Pleasures* (all chapter 19, "Comic Horror")

Hardy, Robin:
> *The Wicker Man* (film) (chapter 13, "Small-Town Horror")

Hardy, Robin, and Anthony Shaffer:
> *The Wicker Man* (chapter 13, "Small-Town Horror")

Harris, Thomas:
> *The Silence of the Lambs* (chapter 14, "Maniacs and Sociopaths, or the Nuclear Family Explodes")

Hautala, Rick:
> *Impulse* (chapter 14, "Maniacs and Sociopaths, or the Nuclear Family Explodes")

Hawkins, Barry T.:
> *Puppet Master* (chapter 14, "Maniacs and Sociopaths, or the Nuclear Family Explodes")

Heim, Scott:
> *In Awe* (chapter 17, "Psychological Horror")

Hitchcock, Alfred:
> *The Birds* (film) (chapter 16, "Rampant Animals and Other Eco-Monsters")
> *Psycho* (film) (chapter 14, "Maniacs and Sociopaths, or the Nuclear Family Explodes")

Hoffman, Barry:
> *Hungry Eyes* (chapter 14, "Maniacs and Sociopaths, or the Nuclear Family Explodes")

Huff, Tanya:
> The Blood series (chapter 9, "Vampires and Werewolves")

Hynd, Noel:
>	*A Room for the Dead* (chapter 17, "Psychological Horror")

Killough, Lee:
>	*Blood Hunt*
>	*Bloodlinks* (both chapter 9, "Vampires and Werewolves")

Kimball, Michael:
>	*Undone* (chapter 17, "Psychological Horror")

King, Stephen:
>	*Bag of Bones* (chapter 7, "Ghosts and Haunted Houses")
>	*The Dark Half* (chapter 8, "Golems, Mummies, and Reanimated Stalkers")
>	*The Tommyknockers* (chapter 10, "Demonic Possession, Satanism, Black Magic, and Witches and Warlocks")

Kiraly, Marie:
>	*Leanna* (chapter 10, "Demonic Possession, Satanism, Black Magic, and Witches and Warlocks")

Koontz, Dean:
>	*The Bad Place* (chapter 14, "Maniacs and Sociopaths, or the Nuclear Family Explodes")
>	*Dark Fall* (chapter 10, "Demonic Possession, Satanism, Black Magic, and Witches and Warlocks")
>	*The Face of Fear* (chapter 14, "Maniacs and Sociopaths, or the Nuclear Family Explodes")
>	*Fear Nothing* (chapter 15, "Technohorror")
>	*Hideaway* (chapter 10, "Demonic Possession, Satanism, Black Magic, and Witches and Warlocks")
>	*Lightning* (chapter 14, "Maniacs and Sociopaths, or the Nuclear Family Explodes")
>	*Shattered* (chapter 14, "Maniacs and Sociopaths, or the Nuclear Family Explodes")
>	*The Voice of the Night* (chapter 14, "Maniacs and Sociopaths, or the Nuclear Family Explodes")

Lake, Paul:
>	*Among the Immortals* (chapter 9, "Vampires and Werewolves")

LeFanu, Sheridan:
>	*Carmilla* (chapter 9, "Vampires and Werewolves")

Leiber, Fritz:
>	*The Dealings of Daniel Kesserich* (chapter 15, "Technohorror")

LeRoux, Gaston:
>	*The Phantom of the Opera* (chapter 14, "Maniacs and Sociopaths, or the Nuclear Family Explodes")

Levin, Ira:
>   *The Boys from Brazil* (chapter 15, "Technohorror")
>   *The Stepford Wives* (chapter 13, "Small-Town Horror")

MacMillan, Scott:
>   *Knights of the Blood* (chapter 9, "Vampires and Werewolves")

Martin, David Lozell:
>   *Tap, Tap: A Novel* (chapter 9, "Vampires and Werewolves")

Martini, Steven Paul:
>   *The List* (chapter 9, "Vampires and Werewolves")

Matheson, Richard:
>   *Now You See It* (chapter 17, "Psychological Horror")

Matthews, Anne McLean:
>   *The Cave* (chapter 14, "Maniacs and Sociopaths, or the Nuclear Family Explodes")

McNally, Clare:
>   *Good Night, Sweet Angel* (chapter 7, "Ghosts and Haunted Houses")

Michaels, Barbara:
>   *The Crying Child*
>   *House of Many Shadows*
>   *Houses of Stone* (all chapter 7, "Ghosts and Haunted Houses")

Naylor, Gloria:
>   *Linden Hills* (chapter 10, "Demonic Possession, Satanism, Black Magic, and Witches and Warlocks")

Neiderman, Andrew:
>   *The Maddening* (chapter 13, "Small-Town Horror")

O'Rourke, Michael:
>   *The Bad Thing* (chapter 14, "Maniacs and Sociopaths, or the Nuclear Family Explodes")

Palmer, Michael:
>   *Critical Judgment*
>   *Extreme Measures*
>   *Natural Causes*
>   *Silent Treatment* (all chapter 15, "Technohorror")

Poe, Robert:
>   *Return to the House of Usher* (chapter 17, "Psychological Horror")

Preston, Douglas, and Lincoln Child:
>   *The Relic* (chapter 11, "Mythological Monsters and 'The Old Ones' ")

Rangel, Kimberly:
>   *The Homecoming* (chapter 10, "Demonic Possession, Satanism, Black Magic, and Witches and Warlocks")

Spruill, Steven:
> *Before I Wake* (chapter 15, "Technohorror")
> *Painkiller* (chapter 15, "Technohorror")
> *Rulers of Darkness* (chapter 9, "Vampires and Werewolves")

Stevenson, Robert Louis:
> *Dr. Jeykll and Mr. Hyde* (chapter 14, "Maniacs and Sociopaths, or the Nuclear Family Explodes")

Straub, Peter:
> *KoKo* (chapter 14, "Maniacs and Sociopaths, or the Nuclear Family Explodes")
> *The Hellfire Club* (chapter 17, "Psychological Horror")
> *The Throat* (chapter 14, "Maniacs and Sociopaths, or the Nuclear Family Explodes")

Strayhorn, S. J.:
> *Black Night* (chapter 17, "Psychological Horror")

Strieber, Whitley:
> *Billy* (chapter 14, "Maniacs and Sociopaths, or the Nuclear Family Explodes")
> *The Wolfen* (chapter 9, "Vampires and Werewolves")

Sullivan, Mark T.:
> *The Purification Ceremony* (chapter 14, "Maniacs and Sociopaths, or the Nuclear Family Explodes")

Swiniarski, S. A.:
> *Raven* (chapter 9, "Vampires and Werewolves")

Tryon, Thomas:
> *Harvest Home* (chapter 13, "Small-Town Horror")

Weaver, Michael:
> *Impulse* (chapter 14, "Maniacs and Sociopaths, or the Nuclear Family Explodes")

Westlake, Donald:
> *The Ax* (chapter 14, "Maniacs and Sociopaths, or the Nuclear Family Explodes")

Wilson, Charles:
> *Nightwatcher* (chapter 14, "Maniacs and Sociopaths, or the Nuclear Family Explodes")

Wolf, Silver Raven:
> *Beneath a Mountain Moon* (chapter 10, "Demonic Possession, Satanism, Black Magic, and Witches and Warlocks")

Zachary, Fay:
> *Blood Work*
> *A Poison in the Blood* (both chapter 14, "Maniacs and Sociopaths, or the Nuclear Family Explodes")

Chapter 21

Bibliographies of Notable and Important Horror-Fiction Authors

Because these writers are perennial favorites, we have included bibliographies that span virtually the entirety of their writing careers. These bibliographies will be particularly useful for patrons who want to read "everything" by Ramsey Campbell, Stephen King, Dean Koontz, Ira Levin, Bentley Little, Anne Rice, John Saul, Dan Simmons, or Peter Straub.

Ramsey Campbell

The Doll Who Ate His Mother—Bobbs-Merrill, 1976

The Face That Must Die—Tor Books, 1979

The Nameless—Macmillan, 1981

Dark Companions—Macmillan, 1982

Incarnate—Macmillan, 1983

Night of the Claw—St. Martin's Press, 1983

Cold Print—Scream Press, 1985

Obsession—Macmillan, 1985

Black Wine—Dark Harvest, 1986

The Hungry Moon—Macmillan, 1986

Scared Stiff: Seven Tales of Seduction and Terror—Scream Press, 1986

Scared Stiff: Tales of Sex and Death—Scream Press, 1987

The Influence—Macmillan, 1988

Ancient Images—Tor Books, 1989

Demons by Daylight—Carroll and Graf, 1990

Midnight Sun—Tor Books, 1991

Waking Nightmares—Doherty, 1991

The Count of Eleven—Tor Books, 1992

Alone with the Horrors—Arkham House, 1993

Strange Things and Stranger Places—Tor Books, 1993

The Long Lost—Tor Books, 1996

The One Safe Place—Tor Books, 1996

Nazareth Hill—Doherty, 1997

The Last Voice They Hear—Forge, 1998

Stephen King

Carrie—Signet Books, 1972

Salem's Lot—Doubleday, 1975

The Shining—Plume, 1977

Night Shift—Doubleday, 1978

The Stand—Doubleday, 1978

The Dead Zone—Viking, 1979

Cujo—Plume, 1981

Danse Macabre—Everest House, 1981

Firestarter—New American Library, 1981

Creepshow—New American Library, 1982

The Dark Tower: The Gunslinger—New American Library, 1982

Different Seasons—Viking, 1982

Christine—Viking, 1983

Pet Sematary—Doubleday, 1983

The Talisman—Viking, 1984

Thinner—Signet Books, 1984

The Bachman Books—Viking, 1985

Cycle of the Werewolf—New American Library, 1985

Skeleton Crew—Putnam, 1985

It—Viking, 1986

The Dark Tower II: The Drawing of the Three—New American Library, 1987

The Eyes of the Dragon—Viking, 1987

The Dark Tower III: The Wastelands—Plume, 1988

Misery—New American Library, 1988

The Tommyknockers—Signet Books, 1988

The Dark Half—Signet Books, 1989

Four Past Midnight—Viking, 1990

Needful Things—Penguin, 1991

Gerald's Game—Viking, 1992

Dolores Claiborne—Viking, 1993

Nightmares and Dreamscapes—Viking, 1993

Insomnia—Penguin-Signet, 1995

Rose Madder—Viking, 1995

Desperation—Viking, 1996

The Dark Tower IV: Wizard and Glass—Plume, 1997

Bag of Bones—Scribner's, 1998

Dean Koontz

The Fall of the Dream Machine—Ace Books, 1969

Fear That Man—Ace Books, 1969

Anti-Man—Paperback Library, 1970

Beastchild—Lancer, 1970

Bounce Girl—Cameo, 1970

Dark of the Woods—Ace Books, 1970

The Dark Symphony—Lancer, 1970

Hell's Gate—Lancer, 1970

Soft Come the Dragons—Ace Books, 1970

The Crimson Witch—Curtis Books, 1971

A Darkness in My Soul—Daw Books, 1972

The Flesh in the Furnace—Bantam, 1972

Starblood—Lancer, 1972

Time Thieves—Ace Books, 1972

Warlock—Lancer, 1972

Demon Seed—Bantam, 1973

Hanging On—M. Evans, 1973

The Haunted Earth—Lancer, 1973

A Werewolf Among Us—Ballantine, 1973

After the Last Race—Fawcett Crest, 1974

Nightmare Journey—Berkley, 1975

Night Chills—Atheneum, 1976

Whispers—Putnam, 1980

Phantoms—Putnam, 1983

Dark Fall/Darkness Comes—Berkley, 1984

The Servants of Twilight—Fontana, 1985

Twilight Eyes—Berkley, 1985

Strangers—Putnam, 1986

Watchers—Putnam, 1987

Oddkins: A Fable for All Ages—Warner Books, 1988

Lightning—Berkley, 1989

Midnight—Putnam, 1989

The Bad Place—Berkley, 1990

Cold Fire—Berkley, 1991

Hideaway—Putnam, 1992

Dragon Tears—Putnam, 1993

Mr. Murder—Berkley, 1993

Dark Rivers of the Heart—Knopf, 1994

Winter Moon—Random House, 1994

Icebound—Putnam, 1995

Intensity—Ballantine, 1995

Strange Highways—Warner Books, 1995

Santa's Twin—HarperCollins, 1996

Sole Survivor—Headline, 1996

Ticktock—Ballantine, 1996

Demon Seed—Berkley, 1997

The Vision—Putnam, 1997

Fear Nothing—Bantam, 1998

Ira Levin

A Kiss Before Dying—Simon & Schuster, 1953

Rosemary's Baby—Joseph (London), 1967

This Perfect Day—Fawcett, 1970

The Stepford Wives—Random House, 1972

The Boys from Brazil—Random House, 1976

Deathtrap—Samuel French, 1979

Veronica's Room—Samuel French, 1974

Cantorial—1990

Sliver—Bantam, 1991

Son of Rosemary—Dutton, 1997

Bentley Little

The Revelation—St. Martin's Press, 1990

The Mailman—Penguin, 1991

The Summoning—Zebra, 1993

Death Instinct—Signet Books, 1992

University—Signet Books, 1995

Dominion—Signet Books, 1996

Guests—Headline, 1997

The Ignored—Signet Books, 1997

The Store—Signet Books, 1998

The House—Signet Books, 1999

Anne Rice

Interview with the Vampire—Ballantine, 1977

The Feast of All Saints—Simon & Schuster, 1979

The Vampire Lestat—Ballantine, 1985

The Mummy, or Ramses the Damned—Ballantine, 1989

The Queen of the Damned—Ballantine, 1989

The Witching Hour—Ballantine, 1991

The Tale of the Body Thief—Ballantine, 1992

Cry to Heaven—Random House, 1993

Lasher—Knopf, 1993

Memnoch the Devil—Knopf, 1995

Taltos: Lives of the Mayfair Witches—Ballantine, 1995

Servant of the Bones—Random House, 1996

Violin—Knopf, 1997

Pandora—Knopf, 1998

The Vampire Armand—Knopf, 1998

John Saul

Suffer the Children—Dell, 1977

Punish the Sinners—Dell, 1978

Cry for the Strangers—Dell, 1979

Comes the Blind Fury—Dell, 1980

When the Wind Blows—Dell, 1986

The God Project—Bantam, 1982

Nathaniel—Putnam, 1984

Brainchild—Bantam, 1985

Hell Fire—Bantam, 1986

The Unwanted—Bantam, 1987

The Unloved—Bantam, 1988

Creature—Bantam, 1989

Second Child—Bantam, 1990

Darkness—Bantam, 1991

Sleep Walk—Bantam, 1991

Shadows—Bantam, 1992

Guardian—Fawcett, 1993

The Homing—Fawcett, 1994

Black Lightning—Fawcett Crest, 1996

The Presence—Fawcett, 1997

Dan Simmons

Song of Kali—Doherty, 1985

Carrion Comfort—Warner Books, 1989

Hyperion—Bantam, 1989

Phases of Gravity—Bantam, 1989

Entropy's Bed at Midnight—Lord John, 1990

The Fall of Hyperion—Bantam, 1990

Prayers to Broken Stones—Dark Harvest, 1990

Summer of Night—Putnam, 1991

Children of the Night—Putnam, 1992

The Hollow Man—Bantam, 1992

Summer Sketches—Lord John, 1992

Lovedeath—Warner Books, 1993

The Fires of Eden—Putnam, 1994

Endymion—Bantam, 1996

The Rise of Endymion—Bantam, 1997

The Crook Factory—Avon, 1998

Peter Straub

Marriages—Pocket Books, 1973

Julia—Pocket Books, 1976

If You Could See Me Now—Pocket Books, 1977

Ghost Story—Simon & Schuster, 1979

Shadowland—Berkley, 1981

Floating Dragon—Putnam, 1983

The Talisman (with Stephen King)—Viking, 1984

KoKo—Dutton, 1988

Mystery—Dutton, 1990

The Throat—Dutton, 1993

The Hellfire Club—Random House, 1996

Pseudonyms

Many authors write under pseudonyms. Although most of these titles are eventually republished or reprinted under the author's real name, older copies may appear with (or be listed under) the pseudonym. The following list cites some of the pseudonyms used by well-known horror authors.

Suzy McKee Charnas	Deanna Dwyer	Aaron Wolfe
Rebecca Brand	K. R. Dwyer	
	John Hill	Barbara Michaels
Stephen King	Leigh Nichols	Barbara Mertz
Richard Bachman	Anthony North	Elizabeth Peters
	Richard Paige	
Dean Koontz	Owen West	Anne Rice
David Axton		Anne Rampling
Brian Coffey		A. N. Rocquelaire

Chapter 22

History and Criticism

One of the most noticeable trends concerning the horror genre has been that of its gradual acceptance into university curricula, which indicates that more and more academics are beginning to realize how important the genre is as a cultural barometer. As more of them understand how *Carrie* chronicles the sexual revolution of the 1960s, or get interested in how the evolution of the vampire reveals something about the society in which the writer who "produced" the vampire lives, university students are flocking to horror classes as quickly as they are offered. At Louisiana State University, where we team-taught courses in horror fiction/film and vampire fiction/film, classes would fill up in two hours or less, and we often ended up with standing room only. Honors students especially enjoyed the chance to seriously study works they had previously read for pure pleasure.

The reserve reading materials for these classes always consisted of works concerned with the history of the genre and with critical interpretations of its most historically famous texts. We include these same secondary sources in *Hooked on Horror* for the same reasons that we included them in our course descriptions: they help readers to better understand and appreciate horror. In general, the works listed in this chapter reflect the differing interests we noted among the critics of the genre. Some studies examine the nature of horror itself, or why it appeals to the human emotions, as do Stephen King's *Danse Macabre,* James Twitchell's *Dreadful Pleasures*, William Patrick Day's *In the Circles of Fear and Desire*, and Terry Heller's *The Delights of Terror: An Aesthetics of the Tale of Terror*. Other texts seem more concerned with what horror fiction has to say about the societies in which we live or in which our ancestors lived. Such studies as David Punter's *The Literature of Terror*; Nina Auerbach's *Woman and the Demon* and *Our Vampires, Ourselves*; Carol J. Clover's *Men, Women, and Chain Saws*; Teresa Goddu's *Gothic America*; and Kelly Hurley's *The Gothic Body* speak to us of our cultural fears and desires.

However, to view horror scholars as merely social or historical critics would be a great oversimplification. Many writers who are, for want of a better term, aficionados of horror literature publish their work simply to share their love of the genre and their individual insights concerning its value as a storytelling device. Jack Sullivan's *Elegant Nightmares* and Tony Magistrale and Michael Morrison's *A Dark Night's Dreaming* are excellent examples of texts that not only analyze what horror literature has to say, but also show an appreciation for how horror literature delights fans while saying it.

This chapter lists most of the recently published criticism, and some of the better but older secondary sources, of and for the horror genre. We include both histories of the genre and focused analyses of specific themes and trends in the genre and its various subgenres. Aside from the texts discussed in this introduction, it includes such important publications as Julia Briggs's *Night Visitors* and S. S. Prawer's *Caligari's Children*. Because the focus of this book is fiction rather than criticism, our annotations in this chapter are brief, but we append an appeal note to each entry to facilitate identification of publications in which the reader may be interested. Additionally, this appeal note can aid librarians in suggesting and collecting sources to meet user community needs.

Andriano, Joseph.

Our Ladies of Darkness: Feminine Daemonology in Male Gothic Fiction. *University Park: Pennsylvania State University Press, 1993. 182p.* Psychological theories on Otherness and the Feminine in gothic/horror fiction. Appeal: Academic.

Auerbach, Nina.

Our Vampires, Ourselves. *Chicago: University of Chicago Press, 1995. 231p.* The cultural significance of vampires, from Dracula to Lestat. Appeal: Academic/Popular.

Woman and the Demon: The Life of a Victorian Myth. *Cambridge, Mass.: Harvard University Press, 1982. 255p.* Study of the relationship between women and monsters in Victorian gothic/horror fiction. Appeal: Academic.

Bayer-Berenbaum, Linda.

The Gothic Imagination: Expansion in Gothic Literature and Art. *London: Associated University Press, 1982. 155p.* Study of the psychology behind gothic literature and of writer motivation. Appeal: Academic.

Belford, Barbara.

Bram Stoker: A Biography of the Author of *Dracula. New York: Knopf, 1996. 381p.* Biographical information on and criticism of Bram Stoker, with emphasis on his theatrical ties. Appeal: Academic/Popular.

Benshoff, Harry M.

Monsters in the Closet: Homosexuality and the Horror Film. *(Inside Popular Film series.) Manchester, England: Manchester University Press, 1997. 328p.* Chronicles the role of homoeroticism and homosexuality in horror films. Appeal: Academic/Popular.

Berenstein, Rhona J.

Attack of the Leading Ladies: Gender, Sexuality, and Spectatorship in Classic Horror Cinema. *New York: Columbia University Press, 1996. 274p.* Interesting arguments concerning sex roles in horror film. Appeal: Academic/Popular.

Bloom, Harold (editor).

Stephen King. *Philadelphia: Chelsea House, 1998. 242p.* History and criticism of American horror, with emphasis on the fiction of Stephen King. Appeal: Academic/Popular.

Botting, Fred.

The Gothic. *(New Critical Idiom series.) New York: Routledge, 1996. 201p.* Explains the fundamental premises of gothic literature and defines its parameters. Appeal: Academic.

Briggs, Julia.

Night Visitors: The Rise and Fall of the English Ghost Story. *London: Faber, 1977. 238p.* Emphasis on the traditional ghost tale à la M. R. James, with argument that the subgenre is dead. Appeal: Academic.

Carlson, Eric W. (editor).

A Companion to Poe Studies. *Westport, Conn.: Greenwood Press, 1996. 604p.* Lengthy study of Poe's detective and horror fiction, including bibliographical references. Appeal: Academic/Popular.

Carter, Lin.

Lovecraft: A Look Behind the Cthulhu Mythos. *San Bernardino, Calif.: Borgo Press, 1997. 198p.* Biographical study of Lovecraft, with emphasis on the history of the mythos itself.

Clover, Carol J.

Men, Women and Chain Saws: Gender in the Modern Horror Film. *Princeton, N.J.: Princeton University Press, 1992. 260p.* Critically acclaimed study of women's roles in slasher films, from *Psycho* to *Silence of the Lambs.* Appeal: Academic/Popular.

Collings, Michael R.

Scaring Us to Death: The Impact of Stephen King on Popular Culture. *2d ed. (Popular Writers of Today #63.) San Bernardino, Calif.: Borgo Press, 1997. 168p.* Discusses the role of Stephen King in American horror. Appeal: Academic/Popular.

Day, William Patrick.

In the Circles of Fear and Desire: A Study of Gothic Fantasy. *Chicago: University of Chicago Press, 1985. 208p.* Analysis of the attraction/repulsion reaction to horror. Appeal: Academic/Popular.

DeLamotte, Eugenia C.

Perils of the Night: A Feminist Study of Nineteenth-Century Gothic. *Oxford: Oxford University Press, 1990. 352p.* Feminist study of Victorian gothicism. Appeal: Academic.

Duclos, Denis.

Le Complexe du loup-garou (The Werewolf Complex: America's Fascination with Violence). *(Amanda Pingree, trans.) Paris: Berg, 1994; Oxford: Oxford International, 1998. 246p.* Study of werewolves in literature, film, and popular culture, from the director of the Centre National de la Recherche Scientifique (CNRS) in Paris. Appeal: Academic/Popular.

Glover, David.

Vampires, Mummies, and Liberals: Bram Stoker and the Politics of Popular Fiction. *Durham, N.C.: Duke University Press, 1996. 212p.* Analysis of what vampires, mummies, and eroticism reflected in the popular culture of nineteenth- and twentieth-century England. Appeal: Academic.

Goddu, Teresa A.

Gothic America: Narrative, History, and Nation. *New York: Columbia University Press, 1997. 226p.* Examines the roles of women and African Americans in American gothic fiction. Appeal: Academic.

Gordon, Joan, and Veronica Hollinger.

Blood Read: The Vampire as Metaphor in Contemporary Culture. *Philadelphia: University of Pennsylvania Press, 1997. 264p.* Collection of essays on post-1970 horror fiction and film; some are very readable. Appeal: Academic/Popular.

Grant, Barry Keith (editor).

The Dread of Difference: Gender and the Horror Film. *(Texas Film Studies series.) Austin: University of Texas Press, 1996. 456p.* A collection of essays that examine gender and the horror film. Appeal: Academic.

Halberstam, Judith.

Skin Shows: Gothic Horror and the Technology of Monsters. *Durham, N.C.: Duke University Press, 1995. 215p.* Comprehensive view of the gothic revival in England, chronicling the roles of monsters in British film and literature. Appeal: Academic.

Heller, Terry.

The Delights of Terror: An Aesthetics of the Tale of Terror. *Urbana: University of Illinois Press, 1987. 218p.* Analysis of the appeal of horror to the reader/viewer. Appeal: Academic/Popular.

Ingebretsen, Ed.

Maps of Heaven, Maps of Hell: Religious Terror as Memory from the Puritans to Stephen King. *Armonk, N.Y.: M. E. Sharpe, 1996. 239p.* The role of Christianity in American gothic and horror literature. Appeal: Academic.

Jancovich, Mark.

Horror. (Batsford Cultural Studies.) *London: Batsford, 1992. 128p.* Good beginner's guide to the study of horror. Appeal: Academic/Popular.

Rational Fears: American Horror in the 1950s. *Manchester, England: Manchester University Press, 1996. 324p.* Historical and critical accounts of horror films of the 1950s. Appeal: Academic.

Jensen, Paul M.

The Men Who Made the Monsters. (Twayne's Filmmaker series.) *New York: Twayne, 1996. 401p.* Biographical and critical notes on horror producers and directors in the United States and Britain. Appeal: Academic/Popular.

Joshi, S. T.

The Annotated H.P. Lovecraft. *New York: Dell, 1997. 360p.* Joshi, a Lovecraft scholar and co-editor of *Necrofile*, annotates the work of Lovecraft. Appeal: Academic/Popular.

Kendrick, Walter M.

The Thrill of Fear: 250 Years of Scary Entertainment. *New York: Grove-Weidenfeld, 1991. 292p.* Popular study of English and American horror tales and film. Appeal: Academic/Popular.

Kilgour, Maggie.

The Rise of the Gothic Novel. *New York: Routledge, 1995. 280p.* Analysis of what gothic fiction is and what movements led to its beginning in England. Appeal: Academic.

King, Stephen.

Danse Macabre. *New York: Everest House, 1981. 400p.* Study of the psychology of the horror writer and the appeal of horror, with emphasis on sociological theories. Appeal: Academic/Popular.

Kotker, Joan G.

Dean Koontz: A Critical Companion. *Westport, Conn.: Greenwood Press, 1996. 184p.* Criticism and interpretation of American horror, with emphasis on Dean Koontz. Appeal: Academic.

Leonard, Elizabeth Anne (editor).

Into Darkness Peering: Race and Color in the Fantastic. *Westport, Conn.: Greenwood Press, 1997. 198p.* Collection of essays about race in horror, science fiction, and fantasy. Appeal: Academic.

Magistrale, Tony, and Michael A. Morrison.

A Dark Night's Dreaming: Contemporary American Horror Fiction. *Columbia: University of South Carolina Press, 1996. 141p.* Part of the Understanding Contemporary American Literature series dealing with history and criticism in the genre. Appeal: Academic/Popular.

Malchow, Howard L.

Gothic Images of Race in Nineteenth-Century Britain. *Stanford, Calif.: Stanford University Press, 1996. 335p.* Discusses the role of race and racial representations in nineteenth-century English fiction, with emphasis on vampirism and cannibalism. Appeal: Academic.

Marrero, Robert.

Godzilla: King of the Movie Monsters. *Key West, Fla.: Fantasma Books, 1996. 143p.* History of horror film, with emphasis on the Japanese creation, Godzilla. Appeal: Academic/Popular.

McCarty, John.

The Fearmakers. *New York: St. Martin's Press, 1994. 198p.* Discussion of detective, mystery, and horror films. Appeal: Academic/Popular.

Meikle, Denis.

The History of Horrors: The Rise and Fall of the House of Hammer. *(Filmmakers Series #51.) Lanham, Md.: Scarecrow, 1996. 420p.* Discusses the history of British horror film, especially of Hammer productions. Appeal: Academic/Popular.

Paul, William.

Laughing, Screaming: Modern Hollywood Horror and Comedy. *New York: Columbia University Press, 1994. 510p.* Examination of the roles of comedy, sensationalism, sex, and violence in horror film. Appeal: Academic.

Pinedo, Isabel Cristina.

    Recreational Terror: Women and the Pleasures of Horror Film Viewing. *Albany, N.Y.: SUNY Press, 1997. 177p.* Analysis of women's roles in horror film as both actors and audience members. Appeal: Academic.

Prawer, S. S.

    Caligari's Children: The Film as Tale of Terror. *New York: Oxford University Press, 1980. 307p.* Study of horror film, with emphasis on early Universal Studio productions. Appeal: Academic.

Punter, David.

    The Literature of Terror: A History of Gothic Fictions from 1765 to the Present Day. *New York: Longman, 1980. 449p.* One of the first studies of horror fiction; elaborates on both English and American horror. Appeal: Academic.

Ramsland, Katherine.

    The Anne Rice Reader. *New York: Ballantine, 1997. 359p.* Biographical criticism and interpretation of America's top vampire fiction writer. Appeal: Academic/Popular.

    Dean Koontz: A Writer's Biography. *New York: HarperCollins, 1997. 508p.* Illustrated biography of one of America's most famous horror writers. Appeal: Academic/Popular.

Rogers, Deborah D.

    Anne Radcliffe: A Bio-Bibliography. *Westport, Conn.: Greenwood Press, 1996. 209p.* Biographical facts about Anne Radcliffe, concentrating on how her life and writing were interrelated. Appeal: Academic.

Russell, Sharon A.

    Stephen King: A Critical Companion. *Westport, Conn.: Greenwood Press, 1996. 174p.* History and criticism of American horror, with emphasis on Stephen King. Appeal: Academic.

Schmitt, Cannon.

    Alien Nation: Nineteenth-Century Gothic Fictions and English Nationality. *Philadelphia: University of Pennsylvania Press, 1997. 219p.* Analysis of nineteenth-century English gothic fiction and its relationship to national identity. Appeal: Academic.

Schweitzer, Darrell.

    Discovering H.P. Lovecraft. *Mercer Island, Wash.: Starmont House, 1987. 153p.* Collection of essays concerned with the fiction of H.P. Lovecraft. Appeal: Academic/Popular.

Senn, Bryan.

    Golden Horrors: An Illustrated Critical Filmography of Terror Cinema, 1931–1939. *Jefferson, N.C.: McFarland, 1996. 518p.* History and criticism of 1930s horror cinema. Appeal: Academic/Popular.

Skal, David J.

    Dark Carnival: The Secret World of Tod Browning—Hollywood's Master of the Macabre. *New York: Doubleday, 1995. 359p.* Chronicles the life and filmmaking career of Tod Browning. Appeal: Academic/Popular.

    The Monster Show: A Cultural History of Horror. *New York: W. W. Norton, 1993. 432p.* Cultural study of horror film and fiction, from the early Universal Studio flicks to Stephen King and beyond. Appeal: Academic/Popular.

Screams of Reason: Mad Science in Modern Culture. *New York: W. W. Norton, 1998. 368p.* A study of the madman in the lab coat, and the American obsession with weird science. Appeal: Academic/Popular.

Smith, Jennifer.

Anne Rice: A Critical Companion. *Westport, Conn.: Greenwood Press, 1996. 193p.* Criticism and interpretation, with emphasis on Rice's use of witchcraft, mummies, women, and vampires. Appeal: Academic.

Spignesi, Stephen J.

Lost Work of Stephen King: A Guide to Unpublished Manuscripts, Story Fragments, Alternative Versions and Oddities. *Secaucus, N.J.: Carol Publishing Group, 1998. 361p.* A guide to Stephen King's unpublished works. Appeal: Academic/Popular.

Sullivan, Jack.

Elegant Nightmares. *Athens: Ohio University Press, 1978. 155p.* Study of horror in general. A nice basic text for the uninitiated horror fan interested in horror criticism. Appeal: Academic/Popular.

Twitchell, James B.

Dreadful Pleasures: An Anatomy of Modern Horror. *Oxford: Oxford University Press, 1985. 353p.* Analysis of the appeal of horror fiction and film. Appeal: Academic.

Ursini, James.

More Things Than Are Dreamt of: Masterpieces of Supernatural Horror, from Mary Shelley to Stephen King, in Literature and Film. *New York: Limelight, 1994. 226p.* Notes on horror tales, in both literature and film. Appeal: Academic/Popular.

Williams, Tony.

Hearths of Darkness: The Family in the American Horror Film. *Madison, N.J.: Fairleigh Dickinson University Press, 1996. 320p.* The role of the family in American horror films. Appeal: Academic.

Wolf, Leonard.

Dracula: The Connoisseur's Guide. *New York: Broadway Books, 1997. 321p.* Explanation of the role of vampires, especially the famous Dracula, in horror literature and film. Appeal: Academic/Popular.

Chapter 23

Periodicals: Journals, Magazines, and E-Zines

Some of the recent trends in horror account for the variety of journals, fan magazines, and electronic magazines (e-zines) that can be found on the local newsstand or on the World Wide Web. For one, the move toward dark erotica in the genre has spawned e-zines such as *Blue Blood*, an adults-only celebration of sadomasochism; the less erotic, more politicized gothic alternative movement has found its voice in the print fan mag *Carpe Noctem*, which exhibits the same macabre and self-effacing sense of humor that the movement itself possesses. Additionally, the trend toward incorporating horror into the literary canon in colleges and universities across the nation (Stephen King in the classroom? Ivory-towered Conradians must be running through the halls of academe screaming, "The horror! The horror!") has led to the surging popularity of scholarly studies of horror, as seen in *The Journal of the Fantastic in the Arts* and *Necrofile*. As always, fan-oriented magazines, such as *Cemetery Dance*, that simply strive to entertain hard-core horror fans continue to thrive.

The popularity of the Internet has also left its mark on horror periodicals, as the proliferation of e-zines and small-press magazines with Web sites makes it possible for amateur and rookie writers of dark fiction to publish. This will ultimately help publishers and fans alike discover new voices in horror—some of which may be of high quality. Additionally, some e-zines allow interactive storytelling, whereby writers can add to stories in progress or even sell their characters (if their characters are marketable) to be used by other writers for future tales.

In short, horror periodicals, like periodicals in all fields, range from the sublime to the ridiculous, from the innocent to the graphically erotic. In this chapter, we list and annotate some of these periodicals, from the established horror journals and magazines, such as *Necrofile* and *Cemetery Dance*; to the lesser-known, small-press journals, such as *Grue*, *Crimson*, and *Hellnotes*. Although we do not assume that librarians will rush to purchase these journals, we hope to remind librarians and patrons alike that much good horror short fiction, as well as many excellent reviews and interviews, are being published by these periodicals. Readers will want at least to be aware of their existence.

NOTE: Librarians should be aware that many "fanzines" in the genre go in and out of print, and may, at a moment's notice, cease altogether, be incorporated into another publication, or die and be resurrected as a totally new 'zine.

Aberrations publishes a broad range of fiction in the sister genres of science fiction, adult horror, and dark fantasy, from the pulp style of storytelling of the 1930s and 1940s to the more experimental and literary fiction of today. It promises "a wild literary ride going where most fiction does not go." *Aberrations* is edited by Richard W. Blair and published monthly by Sirius Fiction of San Francisco. Includes book reviews. Circulation 15,000. Price $31.

Alsirat is an online magazine maintained by Joel Gazis-Sax at www.best.com/~gazissax/ alsirat.html. It seeks to entertain with short stories, interactive adventures, and articles. Alsirat includes role-playing games, in recognition of their importance to the literary genre. In addition, it publishes poetry and drama, and in 1997–1998 reenacted the "game" that led to the writing of Mary Shelley's *Frankenstein*. Free.

Carpe Noctem is an online alternative magazine at http://www.carpenoctem.com. It includes artwork, exclusive interviews, and short stories. It is now in its fourth year of publication, and past issues of the print version are still available via special order.

Cemetery Dance is the genre's most revered popular magazine, and in 1997 it was in its seventh year of publication (27 issues). This quarterly out of Baltimore, Maryland (edited and published by Richard T. Chizmar), has won the World Fantasy Award. *Cemetery Dance* uses regular columnists and has published works by King, Barker, Rice, Straub, Campbell, Simmons, Bloch, Ellison, and Matheson, as well as by hundreds of others. Includes original fiction and book and film reviews. Price $15.

Crimson is a newsletter of stories, case studies, and news and reviews on vampires. A refereed serial, it is published quarterly by the Vampire Guild in Dorset, England, and edited by Phill White. Circulation 1,000. Price £15.

Crypt of Cthulhu is a pulp thriller and theological journal that publishes general critical articles on the fiction of H.P. Lovecraft and his literary disciples. Regularly includes fiction and poetry by fans and major writers. Published irregularly by Necronomicon Press out of West Warwick, Rhode Island; edited by Robert M. Price. Circulation 650. Price $5.95 per issue.

The Dark Planet Webzine (located at http://www.sfsite.com/darkplanet/) is edited by Lucy A. Snyder. It publishes science fiction, fantasy, horror, and reviews. Free.

Dead of Night is a refereed serial containing horror fiction, fantasy, mystery, and science fiction. Published by Dead of Night Publications in Longmeadow, Massachusetts, and edited by Lynn Stein. Circulation 3,200. Price $9.

Fangoria is one of the all-time most popular horror 'zines, and one of the oldest. Published 10 times a year out of New York by O'Quinn Studios, Inc., and edited by Anthony Timpone and Rita Eisenstein. This visually appealing fan magazine covers horror in film, on television, in literature, in comics, in videos, and on video games and laser discs. Circulation 214,000. Price $43.47.

Grue magazine contains horror and dark fantasy fiction and poetry. Published triennially by Hell's Kitchen Productions in New York City. Circulation 2,000. Price $13.

Haunts publishes tales of unexpected horror and the supernatural. Appears triennially; produced by Night Shade Publications of Cranston, Rhode Island. Circulation 2,500. Price $16.

Hellnotes, formerly titled *Horror Show,* is "your weekly insider's guide to the horror field." It includes nonfiction, interviews, best-seller lists, publicity trends, and other horror-related information, and is published by Phantasm Press of Oak Run, California. Circulation 1,000. Price $40.

Horror: The Newsmagazine of the Horror and Dark Fantasy Field is published quarterly by Wildside Press out of Berkeley Heights, New Jersey. (Wildside specializes in horror, science fiction, and fantasy, and publishes anthologies, collections, and the like as well as this magazine.) Edited by John G. Betancourt. Includes reviews, illustrations, and information on the horror publishing and book trade industries in the United States and Canada. Price $36.

The Journal of the Fantastic in the Arts is published quarterly by the International Association for the Fantastic in the Arts, a collection of academics, scholars, researchers, writers, and fans of science fiction, fantasy, and horror. Edited by Roger C. Schlobin and produced by Florida Atlantic University (Jade Seas Publishing). *JFA* includes some original work by big-name writers such as Dan Simmons, but is composed mainly of articles and studies in horror, science fiction, and fantasy. The journal also publishes, on occasion, guest speeches delivered at the annual International Conference on the Fantastic in the Arts.

Lovecraft Studies is a scholarly journal concerned with the writings of H.P. Lovecraft. Published biannually by Necronomicon Press of West Warwick, Rhode Island; edited by S. T. Joshi. Price $12.

Necrofile: The Review of Horror Fiction is an indispensable publication for librarians in horror collection development, as it publishes, on a quarterly basis, the most comprehensive listing of all new horror published in the United States and Britain. The bulk of this small journal (produced by Necronomicon Press of West Warwick, Rhode Island, and edited by horror experts Stefan Dziemianowicz, S. T. Joshi, and Michael A. Morrison) is made up of its authoritative, extended book reviews of both current fiction and newly released older fiction. Although not very visually appealing, this scholarly publication is packed with information. This will be an all electronic format in 2000 at www.necropress.com/necrofile. Price $12.

Terminal Fright, a magazine of traditional horror literature, is produced by Terminal Fright Publications and edited by Ken Abner. Published quarterly. Circulation 3,000. Price $18.

Wetbones, out of Akron, Ohio, is edited by horror writer Paula Guran. *Wetbones* was first printed in 1997. Its preference is for nontraditional, cutting-edge excursions into dark fiction that stress characterization, originality, the bizarre, and the revolutionary. Its Web site claims that its goal is to "publish stories that will change the reader's life. Stories that, once read, won't leave you. . . . Stories that will make you afraid to sleep or maybe, even more frightening, make you THINK."

Chapter 24

Ready Reference Sources

Although there are a limited number of reference works in the horror genre, they are important to readers because they make available insights that shed light on many a horror novel, and because they often offer other information of interest to horror fans. They remind us that the monsters populating the works of Campbell, Erskine, King, Koontz, Little, Lovecraft, McCammon, Newman, Oates, Poe, Rickman, Straub, and countless other writers of the grotesque and the horrific are the descendants of folkloric and fairy-tale creatures that once were invoked to teach young and old alike tough lessons about the dangers of the world.

In this chapter, we list and briefly annotate encyclopedias, dictionaries, and bibliographies that deal with the horror genre. This section includes titles such as Mike Ashley's *Who's Who in Horror and Fantasy Fiction*, which, although dated, makes accessible biographical and bibliographical information on some notable writers in the genre. This and older titles may not be in print, but may be available through other means, such as interlibrary loan or World Wide Web services that find out-of-print texts. Librarians will find that acquiring them is well worth the trouble. Also included in this chapter is Neil Barron's *Horror Literature*, perhaps the single most important reference work dealing with the genre as a whole.

Our mission here is to draw attention to the usefulness of these sources in answering readers' advisory questions, as many of these texts contain bibliographies and/or brief discussions of fictional treatments (examples) of the terms they define. In addition, we hope to remind librarians and readers alike that these works are valuable in and of themselves, as secondary sources on the genre that offer valuable information not accessible elsewhere.

General Readers' Advisory Tools

Barron, Neil (editor).
> **What Fantastic Fiction Do I Read Next? A Reader's Guide to Recent Fantasy, Horror, and Science Fiction.** *Detroit, Mich.: Gale Research, 1998. 1,679p.* An annotated list of some 4,800 books in the fantasy, horror, and science-fiction genres. Includes series, time period, geographic, short story type, character, character description, author, and title indexes.

Barron, Neil, Wayne Barton, Kristen Ramsdell, and Stephen A. Stilwell.
> **What Do I Read Next? A Reader's Guide to Current Genre Fiction.** *Detroit, Mich.: Gale Research, 1998. 649p.* An annual publication that covers current genre fiction, including horror.

Herald, Diana Tixier.
> **Genreflecting: A Guide to Reading Interests in Genre Fiction, 4th ed.** *Englewood, Colo.: Libraries Unlimited, 1995. 393p.* Includes a chapter on horror fiction.

NoveList.
> *CD-ROM. Denver, Colo.: EBSCO. 1994– .* An electronic readers' advisory tool with access to more than 50,000 adult, young adult, and children's titles. Also available soon on the World Wide Web.

What Do I Read Next?
> *CD-ROM. Detroit, Mich.: Gale Research. September 1996– .* Descriptions of more than 63,000 adult, young adult, and children's titles, compiled from multiple volumes of the annual (above).

General Horror Reference

Aguirre, Manuel.
> **The Closed Space: Horror Literature and Western Symbolism.** *Manchester, England: Manchester University Press, 1990. 234p.* Psychological/sociological theories of horror and horror symbolism.

Ashley, Mike.
> **Who's Who in Horror and Fantasy Fiction.** *New York: Taplinger, 1977. 240p.* List of important horror writers, with a brief biography and bibliography of each.

Barron, Neil.
> **Horror Literature: A Reader's Guide.** *(Garland Reference Library of the Humanities 1220.) New York/London: Garland, 1990. 596p.* Bibliography and critical introduction of the horror genre. Good basic source, but somewhat dated.

Bloom, Clive (editor).
> **Gothic Horror: A Reader's Guide from Poe to King and Beyond.** *New York: St. Martin's Press, 1998. 301p.* Excerpts of writings by horror writers, psychologists, and well-known horror critics.

Castle, Mort (editor).

>   **Writing Horror.** *Cincinnati, Ohio: Digest Books, 1997. 224p.* A "how-to" book on horror, including sample tales and interviews with writers.

Clute, John, and John Grant.

>   **The Encyclopedia of Fantasy.** *New York: St. Martin's Press, 1997. 1,049p.* More than 1,000 pages of entries on science fiction, horror, and fantasy.

Jones, Stephen (editor).

>   **Clive Barker's A-Z of Horror.** *New York: Harper Prism, 1997. 256p.* One of the masters of horror, Clive Barker, takes readers on an encyclopedic tour of the genre. Based on a BBC-TV series that inspired an Arts and Entertainment–channel series.

Jones, Stephen, and Kim Newman (editors).

>   Ⓑ**Horror: The Best 100 Books.** *New York: Carroll and Graf, 1998. 366p.* Reissue of a Bram Stoker Award–winning survey of horror scholarship. Appeal: Popular/Academic.

Mulvey-Roberts, Marie (editor).

>   **The Handbook to Gothic Literature.** *Washington Square: New York University Press, 1998. 294p.* Encyclopedia-like treatment of gothic literature from Brontë to Melville.

Pringle, David (editor).

>   **St. James Guide to Horror, Ghost and Gothic Writers.** *Detroit, Mich.: St. James–Gale, 1998. 746p.* Bio-bibliographic information on ghost stories, gothic literature, and horror.

Wiater, Stanley.

>   Ⓑ**Dark Thoughts on Writing.** *Grass Valley, Calif.: Underwood Books, 1997. 200p.* Based on interviews with 50 horror writers. Wiater's text examines why writers of horror enjoy the genre, where they get their ideas, and how they deal with censorship. Winner of a Bram Stoker Award.

Specific Interests

Barber, Paul.

>   **Vampires, Burial and Death.** *New Haven, Conn.: Yale University Press, 1988. 211p.* An ethnographic/folkloric examination of mainly Eastern European vampire mythology. A favorite among vampire fans.

Bunson, Matthew.

>   **The Vampire Encyclopedia.** *New York: Crown, 1993. 303p.* Excellent source on vampire lore and beliefs.

Gottlieb, Sidney.

>   **Hitchcock on Hitchcock: Selected Writings and Interviews.** *Berkeley, Calif.: University of California Press, 1977. 339p.* Hitchcock's ruminations on technique, acting, casting, production, and audience.

Mayo, Mike.

Videohound's Horror Show: 999 Hair-Raising, Hellish, and Humorous Movies. *Detroit, Mich.: Gale–Visible Ink, 1998. 542p.* Large catalog of horror and suspense films, with a brief annotation of each.

McNally, Raymond T.

Dracula: Truth and Terror. *(CD-ROM.) South Burlington, Vt.: Voyager Software, 1996.* Contains a searchable text of *Dracula*, movie clips of various vampire films, and a searchable vampire folklore (worldwide) index.

McNally, Raymond T., and Radu Florescu.

In Search of Dracula: The History of Dracula and Vampires. *New York: Houghton Mifflin, 1994. 297p.* One of the first books to examine the history and folklore of the fifteenth-century Romanian berserker, Vlad Tepes (thought to be the historical basis for Dracula), and the folklore of vampires in general. Includes a filmography, an appendix of folk stories about Vlad Tepes, a bibliography of vampire fiction and nonfiction sources about Vlad Tepes and vampires, and a travel guide to Dracula-related places in Romania and the United Kingdom.

Melton, J. Gordon.

The Vampire Book: The Encyclopedia of the Undead, 2d ed. *Detroit, Mich.: Visible Ink, 1998. 852p.* An encyclopedia of literary and historical vampires; includes notes on history, folklore, and societies.

Vampire Gallery: A Who's Who of the Undead. *Detroit, Mich.: Visible Ink, 1998. 852p.* Covers the spectrum of vampirism, from terminology to geography to organizations to literary characters.

Weaver, Tom.

They Fought in the Creature Features: Interviews with 23 Classic Horror, Science Fiction, and Serial Stars. *Jefferson, N.C.: McFarland, 1995. 318p.* Interviews with famous actors in the subject genres.

Chapter 25

Horror-Related Organizations

This chapter lists the sources that are the most difficult to find: human sources. Horror fans often join societies and attend conventions, such as the World Horror Convention, the International Association for the Fantastic in the Arts Convention, the Popular Culture Association's Conference, and NECON (Northeast Coast Horror Convention). These conventions are excellent places to hear early drafts of both primary and secondary works in the genre, to meet writers and critics, and to exchange ideas and e-mail addresses with other readers and fans. This chapter also notes various smaller societies, such as the Lord Ruthven Assembly (International Vampire Society). We briefly describe each and give enough information for interested patrons and librarians to contact these societies if desired.

The British Fantasy Society promotes enjoyment of fantasy, science fiction, and horror in all its forms, and hosts FantasyCon (conference for fantasy, science fiction, and horror) annually. Members receive a newsletter six times per year (*Prism UK*) and a free copy of *Dark Horizons*. Members also receive a preferential rate at FantasyCon. The current president is horror writer Ramsey Campbell. Its mailing address is 2 Harwood Street, Stockport, SK4 1JJ, England; its home page can be found at www.geocities.com/SoHo/6859/about.htm.

The Horror Writers' Association brings together writers and others with a professional interest in horror. Members receive a newsletter, e-mail bulletins, and access to private online services. Its mailing address is Robert Weinberg, Vice-President, Horror Writers' Association, P.O. Box 423, Oak Forest, IL 60452-2041; its home page is found at www.horror.org/hwa/.

The International Association for the Fantastic in the Arts is an organization of scholars and fans of horror, science fiction, and fantasy who meet at an annual conference in Ft. Lauderdale, Florida. The horror literature division is headed by Tony Magistrale. For further information, contact William A. Senior at Broward Community College. Its mailing address is Prof. Martha Bartter, IAFA Treasurer, Department of Languages and Literature, Truman State University, Kirksville, MO 63501; its home page is found at http://ebbs.english.vt.edu/iafa/iafa.home.html.

The Lord Ruthven Assembly is a scholarly organization recognized as a special-interest group within the International Association for the Fantastic in the Arts. Its objectives include the serious pursuit of scholarship and research focusing on the vampire/revenant figure in a variety of disciplines. The current president is Dr. Elizabeth Miller. Prospective members should address e-mail to moss@chuma.cas.usf.edu. Its home page can be found at http://ebbs.english.vt.edu/LRA/lra.html.

Popular Culture Association is dedicated to the study of popular culture in all forms, including horror. Phil Simpson is the current area chair for the horror section of PCA. For further information, contact Ray Browne at Bowling Green State University, Bowling Green, OH. Prospective members should contact Dr. Nancy Ellen Talburt, Vice-Chancellor for Academic Affairs, University of Arkansas, Fayetteville, AR 72701. The PCA's home page is found at http://h-net2.msu.edu/~pcaaca/popindex.html.

Transylvanian Society of Dracula, Canadian Chapter, is a nonprofit, cultural-historical organization that acts as a clearinghouse for information pertaining to the serious study of Dracula and related topics. Its members include historians, folklorists, literary critics, researchers, students, and film enthusiasts. Its current president is Dr. Elizabeth Miller, who can be contacted by prospective members using her e-mail address: emiller@plato.ucs.mun.ca. Its home page can be found at www.ucs.mun.ca/~emiller/tsd.htm.

Chapter 26

Major Awards

This chapter lists and briefly describes the major awards given annually in horror fiction, from the prestigious Bram Stoker Award for best horror to the smaller but just as meaningful International Horror Guild Awards.

The Bram Stoker Awards: Winners and Nominees

The Horror Writers' Association (HWA) gives the Bram Stoker Awards for Superior Achievement in fiction annually. The winners are determined by vote of the active members of the HWA, and the awards themselves are presented at the HWA's annual meeting and awards banquet.

Winners are denoted in boldface. Stoker Awards are also given for best novella and short story, but the collections in which they appear are generally out of print and unavailable in libraries. For that reason, we did not include these categories.

1998

Ⓑ *Novel*

Children of the Dusk by Janet Berliner and George Guthridge (White Wolf)
The Church of Dead Girls by Stephen Dobyns (Henry Holt)
Earthquake Weather by Tim Powers (Tor Books/Legend)
My Soul to Keep by Tanarive Due (HarperCollins)

Ⓑ *First Novel*

The Art of Arrow Cutting by Stephen Dedman (Tor Books)
Drawn to the Grave by Mary Ann Mitchell (Leisure Books)
Hungry Eyes by Barry Hoffman (Gauntlet Press)
The Inquisitor by Mary Murrey (Lapwing Books)
Lives of the Monster Dogs by Kirsten Bakis (Farrar, Straus & Giroux)

ⓑ Fiction Collection

Exorcisms and Ecstasies by Karl Edward Wagner (Fedogan & Bremer)
Painted in Blood by Lucy Taylor (Silver Salamander)
Things Left Behind by Gary A. Braunbeck (Cemetery Dance Publications)
The Throne of Bones by Brian McNaughton (Terminal Fright)

ⓑ Nonfiction

Clive Barker's A-Z of Horror by Stephen Jones (Harper Prism)
Dark Thoughts on Writing by Stanley Wiater (Underwood Books)
Dean Koontz: A Writer's Biography by Katherine Ramsland (HarperCollins)
The Encyclopedia of Fantasy by John Clute and John Grant (St. Martin's Press)
The Hammer Story by Marcus Hearn and Alan Barnes (Titan Books)
Video Watchdog by Tim Lucas, ed.

ⓑ Lifetime Achievement

William Peter Blatty
Jack Williamson

1997

ⓑ Novel

Crota by Owl Goingback (Donald I. Fine)
Exquisite Corpse by Poppy Z. Brite (Scribner's)
The Green Mile by Stephen King (Signet Books)
The Hellfire Club by Peter Straub (Random House)

ⓑ First Novel

Crota by Owl Goingback (Donald I. Fine)
Dead Heat by Del Stone, Jr. (Mojo Press)
Flute Song by Donald Burleson (Black Mesa)
Horror Show by Greg Kihn (Tor Books)

ⓑ Fiction Collection

The Convulsion Factory by Brian Hodge (Silver Salamander)
The Nightmare Factory by Thomas Ligotti (Carroll and Graf)
The Pavilion of Frozen Women by S. P. Somtow (Victor Gollancz)
Shadow Dreams by Elizabeth Massie (Darkside Press)
With Wounds Still Wet by Wayne Allen Sallee (Silver Salamander)

ⓑ Nonfiction

Bram Stoker: A Biography of the Author of Dracula by Barbara Belford (Knopf)
The Great Pulp Heroes by Don Hutchison (Mosaic Press)
H.P. Lovecraft: A Life by S. T. Joshi (Necronomicon Press)
The Illustrated Werewolf Movie Guide by Stephen Jones (Titan Books UK)
V Is for Vampire by David Skal (Penguin)

ⓑ Lifetime Achievement

Forrey Ackerman
Ira Levin

1996

ⓑ Novel

Bone Music by Alan Rodgers (Longmeadow)
Deadrush by Yvonne Navarro (Bantam)
Widow by Billie Sue Mosiman (Berkley)
Zombie by Joyce Carol Oates (Dutton)

ⓑ First Novel

The Between by Tanarive Due (HarperCollins)
Diary of a Vampire by Gary Bowen (Masquerade)
Madeleine's Ghost by Robert Girardi (Delacorte Press)
The Safety of Unknown Cities by Lucy Taylor (Silver Salamander)
Wyrm Wolf by Edo van Belkom (Harper Prism)

ⓑ Fiction Collection

The Black Carousel by Charles Grant (Tor Books)
Cages by Ed Gorman (Deadline Press)
The Panic Hand by Jonathan Carroll (HarperCollins UK)
Strange Highways by Dean Koontz (Warner Books)

ⓑ Nonfiction

An Encyclopedia of Claims, Frauds, and Hoaxes of the Occult and Supernatural by James Randi (St. Martin's Press)
Immoral Tales: European Sex & Horror Movies 1956–1984 by Cathal Tohill and Pete Tombs (St. Martin's Press/Griffin)
Psycho: Behind the Scenes of the Classic Thriller by Janet Leigh and Christopher Nickens (Harmony)
The Supernatural Index by Michael Ashley and William Contento (Greenwood Press)

Ⓑ *Lifetime Achievement*

Harlan Ellison

1995

Ⓑ *Novel*

The Alienist by Caleb Carr (Random House)
The Butcher Boy by Patrick McCabe (Dell)
Dead in the Water by Nancy Holder (Bantam)
From the Teeth of Angels by Jonathan Carroll (Doubleday)
Insomnia by Stephen King (Penguin-Signet)

Ⓑ *First Novel*

The Black Mariah by Jay R. Bonansigna (Warner Books)
Deadweight by Robert Devereaux (Dell)
Grave Markings by Michael Arnzen (Dell)
Near Death by Nancy Kilpatrick (Pocket Books)

Ⓑ *Fiction Collection*

Born Bad by Andrew Vachss (Vintage)
The Early Fears by Robert Bloch (Fedogan & Bremer)
The Flesh Artist by Lucy Taylor (Silver Salamander Press)
Writer of the Purple Rage by Joe R. Lansdale (Cemetery Dance Publications)

Ⓑ *Lifetime Achievement*

Christopher Lee

1994

Ⓑ *Novel*

Anno Dracula by Kim Newman (Avon)
Blackburn by Bradley Denton (St. Martin's)
Drawing Blood by Poppy Z. Brite (Dell)
The Summoning by Bentley Little (Kensington)
The Throat by Peter Straub (Dutton)

Ⓑ *First Novel*

Afterage by Yvonne Navarro (Bantam)
Created By by Richard Christian Matheson (Bantam)
Suckers by Anne Billson (Atheneum)

The Thread That Binds the Bones by Nina Kiriki Hoffman (Avo Nova)
Wet Work by Philip Nutman (Jove Books)

ⒷFiction Collection

Alone with the Horrors by Ramsey Campbell (Arkham House)
Close to the Bone by Lucy Taylor (Silver Salamander Press)
A Good and Secret Place by Richard Laymon
Lovedeath by Dan Simmons (Warner Books)
Nightmares and Dreamscapes by Stephen King (Signet Books)

ⒷNonfiction

The Diary of Jack the Ripper by Shirley Harrison and Michael Barrett (Warner Books)
The Monster Show by David J. Skal (W. W. Norton)
Once Around the Bloch by Robert Bloch (Tor Books)

ⒷLifetime Achievement

Joyce Carol Oates

ⒷSpecial Trustees Award

Vincent Price

The International Horror Guild Awards

The International Horror Guild was created in 1995 as a way to recognize the achievements of those who toil in the horror field. Before that date, only the Bram Stoker Award, which is presented by the Horror Writers Association, was considered a mark of distinction, but voting on it is limited to HWA members. The International Horror Guild Award represents a large, unaffiliated group of writers who are recognized for excellence by their peers.

ⒽBest Novel

1997—*Nazareth Hill,* Ramsey Campbell (Forge)
1996—*The 37th Mandala,* Marc Laidlaw (St. Martin's Press)
1995—*Resume with Monsters,* William Browning Spencer (Permanent Press)
1994—*Anno Dracula,* Kim Newman (Carroll and Graf)

⊕ *Best First Novel*

1997—*Drawn to the Grave,* Mary Ann Mitchell (Leisure Books)
1996—*Dead Heat,* Del Stone, Jr. (Mojo Press)
1995—*The Safety of Unknown Cities,* (Eros Press) Lucy Taylor
1994—*Grave Markings*, Michael Arnzen (Dell)

⊕ *Best Collection*

1997—*The Throne of Bones,* Brian McNaughton
1996—*Conference with the Dead,* Terry Lamsley
1995—*Cages,* Edward Gorman
1994—*Angels and Visitations,* Neil Gaiman

⊕ *Best Anthology*

1997—*Revelations,* Douglas E. Winter (ed.) (Harper Prism)
1996—*Darkside: Horror for the Next Millennium,* John Pelan (ed.) (Penguin)
1995—*Best New Horror #6,* Stephen Jones (ed.) (Carroll and Graf)
1994—*Love in Vein*, Poppy Z. Brite (ed.) (Harper Prism)

⊕ *Best Publication (award given for best periodicals devoted to horror)*

1997—*Necrofile* (Necronomicon Press)
1996—*Cemetery Dance* (Cemetery Dance Publications)
1995—*Death Realm*
1994—*Answer Me!* (Underground Press Publications)

⊕ *Living Legend Award*

1997—No award available for this year
1996—Edward W. Bryant
1995—Clive Barker
1994—Harlan Ellison

Chapter 27

Publishers and Publisher's Series

This chapter lists nearly every publisher and publisher's series mentioned in the annotations of chapters 5 through 19. Omitted are publishers for which we were unable to find any information. When we first set out to write this chapter, we intended to mention only those publishers that either specialized in horror or were responsible for much of the horror currently on the market. However, we soon realized that this task was impossible. A quick glance at this list of publishers and publisher's series will show the reader one thing: there are very few publishing companies, or even imprints, dedicated exclusively to the horror genre. In fact, according to their listings in *Writer's Market*, many publishers actively discourage genre fiction, especially anything from the "degraded" genre of horror. According to Stephen Jones, in his introduction to *The Mammoth Book of Best New Horror, Volume 9* (New York: Carroll and Graf, 1998), "the number of horror titles published in 1997 was down slightly [from] previous years on both sides of the Atlantic."

Furthermore, Zebra cancelled its horror line, and in the United Kingdom, Random House decided to pull out of the SF/fantasy/horror market entirely. Thus, librarians wishing to begin horror collections or to augment previously existing ones cannot simply order catalogs from a few major publishers and expect to do one-stop shopping. True, much horror still comes from Tor Books and Forge, owned by Thomas Doherty, but these publishers also produce science fiction and fantasy. Smaller, independently owned houses such as Necro Press and Arkham House are single-genre publishers, but their offerings are not sufficient to furnish a representative collection. Librarians seeking to build their collections will have to look through the catalogs of large publishers such as HarperCollins, St. Martin's Press, Berkley, Penguin, and White Wolf to find individual horror offerings.

Academy Chicago Publishers, Chicago, Illinois

A mid-size, independent publisher known for its offerings in women's studies.

Ace Books (G. P. Putnam and Sons), New York, New York

An imprint of Berkley Publishing.

Alfred A. Knopf. *See* Knopf.

Alyson Books, Los Angeles, California

Medium-sized press specializing in lesbian- and gay-related material; the horror Alyson publishes features gay or lesbian characters.

Arkham House, Sauk City, Wisconsin

A small press originally created to publish the works of H.P. Lovecraft. Now continues that tradition by publishing reprints of his work, as well as Lovecraftian-type horror.

Atheneum (Simon & Schuster), New York, New York

An imprint of Simon & Schuster.

August House, Little Rock, Arkansas

Small, independent publisher that specializes in storytelling (audiotapes and books), including some collections of scary tales.

Avon, New York, New York

Large publisher of paperback and hardback originals and reprints. One of their imprints, Avon EOS, specializes in fantasy and science fiction; another, Avon Science Fiction, publishes that genre exclusively.

Ballantine (Random House), New York, New York

Publishes major historical fiction, women's mainstream fiction, and general fiction.

Bantam (Bantam Doubleday Dell Publishing Group), New York, New York

Publishes the gauntlet of fiction, from mystery to science fiction to fantasy to romance.

Berkley/Ace Science Fiction (G. P. Putnam and Sons), New York, New York

An imprint of Berkley Publishing.

The Berkley Publishing Group (G. P. Putnam and Sons), New York, New York

Large publisher whose imprints include Berkley/Ace Science Fiction (which also publishes some horror titles) and Jove Books.

Candlewick Press (Walker Books), Cambridge, Massachusetts

Publishes mostly high-quality illustrated children's books.

Carroll and Graf, New York, New York

One of the few remaining independent trade publishers, Carroll and Graf works with first-time as well as established authors. Publications include science fiction, fantasy, and erotica.

Catbird Press, North Haven, Connecticut

Small, independent trade publisher specializing in quality, imaginative prose humor and central European literature in translation.

CD Publications (or Cemetery Dance Publications), Baltimore, Maryland

A small press publishing *Cemetery Dance* magazine as well as a few horror novels.

Circlet Press, Cambridge, Massachusetts

Small, independent publisher specializing in science fiction and fantasy of an erotic nature.

Crown Publishing Group, New York, New York

Large publisher whose fiction offerings include horror.

Dark Horse Comics, Milwaukie, Oregon

Publishes comics and occasionally comic book–related novels.

Daw Books (Penguin Putnam, Inc.), New York, New York

Publishes science fiction, fantasy, and mainstream thrillers.

Delacorte Press (Bantam Doubleday Dell Publishing Group), New York, New York

An imprint of Dell, Delacorte Press publishes mainstream fiction.

Delta Trade Paperbacks (Bantam Doubleday Dell Publishing Group), New York, New York

Imprint of Dell specializing in mostly light, humorous material and books on popular culture.

Dufour Editions, Chester Springs, Pennsylvania

Small independent publisher tending toward literary fiction.

Ecco Press, Hopewell, New Jersey

Small publisher of hardcover and paperback originals and reprints on acid-free paper. Does not publish genre fiction.

Farrar, Straus & Giroux, New York, New York

Mid-size independent publisher of fiction, nonfiction, and poetry. Does not publish genre fiction.

Fawcett (Random House/Ballantine), New York, New York

Major publisher of trade and mass-market paperbacks.

Fine Publications or Donald I. Fine (Penguin Putnam, Inc.), New York, New York

This imprint of Penguin Putnam publishes dark fantasy and psychological horror, as well as mystery and suspense.

Forge (Thomas Doherty Associates), New York, New York

Mid-size company publishing mostly genre fiction, including horror, thrillers, mystery, and suspense.

Gauntlet Press, Springfield, Pennsylvania

Small press that offers science fiction and horror titles.

G. P. Putnam and Sons (Penguin Putnam), New York, New York

An imprint of Penguin Putnam specializing in hardcover originals. Offerings include science fiction and mystery/suspense.

HarperCollins, New York, New York

A large press publishing nearly every sort of fiction and nonfiction. Their imprints include Harper Paperbacks, Harper Perennial, and Harper Prism.

Headline, London, England

Mainstream publisher of popular fiction and nonfiction in hardcover and mass-market paperback.

Henry Holt and Company, New York, New York

Publishes all kinds of books for all sorts of audiences. Imprints include Owl, a paperback line.

Hyperion (Walt Disney Company), New York, New York

Mainstream commercial publisher whose offerings include mystery/suspense, thriller/espionage, and general literary fiction.

Kensington Publishing, New York, New York

Large publisher offering all sorts of fiction. One of its imprints, Zebra, is primarily dedicated to romance.

Knopf/Alfred A. Knopf (Random House), New York, New York

Publishes hardcover literary, contemporary, suspense, and spy fiction.

Leisure Books (Dorchester Publishing Company), New York, New York

Large paperback publisher whose offerings include horror and technothrillers.

Little, Brown & Company, Boston, Massachusetts

Mid-size publisher of paperback and hardback fiction, with diverse offerings.

Llewellen, St. Paul, Minnesota

Mid-size publisher of New-Age and occult fiction and nonfiction.

Morrow. *See* William Morrow and Company

Mysterious Press (Warner Books), New York, New York

An imprint of Warner Books offering crime and mystery fiction.

Necro Press, Orlando, Florida

Small independent publisher of horror.

New American Library (Penguin Putnam), New York, New York

An imprint of Penguin, publishing works by American authors who either have become part of the literary canon or have created their own immortality by remaining on the bestseller list.

New English Library (Penguin Putnam), New York, New York
> An imprint of Penguin, publishing works by British, Scottish, and Irish authors who either have become part of the literary canon or have created their own immortality by remaining on the best-seller list.

Norton. *See* **W. W. Norton.**

Onyx (Dutton Signet), New York, New York
> An imprint of Dutton offering horror and romance.

Oxford University Press, Oxford, England, and New York, New York
> University press whose horror offerings include anthologies of canonical literature from specific periods or regions, such as gothic ghost stories, Victorian ghost stories, and Australian ghost stories.

Penguin Books (Penguin Putnam), New York, New York
> Generally offers editions of the classics, such as *Frankenstein* and *Dracula*.

Picador USA (St. Martin's Press), New York, New York
> An imprint of St. Martin's Press.

Pinnacle Books (Kensington Publishing), New York, New York
> Publishes some horror.

Plume (Dutton Signet), New York, New York
> Another imprint of Dutton; offerings include some horror.

Pocket Books (Simon & Schuster), New York, New York
> Large publisher of paperback and hardback originals and reprints. Their offerings include horror and science fiction.

Putnam. *See* **G. P. Putnam and Sons.**

Random House, New York, New York
> Large publisher of quality hardback and paperback originals, including mystery/suspense and short-story collections.

ROC Books (Penguin Putnam), New York, New York
> An imprint of Dutton Signet devoted to horror, fantasy, and science fiction.

Seal Press, Seattle, Washington
> Mid-size independent publisher of fiction by women.

Severn House Publishers, Surrey, England, and New York, New York
> Mid-size-to-large publisher whose offerings include fantasy, science fiction, and horror.

Signet Books (Penguin Putnam), New York, New York
> A division of Penguin that publishes horror as well as works in other genres.

Simon & Schuster, New York, New York
> Large publisher of adult, mostly commercial mainstream fiction.

St. Martin's Press, New York, New York

Large press whose offerings include gothic, psychic/supernatural, fantasy, and horror fiction.

Story Line Press, Brownsville, Oregon

Small, nonprofit literary press publishing works in various genres.

Tor Books (Thomas Doherty Associates), New York, New York

Publishes fantasy, science fiction, and horror.

Viking (Penguin Putnam), New York, New York

Imprint of Penguin Putnam, publishing a mix of academic and popular fiction and nonfiction.

Vista, Long Branch, New Jersey

Small independent press owned by women and specializing in nurse authors.

Warner Books, New York, New York

Large publisher of paperback and hardback fiction of all genres, including horror, science fiction, and fantasy.

White Wolf, Clarkston, Georgia

Small publisher of horror and dark fantasy.

William Morrow and Company, New York, New York

Large publisher whose offerings include science fiction and horror.

Word Books, Dallas, Texas

Small publisher of Christian fiction. A few fiction titles fall into the horror/dark fantasy genre.

W. W. Norton, New York, New York

Mid-size independent publisher of trade books and college textbooks, best known for its anthologies of literature and music.

Zebra (Kensington Publishing), New York, New York

An imprint of Kensington Publishing, offering mostly romance.

Chapter 28

Horror on the World Wide Web

The World Wide Web is quickly becoming one of the best resources for information. As a whole, the Web offers the strength of comprehensiveness—one of its best (and worst) attributes is that it offers choices of information on every subject imaginable, no matter how trivial. All a researcher need know is how to take advantage of Internet search engines, such as the popular Yahoo! or Alta-Vista, or the less popular but often better engines such as Profusion (www.profusion.com), Highway 61 (www.highway61.com), Metacrawler (www.metacrawler.com), Mamma (www.mamma.com), or Infoseek (www.infoseek.com), to name just a few. For horror fans, these search engines hold the key to information on subjects ranging from vampire folklore, to vampire music, to vampire clans.

Another strength of the World Wide Web is its ability to offer the most current information available; that is, when the author of a Web site makes a conscientious effort to keep that site as current as possible. Those of us who have built and maintained Web pages, either for our personal use or for the libraries and institutions for which we work, know that a Web page can be changed within minutes of information receipt. This means that on a well-maintained site, the "What's New" section can contain information that is mere minutes old. Of course, the great advantage of this to horror readers and fans is that a site like *Fiona's Fear and Loathing* (annotated in this chapter) will list horror titles that were released that same week, or that a site like *Dark Echo Horror* can contain an interview with Poppy Z. Brite that was conducted just a day before it was posted to the Web page.

Of course, there are drawbacks to finding information on the Web. Because the Web is an international and unedited collection of ideas, notes, musings, and personal theories, it will by its nature contain lots of relevant information for the horror fan. Moreover, it will also contain lots of incorrect information. If researchers are not careful, they might be duped into thinking that just because information is on the Web, it is current—this is not necessarily so (in fact, it is more often *not* so). The careful researcher looks for a copyright date at the bottom of the index page (the opening page or main page) of a Web site, and pays attention to this date.

It is the objective of this chapter to help librarians and horror readers avoid some of these pitfalls by listing some of the better horror Web sites we have encountered in our research, both as instructors of horror film and fiction courses and as bibliographers collecting hard-to-find information for *Hooked on Horror*. Site entries give the site name first, then site address, and finally date last accessed. To facilitate the production of a list containing sites that were still actually available, we waited until the last possible second to run a final check on these sites, even though we had been using many of them habitually for three to four years. This turned out to be a good idea; we found that one of the premier sites for horror, *The Dark Side of the Web*, had disappeared since we had last accessed it. The sites listed were chosen because they were still active as of July 7, 1999, and because they contained useful links and correct information. We avoided sites about specific authors and works, as this chapter is intended to list horror Web sites with a general emphasis. The annotations in this chapter, like the other annotations in this guide, are not evaluative. The discussion on how to evaluate Web sites is a voluminous part of the library and information science literature, and we leave it to librarians and readers to educate themselves on this subject and then to try evaluating sites for themselves.

The Cabinet of Dr. Casey.

> **http://www.drcasey.com. Last accessed July 7, 1999.** With the exception of Dark Echo Horror, this site tops all others on the Web for volume of useful information and for the seriousness it accords to fans of the genre and their interests. Links include Horror in Art, Horror in Comic Books, Horror in Literature, Horror in Games, Horror on the Internet, Horror in Movies, Horror in Music, Horror in Radio, Horror in Television, Horror in Theater, and others. Perhaps most useful is the site's search option, which allows researchers to find pages devoted to specific authors.

The Classic Horror and Fantasy Page.

> **http://www.geocities.com/Area51/Corridor/5582/index2.html. Last accessed July 7, 1999.** Pages that "deal with authors who lived and wrote a long time ago, and whose works are not often reprinted in our own time"—Web site. Includes a very useful link to Online Classic Horror Fiction, where works by classic horror writers can be found in their entirety. Currently under construction, but promising.

Dark Echo Horror.

> **http://www.darkecho.com. Last accessed July 7, 1999.** Perhaps the premier horror site currently on the Web. Dark Echo's page, copyrighted by 'zine editor Paula Guran, links to reviews, interviews (often exclusives), workshops, societies, conventions, e-journals, and more than 200 sites devoted to horror writers. Also links to the Dark Echo newsletter, a weekly free e-mail service for writers and fans of horror and dark fantasy. The place to begin when looking for horror on the Web.

Dark Tales Publications.

> **http://oz.sunflower.org/~monolith/darktale.htm. Last accessed July 7, 1999.** A Webring (online community) dedicated to linking together sites of authors, artists, and listservers in the horror and dark fantasy fields. Also offers free e-mail accounts and various chat rooms. Under construction, but promising.

Fiona's Fear and Loathing.

> **http://www.oceanstar.com/horror. Last accessed July 7, 1999.** Subtitled *A Space Devoted to Horror Literature*, this site run by a single individual contains excellent and up-to-date core lists of horror titles, and links to selected reviews. Also includes links to art galleries, amazon.com mini-reviews, and information on where to purchase horror titles.

Horror @ Indiana.

http://php.indiana.edu/~mlperkin/horror.html. **Last accessed July 7, 1999.** An e-mail discussion list based at Indiana University in Bloomington; covers the topics of horror in film and literature. Currently consists of more than 500 members, is international in scope, and sends an average of 20 to 30 messages a day to subscribers. This mailing list has been active since 1987.

The Horror and Fantasy Homepage.

http://www.webfic.com/mysthome/horror.htm. **Last accessed July 7, 1999.** A selective list of horror resources on the Internet; related to "The Mysterious Home Page" (a guide to mysteries and crime fiction on the Internet). Contains links to various home pages that serve as overall "guides" to horror on the Internet, and also contains links to Web sites dealing with individual horror authors. Authored and maintained by Jan B. Steffenson.

Horror News.

http://www.horrornews.com. **Last accessed July 7, 1999.** A site related to "The Cabinet of Dr. Casey" (annotated in this chapter) but that also contains links to information about comics, the Internet, literature, movies, music, television, and theater.

Horror Online.

http://www.horroronline.com. **Last accessed July 7, 1999.** Commercial site maintained by Universal Studios, but useful for its 1,200 horror movie reviews, as well as for its links to reviews of television, video, literature, comics, and games. Other links include chat rooms and interviews, and these are often linked to those of other Web sites, such as the interviews in Dark Echo Horror.

HorrorNet Home Page.

http://www.horrornet.com. **Last accessed July 7, 1999.** Visually appealing Web site that contains links to various horror presses, as well as links to new releases, events, book reviews, interviews, chat rooms, and articles. Also includes links to individual-author Web sites and some e-mail addresses for authors.

Literature of the Fantastic.

http://www.sff.net/people/DoyleMacdonald/LIT.HTM. **Last accessed July 7, 1999.** This site, which has been around for a few years now, is a selective listing of online texts by various classic horror writers, including Poe, LeFanu, Blackwood, Byron, and Mary Shelley. Particularly useful is its link to the "Varney the Vampire" project, a site that releases, on a regular basis, chapters from the first vampire novel ever (which was originally released in serial fashion).

LitGoth: The Gothic Community.

http://www.siue.edu/~jvoller/commun.html. **Last accessed July 7, 1999.** A listing of links to various interest groups on the Web that cater to fans of gothicism and horror. Links include The International Gothic Association, The Ghost Story Society, and other discussion groups in subjects such as folklore, ghost stories, and mystery/weird tales. The index page contains links to information on authors, titles, and general horror resources.

Masters of Terror.

http://members.aol.com/andyfair/mot.html. **Last accessed July 7, 1999.** Subtitled *A Website Devoted to the Darker Side of Fiction*. Contains links to new releases by specific authors, as well as chat rooms, a "master list" of some 500 writers and 2,500 titles, book reviews, online fiction, exclusive interviews, and articles about writing dark fiction. Edited by Andy Fairclough and Rick Kleffel.

Short Story Index

This index lists short stories by title. Each entry includes the author and the volume(s) the story appears in, as well as page number of the volume's annotation.

Subject Index

Author/Title Index